D0773119

The collaboration of Schubert and the poet Wilhelm Müller produced some of the best loved of nineteenth-century lieder – in particular the song cycle *Die schöne Müllerin*. Professor Youens shows us how this archetypal tale of love and rejection, which has its origins in medieval romance, Minnesong, and popular German legend, is reflected in the poet's own experience, the realms of art and life intertwining. Professor Youens considers other poets' explorations of the theme of a miller maid and her suitors, and looks at other musical settings of Müller's mill poems. But above all she examines Müller's permutation of the literary legends as an exploration of erotic obsession, delusion, frenzy, disillusionment, and death and the ways in which Schubert crucially altered Müller's vision when the poetic cycle became a musical text.

Schubert, Müller, and
Die schöne Müllerin

Was sag ich denn vom Rauschen?/Das kann kein Rauschen sein. Wood engraving, after a drawing by Rudolf Schuster (1848–1902), from Franz Schubert, *Die schöne Müllerin*, op. 25, D. 795, text by Wilhelm Müller. Berlin: s. n., 1878.

Schubert, Müller, and
Die schöne Müllerin

SUSAN YOUENS

UNIVERSITY OF NOTRE DAME

CAMBRIDGE
UNIVERSITY PRESS

Published by the Press Syndicate of the University of Cambridge
The Pitt Building, Trumpington Street, Cambridge CB2 1RP
40 West 20th Street, New York, NY 10011-4211, USA
10 Stamford Road, Oakleigh, Melbourne 3166, Australia

© Cambridge University Press 1997

First published 1997

Printed in Great Britain at the University Press, Cambridge

A catalogue record for this book is available from the British Library

Library of Congress cataloguing in publication data

Youens, Susan.
Schubert, Müller, and *Die schöne Müllerin*/Susan Youens.
p.   cm.
Includes bibliographical references and index.
ISBN 0 521 56364 X (hardback)
1. Schubert, Franz, 1797–1828. Schöne Müllerin.   2. Müller,
Wilhelm, 1794–1827. – Schöne Müllerin.   I. Title.
ML410.S3Y72 1997
782.4´7–dc20   96-14037   CIP   MN

ISBN 0 521 56364 X hardback

Contents

Illustrations

Examples

Preface

"*Another* book on *Die schöne Müllerin?* Why?", friends familiar with my handbook on this work (Cambridge University Press, 1992) ask me. In reply, I can only plead the brevity of handbooks and the plethora of material I have somehow managed to accumulate on this endlessly fascinating work over the years. Because various aspects barred from the previous investigation in the interests of concision have continued to tease my mind, I decided to return to the cycle and explore those topics further, including what transpired before and after Schubert in the realms of poetry, folklore, song, and opera – Schubert inherited a topos that had already attracted many artists before him and would continue to do so after his death. What began as desultory explorations into sundry topics *autour de* Schubert eventually converged once again at the great crossroads of D. 795, illuminating facets of the work I had not glimpsed before. It is my hope that others, similarly fascinated by the tribulations of the miller lad and his beloved, will find this broadening of the frame around *Die schöne Müllerin* helpful.

This book, like the handbook before it, originated with a question posed many years ago in a seminar I taught at the University of Notre Dame on the lied: what gave rise to Wilhelm Müller's poetic cycle? When and under what circumstances, for what reasons, did he write this work? Despite enigmas and missing information, enough remains of the biographical backdrop for us to realize that the drama behind the scenes was just as compelling as the *Liederspiel* (song-play) Müller and his friends created in the autumn and winter of 1816. The members of a young artistic salon which met at the house of the Berlin councillor Friedrich Stägemann concocted a new variation on the old erotic theme of a miller maid and her various suitors, chief among them a miller lad and a hunter, but they also enacted the archetypal tale of love and rejection in their own lives, the realms of life and art intersecting with one another in fascinating ways. The resulting *Liederspiel*-by-committee, with the young hostess Hedwig von Stägemann as the title character "Rose, die Müllerin" (Rose, the Miller Maid), can be reconstructed only partially, but the remnants are revealing. The poetic cycle *Die schöne Müllerin*, Müller's final permutation of the mill tale as a monodrama, was, I believe, a reflection in some measure of the artistic and biographical crises which enveloped those in whose company the cycle was born. The reverse may also have been true: life as an imitation of art. For young artists to choose an archetypal role they dimly sense will educate their hearts is not an unknown phenomenon. But whatever the complexities that lie beyond

xiii

certainty in the interplay between life and art, the known facts of the matter are compelling, a real-life *Liederspiel* whose dramatis personae include some of the foremost writers, artists, and intellects of their generation, in particular, the artist Wilhelm Hensel and his sister Luise Hensel, the great Romantic writer Clemens Brentano, and Wilhelm Müller. Their story is told in chapter 1, "Behind the scenes: the genesis of Wilhelm Müller's cycle" which is a revised and augmented version of an article entitled "Behind the scenes: *Die schöne Müllerin* before Schubert," published in *19th-Century Music* 15/1 (Summer 1991): 3–22. I am grateful to the editors of *19th-Century Music* for permission to reprint this material.

Most major works have both a rich pre-history, extending farther back than the circumstances immediately surrounding their genesis, and a long aftermath. Many factors, some determinable, some not, conspire to produce a particular artifact at a certain moment, and that artifact then impinges upon the creation of later works. Why, of all the themes available to them, did Wilhelm Müller and his youthful friends choose the tale of the miller, hunter, and miller maid for their song-play? None of the participants ever stated a reason for their choice of subject, although one can speculate about certain influences; the paterfamilias of the household in which the youthful artists composed their *Liederspiel*, a Berlin statesman named Friedrich Stägemann, was interested in old German literature and folklore – and few folkloric themes were more venerable or more "in the air" at the time than this one. Müller, who studied folk poetry himself, would have known the characters and their traditional amatory vicissitudes from anthologies such as Achim von Arnim's and Clemens Brentano's *Des Knaben Wunderhorn*, Gustav Büsching's and Friedrich von der Hagen's *Sammlung deutscher Volkslieder* (Berlin, 1807), and Friedrich Nicolai's eighteenth-century compendium *Eyn kleyner feyner Almanach* (ironically, the latter was compiled by someone inimical to the fashion for folk poetry). Müller would also have known the scenario from Goethe: the *Liederspiel* belongs in part to the story of Goethe's mammoth impress on his contemporaries. Müller, wont to acknowledge his borrowings even as he varied them, quotes one of Goethe's four mill ballads in his own narrative; Goethe's mini-cycle mimicking different nationalistic versions of romance-at-the-mill – French, English, Spanish, German – reminds us that mill-wheels turned throughout the Continent and England, not only in German-speaking lands. Goethe's mill ballads were almost certainly inspired at least in part by still another source Müller and his friends might have known: the *commedia per musica L'amor contrastato, o sia La bella molinara* (Love Contested, or The Beautiful Miller Maid) by Giovanni Paisiello, a work which was first performed in 1788 in Naples and subsequently became popular in Germany under various titles (*Die schöne Müllerin*, *Die Müllerin*, *Die streitig gemachte Liebschaft*, and *Die Launen der Liebe*), mostly in a two-act version with spoken dialogue in place of Paisiello's recitatives. The miller maid originally named Rachelina in Italy becomes the archetypal German Röschen (it is she who sings the familiar, wistful melody of "Nel cor più non mi sento" to the words "Mich fliehen alle Freuden") wooed by men from several walks of life and differing social classes; both in Paisiello and Goethe, the serious sermonette beneath the frothy comedy is that one should marry within one's own station, aristocrat to aristocrat, villager to villager, miller lad to miller maid.

The Romantics and their inheritors treated the old theme differently, however. Poets such as Joseph von Eichendorff, Friedrich Rückert, Adelbert von Chamisso, and others preferred lyric poetry to light opera, tragic versions of the tale to comic renditions, and they took their cue from folk tradition. What then was this topos before either Goethe or Müller appropriated it? What do these characters represent in Teutonic folklore, and what did they become when educated poets, philologically-trained *Kunstdichter*, took them over? Chapter 2, "Variations on a poetic theme: hunters, millers, and miller maids," goes even farther behind the scenes to explore the origins of the mill tale in popular German legend, folk song, medieval romance and Minnesong – Müller was among those of his generation fascinated by medieval secular literature and was most intensely engaged with this literary repertoire shortly before the *Liederspiel* came into being – and to peer briefly at poems by Müller's contemporaries, both older and younger, on these same themes. When Müller took the forest path to myth, how did he make it his own? What was modernized and made new, and what was retained of the mythical elements? Present-day listeners to Schubert's cycle might not realize either from whence the characters in *Die schöne Müllerin* came or what other nineteenth-century writers made of them, and hence, they might miss some of the resonances the cycle would have had for the original listeners. The second chapter is an attempt to reclaim some of those nuances.

Schubert was neither the first nor the only composer to discover that Müller's monodrama was "komponabel." The piano virtuoso Ludwig Berger was invited by the Stägemann poets to set their verses to music; his ten *Gesänge aus einem gesellschaftlichen Liederspiele 'Die schöne Müllerin'*, published in 1818, are discussed in chapter 3, "Before and after Schubert: at the mill with other composers," along with Reichardt's settings of Goethe's mill ballads and a medley of songs fashioned from Müller's *Die schöne Müllerin* by Otto Claudius, Bernhard Joseph Klein, Carl Gottlieb Reissiger, Carl Friedrich Curschmann, Louis Spohr, Heinrich Marschner, Wilhelm Taubert, and others. If a full-fledged compendium is not possible, a sampling is, including such attractive and unknown works as the song cycle *Des Müllerburschen Liebesklage in Mond und Morgenliedern* (The Miller Lad's Love-Laments in Moon- and Morning Songs), op. 18 by Carl Banck, one of the most interesting song composers of Schumann's generation. The repertoire of unexplored nineteenth-century song is immense (dissertation students, take note): anyone confronted with Ernst Challier's *Grosser Lieder-Katalog* (Berlin: Published by the author, 1885, with supplements until 1914) or the "Textdichter" catalogue of the Staatsbibliothek zu Berlin at the Unter den Linden branch – the catalogue occupies an entire wall – quickly realizes how few lieder have remained available to musicians in modern editions. Many songs have vanished into the oblivion that always imperils such ephemeral publications or were destroyed in this century's world wars (it always saddens me when I see the double asterisk that means "zerstört," "destroyed," in the Berlin card catalogue), but much is still extant, albeit unsung and unknown. If there is, inevitably, considerable dross in the troves of lieder by *Kleinmeister*, there are also riches ripe for revival. Perhaps the music examples both in this chapter and in chapter 2, where several of the many hunting songs and mill songs by composers other than Schubert proved an irresistible lure, will whet readers' appetites for more of this repertoire.

Berger's and Müller's *Gesänge* were not the only musical works born of the Stägemann *Liederspiel*. On April 16, 1820, the "rustic" (Ländliches) Singspiel *Rose, die Müllerin*, with a libretto by Adalbert vom Thale (a pseudonym for General Karl von Decker) and music by Baron Adolph von Lauer von Münchofen, was performed for the first time at the Royal Opera in Berlin. The specific connection with the young artists of the Stägemann salon is not known, but both the composer and the dramatist were highly placed in Berlin society – the Singspiel may have been rustic, but its creators were not – and could well have moved in the same circles. Unlike the doubly tragic dénouement of the *Liederspiel*, this work has a happy ending, but before its *lieto fine*, the librettist borrowed openly from the poems of the 1816 song-play; even the title is the same. Was the Thale/Lauer work perhaps a "correction" of the *Liederspiel*, a restoration of the comedic character of the topos in eighteenth-century comic opera? In the Singspiel *Rose, die Müllerin*, discussed in chapter 3, the mill is once again the site for mostly merry erotic complications, a Germanized version of the pranks at Paisiello's mill, with a hunter from the Schwarzwald in place of the Italian baron. Unlike the *Liederspiel*, the hunter in Thale/Lauer's version, far from being the successful seducer, is unmasked as a fortune-hunting blackguard, and the miller maid and miller lad are happily affianced at the close. What goes terribly wrong at Müller's mill ends in "tutti a festa e cena" gaiety on the operatic stage.

In this book, however, all roads lead back to Schubert. What did *he* make of the folk-figures Müller borrowed from tradition and bent to his own un-folkish purposes? Müller's tale, after all, is highly disturbing when one examines it closely and discovers a compound of erotic obsession, delusion, sexual bad faith, frenzy, disillusionment, and death. If this poet borrowed eclectically from the Minnesingers, Sir Philip Sidney, Goethe, folk song, and much else for his cycle, he made of his mélange of sources an acute diagnosis of what was wrong with romantic love as inherited from chivalric literature. In sum, he made an old tale modern, in part – a wonderful paradox – by harking back to medieval Germanic culture. Some composers, perhaps blinded by the rustic garb and *mise-en-scène*, ignored the multiple pathologies at the heart of these poems in their musical settings, but Schubert was not given to such naiveté; he did not miss the sophisticated delineation of psychological distress, nor did he expunge it from his music – far from it. The mill songs, one notices, are more virtuosic than the songs of the second Schubert-Müller cycle, *Winterreise*: the miller lad's delusional raptures and doubts find expression in deliberately difficult music, the musical strains often as over-reaching as the mental strains. Even near the beginning, one can find premonitions aplenty of obsession in the making.

But Schubert's miller is not Müller's as the cycle shades into tragedy. Such differences are an inevitability to some degree in any composer's setting of poetry by someone else, but Schubert's revision of Müller is an especially compelling example of the phenomenon both because the composer rejected portions of his poetic source – rejected by outright deletion – and because he imposed a contradictory musical reading on Müller's words at a crucial point in the cycle. Schubert omitted five poems from Müller's complete monodrama, a prologue and epilogue framing the cycle proper on both sides and three poems from the body of the poetic narrative; if one might reasonably expect prefatory poems and concluding morals to be deleted so that no attention would be diverted from the tale itself, one does not expect portions of the poetic story to be excised. Because Schubert did not set them to music, musicologists have not paid them much attention, but Schubert, of course, did; he had reasons to reject them, and those conjectural reasons belong to the story of his musical vision of the work. In particular, the last of the poems Schubert omitted from his cycle is the darkest, most shocking poem in the entire text, an astonishing glimpse into early nineteenth-century notions of sexuality: Müller's seventeenth poem, "Blümlein Vergißmein" (Little Forget-me Flower), a poem which belongs to the last stage of the cycle's four-year-long transformation from *Liederspiel* to lyric monodrama. With this poem no longer present in D. 795, our understanding of what impels the lad to commit suicide is altered, nor is this omission (and two others) the only revision Schubert wrought on Müller's text. The poet's twelfth poem – the exact midpoint of the cycle and its crux, the emotional center of the entire work – "Mein!" is necessary to the plot and Schubert retains it, but he drastically "rewrites" it in music. What in the poem can be read as acute psychological disturbance becomes untainted rejoicing in song, devoid of all but a few traces of the distress which pervades the words. The differences between the two cycles and speculations about Schubert's possible reasons for diverging so radically from the poetic work are the subjects of the fourth and final chapter, "'Lilies that fester': sex and death in Müller's and Schubert's cycles."

It will be apparent to the reader by now that these chapters are not a series of like-minded explorations, each one developing from the preceding chapter in serial fashion, but rather four different angles of investigation converging on *Die schöne Müllerin*. The thread linking these separate studies together is a fascination with the enmeshing of life and literature, the emphasis necessarily shifting from one essay to the next; life (biography) comes to the fore in the first chapter, for example, and literature in the second. Even in the third chapter, where this thread is at its weakest, it is not altogether absent; for composers post-1830, Schubert too became quasi-myth of a different sort than the hunter, miller maid, and miller, his life and lieder impinging on the songs of composers who followed in his wake. I have hoped in particular to build a bridge between the first and last chapters, to make of this book a tonally closed cycle, by returning at the end to themes adumbrated in the beginning. In the first chapter, I have guessed that exigencies of life and literature alike shaped the formation of the poetry in certain ways, and in the last chapter, I have similarly speculated that life's travails led Schubert to alter what the poet had created, and to do so in a terribly moving manner. Eros kills the miller lad, and it would, Schubert knew, kill him as well, and yet he spares *his* creation some, if not all, of the degradation Müller's lad suffers. Whatever his reasons for doing so, I would like to think that the emendations stem in part from a vision of love, from a refusal to allow death to obliterate its ultimate meaning.

Acknowledgments

Any book is a collaborative endeavor between the author and those who supply writers with information and aid. I wish to thank in particular the curators of both houses of the Staatsbibliothek zu Berlin, the Bartsteingasse music collection of the Wiener Stadt- und Landesbibliothek, the music collection of the Österreichische Nationalbibliothek, the Beinecke Library at Yale University, the Eda Kuhn Loeb Music Library at Harvard University, the Newberry Library in Chicago, the New York Public Library, the Brown Collection of the Boston Public Library, the Regenstein Library of the University of Chicago, the Archiv für Kunst und Geschichte in Berlin/Archive for Art and History in London, and the Library of Congress for coping both with large orders for photocopies, photographs, and microfilm and, on numerous occasions, with my presence. My friends and colleagues James Parakilas of Bates College, John Wustman at the University of Illinois, Lisa Feurzeig of the University of Chicago, John Sienicki, Albert Wimmer at the University of Notre Dame and Roger Parker at Oxford University have read drafts of these chapters and have made numerous suggestions resulting in a greatly improved latter-day version of the original book. I have depended on their generosity in the past and am grateful that they once again volunteered to help me. I am also indebted to the National Endowment for the Humanities for a research grant during the academic year 1994–95, to the Deutscher Akademischer Austauschdienst for their support of a research trip to Berlin in 1995, and to the Institute for Scholarship in the Liberal Arts at the University of Notre Dame for funding a research trip to Vienna and Berlin in 1993. This book would not have been possible without the financial support and the time such grants make available to scholars.

My greatest debt, however, will always be to a dear friend now deceased, someone whose heartfelt support of my endeavors for many years enabled me to continue working, despite the difficulties I encountered along the way: the composer, critic, teacher, and musicologist Paul Amadeus Pisk, who died on January 12, 1990. If the middle name was borrowed from Mozart, it was apt for him as well, "beloved of God." He was certainly beloved to me, and it is to his memory, which sustains me to this day, that I dedicate this work.

Chapter 1

Behind the scenes: the genesis of Wilhelm Müller's cycle

Seven years before Franz Schubert discovered the poetic cycle *Die schöne Müllerin* (*Im Winter zu lesen*), or *The Beautiful Miller Maid* (*To Read in Wintertime*), in the first volume of Wilhelm Müller's extravagantly entitled anthology *Sieben- und siebzig Gedichte aus den hinterlassenen Papieren eines reisenden Waldhornisten* (Seventy-seven Poems from the Post-humous Papers of an Itinerant Horn-Player), a real-life drama surrounded the creation both of the poetry and the first musical settings of Müller's miller poems.[1] The biograph-ical entanglements were as complex as any Baroque opera plot and as perfervid as any Romantic melodrama – religious torment, unrequited love, four men in love with the same poetess, and a great writer at a literary crossroads – but the players were real, not fictional, and included some of the foremost artists, composers, and poets in Berlin after the Prussian War of Liberation from Napoleon's armies. From the evidence of their diaries, autobiographies, *Denkmäler*, chronicles, poems, and letters, it is clear that this was a time of crisis for the artists who together created a series of works based on the familiar theme of the beautiful miller maid and her multiple suitors and that their artis-tic and personal trials form the backdrop, even the subtext, for those works. Art and life intertwine in fascinatingly complex ways in the original drama-within-a-drama – a playlet within the larger framework of a *Sturm und Drang* play in real life – and there-after. In particular, the record of what these remarkable people both created and experi-enced in 1816–17 offers a unique insight into the genesis of an emerging art form (the song cycle), the world of private salons in a city where they flourished with particular brilliance, the life and literary aesthetic of Wilhelm Müller, the formative years of a female poet of considerable merit, and much else besides. Yet the chronicle has virtually disappeared from sight in the twentieth century: we know little of the history and the works, fascinating in themselves, that preceded Schubert's cycle.

It was not always so. Literary scholars of both the past and present centuries were fas-cinated by the tale. Max Friedländer, a friend of Hedwig von Stägemann, one of the par-ticipants in the real-life drama, reported an abbreviated version of events in the *Deutsche Rundschau* for 1892 and in the introduction to his 1922 edition of Schubert's *Die schöne Müllerin*.[2] The chronicle is less well known to present-day musicians, disinclined to respect Müller and therefore to take an interest in the genesis of verse they wrongly con-sider negligible or in lieder at levels less empyrean than Schubert's song *oeuvre*.[3] Friedländer was enchanted with the realization that he actually knew the original "Rose,

1

die Müllerin" (Rose, the miller maid) from that winter long ago, although he did not confuse the artist with the art-work, life with art, as some nineteenth-century chroniclers were prone to do. In fact, biographical and historical details are in short supply in Friedländer's account, although he includes much else that is valuable. Recognizing implicitly that poetry is always, whatever else it may be, a response to other poems, he cites various literary models for the song-play of 1816–17 and presents an abbreviated history of Müller's painstaking revisions throughout the lengthy genesis of the poetic cycle – a work Schubert set to music not two years after its first appearance in print.

But Friedländer was interested in the song-play and its creators only as lesser precursors to Schubert and not as events and persons of intrinsic interest. When I in turn recount the story of Wilhelm Müller, Luise Hensel, Ludwig Berger, and the genesis of the first *Die schöne Müllerin* songs, it is not solely for the light it sheds on Schubert or to imply naive parallels between the dramatis personae of the poetry and the people who created them – although I believe parallels *do* exist, on subtler, more subterranean levels – but to bring back to life a privileged moment in the history of poetry and song. How often, after all, are we able to peer into the long-distant chambers from which a major genre of European music was emerging newly defined and reinvigorated, and look into the lives and hearts of those who were among its early creators? How often do we actually witness nineteenth-century poets and composers working together in the early years of the lied? From this story of youthful artists at play (but this is *serious* play), we can see all that and more.

THE VIEW FROM OUTSIDE: THE ARTISTS AND THEIR CREATION

The poetic cycle and the first musical settings began with a series of events that took place in the autumn of 1816 and early 1817 on the Bauhofstrasse in Berlin, at the home of the eminent banker and privy councillor Friedrich August von Stägemann (1763–1840). Every Thursday, beginning in 1815, Friedrich August, an amateur poet whose *Kriegsgesänge aus den Jahren 1806–1813* (War Songs from the Years 1806–1813) enjoyed some measure of success, and his gifted wife Johanna Elisabeth Fischer Graun Stägemann (1761–1835), hosted a salon that met on Thursday evenings.[4] For the sake of their children, August and his sister Hedwig (1799–1891),[5] Elisabeth also gathered together a circle of younger writers, poets, composers, and performers in the autumn and winter of 1816–17; evidently, the older and younger guests mingled freely. The group of young people included Wilhelm Müller (1794–1827), then twenty-three years old; the twenty-two year-old Wilhelm Hensel (1794–1861), who became a noted portrait artist; his eighteen year-old sister Luise Hensel (1798–1876), later a respected poet of Catholic religious verse; the poet and pianist Ludwig Rellstab (1799–1860), who became an important music critic; the later historian Friedrich Förster (1791–1868), whose influential literary and artistic anthology *Die Sängerfahrt* (The Minstrels' Voyage) of 1818 includes numerous poems originating from the Stägemann salon; Adelbert von Chamisso's fiancée Emilie Piaste; a young woman named Laura Gedike who later became Förster's wife; and others.[6] Two older artists were also closely associated with the younger circle: the great Romantic writer Clemens Brentano (1778–1842), thirty-eight at the time, met Luise Hensel, with whom he fell in love, at the Stägemann's house, and the thirty-nine year-old composer and piano virtuoso Ludwig Berger (1777–1839), also in love with the dark-haired, blue-eyed Luise, was invited in December 1816 to set some of their poems to music. These are the principal players both in the *Liederspiel* "Rose, die Müllerin" and in a biographical drama that reached flash-point at the same time.

The performance of *Liederspiele* (narrative plays in verse and song) was a popular artistic diversion both at salons and professional theatrical companies in Berlin. Johann Friedrich Reichardt (1752–1814) invented the genre, a cross between the *Singspiel* and the *Liederkreis*, at the turn of the century in order to provide a *volkstümlich* alternative to what he amusingly characterized as the "throat-rending hurtles and deafening noise" of the bravura arias in opera. In the 1801 essay, "On the Liederspiel," he writes that he dubbed his venture into "the simple and the simply pleasant" by this name because the musical content consisted of "lied and only lied"; he did not want audiences to expect anything other than songs in a folk-like, "natural" style.[7] A figure notorious in Berlin for his political views (he had backed the French Revolution and was disgraced for it), Reichardt was a friend – at one time, an amorously inclined friend – of Elisabeth Stägemann, an accomplished amateur actress and singer who had sung the part of Rose in Reichardt's first *Liederspiel Lieb' und Treue* (Love and Fidelity) of 1800 and might well have influenced, even determined, the group's decision to create a *Liederspiel* of their own; her daughter Hedwig, who subsequently played Rose the miller maid, was sufficiently adept at singing to perform Carl Friedrich Zelter's setting of Goethe's "Blumengruß" with the composer himself accompanying. For whatever reasons, the habitués of the Stägemann house chose for their subject the venerable topos of a beautiful miller maid wooed by various suitors, perhaps because it was a theme familiar from folk poetry and therefore well known to Müller and Brentano, perhaps because it was germane to the group's personal involvements, perhaps because it reflected the *alt-Deutsch* interests of their host Friedrich Stägemann, perhaps as an offspring of Goethe's four mill ballads, "Der Edelknabe und die Müllerin," "Der Junggeselle und der Mühlbach," "Der Müllerin Verrat," and "Der Müllerin Reue" (The Aristocratic Youth and the Miller Maid, The Young Apprentice and the Millstream, The Miller Maid's Betrayal, The Miller Maid's Remorse) – possibly all four speculative reasons.[8] Goethe's journeyman in "Der Junggeselle und der Mühlbach" who bids the talking brook "Geh', sag ihr gleich und sag ihr oft" (Go tell her the same and tell her often) was clearly the model for Müller's "Eifersucht und Stolz" (Jealousy and Pride), in which his miller tells the brook "Geh', Bächlein, hin und sag ihr das" (Go, little brook, and tell her that).

Der Junggeselle und der Mühlbach	The Young Apprentice and the Millstream
(stanzas 1 and 9 of 9)	
Wo willst du, klares Bächlein, hin So munter?	Where are you going so merrily, clear little brook?
Du eilst mit frohem, leichtem Sinn Hinunter.	You hurry with a light heart, happily, down below.
Was suchst du eilig in dem Tal?	What are you seeking hurriedly in the valley?
So höre doch und sprich einmal!	Hear and speak!

Geselle meiner Liebesqual,	Companion of my sorrow in love,
Ich scheide;	I depart.
Du murmelst mir vielleicht einmal	Perhaps you will whisper to me once more
Zur Freude.	of happiness.
Geh, sag ihr gleich und sag ihr oft,	Go, tell her the same, tell her often,
Was still der Knabe wünscht und hofft.	what this lad secretly desires and hopes.

Goethe, wrestling with the Romantic in himself, gives the miller tale a happy ending of mutual love reconciled, but the Stägemann circle did not follow his lead. On the contrary, their miller and miller maid, like a rustic Tristan and Isolde, both die; Müller, who published his *Blumenlese aus den Minnesingern* (Selection from the Minnesingers) earlier in 1816, before the creation of the *Liederspiel*, knew medieval literature well and modeled his mill romance in part on the conventions of courtly love (see chapter 4).[9] In 1815, along with his Minnesong translations, he also busied himself with a work, never finished, about the troubadour Geoffroi Rudel, who is credited with the invention of "amor londanh," or a knight's worship from afar of an unavailable love-object; according to the *vidas* (capsule biographies) in medieval manuscripts, Rudel pined for the Countess of Tripoli, became a crusader for her sake, and died in her arms – their first and last meeting. On October 25, 1815, Müller writes of his enthusiasm for the tale of Tristan (presumably, Gottfried von Strassburg's version of the tale), adding that Luise must read it.[10]

There were prototypes aplenty for works small and large on the venerable theme of love-at-the-mill – it seems to have been "in the air" at the time. This is a tale with both a tragic and a comic mask: the death-haunted double tragedy that was the Stägemann parlor game was born in part from eighteenth-century comic opera, as well as from folk songs (and the folk songs too come in both ribald and melancholy incarnations). In the chain reaction by which one work gives rise to another, the *commedia per musica L'amor contrastato, o sia La bella molinara* (Love Contested, or The Beautiful Miller Maid) by Giovanni Paisiello (1741–1816, the latter being the same year that the young Stägemann circle conceived their *Liederspiel*), to a libretto by Giuseppe Palomba, was one source of inspiration for Goethe's mill ballads. Goethe, whose multitudinous positions included that of theatrical manager, knew Paisiello's opera well and oversaw numerous performances of the work, translated into German by Christian August Vulpius, at Weimar during the winter season of 1797–98 and after; in a letter to Schiller of July 1802, he writes that "die Müllerin" had drawn an audience of 226 people.[11] The original Italian version – a hit from the moment of its first performance at the Teatro Fiorentini in Naples during the autumn carnival season of 1788 (it was even revived for the following carnival season, a notable occurrence in the novelty-crazed Italian operatic market) – had made its way to Dresden in 1790 and to Brünn in 1791 in a translation entitled *Die Launen der Liebe* (The Caprices of Love) and thereafter migrated elsewhere with the titles *Die streitig gemachte Liebschaft*, *Die Müllerin*, and *Die schöne Müllerin*.[12] Paisiello's lively comedy has more to commend it than the second-act duet "Nel cor più non mi sento" for the miller maid Rachelina and the nobleman Calloandro (who become Röschen and the allegorically dubbed Baron Felsenherz in the German translations), as lovely as that famous air indisputably is;[13] one wonders whether Schubert could have heard the opera and remembered it at some subterranean level when he began *his Die schöne Müllerin* in the same B flat major tonality of Paisiello's overture, although that could be the merest of coincidences. Did Müller and his friends know the opera? It was popular in Berlin, and a vocal score was published in the early years of the century by E. H. G. Christiani, the same publisher who later brought out their own mill songs in 1818, although this too could be no more than happenstance.[14]

The beginning of the second act, traditionally where a buffa plot is at its most entangled, is of particular interest in the context of Schubert's and Müller's cycle. At this juncture of the plot, Baron Felsenherz and the notary public Pistofolus, both wooing the beautiful miller maid, are hiding in the mill from the Baroness Eugenia (Felsenherz's betrothed). When Eugenia and the elderly judge Knoll (another would-be suitor) show up, angrily looking for the two miscreants, Röschen brings them out as her gardener Wilhelm and her mill apprentice Christoph and bids them perform a song for the Baroness's amusement. When the false gardener Felsenherz, accompanying himself on the zither, sings "Geht der Gärtner in den Garten, / Abends oder in der Früh, / und er sieht sein Mädchen, / dann vergisst er alle Müh" (The gardener goes into the garden, in the evening or in the morning, and he sees a maiden; then he forgets all care) and the false miller Pistofolus sings, "Hat der Müller brav gemahlen, und die Feyerstunde schlägt, / so kann ihm die Liebe zahlen, / die sein Mädchen für ihn hegt" (The miller has milled well and the hour of recreation has sounded, and he can tally the love his sweetheart cherishes for him), one can hear the traditional innuendos of "mahlen" as a metaphor for sexual intercourse and see the play-acting predecessors for the gardener and miller of the Stägemann *Liederspiel*. In Paisiello's quintet, the principal characters enter into the spirit of this entertainment-within-an-entertainment and hymn the supposed innocence of rustic love as opposed to love in cities: "Nur allein bei den ländlichen Schönen / herrscht der Unschuld so süßes Gefühl. / Wie verschieden ist die Liebe, / in der Stadt und auf dem Land" (Only with rustic beauties can such a sweet feeling as innocence reign. How different love is in the city and the country), they all sing. It is precisely this notion of innocence in country love at which Müller takes aim in his *Die schöne Müllerin*; he knew (Paisiello assuredly did as well) that this was a fashionable fiction, not reality, although it was to prove an enduring fiction, and he disabuses it from within other fictions, other realities. He too tells his audience that this is rustic stuff artfully imitated and transformed for their amusement, and in his prologue, bids his readers amuse themselves (he is, however, setting them up for a fall). Paisiello, tongue-in-cheek, does likewise, but without the darker undertones of the later mill poet; librettist and composer simultaneously congratulate themselves from within their own work and direct the audiences how they should respond when Eugenia says, "This music has cheered me up enormously" and Knoll chimes in, "It was a very artful little song." Still more artful songs, little and not-so-little, would follow from it.

Most of the younger lyric poets who followed in Goethe's wake preferred the tragic versions of the romance-at-the-mill; Müller was of his time and place in choosing tragedy over comedic complications en route to marriage. Friedrich Rückert, a friend of Müller's in their youth, wrote a poem on the familiar theme in his *Jugendlieder* of 1810–13 ("Die

Mühle wogt wohl Tag und Nacht," or "The Mill Grinds by Day and Night," later set to music by Heinrich Marschner as "An die schöne Müllerin," op. 106, no. 6).

Die Mühle wogt wohl Tag und Nacht	The Mill Grinds by Day and Night
(stanza 2 of 4)	
O wenn ich doch das Rädlein wär,	Oh, if only I were the little wheel,
So wollt ich Lieb ihr sausen;	I would murmur to her of my love,
Und wär ich der Mühlbach unterher,	and if I were the millstream down below,
So wollt ich Lieb' ihr brausen.	I would shout to her of my love,
Und wär ich im Wasser der Wasserman,	and if I were the merman in the waters,
Mit starkem Arm faßt ich sie an,	I would grasp her with my strong arms
Und zög sie in mich hinunter.	and drag her down with me.

Müller may have borrowed the motif of "sausendes-brausendes" activity to impress the miller maid and improved on it for his poem "Am Feierabend." Even more important, he may have found the tragic dénouement of the *Liederspiel* and the later poetic cycle here in this poem. At the end of the fourth and last verse, the love-sick poetic persona threatens to drown himself in the millstream if the miller maid does not return his love ("Und wenn ich nicht ruh' in der Müllerin Arm, / So ruh' ich in ihren Wassern"), a threat that becomes actuality in Müller's versions of the mill drama. Theodor Körner (1789–1813), the facile young poet and hero of the War of Liberation,[15] wrote both a tragic ballad entitled "Treuröschen" (Faithful Rose) about a bold huntsman and his bride and "Der Jüngling und der Bach" (The Youth and the Brook), probably also inspired by Goethe's miller poems and not published until after the inception of Müller's cycle. The latter poem tells of a youth – but not a miller lad – who befriends a confidant-brook in his native land and then is overcome by the twin forces of *Sehnsucht* and *Wanderlust*. After wandering for many years and through many travails, he returns to the brook and drowns himself in it; like Müller's brook several years later, this brook lovingly enfolds the lad's body. That the liquid embrace is in one sense a return to the womb, life coming full circle to death, seems evident in both of these poetic tales, especially in Müller, whose lad repudiates the betrayals of adult female sexuality and goes back to the maternal element and to oblivion. Körner's lad too wishes to regress, first to youth, then even farther back, to non-existence.

Der Jüngling und der Bach	The Youth and the Brook
(stanzas 8 and 9 of 9)	
Und plötzlich hält er still und weint,	And suddenly he stops and weeps.
Er steht an des Stromes Rande	He stands at the banks of the stream
Und erkennt den alten treuen Freund,	and recognizes his old, faithful friend
Aus dem seligen Jugendlande,	from the blessed land of his youth
Und gedenkt der fröhlichen Knabenlust,	and thinks of the happy boyhood pleasures,
Und auf's neue erwacht der Schmerz in der Brust.	and sorrow reawakens in his heart once again.
Und er ruft: wohl versteh' ich den dumpfen Gruß,	And he cries out: now I understand the muffled greeting.
Wohl erkennen die Freunde sich wieder;	Truly the friends recognize each other again;
So empfange den ewigen Bundes-Kuß!	so receive the eternal kiss of brotherhood!

Und er stürzt in die Wogen sich nieder,	And he throws himself into the waves,
Und treu umarmen die Wellen den Freund.	and the waves faithfully embrace their friend.
Sein Auge bricht – er hat ausgeweint.[16]	He has passed away – he has finished crying.

One notes in particular the beautiful idiom, "sein Auge bricht" in the last line, signifying the moment when the living quality of the eyes vanishes, as if suddenly broken, and is replaced by the glaze of death.

For their *Liederspiel*, the younger Stägemann circle assigned roles as follows: Hedwig, the hostess of the gathering, was to be Rose, the miller's beautiful daughter. Her suitors were Friedrich Förster as a country squire;[17] Wilhelm Müller, predestined by his name, as the journeyman miller; Wilhelm Hensel as the hunter (Hedwig was secretly in love with him at the time); and Luise Hensel as a gardener. With their roles assigned, the game of "Rose, die Müllerin" began, perhaps as early as October, perhaps in November. According to his diary, Müller spent the entire month of October in his native Dessau,[18] and Luise Hensel fell ill in December, shortly before her sister Frau Karoline Rochs died of puerperal fever on December 23 after giving birth to her second child; both eventualities would have removed two of the most proficient poets in the group from participation in the Berlin salon, especially as the Hensels lived in the town of Schöneberg, a little distance away from the city.[19] We know from one of Brentano's letters of December 1816 that the *Liederspiel*, like the earlier exemplars of the genre by Reichardt, was acted with whatever gestures and vocal inflections the amateur actors deemed appropriate; he particularly notes and praises Luise's reticence as an actress.[20] Given his love for her and his transmutation of her into an angelic figure, he would not have wanted her purity sullied by imputations of acting skill.

As Hedwig von Stägemann, by then Frau Ignaz von Olfers, later told one of Luise's biographers, the verses for the *Liederspiel* were improvised on the spot and written down quickly, hence, the subsequent loss of many of the poems and the impossibility of full reconstruction.[21] Indeed, Ruth Bingham has speculated that the Stägemann *Liederspiel* may never have existed as "a work," but only as numerous poems, their order beyond determination, held together by an unwritten general story; it is also possible that the poems were improvised as a group rather than being the product of individual authorship.[22] Of certain roles, such as Friedrich Förster's *Junker*-suitor, little or nothing remains, although it is possible that his poem "Mein Verlangen" (My Longing), published in *Die Sängerfahrt*, comes from the *Liederspiel*; the title hints that it could be a response or poetic twin to Hedwig von Stägemann's poem "Mein Sinn" (My Wish), printed in the same source. "She plucked a little rose from the branch," Förster writes in stanza 2, "All the other colors seem dead next to the crimson of her cheeks." The sappy effusion – she plucks a violet in stanza 3, upon which the poetic persona sighs, "Thou violet, close your eyes, go to rest for a little while" – gives no clue to the unfolding of the miller tale, if indeed it was born of the *Liederspiel* at all.[23] The rose, the invocation of death, the motif of closing one's eyes are all elements repeated elsewhere in the songplay, however, while the miller maid's act of plucking a rose symbolically suggests either sexual experience or the willingness to engage in lovemaking – it is she who picks the flower, not her besotted suitor.

Other poems can be more securely identified as coming from the *Liederspiel*. Eleven previously unpublished poems from Luise Hensel's fourteen gardener poems were later found among her *Nachlass* by Frank Spiecker, who included the seven courtship poems and seven mourning poems in his 1936 book *Luise Hensel als Dichterin* (Luise Hensel as Poetess). In those poems, the gardener confides his love to his beloved flowers, appoints the flowers and birds his intermediaries to "the beautiful Rose," and plants flowers all around her house so that she will always live in the midst of his love. (When the miller in Müller's "Des Müllers Blumen" speaks of planting little blue flowers beneath the maiden's window, he either echoes the gardener's motif or provides the model for it.) In his remaining poems, the gardener sings a night song that is both prayer and serenade, weeps when a great stone inexplicably smashes his flowers (the great stone a symbol of inexplicable adversity, destroyed hopes, and Fate's malice – evidence as well of the alle- gorical substratum in the *Liederspiel*), dreams of enveloping Rose in a mantle of flowers so that noblemen and millers cannot see her, and mourns her death, the seven mourn- ing songs themselves constituting a cycle-within-the-play, as Bingham has perceptively pointed out.[24] In these poems, which retain their original improvisatory quality, one can see how the members of the salon echoed one another's themes: the gardener, like the miller, looks into the millbrook and sighs for love.

Am Bach	**At the Brook**
(stanza 1 only)	
Ich sitz' in meinen Blumen,	I sit amidst my flowers,
Seh' still der Welle nach,	looking quietly into the waves.
Sie rinnt, sie rauscht so schnelle,	The brook runs along, it rushes so quickly,
Nimmt hin mein leises Ach.	carrying away my soft sigh, "Ah!"
Du Welle, liebe Welle	thou waves, dear waves
In Liebchens Mühlenbach!	in the beloved's millstream!

The sexual ambiguity of the gardener's role is especially piquant because at the time Luise Hensel herself was wooed by many suitors, and because the gardener is never a serious contender for the miller maid's affections; he remains an eloquent outsider, a pained witness to the miller's and hunter's successful suits. Not even in company and at play could Luise keep her acute psychic conflicts (of which more later) at bay: her noc- turnal serenade to the miller maid swerves near the end from formulaic lover-like speech to tearful prayer for relief of the *gardener's*, not the maiden's, fears. One notices as well the *volkstümlich* chain-link construction by which the third line of each quatrain gives rise to the next quatrain and the words "Schwester, gute Nacht" in stanza 4 ("Sister, good night" – she converts any erotic object into the safer form of a "brother" or "sister").

Nachtlied	**Night song**
(stanzas 1–2 and 4 of 5)	
Bist du schlafen gangen,	Have you gone to sleep?
Hast genug gewacht?	Have you kept vigil long enough?
Hält' dich Traum umfangen?	Do dreams enclose you?
Liebe, gute Nacht.	Beloved, good night.
Hält der Traum umfangen	Do soft dreams, still dawning,
Dämmernd still und sacht	envelope your
Deine rosen Wangen?	rosy cheeks?
Süße, gute Nacht.	Sweet one, good night.

Wenn der Sternlein Prangen	When the little stars' brilliance
Mir durch Thränen lacht,	smiles at me through tears,
Weicht von mir das Bangen	fear departs from me.
Schwester, gute Nacht.	Sister, good night.

We are fortunate to have these poems. Luise did not revise her gardener poems for later publication, as her brother, Hedwig, and Müller would do. She did, however, keep them.

Enough remains of the *Liederspiel*-by-committee to guess that it was of considerable heft and length and to know that it differed in significant ways both from Müller's first published version of the cycle in 1818, containing twelve poems, and the final poetic monodrama, completed in 1820.[25] Both plot and characters undergo a sea-change by the end of this protracted metamorphosis, a transformation in which everything is refracted through the prism of the miller's consciousness alone. In the Stägemann drama, we hear the tale from a variety of different viewpoints, including a supporting cast taken from nature – a talking stone, birds, a brook, flowers – according to eighteenth-century convention. For example, birds, traditionally erotic symbols (Papageno's "Ein Vogelfänger bin ich ja" comes to mind) and message-bearers for faithful or faithless lovers in folk poems, bring Rose the hunter's messages of love in "Vogelgesang vor der Müllerin Fenster" and convey his seductive flattery, his braggart's pride in supplanting the miller, and his not-so-veiled misogyny in calling her "Rose, Lose." The Stägemann song-play, furthermore, extends beyond the point where the later monodrama ends, closing not with the miller lad's death but with Rose's. In the *Liederspiel*, the young miller prevails briefly over the other suitors and then commits suicide when she spurns him for the hunter. The miller maid, whose guilty awareness of the miller's suffering is evident even as she expresses her attraction to the hunter, is overcome by remorse and throws herself into the brook, after which the others compose songs of mourning for her. The gardener alone sings seven *Klagelieder*; even if one assumes that the more proficient poets in the group (Müller as the miller and Luise as the gardener) would naturally be more fluent and prolific in their contributions, the amateur poets less so, the *Liederspiel* must have been formidable in scope.

As one might expect, it is the hunter and the miller maid who differ most drastically from their later incarnation in Müller's monodrama – in the *Liederspiel*, they were brought to life by poets other than Müller, and they speak for themselves, rather than appearing through the miller lad's eyes. Wilhelm Hensel's hunter is, if one will pardon the paradox, a conventional "free spirit," a bold, merry figure based on a pattern taken from centuries of German folk song (see chapter 2). His poems possibly included the "Jägerlied" (Hunter's Song), later published in Friedrich de la Motte-Fouqué's *Frauentaschenbuch für das Jahr 1820* (Women's Periodical for the Year 1820):

Jägerlied	**Hunter's Song**
Morgenhell	Morning's brightness
Zieht der lustige Waidgesell	draws the merry huntsman
Singend hin durch Flur und Forst,	singing onward through field and forest,
Stehet frank auf Adlers Horst	he stands free by the eagle's eyrie,
Wolkennah.	close to the clouds,
Trararah!	Trararah!

Wie die rothe Morgenzeit	Like the crimson morning,
Hat den Leib in Grün gekleidt	he has clad his body in green;
Blüht sein Antlitz roth aus grün	his countenance blossoms redly from the green
Und den Brüder grüßend, ziehn	and, greeting his brothers,
Hornesklänge fern und nah.	he blows horn-calls near and far.
Trararah!	Trararah!
Morgen zählt die Strahlen nicht,	Morning does not count
Die er um die Erde flicht,	the rays it sheds over the world;
Jäger zählt nicht Wort und Klang	the huntsman does not count his words and tones.
Frisch und fröhlich läßt er schwingen	His music resounds boldly and happily –
Klingen, Singen	echoing, singing –
Frei ob freiem Bergeshang,	from the mountain peak,
Schweben, weben jubelnd da	swaying, hovering, rejoicing . . .
Trararah!²⁶	Trararah!

One reads this poem with a certain indulgence (Hensel also wrote other poems and a one-act play entitled *Ritter Hans*) and is glad he chose to pursue a vocation as an artist. If Wilhelm Hensel was uncritical of the model he emulated, Müller would later devise a more complex version of the huntsman topos for *Die schöne Müllerin* in which the hunter represents sexual license and freedom from civilization's constraints, a folk hero Müller castigates from within his poetry.

Hedwig von Stägemann's miller maid was also different from the character we encounter only in glimpses in the monodrama, where she is first idealized as the object of troubadour-like veneration and then excoriated as a heartless coquette. In the *Liederspiel*, however, she is someone to mourn sincerely, a lively, three-dimensional creature of considerable strength of will and a loving heart. In one of Hedwig's four extant poems from the *Liederspiel*, "Müllers Liebchen" (Miller's Sweetheart), the miller maid awakens from "wondrous dreams," springs out of the house, and looks about for her beloved white-clad miller with his friendly blue eyes, thick shock of hair, and sweet disposition – or so it seems at the beginning of the poem. A surprise lies in wait: she has had a change of heart, and the miller is transformed from beloved to ex-beloved in mid-poem. (Both this poem and "Mein Sinn!" were published in Friedrich Förster's *Die Sängerfahrt* under the allegorical pseudonym "Liebetraut." The full names and even birthplaces of most of the male poets appear on the title page and in the table of contents, but the two women writers, Luise Hensel and Hedwig von Stägemann, are not similarly acknowledged.)

Müllers Liebchen	**Miller's Sweetheart**
(stanzas 1–7 of 15)	
Ei, sieht ins kleine Fensterlein	Is not the light of dawn already
Das Frühlicht mir nicht schon herein?	peering into my little window?
Entflohen ist der Träume Schaar,	The multitude of dreams that fluttered
Die mich umgaukelt wunderbar.	about me so wonderfully has vanished.
O! wie verjüngt dem muntern Augenpaare	Oh, how rejuvenated to my merry eyes
Das lichterhellte Weltall nun erscheint,	the bright, light-drenched world now seems!

Ich flechte rasch die aufgelösten Haare,	I hurriedly comb my unbound hair;
Um diese Zeit erwart' ich meinen Freund.	I am expecting my sweetheart at this time.

Schnell spring ich aus dem kleinen Haus,	Quickly I run from the little house,
Vor meine niedre Thür hinaus,	stand before my low door,
Und sauge ein die Morgenluft	drink in the morning breeze,
Und lausche, ob mich jemand ruft.	and listen for someone calling to me.

Hör' ich das Rasseln schwerer Wagen,	If I should hear heavy carts rattling,
Wie horch ich auf in ahnungsvoller Lust,	how I listen in pleasurable foreboding,
Und seh ich, daß sie Mehl in Säcken tragen,	and if I should see that they carry sacks of flour,
Wie klopft das Herz mir in der kleinen Brust.	how my heart beats in my little breast!

Wie pochts, wie wird es groß und weit,	How it beats, how it swells,
Gewahrt's ein weißes Müllerkleid,	awaiting a white-clad miller.
Dein Liebling ist es, ruft's in mir,	It is your beloved, a voice cries within me,
Dein Trauter ist's, er kommt zu dir!	it is your darling – he is coming to you!

Doch giebt es gleich viel Müllersknechte,	But there are many miller lads,
Sind all' wie Einer angethan,	they are all dressed alike,
So ist doch Einer nur der Rechte,	yet only one is the right one;
Nur Einem bin ich zugethan.	I am devoted only to one.

Nur Einer hat so reiches Haar,	Only one of them has such thick hair,
So freundlich blaues Augenpaar,	such friendly blue eyes,
Nur Einem liegt so frommer Sinn,	only one has such a pure heart,
So holde Sittlichkeit.[27]	such good breeding.

But "holde Sittlichkeit" is less compelling than the twin forces of nature and erotic novelty. Despite her attempts to persuade herself that she still loves the miller, that she is both physically attracted to him and captivated by his moral worth, she is unsuccessful and abandons the effort, bidding Nature bear messages to her new beloved, whom she coyly refuses to identify.

(stanzas 8–13 of 15)

Geschwinde ist er abgestreichelt,	Quickly he wipes off
Der weiße Staub von dem Gesicht,	the white dust from his face.
Den Müller hab' ich fortgeschmeichelt,	I have wheedled the miller away,
Den Müller – doch den Liebsten nicht.	the miller – but not my beloved.

Ist Liebe doch, wie Sonnenschein,	Is love then like sunshine?
Sie blicket überall hinein	It shines down on everyone
Und folgt ihr auch kein Dienerschwarm,	and if no crowd of servants follows it,
Ist sie doch nie an Dienern arm.	it is never lacking in followers.

Lieblicher Bote im wolkigen Wagen,	Gentle messenger in cloudy carriages,
Rege die flüsternden Flügel geschwind,	stir your fluttering wings quickly;
Eile den Kuß ihm hinüber zu tragen,	hurry to take my kiss to him,
Grüß den Geliebten mir, plaudernder Wind.	greet the beloved for me, chattering wind.

Dring ein zu ihm, du Sonnenlicht,	Surround him, sunlight,
Umspiele mild sein Angesicht,	play gently about his face,

Doch stich ihn scharf, doch triff ihn schwül,	but prick him sharply, oppress him with sultry heat,
Treibt er mit andern loses Spiel.	if he plays wicked games with someone else.
Lüftchen, ihr lieblichen, kühlt seine Wangen,	Gentle little breezes, cool his cheeks;
Vöglein, ihr flatternden, ruft mir ihn her,	fluttering little birds, call him to me.
Stille! – dort kommt er schon selber gegangen,	Quiet! – there he comes;
Freundlicher Boten bedarf ich nicht mehr.	I do not need friendly messengers any more.
Also sprach das Müllersliebchen,	Thus spoke the miller's beloved,
Sprang hinweg vom Fensterlein,	sprang away from the little window,
Hüpfte tänzelnd aus dem Stübchen	skipped dancing from the little room
Nach dem duftumhauchten Hain.	to the fragrant meadow.

Poetic images echo between the participants in the *Liederspiel*: Hedwig's lines "Entflohen ist der Träume Schaar, / Die mich umgaukelt wunderbar" in "Müllers Liebchen" are kin to the miller's "Morgengruß," in particular, the lines "Hat es die Nacht so gut gemeint, / Daß ihr euch schließt und bückt und weint / Nach ihrer stillen Wonne?" and the injunction, "Nun schüttelt ab der Träume Flor." Implicit in Hedwig's allusions to birds, breezes, and sunshine as messengers of love is an understanding of sexual attraction as a natural force; the young artists of the Stägemann circle were rather bold in their exploration of "natural" morality, of rejuvenated sexual drives on the loose in springtime.

The theme of youthful sexuality is even more frankly explored in "Mein Sinn!" (My Wish!), in which Hedwig's Rose asserts her erotic freedom to be with the man she loves, yet again unnamed but surely the hunter, as implied by the hunting calls "Wohlauf, wohlauf" in the third stanza and the references to green, the forest, and roguishness. Women too, she asserts, feel the need to roam from love to love as will and whim dictate, to revel in sensual pleasures in the midst of Nature, whose amorally instinctual laws second her own desires.

Mein Sinn!	**My Wish!**
Durch Felsgestein und Büsche	Through rocks and bushes,
In mailich grüne Frische	in the Maytime green freshness,
Treibt es mich hin.	it drives me forth
Durch Wies' und Wald zu springen	to leap through meadow and forest,
Und schallend drein zu singen,	there to sing loudly –
Das ist mein Sinn.	That's what I want.
Die Blumen mir zu Füßen	The flowers at my feet
Bescheiden nach mir grüßen,	seem to greet me modestly;
Ich schreite drüber hin.	I stride over them.
Mein Muthwill läßt sie sterben,	In my mischievousness, I let them die,
Kann sorglos sie verderben	can destroy them without a care –
Das ist mein Sinn.	That's what I want.
Wohlauf, geschmückt mit Kränzen,	Let's go, bedecked with garlands,
Wohlauf zu muntern Tänzen,	to the merry dances,
Zum lauten Reigen hin;	to the gay round-dances –
Die Weisen und die Gecken	The wise ones and the dandies,
Ich will euch alle necken,	I'll flirt with all of you –
Das ist mein Sinn.	That's what I want.

Mit dem Geliebten wallen
Im Sang der Nachtigallen,
Ins einsam dunkle Grün,
Und freundlich nach ihm nicken
Und in die Sterne blicken,
    Das ist mein Sinn.

Und ist er recht versunken,
In Träumen wonnetrunken,
Dann schüttl' und neck ich ihn,
Und thu, als ob ich zürne,
Und ziehe kraus die Stirne,
    Das ist mein Sinn.

Dann laß ich mich versöhnen
Und lach ihn aus durch Thränen
Und knie vor ihn hin;
Mit Sternchen nach ihm zielen,
Mit seinen Locken spielen,
    Das ist mein Sinn!

April der wandelbare
Hat meinem Augenpaare
Sein schelmisch Licht verliehn;
Drum bald wie Sonnen scheinen
Und bald im Lächeln weinen,
    Das ist mein Sinn.[28]

To stroll with my lover
to the song of nightingales
into the lonely dark greenness,
to beckon him in encouragement –
to look at the stars –
    That's what I want.

And if he sinks deep
in dreams filled with joy,
then I'll shake him and tease him,
and pretend that I'm angry,
and wrinkle my brow –
    That's what I want.

Then I let myself be reconciled
and laugh at him through my tears
and kneel before him;
to give him a soulful look,
to play with his hair –
    That's what I want!

Fickle April
has lent my eyes
their roguish glint;
now to shine like the sun
and then to weep through smiles –
    That's what I want.

Was Müller in 1820 remembering Hedwig's second stanza when his miller cannot bring himself to tread on the forget-me-not flowers underfoot in "Blümlein Vergißmein" (see chapter 4)? Given the echoes between poets and poems in the *Liederspiel*, it seems likely. Hedwig's miller maid is only too willing to trample the flowers emblematic of women, in particular, of female modesty and lowliness, but for her erstwhile lover, it is an ideal that literally dies hard.

With "Mein Sinn!", the stage is thus seemingly set for a morality play in which female fickleness, however attractive it may be in its high-spirited élan, and willfulness – "That's what I want," she declares over and over again – will meet with doom, not because of condemnation by the outside world but because she herself is so conscience-stricken by her own perfidy and by the lad's suicide. Even as she declares her love for the hunter in "Wie's Vöglein möcht' ich singen" (Like a little bird would I sing), she feels compunction for the miller and pleads with him not to be so sad. This maiden is a more sympathetic character (certainly, a more fully adumbrated one) than the uncaring creature Müller sketches in the final lines of "Tränenregen," composed for the cycle, not for the *Liederspiel*. What sort of person, after all, would notice tears in the eyes of someone obviously smitten with her, make a humorless crack about it ("It's raining"), and leave? "Tränenregen" ends there, in a silence filled with the miller's refusal to acknowledge the true import of what his beloved has just said and done. At one level, Müller's *Die schöne Müllerin* is an exemplary study of the virgin–whore dichotomy in the European romance tradition: the miller invokes his beloved as an icon of perfection for the first half of the

13

cycle, a household-goddess (in "Das Mühlenleben," or "Life at the Mill," she is compared to "the eye of God," all-seeing and all-knowing), and then rails at her for her immoral behavior when she falls out of love with him (see chapter 4).

There are other changes en route from *Liederspiel* to monodrama as well, the result of a shift of focus in which events clearly delineated in the song-play become more enigmatic in the lyrical cycle, more a matter of doubt. In the *Liederspiel*, the miller lad's suit for Rose's affections is successful, however briefly, and the assurances of reciprocated love are not delusory. Nor is that love confined merely to heart palpitations and serenades: both Rose and the miller lad sing frankly of lovemaking, the latter in the jubilant song "Ein ungereimtes Lied" (An Unrhymed Song), a remarkably improvisatory-seeming work. Here, in a breathlessly enchained series of brief phrases beginning with "und," we are told openly that the miller and miller maid do not meet under the linden tree (the archetypal meeting-place for lovers with no other bedroom at hand) merely to chat, but to kiss, to embrace "Herz an Herz," and to weep, the "tears therein, tears so blissful" not difficult to decode as post-coital *tristesse*. The delicate hints of sexualized motion as the little blue flowers emblematic of the miller maid wave to and fro are also notable, the inferences stopping just short of triumphal announcement.

Ein ungereimtes Lied	**An Unrhymed Song**
Kein Liedchen mehr!	No more little songs,
Aber Küsse, Küsse!	but kisses, kisses!
Und Herz an Herz,	And heart to heart,
Und schwimmende Blicke,	and swimming glances,
Und Tränen drin!	and tears therein!
Und Tränen so selig,	And tears so blissful,
Und Seufzer dazu,	and also sighs,
Und Seufzer so süß!	and sighs so sweet!
Und wer sie sucht –	And whoever seeks her –
Und will nicht plaudern –	and does not want to chat –
Am Erlenbach,	at the alder-brook
Wo die Blümlein stehn,	where the little flowers grow,
Die kleinen, die blauen,	the small ones, the blue ones,
Und unter der Linde	and beneath the linden tree
Im Mühlengarten,	in the mill garden,
Da wird er sie finden,	there he will find her.
Da wehen sie hin	There they wave,
Und wehen sie her,	and wave to and fro,
Im Abendwind,	in the evening breeze,
Im Sternenschimmer!	in the starlight glow!
Ach, wer sie hörte,	Ah, whoever would hear them,
Und recht verstände,	and rightly understand,
Und wieder sänge	and would sing again
In Vers und Reim:	in verse and rhyme:
Die Lieder dort![29]	the songs there!

Sex, not song, the poet proclaims – but he does so in song, however unmetered; free love slyly equals free verse. Here, Müller devises his own variation on the Romantic play with multiple authorial presences (even more blatant in the prologue and epilogue to the later monodrama): the poet-singer miller lad supposedly abjures song, or versifying, for the more satisfying occupation of lovemaking and yet, poet that he is, he fantasizes that someone might come along, hear the unsung songs in the very air, and sing them yet again, this time ordered "in verse and rhyme" by someone who will presumably be less distracted by sensual delights. The call for future poetry spun from this ineffable exercise is likewise in poetry, the very world poeticized and resonant with song.

The excision of "Ein ungereimtes Lied" was not the only major change Müller wrought on the *Liederspiel* when he converted it into lyric monodrama. The original version of "Mein!" was entitled "Das schönste Liede" (The Most Beautiful Song) and was much simpler in form and tone than the later version.

Das schönste Liede	The Most Beautiful Song
Bächlein, laß dein Rauschen,	Little brook, stop your babbling;
Räder steht nur still!	mill-wheels, stand still!
Kommt heran zu lauschen,	Come here and listen,
Wer das schönste Liedchen hören will!	whoever would hear the most beautiful little song of all!
Still, ihr Nachtigallen,	Be quiet, nightingales;
Lerchen, Finken, still!	larks and finches, stop singing!
Laß ein eitel Schallen,	Cease your vain sounds,
Wer das schönste Liedchen hören will!	whoever would hear the most beautiful little song of all!
Sonne, gib herunter	Sun, give forth
Deinen hellsten Schein:	your most brilliant light;
Frühling, strahle bunter:	Spring, beam brightly.
Die geliebte Müllerin ist mein![30]	The beloved miller maid is mine!

The a b a b rhyme scheme, devoid of irregularities and simple to a fault, and the symmetrical quatrains consisting of three lines of trochaic trimeters and an exuberant refrain-line in pentameters – if the last line overflows the boundaries of the previous lines, it does so in the same fashion each time – bespeak an ordered poetic world in which love leads to reciprocity and consummation. But in the revised version for the cycle, love is a *disordering*, not an ordering force, and therefore a single rhyme chimes throughout the poem, the line lengths and rhythms changing unpredictably from line to line in a precise mirror of a mind disordered. Too manic and panic-stricken to devise symmetrical quatrains, the miller babbles an unbroken, irregular, single "stanza" and thereby throws his claim of possession into doubt. Is he delusional and raving, or is she really his? The youth of the *Liederspiel* is, briefly, luckier: sex for him is ecstasy. In the monodrama, it becomes sheerest hell (see chapter 4).

According to Ludwig Rellstab in *Ludwig Berger, ein Denkmal*, a two-volume memorial to Rellstab's teacher and friend, the Stägemann poets decided, when their poems were completed and assembled, that the play needed music. I wonder whether Müller might have been the impetus for the decision, as he actively sought musical settings of his verse; he once thanked the Berlin composer Bernhard Klein (1793–1832), who had published settings of six of his poems (including "Trock'ne Blumen" from *Die schöne Müllerin*) by saying, "For indeed my songs lead but half a life, a paper existence of black-and-white, until music breathes life into them, or at least calls it forth and awakens it if it is already dormant in them."[31] Berger, who was Luise Hensel's piano teacher, became their musical collaborator, and the work inevitably changed under his influence; here, the miller becomes the focal character in a tale, albeit a tale with many gaps, that begins with his arrival and ends with his death. The tension between the various male suitors comes more to the fore, while Rose becomes a stereotypical love-interest, far less important than in the Stägemann song-play. Her choice from among the male suitors seems quixotic, her anguish over the decision is diminished to next-to-nothing, and her death is eliminated altogether. As in all later versions of the cycle, Berger's work ends with the brook's lullaby; as Ruth Bingham so beautifully writes, "The miller, twice drowned in blue, is embraced by his true and loyal friend."[32] In his unreciprocated love for Luise Hensel, did Berger identify with the miller's pain and thereby alter the configuration of the drama? He included two of her gardener's poems in op. 11, despite the fact that they dis-order the coherence of his version of the tale; the miller maid never mentions him, nor does anyone else in the story. Each of the suitors is allotted two songs in nos. 1–6, but despite this symmetry, it was, one guesses, out of love for Luise that Berger chose thus to inter-rupt the more important relationship between the hunter, miller lad, and miller maid.

Whatever the reasons for his choice of poetry-for-music and his ordering of those poems to form a different story, he first set "Ich habe das Grün so gern" (I like green so much, the refrain of Hedwig von Stägemann's "Wie's Vöglein möcht' ich ziehen") and then continued with the other settings after the group expressed their approval of the first lied. Müller writes in his diary for December 14, 1816 that Berger had requested his and Wilhelm Hensel's presence that evening, possibly in order to work on their contribu-tions to the song cycle.[33] Five of the ten poems Berger set to music are by Müller, whose poetry he evidently considered the most *komponabel*, but not without emendation. According to Rellstab, the composer worked slowly and painfully, making many revi-sions and torturing Müller with criticism and demands for change. Upon seeing the beautiful musical results, the poet reportedly complied gladly with Berger's tyranny, although one wonders if Müller was really so amenable or if he simply acceded author-ity to someone far more eminent than he was at the time.[34] Rellstab does not say how long the "slow and painful" process required, but Müller's departure from Berlin in August 1817 must be the *terminus ad quem* for the collaboration. When the composition was completed, Rellstab and others persuaded Berger to give his songs to the newly founded Berlin music publishing firm of E. H. G. Christiani, who published them as *Gesänge aus einem gesellschaftlichen Liederspiele 'Die schöne Müllerin'* (Songs from a Sociable Song-play, "The Beautiful Miller Maid") of 1818, the first of many musical works born of the Stägemann salon (see chapter 3).

INSIDE THE LIEDERSPIEL: BEHIND THE SCENES

Here at the midway point, we move from the song-play to its creators, from art to life. A cautionary word before embarking on biographical matters – whatever the flamboyant poses or eccentric behavior expected of geniuses in the nineteenth-century mythology of the artist, the intellectual labor required for Heine to craft a poem (if there were ever poetry suffused with the poet's personality, this is it) or for Chopin (who lived the myth) to construct his compositions was another matter, then as now. Müller knew the difference: Arthur, the semi-autobiographical protagonist of his second novella *Debora* may invoke white-hot creation as if seized by divine forces, but his creator told the Leipzig publisher Friedrich Arnold Brockhaus in 1826, "I am very scrupulous about style and count syllables anxiously."[35] It was a habit begun early – the protracted history of his miller cycle reveals that he tinkered with the poems first written for the *Liederspiel* at each stage of their publication in various literary periodicals, in Berger's cycle, and in Müller's *Waldhornisten-Gedichte I*. Seeing the Stägemann circle's romantic and artistic travails mirrored in the *Liederspiel* is one thing; "counting syllables" is another, and both are germane to an understanding of the song-play, the poetic cycle, and the *schöne Müllerin* song cycles.

The crisis in the various erotic entanglements among the Stägemann circle coincides directly with the genesis of the *Liederspiel*. The woman at the center of the tensions was Luise Hensel, and one of those who fell in love with her was Wilhelm Müller.[36] We begin disentangling the complex web of emotions stated and unstated, requited and unrequited, with these two.

Wilhelm Hensel's pencil sketches and charcoal drawings of his sister from 1815–16 show a reserved young woman with downcast eyes and an oval face, pretty but quietly so (Figs. 1a and 1b). Luise was born on March 30, 1798 as the fifth child of a Lutheran pastor, Johann Jakob Ludwig Hensel, from humble origins (he was a baker's son) who died in 1809 when she was eleven.[37] The impoverished family of five (Luise's mother, the former Luise Trost; Wilhelm (Fig. 2); an older sister Karoline; and a younger sister Wilhelmine) moved in 1810 to Berlin, where Luise attended the Realschule. She too, like her brother, was talented artistically and even briefly considered training as a painter, although her mother forbade it; unlike her brother, she was musically gifted – she played the harp and studied piano with Berger. It is through her poetry, however, that we know her best; her most famous poem, "Nachtgebet" (Nighttime Prayer), or "Müde bin ich, geh zur Ruh'" (I am tired and go to rest), written in the autumn of 1816 when the miller play was created, is often anthologized and was set to music by Ferdinand Ries and Carl Reinecke, among others.[38]

Poetry evidently ran in the family: her mother and older sister Karoline wrote occasional verse commemorating family celebrations, her brother Wilhelm had collaborated with Müller on another volume of poems entitled *Die Bundesblüthen* (Blossoms of the League), published that same fateful year (Berlin: Maurer, 1816), and Luise herself began writing poetry when she was only eight years old. Her first published poems appeared in Förster's *Die Sängerfahrt* (The Minstrels' Voyage) under the pseudonym Ludwiga, a name that almost certainly alludes to her unrequited love for a young statesman-in-the-making named Ludwig von Gerlach (of whom more shortly).[39] Her poetry was known and circulated among the members of the Stägemann circle for several years before the appearance of Förster's anthology, however – Elisabeth Stägemann spoke of Luise's "very pretty little poems" in a letter to her husband on February 20, 1815.[40] She must not have seen any of the more anguished religious works.

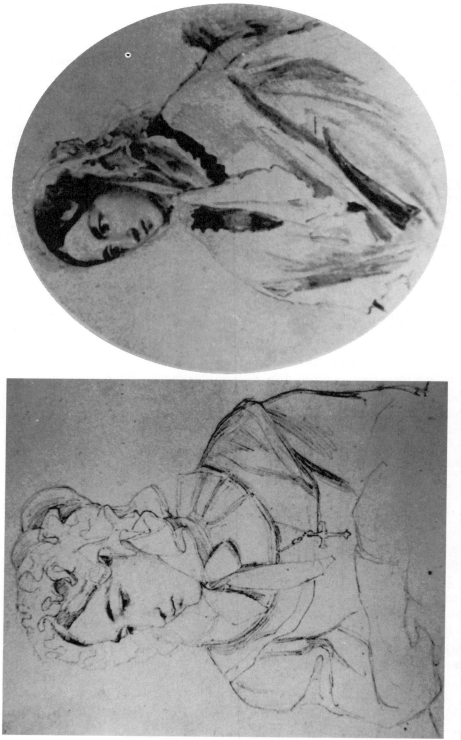

Figure 1a Pencil sketch of Luise Hensel (1798–1876) by her brother Wilhelm, dated October 14, 1828. KdZ 3(7/26). Figure 1b Pencil drawing, heightened with white chalk and inscribed "Herr, bin ich's?" (Lord, is it I?), dated January 9, 1856. KdZ 4(31/15).

Figure 2   Wilhelm Hensel (1794–1861), Self-portrait in 1829.

Luise Hensel was a complex personality, and interior conflicts between asceticism and sensuality dominate her early poetry, with titles such as "Sehnsucht nach Ruhe" (Longing for Peace), "Sursum corda!", "Gebet um Beharrlichkeit" (Prayer for Perseverance), "Immer–Nimmer" (Ever–Never), "Rat von oben" (Advice from Above), and "In schwerer Krankheit" (In Great Illness).[41] Although it should always be kept in mind that the subjects of poetry are dictated as much by generic choices (for example, the themes endemic to German Protestant penitential verse) as by personality, an idiosyncratic torment peers through the conventional sentiments and subjects. There is very little light and air and youthfulness in her poems; "Die Siebzehnjährige auf dem Balle" (The Seventeen Year-Old Girl at the Ball) of 1815, for example, is a *memento mori*, the poetic persona telling her hapless suitor – Wilhelm Müller? or someone else? or no one? – that he loves only the transitory youthful beauty doomed to wither and die all too quickly.

Die Siebzehnjährige auf dem Balle

Du liebst mich, weil durch braunes Haar
Sich schlingt der grüne Lebenskranz,
Weil frisch und voll der Wangen Paar
Und leicht der Fuß sich hebt im Tanz.

O, armer Jüngling! wisse, bald
Ist all das hin, was du geliebt,
Geknickt die blühende Gestalt,
Die jetzt den Zauber auf dich übt.

Denn eine Blume bin ich nur,
Und kurz ist alles Erdenblühn;
Drum suche ew'ger Schöne Spur,
Ihr weihe deines Herzens Glühn.

Sieh, wenig Lenze gehn ins Tal
Und hin ist dieser Augen Schein,
Gewelkt der Mund, die Wange fahl,
Man sargt die kalte Hülle ein.

Und nur das Kreuz am Hügelrand
Sagt, daß ein Leben hier geblüht,
Und betend faltet wohl die Hand
Der Pilger, der vorüberzieht.[42]

The Seventeen Year-Old Girl at the Ball

You love me, so long as life's green
garland is wound in my brown hair,
so long as my cheeks are rosy and plump,
and I can dance lightly and fleetly.

Oh, poor youth! Know that soon
everything you loved will be no more,
the blossoming form, that now
works its magic on you, cast down.

For I am only a flower,
and all earthly blossoms last but a brief while;
therefore seek the traces of eternal
beauty, dedicate your glowing heart to it.

See, the brief springtime goes into the valley.
Gone is the lustre from these eyes,
the mouth wrinkled, the cheeks faded;
they bury the cold, dead husk.

And only the cross on the grave-mound
says that a life once blossomed here,
and the pilgrim who passes by
folds his hands in prayer.

In "Die Kinder in der Fremde" (The Children in a Strange Land) of 1815, the elements of her style are already fully formed, and her favorite themes emerge full-blown. In this allegory of life-as-pilgrimage, the human wanderers are all, spiritually speaking, children who have been promised a return home to the heavenly father and mother after the trials of their journey:

Die Kinder in der Fremde

Ach Mutter! bleibst so lange,
Es wird uns Kindern bange,
Der Abend ist so kalt;
Die Winde schaurig wehen

The Children in a Strange Land

Oh mother, stay with us,
your children are afraid.
The evening is so cold,
the wind blows terrifyingly,

Und lange Schatten gehen
Und Löwen brüllen durch den Wald.

long shadows move about
and lions roar in the forest.

Weit sind wir heut gegangen,
Und tragen nun Verlangen,
Nach unsrer Mutter Schoß;
Komm, trockne unsre Tränen,
Lös' auf dies bange Sehnen,
Mach' unsre müden Herzen los.

We have gone far today
and now long
for our mother's lap.
Come, dry our tears,
release us from this fearful longing,
put our weary hearts at ease.

Du sagtest uns am Morgen:
Wir sollten ohne Sorgen
Von deiner Schwelle gehn;
Wenn wir den Berg erklommen
Und wenn die Nacht gekommen,
Dann würden wir dich wiedersehn.

You told us in the morning,
we should go from your threshold
without worry.
When we reached the peak of the mountains
and when night came,
then we would see you again.

Wir mußten mühsam wallen
Und viele sind gefallen
Und mancher ging voran.
Oft mußten wir auch weinen;
Durch Dornen und auf Steinen,
Durch Hitz' und Sturm ging unsre Bahn.

We had to wander with great effort,
and many fell
and many went ahead.
Often we had to weep.
Our path took us through thorns and stones,
through passion and storm.

Nun geht der Tag zu Ende,
D'rum heben wir die Hände
Und suchen deine Hand;
Tu' auf die traute Zelle!
Sind wieder an der Stelle,
Da du uns hast hinausgesandt.

Now the day draws to an end,
now we raise our hands
and look for thy hand.
Make ready the snug cell!
We are once again at the place
from which you sent us forth.

Laß uns in grünen Wiegen
Im weißen Hemdlein liegen
So tief und still und dicht;
Laß Tränen uns befeuchten,
Laß auf uns niederleuchten
Dein ewig klares Mondgesicht.

Let us lie in our white garments
in green fields,
so deep and quiet and close;
let tears bedew us,
let your eternally clear moon-visage
shine down upon us.

Den Schleier, blau gewoben,
Den breite weit aus oben,
D'rin laß uns hoffend ruhn.
Einst wird es wieder tagen,
Dann wird der Vater sagen:
"Steht auf, ihr Kindlein, alle nun."

The veil woven of blue
that spread out wide above us,
there let us, hoping, rest.
One day, dawn will come again,
Then the Father will say to us:
"All now arise, my children."

Her characteristic poetic rhythm is nervous and Angst-ridden. The fearfulness before the world one so often finds in her poetry is here emphasized by the addition of a fourth foot to the final line, weighing down the conclusion of each stanza; the allegorical lions who roar in the wild forests of life are all the more threatening for it. Was it here in Luise's seventh stanza, with its blue veil of the sky "spread out wide above us," that Müller found, and turned to his own purposes, the perspective from the grave that is so moving an element of "Des Baches Wiegenlied"? From what other vantage point can one see "der Himmel da droben, wie ist er so weit!"?

21

Determined to find everything she did perfect but perturbed by the tone and content of her verse, Müller in 1815 characterized her works in his diary as "wonderful poems, but dark, or rather not so much dark, because they glow with fiery piety, but without love, [filled with] a longing for the afterlife, lost hopes, weariness with life."[43] The diagnosis was apt (Müller would later become an astringent literary critic who did not shrink from harsh judgments). Luise had absorbed her parents' piety in a concentrated and anguished form, psychologically all the more powerful because of her search for spiritual authority in the wake of her father's death. For her, the religious obligations absorbed in childhood and adolescent sexual awakening, *caritas* and *eros*, were incompatible, and the strength of her sensual impulses something to be fought with considerable desperation. In another of the early poems, "Untreue, Reue, neue Treue" (Betrayal, Repentance, New Faith), she again renounces earthly love, declaring "I have found a lover / who is not of this world; / to him alone am I bound."[44] But the declaration was easier said than done, and "Untreue," or surrender to earthly love, beckoned; indeed, one version of the 1816 poem "Ergebung" (Submission) is subtitled "Nach einem schweren Kampfe" (After a Bitter Struggle). Those struggles are recorded in her diaries, in the sheaves of poetry she wrote throughout the years of young womanhood, and in her extant letters to her family and members of the Stägemann circle. In one letter written in early 1817 to Brentano, when he was attempting to win her hand by means of psychological blackmail, she wrote, attempting to explain her reliance on Christian precepts and her determination to direct all feeling into the single channel of religious sublimation:

If I had not come to know Holy Scripture and if I had not learned to believe and understand it in all simplicity, by the unmerited grace of God, I believe, I tell you in all honesty, that I would have become a witch, or more, if I had not come to that, I would have gone mad, or I would have sought frenetically to plunge into all the vanities of the world. I would without doubt have become the devil's prey.[45]

To accede to desire for human love on earth was indulgence in self-will and therefore counter to God's wishes. Because she did in fact fall in love and because others fell in love with her, the pitched battles between heavenly and earthly bridegrooms continued for two crisis-fraught years from 1816 to 1818.

It was with this tormented, gifted young woman that Wilhelm Müller, himself at a crossroads in life, fell in love in 1815. Wilhelm Hensel's pencil sketch of Müller in 1816 shows a slender, refined youth with large, intense eyes (Fig. 3), the image in keeping with Friedrich de la Motte-Fouqué's description of the young poet:

His countenance bloomed in its first youth, and an almost feminine embarrassment colored the transparent skin of his cheeks with red that quickly waxed and waned. In his eyes gleamed the pride of the budding poet; a full garland of blond, dishevelled hair adorned his high forehead.[46]

He was, from all accounts, a charming creature whose literary talent was already manifest in his contributions to *Die Bundesblüthen* and his translations of Minnesong (*Blumenlese aus den Minnesingern*), both published in 1816. In his love for Luise, he lived a medievalizing romance redivivus on a German middle-class stage, its ending more in accord with the tragic traditions of romance than he might have preferred.

Figure 3   Wilhelm Müller (1794–1827), sketched by Wilhelm Hensel in 1816.

That love is recorded in his diary, which begins on October 7, 1815, his twenty-first birthday, and ends in December 1816. Müller had returned to Berlin and his studies in philology, history, and literature at the University in late November 1814, after a stint at a wartime post in Brussels. There, he had an affair with a woman we know only as Thérèse, an episode that evidently caused his father much concern and ended badly. Chastened, Müller next fell in love with Luise; while they discussed literature (she was fond of Novalis – was he the source of the blue flowers symbolic of the miller maid in the *Liederspiel* and the cycle? – and of Hartmann von der Aue's *Der arme Heinrich*[47]), he day-dreamed of marriage. Müller recognized at the time that it was his pattern "since earliest childhood" to fall in love with those who did not reciprocate his feelings. In his timidity and reticence, it required, he writes, only the slightest of circumstances for the flame in his heart to be entirely extinguished; his love for Luise was in the same mold, but lasted longer and ran deeper, possibly a transitional stage between the infatuations that preceded it and the happy marriage to Adelheid von Basedow that came after.[48] The diary entry for November 8, 1815 is typical:

I must write to you, my Luise, before I go to sleep. I know that this letter will reach you, if not in words and in writing. You are truly within me, and whatever I say and write, I say and write as well to you, and you are that which I write to you. It is truly a rapturous thought that I am so entirely one with you, that your love has so penetrated me, that I have banished the person I once was and created [ersprießen] a new inner being out of your love. Whatever I have done, thought, felt, spoken, or created that is good and beautiful, I have created, spoken, and felt through you. What remains in me that is evil and hateful is the remains of the time of sensuality and freethinking that held me too long in its chains [a reference to Brussels and Thérèse]. Luise, my thanks to you are inexpressibly numerous: you have saved my soul, my immortal soul. I have you to thank for eternal blessedness – you alone – also perhaps for transitory earthly blessedness as well . . .[49]

He then re-reads the heated effusion critically and finds it "incomprehensible, excessive, and full of commonplaces" but refuses to alter what he has written because his emotion is too great for artistic constraint – a precursor of the miller in "Pause" who says "I cannot sing anymore; my heart is too full; I do not know how I can restrain it in rhyme." It is highly significant that he thus makes a literary judgment about his "feelings" – indeed, it is very difficult in this entire circle to differentiate between "real" feelings and literary poses. "All of my poetry," Müller confided in his diary, "comes from her – they [the poems] pass through my heart and then return to her."[50] Elsewhere, he speculated that if she liked his poetry, it is because there must be an affinity between them, and he sought every opportunity to visit the Hensel household. One day, he wrote the question "Luise, do you love me?" and the words "Yes" and "No" on pieces of paper and was playing with them; at first, the answer was "Yes," but an unlucky rearrangement produced a conjunction of "Yes" and "No": "Ja, nein Wilhelm."[51] In such youthful romantic play is possibly the origin of "Der Neugierige" and a world that shrinks to two little words.

Luise seems not to have discouraged his attentions. At the same time, however, she made no secret of her renunciatory impulses, not because Müller ever spoke openly to her of marriage but because the matter was so much on her mind. When she spoke of her wish to flee earthly chaos and reserve her heart for other-worldly things, Müller's private reaction was to think that at least no one else would have her if she and Heaven thus claimed one another.[52] He paid little heed to her religious turmoil (although at the time, he assumed, as if it were an actor's costume, the piety of a *Minnesänger* or an *echt* German patriot, he was not truly of a religious inclination); in his youthful narcissism, she was supposed to save his soul, not the other way around, and her avowals of renunciation did not keep him from fantasizing that Luise, who looked so charmingly domestic, might become his wife.[53] It mattered little to him of what she spoke, so long as she was there in the room with him: on one occasion in December 1815, he writes that they conversed of "biblical things," a comically vague designation.[54] It was Luise's misfortune that none of the men in love with her was truly attentive to her, to the significance of what she said and did in their presence.

By 1816, the diary had palled. Throughout the first half of the year, Müller wrote only a brief chronicle covering the span from February to late May, with only a few highlighted events summarized in chronological order. The gravest news came early: Luise was accidentally poisoned by escaping coal-gas on February 13 and came close to death.[55] Despite his concern, Müller was more interested in recording that he kissed her hand for the first time on the 15th, after she was out of danger. After May, Müller wrote nothing further in the diary until November 10, 1816, the same month in which the *Liederspiel* probably began. He does not mention the song-play, only that he kissed Luise on the right cheek in the course of a game at her house, after which he dreamed of "a new, pure life" in which Luise would be his; she "seems to know everything that I think, say, and do," he naively writes, unaware that he was simply imputing to her his own wish that she should be clairvoyant where he was concerned.[56] The diary then ends altogether with brief entries for December 15 and the Advent season:

I was at the Hensels for the holy evening. Luise gave me a songbook. Brentano was also there.

The first day of the holidays, I was also with her. At the Stägemanns in the evening.

On the third day of the holidays came the news of the death of her married sister [Karoline Rochs, who had died on December 23, with her mother at her side]. Luise, Minna [the younger sister Wilhelmine], Wilhelm, Brentano and I were together. Brentano read something aloud. We were in my room.[57]

Clemens Brentano (Fig. 4) was indeed there, and what transpired between the great writer and Luise Hensel put an end to Müller's fantasies of Biedermeier *Traulichkeit* with her. It is no wonder that the diary, devoted in large measure to Luise, ends where it does. Hedwig Stägemann's descendant and biographer, Marie von Olfers, writes that both August Stägemann and Wilhelm Müller "looked too deeply into the gardener-lad's beautiful eyes" but that both men were too young, and the matter was of no real import. (Luise may, speculatively, have been aware of August Stägemann's infatuation as well. In his diary for November 10, 1815, Müller records his fear and jealousy when Luise told him of a dream in which Hedwig's brother gave her a wondrously scented lily-like magic flower. Even though he realized that she had recently been reading Novalis and that the dream-fantasy was patterned upon *Heinrich von Ofterdingen*, he was still hurt and jealous.[58]) The sentiments Müller expresses in the diary are indeed immature, and yet the calf-love, as some would call it, persisted for over a year and undeniably had a great

Figure 4 Portrait of Clemens Brentano (1778–1842) by Wilhelm Hensel in 1819.

effect on the poet who began his first major poetic cycle in Luise's company and with her collaboration.

Brentano met Luise at the Stägemanns, according to Hedwig Stägemann, on October 10, 1816. Hedwig (Fig. 5), writing to her cousin Antoinette Schwinck one week later on 17 October, describes the previous week's Thursday soirée, when her brother August brought a group of young men to the house to join her, the Hensel daughters Luise and Minna, and Laura Gedike in "lively, amusing conversation."[59] Just as they were discussing the sarcastic, scandal-tinged Brentano, comparing him with Tieck, Brentano walked in, to the discomfiture of some and the amusement of others. To salvage an awkward social moment, Hedwig asked him to read aloud from his allegor-ical-patriotic comedy with a typically fantastic title, *Victoria und ihre Geschwister mit fliegenden Fahnen und brennender Lunte* (Victoria and her Sisters with Flying Banners and Burning Fuse), a failure with the Viennese public for whom it was written. According to her letter, Brentano exerted himself to be uncommonly witty, even singing songs he himself had composed, and she and Luise "howled like drunkards." Luise's own account, in a "Lebensskizze" she wrote thirty-nine years later, of their first meeting, differs in almost every particular: according to her, the date was either September 5 or 12, and there were only a few people present, not a large gathering. Luise furthermore records saying to August von Stägemann upon Brentano's entrance, "If he is nothing other than witty, he must be a pitiful and unfortunate man" and that Brentano went over to her immediately, looked at her gloomily, and said, "My God, you look just like my dead sister Sophie!"[60] While it is difficult to imagine Luise laughing like a drunkard and easy to imagine Brentano being simultaneously eccentric and macabre, Hedwig's letter was by far closer chronologically to the events reported. Two people can, and often do, perceive the same circumstances differently, but such extreme differences leave one perplexed.

Behind the amusement he generated that evening, Brentano was struck by a classic *coup de foudre* of the sort common in literature and rarer in life. He had been married twice before, the first time in 1803 to the poet Sophie Schubart Mereau, eight years his senior, who died in childbed on October 31, 1806 (Brentano contemplated suicide after her death), and the second time in 1807 to the immature, unstable seventeen year-old Auguste Bussmann.[61] The second marriage was a disaster right out of Strindberg and culminated in her flight in 1811 and a bitter divorce action in 1812. Auguste married again in 1816, coincidentally (or not) the same year that Brentano fell in love with the eighteen year-old Luise. Luise Hensel and Clemens Brentano may have seemed an odd couple, the cosmopolitan literary lion and a quiet young woman twenty years his junior, but they shared a tortured duality that arose from the search for a *raison d'être*, for some valid means of being in the world. If there were pathological elements aplenty in their relationship, it was nonetheless the impetus for a renewed creative élan that produced several poetic masterpieces and a series of shattering letters that turn on occasion into extended prose-poems of powerful erotic religiosity – there is a medieval intensity to the spiritual experience both sought. "Ach, alles geht vorbei" is one of the most haunting of Brentano's poems inspired by this cataclysmic episode in his life, with its tolling refrain "Alas, everything passes," its lines that wax and wane from pentameters to dimeters, and

Figure 5   Undated pencil and watercolor portrait of Hedwig von Stägemann (1799–1891) by Wilhelm Hensel. KdZ 143(11/3).

the incantatory reiterated ah-sounds, like sighs of grief and wonder, at the close of each stanza.[62]

Ach, alles geht vorbei	**Alas, Everything Passes**
(stanzas 1–3, 7–8 of 8)	
Ach alles geht vorbei	Alas, everything passes
Selbst dieser Unverstand	except this folly
Den ich in einer wundersel'gen Stunde,	that I experienced in a wonderfully blessed hour
An einer Wand empfand	at a wall –
Hat nicht Bestand.	This does not last.
Ja alles geht vorbei,	Yes, everything passes
Doch daß ich auferstand	but that I arose
Und wie ein Irrstern ewig sie umrunde,	and, like an errant star circle her eternally,
Ein Geist den sie gebannt,	a spirit that she captivated . . .
Das hat Bestand.	that is lasting.
Ja alles geht vorbei,	Yes, everything passes . . .
Nur dieses mag'sche Band	only this magic bond
Aus meines Wesens tiefstem Grunde	from the deepest ground of my being
Zu ihrem Geist gespannt,	linked to her spirit . . .
Das hat Bestand.	that is lasting.
Ja alles geht vorbei,	Yes, everything passes,
Doch diese liebe Hand	but this beloved hand
Die ich in dunkler freudenheller Stunde	that I, in a darkling, joyously bright hour
An meinem Herzen fand,	found upon my heart . . .
Die hat Bestand.	that is lasting.
Ja alles geht vorbei,	Yes, everything passes –
Nur dieser heiße Brand,	only this fiery brand,
In meiner Brust die bittre süße Wunde,	the bittersweet wound in my heart
Die ihre Hand verband,	that her hand bound up,
Die hat Bestand.[63]	that is lasting.

There are few more beautiful statements of the paradox, admitted to be irrational folly, that all else may be impermanent but not what love does to the heart. If the beloved herself inevitably vanishes and joy becomes pain, the impress made by love remains.

But at the time he met Luise, Brentano, intellectually and emotionally isolated for several years, had lost his faith in the Romantic creed of poetry, telling E. T. A. Hoffmann in January 1816 that he felt a kind of horror at all poetry that reflected only itself and not God;[64] in one of his letters to Luise, he tells her – and this to another poet – that "Everything becomes a lie in verse, a make-work," that "all art pilfers individuality and turns it into the 'common good.'"[65] The sarcasm of "Gemeingut" is palpable. Lacking his former belief in the power of writing to poeticize the world, Brentano had decided to cease writing imaginative fiction and poetry, and the decision had ignited anew the intermittent brush-fires of his lover's quarrel with Catholicism. In a lengthy letter to his friend Johann Nepomuk von Ringseis written in November 1815 and February 1816, Brentano wrote that although the forms of Catholic ritual were now as incomprehensible to him as services in a synagogue, his deep but unformulated aspirations to God are the most treasured moments of his spiritual life.[66] The tirade-cum-*cri de coeur* continues at length, including among other objections the proto-feminist question, "Why cannot women offer the sacraments, when they can partake of them and when the Savior's mother was a woman?" In Luise, his "angel in the wilderness" (Engel der Wüste), he hoped to find a unity in which all of his metaphysical as well as earthly longings would be stilled. The beloved was to be the supreme power on which his existence depended, now that art and the forms of religion had failed him. In the first version of his poem "Die Erde war gestorben" (The Earth Had Died), written for Luise's birthday on March 30, 1817, the poetic persona writes that everything on earth is dead, with no further meaning, that he only subsists by the grace of his beloved, whose eyes are the sole source of light and life.

Die Erde war gestorben   **The Earth Had Died**

(stanzas 1 and 2 of 3)

Die Erde war gestorben
Ich lebte ganz allein
Die Sonne war verdorben,
Bis auf die Augen dein.

The earth had died,
I lived all alone,
the sun was tainted,
all but your eyes.

Du bietest mir zu trinken
Und blickest mich nicht an
Läßt du die Augen sinken
So ist's um mich getan.[67]

You bid me drink
and do not look at me.
If you cast down your eyes,
it is all over with me.

But Brentano mishandled matters brutally. The profusion of roles he heaps on her head is remarkable: the projections change from moment to moment in a bewildering array – she is savior, angel, devil, mother, sister, bride, Judas-betrayer, and more. To Luise, who was looking for a father-figure, he most often posed as a terrified child, fearing that she would abandon him like a "bad mother," and made her solely responsible for his soul at the tribunal of her conscience; at the thought that she might disown him, "I wept like a lost child who has no home."[68] She could be, he tells her, Pontius Pilate to his Jesus, a female Peter who will deny she knows him, the poisonous serpents' tongues that enmesh his Laocoon-like soul, an angel with the power of life and death over him:

I am very, very sorrowful in my soul; I sway between heaven and earth, like a sad thought. A sword goes through my heart, and yet I cannot die from it because it comes from you . . . oh, if only I had never seen you, if only I had not been resurrected from the dead to stand before you.

Do you know what you have done when you accepted my heart from God's hands? You are charged with it as a duty – you must heal my heart, you must sanctify it [*es zu heilen und zu heiligen*] . . . you yourself have felt it and spoken it, that this heart is yours – you know it, I know it, God knows it!

You madwoman, you lunatic, leave me, go away in all your sanctity, but I tell you this with all my soul that when you appear before the Savior, he will ask you: Where is the heart of the one I confided to your care? And I will pursue you beyond eternity with my cry: in vain!

You are horribly perverse, my angel: with a word, a silence, you take away everything that you have given and promised to me. Even more, you wake the dead, then kill him; you clothe the naked and then tear away the breast over his heart; you feed the hungry and thirsty with hunger and thirst; you bring poison to the sick and free the prisoner in order to trample on him in the sunshine.

These passages are taken from a single letter written in late 1816, the first in an extraordinary bombardment – his second letter was a veritable *lettre-fleuve*, a torrent of confessional prose encompassing a five-day span.[69] He wanted her to know him utterly so that she could solace him utterly ("You have everything that I lack," he told her), but his misery and self-absorption were such that he was unable to respond in kind. He even fantasized transposing her within his breast, inside his heart, by night so that she could dream of how needy he was (the obverse never seems to have occurred to him),[70] and he admitted that his entire understanding of her was a fantasy with only the most minimal foundation in reality.[71] Finally, he proposed marriage on Christmas of 1816 just as Luise learned of her older sister's death in childbed, hardly the sort of news conducive to prompting enthusiasm for the married state; Luise, to whom her dying sister entrusted care of her newborn son Rudolf, was ill with grief for weeks thereafter.[72] (Antoinette Schwinck, in a letter written at the end of February 1817, observed that the grieving Luise did not believe herself deserving of any better fate, that she had "taken leave of herself" and lived only for others, abnegating her talents for music, poetry, and art.[73]) The day Brentano proposed, he wrote her a letter filled with macabre invocations of death:

Do you know the light of life on the face of a dying person? That is what you are to me! Do you know the wreath of flowers set on a bride's head, on the sacrificial lamb, on the dead? That is what you are to me. Do you know the last wish of those who go to their judgment? That is what you are to me. [Do you know] the chalice of wine to a poor sinner, who sees gleaming within it the sun of lost life and, fainting, sinks? Do you know the sunshine in a dying man's chamber and the swaying of the vines at his window? That is what you are to me.[74]

Later, in the poem "Abends am 27. Oktober 1817," he writes that he "lies on your heart like a corpse between tapers" ("Läg ich auch an deinem Herzen / Wie die Leiche zwischen Kerzen").[75] Even making allowances for Romantic extravagance, this is a morbid manner of proclaiming one's love.

How did Luise respond to this siege? At first, she was overwhelmed, telling him after receipt of his marriage proposal that she had "prayed, wept, and read what thy beloved hand wrote to me, my dear brother, the entire night through," that she was unworthy of the God-given Christmas gift of his heart; despite the length and ardor of her letter, the preferred form of address – "Brother" – and the constant references to Christ and her unworthiness boded ill for any earthly marriage.[76] Brentano persisted, however, and Luise soon recoiled from such a pathological suit, comparing herself to a snail who wishes only to withdraw into its shell, while Brentano is the persistent intruder who looks in the windows, knocks at the door, and asks who is there. Although she was deeply affected by his desperation (she too knew what it was to be desperate), she reproached him for not being sufficiently careful about her reputation, accused him of telling others that she loved him, and turned him down flatly.[77] Perhaps recognizing that his wish for utter dependence could only find satisfaction in religion, she urged him to return to the Church, saying that she would not see him any more unless he did so. She would, with God's help, do what she could, she told him, and gladly offered "heartfelt sisterly love and understanding of all your sorrows and joys."[78] This was not what Brentano wanted to hear, and his barrage of recriminations distressed her so much that she briefly considered an asexual, or Josephite, marriage with him (" . . . auch glaubte ich, unsere Ehe würde kinderlos und keusch sein").[79] He had, and exercised to the utmost, the capacity to throw her into a state of confusion, to redouble her already intense sense of guilt, as when she absolved him and blamed herself: "You are not my Devil – I am that myself. Oh, if only I could have blessed peace! . . . I am afraid I am not yet free of myself; I disgust myself."[80] That he could arouse sexual feelings in her, feelings she admitted but did not understand fully, is evident in such passages as the following:

I am doubly ill and weak: I must bear your weakness too, and yet you will not be strong. When you warm my hands in yours, tender and human and intimate (not sinful, I believe) feelings course through my soul and then a pair of wings quivers within me and wishes to fly away with your soul, where, you do not know; and when you lay your head in my lap, I often wish to tear it away and fly off with it, I know not where [und wenn Du Deinen Kopf in meinen Schoß legst, möcht ich ihn Dir manchmal abreißen und damit fortfliegen, ich weiß nicht wohin]. Do you understand? . . . me neither.[81]

Whether or not she understood fully, the passage is vivid revelation of an inchoate attempt to sublimate sexual sensation into religious channels. That the strategy was unsuccessful is evident in the swift modulation from protestations of innocence and angelic metaphors to symbolic violence laden with multiple meanings. Little or no Freud is required to see her panic-stricken desire to separate the head from the sinful body and to remove Brentano's avid mouth from proximity to her sexual organs, nor is the castration fantasy difficult to decode; the double denial of location ("I know not where . . . I know not where") is particularly telling. Despite her distress, however, she replied at length and with spirit to his often wild accusations. And she once again refused to marry him in February 1817.

Brentano had feared that Luise loved someone else, and he was right. In 1818, after Müller's departure from Berlin and little more than a year after the *Liederspiel*, Luise was in love with a young statesman named Ludwig von Gerlach (1795–1877), who in later life became the soul of the *Neue Preußische Zeitung*, a jurist and president of the appeals court, and a staunch conservative opponent of Bismarck (Figs. 6 and 7). In their youth, Gerlach and his brothers Leopold and Wilhelm belonged to a religious-political-literary club – the "Maikäferei" – formed by Brentano in 1815 and moved in the same social circles as the great poet. (Ludwig Gerlach wrote in his diary for October 27, 1816 that "the poet Wilhelm Müller" had come to Brentano in order to read his translation of Christopher Marlowe's *Doctor Faustus* aloud to the older poet. Brentano's opinion is not recorded, but Gerlach was enormously impressed: "[it is] so simple, pure and clear like an old German painting, with its modest coloration. The passage from the turmoil and unrest of our present circumstances into olden times and olden poetry is like emerging from a gloomy chamber into an open green meadow in the cool of evening, the sky unclouded."[82]) In her diary for January 25, 1818, eleven months before her conversion, Luise records the thoughts of marriage that assail her and then prays not to be led into temptation.

Why should you be deprived of marriage? Have you renounced it for God's sake? Because it isn't pleasing to your obstinacy. Good, and if a hand reaches out to you that could draw you farther along the path to God . . . You could choose – but oh, my heart, no other hand! Lord my God, do not lead Your child into temptation . . . To have You alone, Thou beloved, is better![83]

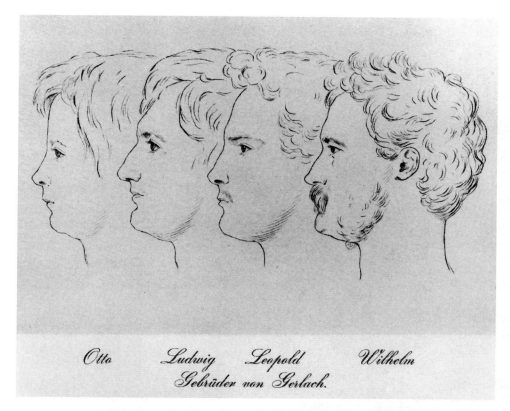

Figure 6 The Gerlach brothers as young men. Frontispiece to Jakob von Gerlach, *Ernst Ludwig von Gerlach. Aufzeichnungen aus seinem Leben und Wirken 1795–1877*, vol. 1 (Schwerin: Fr. Bahn, 1903).

On September 14, Brentano left Berlin at Luise's wish, possibly to settle the question of her attraction to Ludwig Gerlach without Brentano's disturbing presence. On November 15, she began the process of renunciation, writing in her diary:

I lost a brother Ludwig [an older brother who died in 1808 at age thirteen] – he is dead: will you not now be my Brother Ludwig? That you are already, and that is much indeed. More than that you dare not, cannot be for me in this world. All as God wills it! If he sent me ten thousand such Ludwigs like you, I would have to give them to you.[84]

Again as if speaking to Gerlach himself, she wrote on November 23: "If I choose between you and Jesus, I would be tormented and unhappy my entire life, should I place you first ... since the world appears once more so enticing, so promising, through your eyes, I must wholly forsake you, must turn away from you entirely, even though I would gladly become your sister."[85] Two days later, the renunciation was complete:

This youth must now be dead to me, and I have not time and room enough in which to bury him. My beloved brother Ludwig, thou seest well that I must go away, without daring to look back – but won't you go with me? Thou too hast a soul, which is a pity in this wicked world ... I love you very much, but I love God more.[86]

Figure 7 Ludwig von Gerlach (1795–1877) in later life. Frontispiece to Jakob von Gerlach, *Ernst Ludwig von Gerlach*, vol. 2 (Schwerin: Fr. Bahn, 1903).

But Gerlach did not even know of her feelings, according to his testimony in later life. He *did* know of Brentano's passion for Luise and his brief comments in his diary constitute interesting additions to the tale, for example, his astute observation that true love was not to be found in Brentano, who only loved himself in other people[87] and his brother's comment on February 3, 1817 that the matter of "Mlle Hensel and Brentano" could come to no good end.[88] Evidently, the antagonism was mutual; on February 27, Gerlach noted that Brentano "seems to have a special malice toward me"[89] and compared him to Hamlet – a noble soul destroyed – even before they met, on the basis of reports by a mutual friend.[90] And yet, according to Gerlach's diary,

Brentano on August 31, 1818 sought Gerlach out in order to tell him that Luise was "the most wonderful, the most profound of all women, married or unmarried . . . For two years, he [Brentano] has seen her daily and never without renewed astonishment and new gratitude to God, who works such wonders in humankind. She was the only person on earth who helped him and did him good, but she remains enclosed within her personal relationship with God."[91] Did Brentano know the object of Luise's affections and therefore address confidences with an ulterior motive to a man he disliked? Bettina von Arnim, whom Gerlach considered comparable in sheer egotism to Clemens, was apparently convinced that Luise was Brentano's mistress, but Gerlach did not agree, hymning her "profound and quiet modesty" and unaffected bearing, although he told Brentano that taciturnity such as Luise's did not bode well for love. She wanted, not pleasantries and lover-like service, but the innermost heart – it was altogether a pretty kettle of fish, he concluded ironically.[92] A few days later, on September 5, Gerlach records what must have been a rather fraught conversation with Luise and Brentano about divorce, a conversation in which Luise wanted to know how secular courts could possibly dissolve what spiritual powers had joined together – one wonders what led to the topic. When Brentano left, Gerlach told Luise that it had pleased him to see how she had resisted Brentano's seduction, and she replied demurely that in the country, one simply said, "God bless" and went away. To Gerlach, her answer seemed contrived: "Brentano's influence? Her brother artist?"[93] The remark betrays annoyance with Brentano's eccentric behavior and perhaps a touch of impatience with all poets and their poses. Gerlach undoubtedly did not return Luise's unspoken love, but she made a sufficient impression on him that he could copy one of her poems in his diary and counsel her on such a sensitive subject.

Many years later, in late 1874 or early 1875, Gerlach was journeying through Paderborn; when his friend Alfred Hüffer told him that the elderly and bed-ridden Luise lived there, he went to see her. According to a letter of July 30, 1884 from Hüffer to Luise's biographer Franz Binder, Gerlach told Hüffer that he had seen Luise and spoken to her in Berlin society circles, but had come no closer.[94] In his diary for October 21, 1875, Gerlach wrote that he could still recognize her features despite the signs of age, that they had exchanged anecdotes about Brentano and others, and that they spoke of spiritual matters. At the end of the diary entry, he wrote "Ich sprach noch feierliche und förmliche Abschiedsworte" (I said farewell to her solemnly and formally). He knew that she would not live much longer.

Gerlach's ignorance of Luise's feelings and her powers of renunciation were more than enough to put an end to her final flare-up of longings for marriage, but Brentano was taking no chances. In early 1817, he had evidently volunteered to become Protestant if Luise, the daughter of a Lutheran pastor and still Protestant herself, would marry him. When that did not avail, he did what she had asked him to do and made his universal confession at St. Hedwig's in Berlin on February 27, 1817 after many years' absence from the Catholic Church. Berlin society, accustomed to conversions on the part of Romantics with mystic propensities, took note of the fact without surprise and observed that he did so at Luise's behest. When Luise sent him away from Berlin in September 1818, Brentano went to the town of Dülmen to see the stigmatized nun

Anna Katharina Emmerick. From the autumn of 1818 to January 1819, he besieged Luise with letters and a travel diary, begging her to join him at the nun's side.

Luise would later insist that Brentano had little to do with her conversion to Catholicism in December 1818. In old age, she wrote to her friend of almost fifty years, the blind philosopher Christoph Bernhard Schlüter, that "I was already more Catholic than he when we met," that her mother used to say "How did this child come by these Catholic notions?" when she was but six years old, and that when she was confirmed in her father's faith in 1813, she felt she was betraying God.[95] In a letter of June 4, 1820, Luise attempted to explain to her mother, angry at Brentano over the issue of conversion, that it was she (Luise) who had led Brentano to religion, not the reverse. "You know," she writes to her mother, "that he lived for a long time outside of the Church and that the proximity to pious Protestants almost led him (all the more as he had practically forgotten the teachings of the Church) to Protestantism. I disliked this because I felt strongly that this was not the answer; I told Brentano this and urged him to become reconciled with the Church. When he so often spoke to me of his restlessness and unhappiness, of his lost life, I told him he should confess or I would have nothing more to do with him." The letter is remarkable for her defense of Brentano, even though she reminds her mother, "You know I was entirely impatient with him, and he then traveled to Westphalia and Holland."[96] Her younger sister attested after Luise's death that the "shallow rationalism" of their father's faith was insufficient to satisfy Luise's longing for union with God, but the Brentano–Hensel correspondence of 1818 reveals a different story. In truth, he had everything to do with her conversion: he used his persuasive powers and the influence of the stigmatized nun to push her in the direction of Catholicism, in part to prevent her from marrying anyone else and in part so that she might share his brand of sublimation. They would have, or so he intended, a mystic marriage of the spirit at the nun's bedside – he called her "the new bride" of the Church, never Luise, while her journey to conversion was a "Brautfahrt," a bridal journey.[97] The diary-cum-letters he sent her from Dülmen are tantamount to verbal bludgeons, their propagandistic intent blatant. "O my beloved bride," he writes, "I see so well the condition of your heart – you will come to the Church, you will not be afraid, it will all go quite easily," and he has Anna Katharina Emmerick send messages such as, "I hope before my death to embrace my new bride."[98] Luise at first resisted, telling Brentano and the mystic nun on November 23 that "I become frightened when I realize how much is being done for me. The more dearly my soul is bought, the greater my obligation is – oh, how can I bear it? Stop, at least stop saying it to me!"[99] and, in a calmer vein, "You think that I would find peace in your religion; my dear, I don't believe so," but in this sphere and in this way, he could and did prevail.[100] On December 18, 1818, less than one month after her private renunciation of Ludwig Gerlach, she formally converted to Catholicism. Brentano, who hoped that her conversion would bring her closer to him, proposed marriage yet again in 1819, but she refused him for the last time.

Seventeen years after the events of 1816–18, both Brentano and Luise would remember those years as "the most beautiful and the saddest of my life," in Brentano's words from a letter of 1835. (The psychological substratum of this letter is interesting. Brentano at the time was pursuing the last futile love of his life, a woman named Emilie

Linder, the pattern of pursuit and rejection similar to that enacted earlier with Luise Hensel.[101] Luise wrote back on December 9, 1835 to say, "Yes, dear Clemens, there is not a single Christmas that goes by without my remembering you and your beautiful gift [the gift of his heart]... Oh, that was a difficult and yet beautiful, rich and yet so poverty-stricken, period both of my inner and outward lives."[102] Her rejection of him was a long-standing wound, however: when he accidentally encountered her in 1838 at the home of Joseph Görres in Munich, he wrote an epilogue to his exquisite poem "Frühlingsschrei eines Knechtes aus der Tiefe" of early 1816, an epilogue in which her angelic voice becomes the Siren's destructive singing:[103]

Stimme nachtigallenfarben,	Nightingale-colored voice,
Ätzend Liederpulver streuend,	strewing corrosive dust of song,
Daß zu Wunden werden Narben	so that scars become wounds,
Leid und Lied und Schmerz erneuend.	suffering and song and pain renewing.
Torenstimme einer Weisen	Foolish voice of a wise woman,
Weise Stimme einer Törin,	wise voice of a foolish woman,
Stimme aus den Zaubergleisen	voice from the magic paths of Lady Venus,
Der Frau Venus, Klang der Möhrin.	sound of the Moorish woman.
Weh, wie diese den Tannhäuser	Woe, as she enticed Tannhäuser
Lockte mit der Zauberflöte,	with her magic flute,
Lockt den Pilger heiser, leiser,	now from Linum the raucous horn,
Jetzt von Linum die Tralöte!	thus entices the pilgrim, coarser, softer.

And yet, they remained, in a curious manner, friends, united by their passionate inclination to God (Luise would later hope to enter the Carmelite order, but was prevented from doing so by lack of financial means and instead became a lay nun). She had already foreseen the interwoven pattern of their destinies, both the alteration of their relationship as a result of separation and their continuing reliance upon one another, in a letter she wrote to Brentano on September 18, 1818. "I believe," she told him, "that a purer disposition, a better, more noble friendship always crystallizes from outward parting. Other winds blow through my hair [Mir weht ein anderer Wind durch die Haare . . .]"[104] One reads the last phrase and realizes anew the arresting, mystic, crystalline-precise nature of her style. She was reticent about the subject of her relationship with Brentano in later life, lamenting Emilie Brentano's edition of her brother's letters as a heartless exposé of a tormented man's inner being. "It seems to me as if my poor old friend's heart were disclosed to all the world's eyes so that everyone might see what curiosities [Raritäten] it held," she wrote indignantly.[105] One of those "rarities" was his love for her and their thorny path to the same refuge of Catholicism; even though his letters to her from that 1816–17 season of storm and stress were subtitled "To an unknown woman," she was displeased and apprehensive about the possible consequences of Emilie's revelations. Little knowing that this letter too would be revealed, she wrote in later life, "That Clemens in close company was hard to endure is something everyone who has lived with him knows, particularly if he happened to love them, but posterity, I feel, does not need any communiqués on the matter."[106]

Because her early life *was* so difficult and sad, because she did in fact flee to religion as the sole means of subduing her "sinful" self, I will take leave of her by recalling a moment of youthful rebellion, of unfulfilled fantasies about freedom. I have earlier mentioned that five of Luise's poems were published in Friedrich Förster's *Die Sängerfahrt* of 1818, actually a joint editing venture with Brentano. In a letter of April 16, 1852, Luise told Christoph Schlüter, who encouraged her at age seventy-one to publish the first collected anthology of her works, that "several horrible, hateful poems of mine, written when I was fifteen or sixteen years old" were, against her wishes (?), published in *Die Sängerfahrt*, and she singles out "Will auch mit"[107] as a particularly odious specimen.[108] No wonder! – it is entirely secular, even anti-religious, and exudes female rebellion against confinement and against the restrictions that kept women from full participation in the world of ideas. "Will auch mit" is a dialogue poem in which a daughter tells her mother that she wants to follow the enticing music she hears and, by implication, venture forth into the world; the poem thus begins with the defiant assertion that a woman can experience Romantic *Sehnsucht* (the unappeasable longing to journey in search of unknown experience) as well as any man. Her mother, like the archetypal mothers of folk poetry, tells her to stay home with her spinning and warns her about "wild men" and such dangerous places as publishing houses [!]. The daughter, however, pays heed to a sailor instead and goes away with him. When she briefly demurs, telling her prospective seducer that women do not go on ships, the sailor tells her that "the heavenly image of Mary, Lady Propriety, the Muses and Love" are all aboard, a transparent ploy that she is only too happy to accept.

Will auch mit

"Ach Mutter, ein' Laut' ist erklungen,
Da hat sich das Herz mir geregt,
Ach Mutter! ein Lied ist gesungen,
Das hat mir die Seele bewegt."

Ach Töchterlein, bleib mir beim
  Rokken,
Das waren die fahrenden Herrn.
Laß Sang und Klang dich nicht locken,
Das Schifflein zieht gar zu fern.

"Wenn fern das Schifflein ziehet,
Da zieht es gewiß in das Land
Wo Singen und Klingen hinfliehet,
Wo Frühling wohnt, wenn er hier
  schwand."

Kann seyn. Heut hört ich wohl sagen,
Ich ging bei dem Schifflein vorbei,
Es sollte die Herren tragen
Nach Leipzig zur Buchdruckerei.

"Ach Mutter, ich will euch gestehen,
So eine Buchdruckerei
Die hab ich noch gar nicht gesehen.
Nun wär' ich gern auch 'mal dabei, –

I'll Go Too

"Oh mother, a lute is resounding
and the sound has stirred my heart!
Oh mother, I hear a song
that has moved my soul."

Oh my dear daughter, stay here with me by
  your spinning,
those were the travelling men.
Don't let the music lure you . . .
the ships go too far away.

"If the ship goes far away,
then surely it goes to the land
from whence the music is fleeting,
where Spring dwells, when it vanished from
  here."

That could be. Today I heard it said
when I went by the ship
that it should carry men
to the book publishers in Leipzig.

"Oh mother, I want you to tell about
such a book-publishing house;
I have not yet seen one.
I also would like to be there now –

Gott grüß euch, ihr Herren, schöne!	Greetings to you, gentlemen!
Habt ihr wohl ein Plätzchen noch leer?	Do you have a small place still empty?
Wie klingt hier so lieblich Getöne,	Such enticing tones resound here
Das lockte vom Ufer mich her."	that they lured me to the shore."
Der Mann, der das Schifflein will fahren,	The man who will steer the ship
Sagt: Komm, wenn dein Herz ist erweckt.	says: Come when your heart is aroused.
Er sagt auch, er will mich bewahren,	He also tells me that he will protect me
Daß keiner mich ärgert und neckt.	so that no one will tease or annoy me.
"Ach Fährmann, was soll ich beginnen?	"Oh sailor, what should I begin to do?
Ich bin ja so furchtsam und mild,	I am truly so timid and gentle.
Im Schiff noch kein Mägdlein sitzt drinnen,	No maiden sits there within the ship,
Und Mutter sagt, Männer sind wild."	and mother says that men are wild."
Ei, säßen nicht Mägdlein darinne?	Oh, no maidens are here within?
Maria, der himmlischen Bild,	Mary, the heavenly image,
Frau Sitte und Musen und Minne;	Lady Propriety, the Muses, and Courtly Love,
Und Sänger sind artig und mild.	and minstrels are artful and gentle.
Da hab' ich das Fährgeld ihm geben,	So I gave him money for my passage . . .
Es war nur von Blümlein ein Strauß;	it was only a garland of flowers,
Da that er ins Schifflein mich heben,	then he lifted me into the boat,
Ich will auch nicht wieder hinaus.	I never want to leave it.
Da sitzt gar ein Engel am Steuer,	It's really an angel sitting there at the helm;
Nun schäm' ich und gräm' ich mich nicht;	only now I am not ashamed and do not grieve.
Und guckt mir wer durch den Schleier,	And if someone looks at me through the veil,
Dem schneid' ich ein Gesicht.	I'll make a face at him.

What makes this flight of fancy about freedom of several kinds noteworthy is the implied equation of freedom with blasphemy and the guiltless attraction of such devil-may-care behavior. A young girl wishes to become a writer, such that Leipzig publishing houses are her faintly comic El Dorado, and her mother gently discourages her aspirations as unsuitable. In poetry, one can dispose of opposition more handily than in real life, and the mother vanishes from the miniature ballad without a backward glance (Luise's letter-seal in later life was the emblem of a ship in full sail with the letter "L" on the central sail). Luise could not, even in poetry, conceive of venturing out into the world without a man to lead the way, but he is clearly little other than the means of escape. To complete the ambiguities and biographical undercurrents of the situation (a poem by "Ludwiga" about going off with a lover), we may note that all five of Luise's poems in *Die Sängerfahrt* were edited by Brentano. Whatever *he* made of "Will auch mit," it is a revealing document for present-day readers.[109]

Luise evidently gave up writing for a time after her conversion. In a letter of October 2, 1833, she told Schlüter that she had not written poetry "for years, perhaps never again, since I have lacked the solitude and the inclination for it,"[110] but Schlüter helped lead her back to the poetry she had abandoned, despite her scruples about "bluestockings"[111] and the presumption of women's claims to creativity; she did not believe that the terms "poet" or "writer" were proper for women. And yet she did not entirely abandon her early longing to break free from the bounds of women's conventional circumstances, a longing evident in her transformation of commonplace poetic imagery.[112] For example, in the evocatively entitled "Will keine Blumen mehr" (I'll Have no More Flowers), summer roses are symbolic of the unbearable passivity of women's lives, especially when compared to the freedom enjoyed by the poetic persona's brother. He can go out in the world and do battle with its forces, engage fully in its enterprises, but the ephemeral flowers, fixed in place, can only bloom, exude a sweet fragrance, and die. The poetic "I" rebels.

Die Sommerrosen blühen	The summer roses blossom,
Und duften um mich her;	and smell sweetly all around me;
Ich seh' sie all verglühen,	I see them all die –
Will keine Blumen mehr.	I'll have no more flowers.[113]

She had designated herself as a flower, doomed to wither and die, in "Die Siebzehnjährige auf dem Balle," but later, she would have nothing of such feminine ephemerality. Luise even sketches a woman's cosmogony of Christianity in her Marian poems, in which "Mary, the new Eve," is an actual priestess (*Priesterin*), garbed in the sun traditionally reserved for the male Trinity.[114] And it seems possible in retrospect that her refusal to marry any of the small throng vying for her hand and heart or to accede to her own longing for Ludwig Gerlach might have stemmed from recognition that domestic life was incompatible with her larger spiritual desires.

The last of the Stägemann salon members to appear in these pages is Ludwig Berger. We know much less about his courtship of Luise Hensel than we do about Müller's or Brentano's wooing; given Berger's shyness, his younger friend Ludwig Rellstab is discreet about the matter in the chapter "A late blossom of love – its demise" from his biography of Berger.[115] The thirty-nine year-old Berger, whom Rellstab describes as hypochondriacal and depressive (his wife, the singer Wilhelmine Karges, had died in St. Petersburg in 1810 after a mere ten months of marriage), offered Luise his hand in early 1817. According to one source, he sent a young friend, known only as "Dr. K.," to be his emissary.[116] Rellstab does not even mention Luise as one of the participants in the *Liederspiel*, although he names her brother, and he does not link Brentano's name with that of the woman who refused Ludwig Berger's offer of marriage. Luise was still living in 1846, and Rellstab could possibly have wanted to protect her privacy. Instead, he tells the reader that the unnamed young woman refused Berger because her religious aspirations forbade marriage to anyone at all – the same reason Luise had given both Müller and Brentano. The chronicler ends the chapter with a melancholy anecdote: one day when he and Berger were out walking, a woman came over to them, and Berger greeted her, but without looking directly at her. For a few moments, he stood still and then said, "Da geht das geträumte Glück meines Lebens hin!" ("There goes the dreamed-of happiness of my life!").[117] Whatever his dashed hopes for remarriage, he *did* set two of her poems to music in his op. 11 *Gesänge aus einem gesellschaftlichen Liederspiele 'Die schöne Müllerin.'*

If none of those in love with one another that autumn and winter of 1816–17 found heart's-ease with the objects of their desire (Müller, Hedwig, Ludwig Gerlach, and Wilhelm Hensel eventually married others), the artistic fruits were rich indeed. For Luise, this was the most prolific period of her life poetically, while Brentano found through her a new focal point for both verse and life alike. Luise's blue eyes became the blue eyes and blue flowers of one of the world's most famous song cycles, and music born of the *Liederspiel* and its offspring proliferated throughout the century. From much unhappiness was born much that is beautiful and enduring – "Das hat Bestand."

Chapter 2

Variations on a poetic theme: hunters, millers, and miller maids

A booth with books of folk tales and folk songs soon attracted me greatly.

The maids, who came from the nearby well, had gathered in a circle around it and let the merchant lead in singing the beautiful new songs with the accompaniment of a dulcimer.

I also found the hunter and the miller's apprentice here once again.

The hunter from the imperial palace looked first, but it was the miller's apprentice who bought the little book entitled: "The garland in honor of millers."

The hunter, who was a handsome young man, kissed the maidens one after another, and they did not object. The miller's apprentice would gladly have done so as well, I observed, but he was still quite young and not at all bold, although he was in love; he bought the song "If I were a little bird" and then cried aloud the echo, "Greet my sweetheart many thousand times!"

The hunter, however, attracted the maidens like deer in the forest, who all belonged to him; for that reason, he soon held two in each arm.[1]

In this miniature tale, the "Fünfte Vorstellung" (Fifth Performance) of the "Vierte Schattenreihe" (Fourth Row of Silhouettes) from Justinus Kerner's eccentric first novel *Reiseschatten aus dem Schattenspieler Luchs* of 1811 (the untranslatable title refers to scenes cast on the wall by a camera obscura), we are told once again of a gentle, poetically inclined miller lad outdone by a bold hunter. In a witty instance of the Romantic intermingling of authorial presences, the hunter and the miller appear "once again" – thus Kerner makes evident their ubiquity – in multiple roles, as the consumers of folk song anthologies, as the poetic personae of the very songs they buy, and as characters in the novel: song within song within song. Like a hall of mirrors, the images replicate themselves at different distances from the objects reflected. The characters of this episode are in fact walking, talking songs; "Der Jäger aus Kurpfalz" is the title of one of the best-known hunting songs from the folk tradition, and "Wenn ich ein Vöglein wär" had recently been given new life both in Herder's *Stimmen der Völker* and in *Des Knaben Wunderhorn*.[2] (One notes that a merchant leads the maids in singing folk songs; it is the bourgeoisie, Kerner implies, who are the most avid participants in the folk song revival.) Virtually all of the ingredients of Müller's cycle are present in evocative sketch-form in the Swabian writer's novel: Kerner's miller lad is in love (with whom, we are not told), shy, sentimental, inclined to wishful, wistful song, while the bold hunter is irresistible to women. Only the miller maid is absent, but she too is descended from a long literary tradition.

Rather than inventing a playlet *de novo*, the young *literati* of the Stägemann circle took this same subject as their own – from the Nile of folk song, eighteenth- and nineteenth-century poets created their own flood of poems on the same themes, and both rivers flow into *Die schöne Müllerin*. The cycle is thus in one sense a palimpsest of numerous sources collected and criticized from within by a poet who borrowed like a magpie but seldom did so uncritically. Whatever Müller took from others, he transformed, sometimes with mocking intent and always with a mind to modernize his appropriations. He did not disguise his models, as that would have defeated his purpose: we are meant, I believe, to hear both a plethora of folk voices and the echoes of "Schillerandgoethe" beckoning from behind his words in order that we might most fully admire Müller's ingenuity in turning such familiar material – these characters are as formulaic, hence as malleable to variation, as the stock characters in the *commedia dell'arte* – to his own unfolk-like ends. To use and yet to deride what is fashionable is a familiar impulse among artists, a Janus-faced phenomenon perhaps especially evident among latecomers to a movement or trend – and Müller was a latecomer to Romanticism. What its earlier avatars had proposed as models for emulation, he too would use, but selectively and critically.

As additives to the venerable folk story, Müller incorporated elements from the Middle High German romances he had been studying and a savage jab or two both at the folk song movement and the patriotic songs born of the Napoleonic Wars (after a fashion typical of his built-in paradoxes, he was a knowledgeable participant in the former and produced specimens of the latter). A "Jäger," after all, was the military term for a fusilier, and those who wrote the poetry of German nationalism *redivivus* during the Napoleonic years invoked the *Jägerkorps* with all the white-hot jingoistic fervor of those attempting to overthrow one of the great tyrants in European history. "Heimat" and "Wald," "Waidwerk" and "Jäger" (home, forest, hunting, hunter), became multivalent terms, laden with political associations no English translation can adequately encompass; if they were already potent words in the eighteenth century, they become even more so in the combat against the Corsican-born French emperor Napoleon. The traditional association between the pursuit of hunting and the pursuit of war is deliciously underscored when Goethe's erstwhile beloved Charlotte von Stein describes the ceremonial hunting parties organized for the occasion of Napoleon's 1808 visit to Weimar in a letter to her son Fritz and draws a pointed analogy between the "poor stags" routed from their forest dwelling places and the European rulers routed from their lands.[3] "Jäger" as heroes fill the patriotic verse by the likes of Ernst Moritz Arndt and Theodor Körner, along with hundreds of hymns to oak trees – the symbolic emblem of Germany – and the German *Urheld* Arminius/Hermann ("Heer"-plus-"Mann," or "man of the army"), the victor at the battle of the Teutoburger Wald in 9 AD between the ancient Germanic Cherusci tribe and the Romans. (Schubert, one recalls, set Friedrich Klopstock's "Hermann und Thusnelda," D. 322, to music in 1815, at a time of heightened nationalistic sentiment, although he seems to have had far more musical sympathy for the hero's wife Thusnelda than for her sword-swinging husband.) At this fraught juncture in European history, the German *Jäger* becomes a nationalistic emblem, a masculine-heroic model of irresistible bravery and sexual appeal – the hero of Friedrich Baron de La Motte-Fouqué's rabidly nationalistic 1819 drama *Jäger und Jägerlieder. Ein kriegerisches Idyll* (Hunters and Hunting Songs: A Warlike Idyll) is appropriately named Kaspar Keck (Caspar Bold).[4] Earlier, hunters were celebrated for their defiant choice of a life close to Nature rather than "unnatural," effete civilization, and the translation of solitary hunters who bravely stalk and kill large animals to masses of such men on the battlefield, fighting and winning Germany's liberation, was only a small step to take. The composer Friedrich Wilhelm Berner's (1780–1827) setting of Gottfried August Bürger's "Jägerlied" perfectly exemplifies the fusion of hunter and soldier, all the more amenable to song because both types of *Jäger* – those who killed animals and those who killed men – were associated with music.

Jägerlied	**Hunter's Song**
(stanza 1)	
Mit Hörnerschall und Lustgesang,	With the sound of horns and merry song,
Als ging' es froh zur Jagd;	as if going happily to the hunt,
So ziehn wir Jäger wohlgemut,	we merry fusiliers
Wenn's Not dem Vaterlande thut,	when our Fatherland is in need
Hinaus ins Feld der Schlacht.[5]	go forth into battle.

But the protagonist of *Die schöne Müllerin* refutes the antique myth of the hunter-as-hero when he excoriates one of their number as a savage killer and a rapist. In the miller lad's distraught cry, "Die Eber, die schieße, du Jägerheld!" (The boars, kill them, you heroic hunter!), at the end of "Der Jäger," we hear both the conventional designation of hunters as heroes and the bitter denial of any such heroism. If one considers that the lad equates the hunter with the wild boars he hunts, that the syntax of "die schieße" emphasizes "die" ("Shoot *them* [and not my girl]," the lad cries), and that "shooting" must be understood in this context as a metaphor for sex (a traditional metaphor), then the line clearly implies "Go f – yourself." Polite language will not do for the tone and temper of what lies behind the furious words at the close of this poem.[6] Müller thus tells of the darker side of a mythic figure, and he does likewise with the millers and miller maids who also migrated from folk song into opera libretti, poetry by *Kunstdichter*, prose tales and plays. By the time Müller adds elements taken from Edmund Spenser, Goethe, Minnesong, Gottfried von Strassburg, and elsewhere to his folk-figures and then stirs into the pot-au-feu his own post-Romantic skepticism, the very term *Volkstümlichkeit* becomes fraught with idiosyncratic nuances, the enterprise wonderfully Janus-faced. If Müller was modernizing his source material in one sense, he was also rediscovering the olden wildness at the mythic heart of these characters.

Müller was not the first and he was certainly not the last to find new uses for old legends. In particular, the figure of the *Jägerheld* had a radioactive afterlife in twentieth-century culture, evident in such sources as Carl Clewing's three-volume *Musik und Jägerei: Lieder, Reime und Geschichten vom Edlen Waidwerk* (Music and Hunting: Songs, Poems and Tales of the Noble Hunt), published in 1937–38 – the date is significant.[7] Following the title page is a dedicatory folio whose words of invocation, beginning "The love of Nature and its creatures, and the joy of hunting in the forest and field, have roots deep in the German *Volk*," are positioned beneath the emblem of a stag's horns printed in green ink. Between the horns is the swastika of the Third Reich (Fig. 8): it was in part by appealing to carefully selected archetypes such as the *Jägerheld* that Hitler and his pro-paganda ministers constructed their vision of "das Volk."[8] Hermann Göring, who was

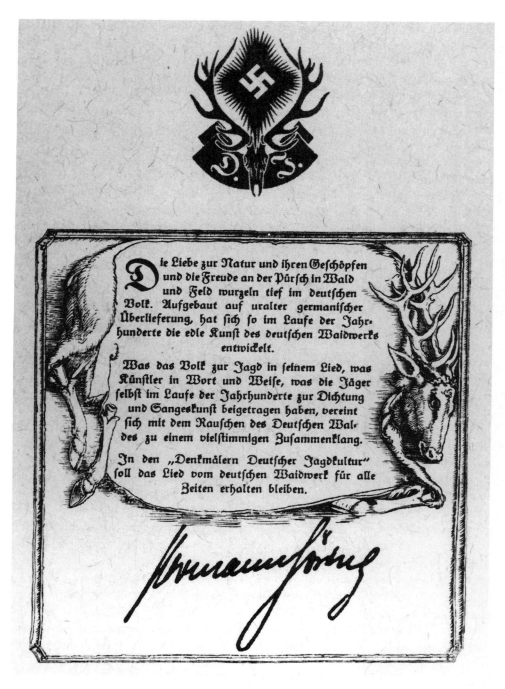

Figure 8 Dedicatory page of Carl Clewing, *Musik und Jägerei: Lieder, Reime und Geschichten vom Edlen Waidwerk*, vol. 1 (Neudamm: J. Neumann and Kassel & Wilhelmhöhe: Bärenreiter-Verlag, 1937–38).

the *Reichsforstminister* and *Reichsjägermeister* of Hitler's Germany as well as commander of the Luftwaffe, was obsessed with hunting (Simon Schama, in *Landscape and Memory,* writes that Göring on the hunt dressed like an extra in *Der Freischütz*[9]) and, in company with many of his vile cohorts, sought to revive an ancient connection between forest cultism and militant nationalism. The image of the stag and the swastika in Clewing's compendium is all the more shocking to those who know that in the legends of Saints Hubertus and Eustachius, the patron saints of hunters, it was a crucifix that appeared between a mystical stag's horns in the visions that supposedly impelled both men to convert to Christianity. The substitution of the *Hakenkreuz,* forevermore a symbol of the worst in humanity, for Christ's cross is enough to make anyone shudder. Müller could not, of course, have foretold the poisonous later use of the *Jägerheld* more than a century later, but he could and did perceive an underlying brutality at work in the notion of a "hero" who is a law unto himself, who rejects civilized precepts, who exalts violence, and who kills as much for pleasure as for food.

WHEN HUNTING HORNS BLOW: HUNTERS IN FOLK SONG AND POETIC TRADITION

In the Viennese playwright Joseph Alois Gleich's (1772–1841) comedy "Der Hölle Zaubergaben" (The Magic Gifts from Hell) of 1819, the hero is a hunter employed by a wealthy man to tend his hunting preserves. After the hunter gains and loses a fortune, aided by his attendant spirits Begierde and Verführung (Greed and Temptation), he does penance by wandering the world as a pauper in order to win back his wife. The climactic scene occurs when the erstwhile hunter finds himself at a mill, where he asks the miller for a glass of wine and receives an entire bottle, this being Austria. The miller agrees to hire him as an apprentice miller, and there is a delightful comic exchange in which the hunter declares his wish to be just one of the boys. The miller responds that it will be great fun calling him "Du Bub," whereupon the hunter-turned-miller – this was one of Ferdinand Raimund's famous roles – replies, "Yes, but in honor of my former better days, why can't you call me Monsieur Bub or Herr von Bub?" This is all very amusing in a *Wiener-lokalisch* sort of way, but it also points out the hierarchy by which the hunter is of higher status on the folk ladder than apprentice-helpers at a mill. Müller's hunter thus begins his conquest of the miller maid with all the advantages of mythified glory and greater status than his rival.[10]

We never see the hunter or hear him speak in *Die schöne Müllerin* – his impact is all the greater for it – and yet this character who is the least visible of all the dramatis personae at Müller's mill is the most ubiquitous in folk poetry and its Romantic descendants. Hunters by the hundreds blow their horns and call their hounds to the ready in poetic tradition, their cries of "Wohlauf zum fröhlichen Jagen!" (Away to the merry hunt!) a leitmotif of the repertoire. Bernhard Pompecki's giant anthology *Hörnerschall und Lustgesang: Ernste und heitere Wald-, Jagd- und Jägerlieder mit leichter Klavierbegleitung* (Horncalls and Merry Song: Serious and Merry Forest-, Hunt- and Hunting Songs with Easy Piano Accompaniment) contains 364 such songs (music for the entire "liturgical year" of hunting, one asks, tongue-in-cheek?) arranged in topical categories; significantly, the patriotic songs come first, and the title of the entire anthology is taken from the Berner–Bürger war song cited above. Browsing through the fat tome, one rapidly becomes satiated with major mode, with fanfare motifs by the thousands, with the unrelenting macho simplicities of the genre.[11] Nuance, harmonic complexity, subtlety of musical expression are not to be found in ninety-nine percent of these songs; the patriotism is always hyperbolic, and no criticism of carnage taints the self-glorifying hunter's conviction of superiority. Where such uninflected certainties reign supreme, their music hardly requires modulation to distant keys or chromatic coloration or rhythmic complexity.

But it is in these bluff, hearty songs that one finds the mythic creature Müller molded to his own distinctive ends in *Die schöne Müllerin*, the folk-figure he deconstructs. What then are the defining elements of this stock character? Pompecki celebrates the myth at its simplest, and the hunters he gathers together in his compilation are models of masculine perfection (as it was then reckoned), self-confident, energetic, patriotic to the hilt, and fiercely independent, although one notes the paradoxes by which "merry minds" kill and patriotism goes hand-in-hand with anti-social solipsism. "In the forest, only merry minds and true German faith reign," sings the poet Friedrich von Wildungen (1754–1821), whose *Jägerlieder für Jagd- und Forstfreunde* (Hunting Songs for Friends of the Hunt and the Hunting Preserve) appeared in 1823, two years after the publication of Müller's cycle and the same year in which Schubert composed his setting of it – the undiluted archetype was very much alive at the time.[12] Two strains perhaps meet and mingle in this model of the *Jägerheld*: the medieval notion that a knight should have mastered venery, or the art of the hunt, hence, hunting as a badge of courtly perfection, and the eighteenth-century conception of closeness to Nature as a *desideratum*, or the exaltation of "natural man" disdainful of cities and civilization. Stir sex into the pot-au-feu, and the mixture is complete: the animal magnetism of those who stalk and kill wild animals is hymned over and over in hunting songs.

Hunters dress in green and are identified by and with that color; when Müller in "Erster Schmerz, letzter Scherz" from *Die schöne Müllerin* invokes "the Green One," we need no other information to know that this is the hunter. The green *Tracht* and feathered cap was, of course, camouflage, designed to make its wearer melt into the shrubbery and forest in which he stalked his prey, but to this pragmatic purpose is joined rich symbolic signification as well. Green is the color most emblematic of Nature's springtime rebirth, and hence, it is the color most evocative of hope, in particular, the hope of finding love. Sexual sap rises in human lovers along with the sap of rejuvenated life in trees and plants; according to antique myth, green was the color associated with Priapus, and the hunter's green garb thus announces his Priapic inclinations before he says or does anything at all.[13] In medieval color symbolism, which Müller would almost certainly have absorbed from his studies of olden German verse, green was either the color of Minne's beginnings or of Love itself – "Nach grüner farb mein hertz verlangt, / da ich elend was, / Das ist der liebe ein anfang, / recht so dz grüne gras" (My heart longs for green, for I was unhappy; that is the beginning of love, as right as green grass) sings a lover in the Ambraser Liederbuch of 1582,[14] while the following lines come from a fifteenth-century "Klopfan-Gedicht" (a lover knocking at the door before launching into a serenade).[15]

Grün in allem meinen Sinn	Green in all my thoughts
Ist der lieb ein anefing.	is the beginning of love.
Grün soltu allezeit haben wert,	Green should you always find worthy
Ob dein Herz dir lieb begert.	if your heart commits you to love.
Grün sol niemant tragen,	Green should no one wear
Der in lieb wil verzagen.	who would despair of love.

"Green, yes, green, are all my colors . . . I love what is green because my sweetheart is a hunter," sings the woman's voice in the folk song "Grün, ja grün" (Green, yes, green), although she then turns right around and proclaims, "White, yes, white are all my colors . . . I love what is white because my sweetheart is a miller."[16] There, in reverse order and less detail, is *Die schöne Müllerin* in the smallest of nutshells. (Black for a coalburner-sweetheart follows in the folk song: this is a mini-catalogue of suitable occupations for a lower-class maiden's dreams of marriage, the catalogue arranged in descending order from highest – the hunter – to lowest.) "Hunter-green, thou happy green!", the hunting poet Johann Wilhelm Bornemann proclaims in "Jagergrün," while Georg Grünbauer (a pseudonym?) compresses into "Jägerfarbe" (Hunter's Color) all of the associations of green with hunters – the greening world in spring, burgeoning love, the green oaks which symbolize Germany, German patriotism, and the joys of the hunting life.[17]

Thus, when Müller's miller angrily, broken-heartedly, sings, "In Grün will ich mich kleiden" in "Die liebe Farbe," he is enveloping himself in a most potent color.[18] Did Müller borrow the language of this poem from one or both of two prior models? In "Mit den Jägern ich es halte" (I Hold with Hunters), later included in Franz von Ditfurth's anthology *Deutsche Volks- und Gesellschaftslieder des 17. und 18. Jahrhunderts* (German Folk and Guild Songs of the Seventeenth and Eighteenth Centuries), we are told that "Cupid is a hunter," while the allegorical meanings of the green motif and the identification of hunters with a world drenched in a single color are spelled out explicitly.[19] The poet even puns on "Grün" and "gründen" (to found, to establish) in stanza 3, the closest to Müller's language in "Die liebe Farbe." Does Müller's lovelorn youth mimic in sorrow the hunter's happiness in this poem? "I will love green even unto the grave," says the hunter of "Mit den Jägern ich es halte"; so too, but with a bitter twist, does Müller's miller.

Mit den Jägern ich es halte	**I Hold with Hunters**
(stanzas 1–3 of 6)	
Mit den Jägern ich es halte,	I hold with hunters
Weil sie sein nach meinem Sinn;	because they are after my own heart;
Wann sie gehen durch den Walde,	when they go through the forest
Mit dem Weidhund suchen hin,	on the prowl with their hunting dogs
In die Hoffnung sich vertiefen,	engrossed in hope
Bis das Wild wird aufgebracht,	'til the wild animals are hunted out.
Busch und Stauden sie durchschliefen,	They sleep in the bushes and hedges
Scheuen nit die dunkle Nacht.	and do not shy away from the dark night.
Fuchs und Hasen ich nit jage,	I do not hunt foxes and hares,
Dachs und Wölf ich nit vermein,	I don't think of badgers and wolves.
Nach Schwarzwildpret ich nichts frage:	I don't ask after wild black boars,
Ein lieb's Thierlein muß es sein;	it must be a gentle little animal.

Wann es schon ist hart zu fangen,	If it is hard to capture,
Wie es leider gar gewiß,	as it, sadly, is indeed,
Hoff ich doch, ich werd's erlangen,	I yet hope I shall succeed
Weil Cupid ein Jäger ist.	because Cupid is a hunter.
Mit Grün will ich mich umgeben,	I will surround myself with green;
Grün ist alles, was ich hab;	everything I have is green.
So lang ich in meinem Leben,	So long as I live,
Grün lieb ich bis in das Grab.	I love green even unto the grave;
In Grün ich mein Leben gründe,	I will found my life in green,
Grün das liegt mir stets im Sinn,	green is always in my heart;
In Grün ich mein Leben finde,	in green I find my life –
In der Hoffnung Jäger bin.[20]	in hope, I am a hunter.

But it is even more likely that Müller might have borrowed the haunting first line of "Die liebe Farbe" from a song which goes back at least to the fifteenth century.

Regina

Regina

(stanza 1 of 9)	
In Schwarz will ich mich kleiden,	In black will I garb myself,
Dieweils Trauren bedeut,	for it means mourning,
Vonwegen meines Buhlen,	because my lover
Der mir ganz Urlaub geht;	has entirely taken leave of me,
Urlaub, ohn alle Schuld:	gone, though I did nothing wrong:
Hilf, reicher Christ vom Himmel,	Help me, Lord Christ in Heaven,
Daß ich's leid mit Geduld![21]	that I suffer this with forbearance!

What follows after this stanza is a catalogue of symbolic colors – "In Weiß will ich mich kleiden," "In Roth," "In Blau," "In Grün," although here, there is no hunter on the scene and green signifies only the desire to go walking in nature with one's sweetheart. Nevertheless, one can hear this folk song lurking just behind Müller's words about another suffering lover whose former sweetheart has left him and for whom green, not black, has become the color of mourning.

From green garb to the psychology of the myth, Müller knew all of the ingredients and assembled them for the hunting songs in his *Ländliche Lieder* (Country Songs) as well as *Die schöne Müllerin*, but with a soupçon of skepticism not to be found in more straightfor-ward celebrations of the *Jägerheld*. In "Jägers Lust" (Hunter's Happiness), the poetic persona's typically boastful assertions are reinforced by a choral refrain glorifying the hunt, but the requisite swaggering – "I am king of the forest" – hints at Müller's dis-approval; the poet who fashions such braggadocio does not, one suspects, think much of those who in real life actually espoused such views. While delight in guns is a common-place of the genre, Müller's threefold verbs "blitzt, dampft, knallt" (flashes, smokes, explodes) in the first solo stanza, like three gunshots in succession, underscore the hunter's love of violence, the *Mordlust* implicit in hunting.

Jägers Lust

Hunter's Happiness

(Chorus following each verse):	
Es lebe, was auf Erden	Long live what on earth
Stolziert in grüner Tracht,	glories in a green costume:

Die Wälder und die Felder,	the forests and the fields,
Die Jäger und die Jagd.	the hunters and the hunt.

(Solo):
Wie lustig ist's im Grünen,	How merry it is in the greenwood
Wenn's helle Jagdhorn schallt,	when the bright hunting horn resounds,
Wenn Hirsch und Rehe springen,	when the stag and deer leap,
wenn's blitzt und dampft und knallt!	when it flashes and smokes and explodes!

Im Walde bin ich König,	In the forest, I'm king;
Der Wald ist Gottes Haus,	the forest is God's house –
Da weht sein starker Odem	there, his stronger breath blows, lively,
Lebendig ein und aus.	in and out.

Ein Jäger will ich bleiben,	I will remain a hunter
So lang die Tannen grün;	as long as the fir-trees grow green;
Mein Mädchen will ich küssen,	I will kiss my girl
So lang die Lippen glühn.	as long as her lips are glowing.

Komm, Kind, mit mir zu wohnen	Come, my child, and live with me
Im freien Waldrevier,	in the free forest hunting ground;
Von immer grünen Zweigen	from evergreen branches,
Bau ich ein Hüttchen dir.	I will build you a little house.

Dann steig ich nimmer wieder	Then I will never again climb down
Ins graue Dorf hinab,	to the gray village;
Im Walde will ich leben,	I will live in the forest –
Im Walde grabt mein Grab!	in the forest, dig my grave!

Daß nicht des Pfarrers Kühe	The pastor's cows shall not go there
Darauf zur Weide gehn,	to graze;
Das Wild soll drüber springen,	the wild animals shall leap over it –
Kein Kreuz im Wege stehn.[22]	no cross stands in the path.

Müller makes explicit the archetypal hunter's stance *contra* civilization, the defiance of both Church and State; his poetic persona abjures towns, equates churchgoing people with cud-chewing cows, and refuses to allow a cross on his grave. Müller thus underscores the belligerence at the heart of the mythic figure, the hunter's isolation from people and sense of superiority – in his forested heights, he is literally lifted above the drab gray village life down below.[23] Could Schubert have known Conradin Kreutzer's (1780–1849) setting of this poem?[24] The younger composer expressed admiration for Kreutzer's settings of Ludwig Uhland's *Wanderlieder*, but there is no mention of "Jägers Lust." Kreutzer omits Müller's final stanza – for fear that it might offend the censors? – and sets the remainder as a hearty hunting song filled with simple fanfare motifs, devoid of any evidence of comprehension on the composer's part that the poet might be mocking the very myth he seems to endorse; if it is not one of Kreutzer's best songs, it is emblematic of the genre in its most common manifestation, untinged by irony or complexity (Ex. 1). Other composers would subsequently do likewise with poems from *Die schöne Müllerin*, its numerous disturbed and disturbing elements expunged from musical mention. Did they, one wonders, notice them at all (see chapter 3)?

As in "Jägers Lust," the hunters of song and story are not a modest lot: it is a leitmotif

Example 1   Conradin Kreutzer, "Jägers Lust," mm. 1–8, to a text by Wilhelm Müller, from Bernhard Pompecki, ed., *Hörnerschall und Lustgesang*. Neudamm: J. Neumann, n.d.

of hunting songs that hunting is boastfully exalted above all other occupations. In "Nur Jagen" (Only Hunting) by an unknown poet, the poetic persona rejects Apollo, the Muses, and Venus – poetry, the arts, and love – as inferior to the joys of hunting. He will dedicate himself to Diana, he declares; that there is something intrinsically pagan in such an obsession with the hunt is implicit in these songs.

Nur Jagen	**Only Hunting**
(stanzas 1–2 of 6)	
Nun ist der feste Schluß,	Here is the strong conclusion
Dabei es bleiben muß:	to which I must hold:
Diana will ich geben,	To Diana will I give
Mein frisch und junges Leben	my lively, young life;
Ein treuer Diener sein	I will be a true servant
Dir, o Diana mein!	to you, o my Diana!
Kein' größre Lustbarkeit,	No greater pleasure,
Kein anders Spiel mich freut,	no other game pleases me
Als nur das edle Jagen,	other than hunting,
Allwo kein' Sorg noch Plagen,	where there is no care nor trouble,
Wo alles freudenreich	where everything is joyous
In der Diana Reich.[25]	in Diana's realm.

Similarly, in "Jagen über Alles" (Hunting Above All), the poet proclaims that all of the other arts and their tutelary gods and goddesses retire *hors de combat* when the hunting horn resounds in the valley of Mount Parnassus and Diana goes hunting.[26] The hunter's existence is ultimate freedom, liberation from the "blauer Dunst" (blue vapor) of learning, which offers neither comfort nor happiness, from the burdens of power and wealth, and so forth at length, the poet running on for thirty-two stanzas of blissfully verbose praise for the hunting life; a beast-by-beast bragging catalogue of all the animals he has caught and killed (a frequent feature of hunting songs) swells the dimensions even more. The version of this song in Ditfurth's anthology is replete with the fanfare motifs endemic in hunting music and requiring two parts in order to produce the requisite harmonic intervals of a perfect fifth as passing tones between intervals of a third and a sixth. Anyone familiar with Schubert's lieder will recognize how frequently he has recourse to this figure in contexts which make its signification evident, as in the setting of Johann Mayrhofer's "Antigone und Oedip," D. 542, where horn-call motifs accompany Oedipus's invocation of "happy days, in the halls of my great fathers, amid the songs of heroes and the peal of horns," in "Ellens Gesang II (Jäger, ruhe von der Jagd)," D. 838, and in "Die böse Farbe" – "Und wenn im Wald ein Jagdhorn schallt," the miller lad sings to the accompaniment of rapid-fire reiterations of this well-known gesture.[27] The musical landscape in Ditfurth is happier by far.

Indeed, happiness is the prerogative above all claimed by hunters. "When I think of the merry life one leads in the fields and forests, then I look for my shelter under the trees and do not long for the gleaming cities," the poetic persona of "Jagdlust" (Hunt Happiness) proclaims – yet again, the refutation of citified life for the greater joys of *Waldleben*.[28] The joys of hunting are enumerated one by one in a song variously entitled "Edles Jagen" (Noble Hunting) or "Vom edlen Jagen" (Of Noble Hunting), a poem whose poetic persona frankly admits pleasure in killing animals large and small. "Stag and deer, fox and hare, leap with joy, as does the beautiful chamois that springs onto the rocky crag until I shoot him in the back and send him to his death . . . that is a hunter's happiness, that is a hunter's joy," this hunter exults. It requires cunning to outwit a wild bear, he continues, and when the bear crashes to the ground, bathed in sweat, that is "hunter's happiness, hunter's joy."

Edles Jagen	**Noble Hunting**
Edles Jagen!	Noble hunting!
Kann's wohl sagen:	It can well be said:
So ein tapfrer Jäger	Just so does a gallant hunter
In den Wäldern,	seek his joy
Grünen Feldern,	in the forests,
Wo Diana ras't,	the green fields
Seinen Muth ergetzet,	where Diana coursed,
Suchet seine Freud	delighting in his courage.
Auf dem schönen grünen Rasen,	On the beautiful green grass,
Thut sein muntres Hörnlein blasen	he blows his merry little horn
Und trach't nach frischer Weid,	and hunts for lively game,
Und trach't nach frischer Weid.	and hunts for lively game.
Hab ich gejaget,	When I have tired of hunting
Mich geplaget,	and am weary,
Leg ich mich in Schatten;	I lay me down in the shadows,
Labe wieder	refreshing my limbs
Meine Glieder	once again
In dem grünen Wald,	in the green forest,
Allwo der Vögelein Musik	where the little birds' music
Lieblich klingen thut;	gently resounds all about;

Unter den grünen Bäumen	under the green trees
Thut mir auch bisweilen träumen;	I can occasionally dream . . .
Wie süß ist meine Ruh,	how sweet is my rest,
Wie süß ist meine Ruh![29]	how sweet is my rest!

The hunter-singer of the Swedish poet-musician Carl Michael Bellmann's (1740–1795) song "Auf lustiger Bahn" (On a Merry Path) echoes the same sentiments, with the added assertion of autonomy as the source of utmost happiness.[30] Hunters disdain as superfluous whatever the forest cannot give them; they do not work for hire, but truly *lead* their own lives as most people cannot. Where mill apprentices must answer to a master and do his bidding, hunters can come and go as they please, beholden to no one but themselves.

Auf lustiger Bahn	**On a Merry Path**
Wir Jäger, wir wandeln auf lustiger Bahn!	We hunters, we travel a merry path,
Wir leben und handeln nach eigenem Plan.	we live and act after our own plan.
Wir führen das Leben im doppelten Sinn!	We lead life in a double sense!
Wir leben und weben in Lust und Gewinn.	We live and move in happiness and gain.
Nicht ackern, nicht spinnen,	Not tilling, not spinning,
Nicht weben um Lohn.	not weaving for hire.
Und dennoch gewinnen,	And yet we already know
Verstehen wir schon.	how to enrich ourselves.
Wir sammeln die Gaben	We gather the bounty
Der süßesten Pflicht.	of the sweetest task,
Und was wir nicht haben,	and whatever we don't have,
Das brauchen wir nicht.[31]	we don't need.

According to the poetic persona of "Rechter Jäger" (A Proper Hunter), the joys of hunting are such that the entire world, even emperors and kings, esteem it above all other pursuits:

Rechter Jäger	**A Proper Hunter**
(stanza 20 of 20)	
Drum so sag ich's treu und frei,	Therefore I proclaim it freely and in truth,
Alles Ander unverdrungen:	ousting all others:
Herrlich ist die Jägerei,	hunting is glorious
So mein junges Herz bezwungen!	and so has overmastered my young heart!
Alle Welt	All the world
Hoch sie hält;	holds it in high esteem:
Kaiser, König, Höchstgestellt,	emperor, king, those highest-placed
Haben selbst ihr Lob gesungen.[32]	have even sung its praises.

Delight in hunting spanned the gamut of class and rank, and for the nobility, it was not an inexpensive hobby – "those highest-placed" could, and did on occasion, severely tax or even drain their royal, ducal, or baronial treasuries in the staging of magnificent hunting parties.

The mini-catalogue of beasts pursued by the hunter in "Rechter Jäger" culminates in an invocation of "the most beautiful wild animal of all": his sweetheart, whose domestic world of interiors and enclosures is contrasted with his wide-open world of the wild.

He is not the only amorous hunter – far from it; the folkloric woods teem with hunters in love or in lust. In "Lob der edlen Jägerei" (Praise of Noble Hunting), Karl Josias Bunsen (1791–1860, a friend of the Schubert poet Ernst Schulze) celebrates both the antiquity of hunting, which existed before there were ever any doctors, lawyers, soldiers, or priests, and the hunter's legendary powers of attraction for the female of the species.

Lob der edlen Jägerei	**Praise of Noble Hunting**
(stanzas 1 and 3 of 5)	
Des Waidmanns Ursprung liegt entfernt,	The origins of the hunter lie far away,
Dem Paradiese nah:	close to Paradise:
Da war kein Kaufmann, kein Soldat,	there were no merchants, no soldiers,
Kein Arzt, kein Pfaff, kein Advokat;	no doctors, no priests, no lawyers,
Doch Jäger wären da.	but hunters were there.
Er zeigt im Wald und beim Gelag	In the forest and at the feast,
Den Helden und den Herrn.	he shows who is the hero and the lord,
Drum sind ihm auch die Weiblein hold	therefore women show him favor
Und zahlen ihm den Minnesold	and gladly accord him above all others
Vor allen andern gern.[33]	the guerdon of love.

When a hunter meets a pretty young haymaker in the folk song "Jäger und Graserin," he declares that "I am the hunter, and you are mine," upon which she responds that if he is the hunter and would have her, "so will ich dir aber was anders sa'n."[34] They are indeed "making hay" with seed of another sort, as is the hunter who leaves "a sweet young maiden clad in white" pregnant in the song "Es wolt gut jäger jagen, / wolt jagen die wilden schwein" from the Ambraser Liederbuch of 1582.[35] (Most of the amatory hunters' songs tell us little or nothing about the aftermath of seduction, but here, we are told that the hunter abandons the maiden-become-mother, who is subsequently rescued from her sad lot by the knight who marries her.) The hunter of the folk song "Es blaset ein Jäger wohl in sein Horn" (A Hunter Blows on his Horn) – to blow the horn is a sexual innuendo of great antiquity[36] – encounters a nobleman's beautiful daughter and, with a minimum of preliminaries, invites himself into her bed. She eagerly acquiesces, but warns him the next morning that he must leave or he will be discovered and shot; the hunter would then become the prey.[37] Similarly, the poetic persona of "Es war ein Jäger" (There was a Hunter) meets a maiden in the woods and asks her if she would like to help him hunt wild boar; cutting right to the chase, she says, "No, but I would not deny another plea," its nature unstated but implicitly sexual.[38] And so on and on – hunters are a seductive lot, and most women willingly capitulate.

The medieval allegory of the *chasse d'amour* in which the beloved is hunted, pursued, and finally captured – woman's supposed animalistic sexual nature is implied in her frequent metamorphosis into a "Tierlein" – lives on in poems such as these. Müller would have known the "Jagdstücke" in the Middle High German romances he studied as a philology student in Berlin,[39] as when Gottfried von Strassburg's Tristan "breaks" a stag, that is, dissects it and parcels out each portion to the proper recipient, foreshadowing the later hunt scene where Marke pursues a white stag's traces to the cave where Tristan and Isolde are dwelling.[40] (White stags appear both in Christian symbolism, in which they bear a crucifix between their antlers, and in secular myth, where the rare coloration, emblematic of purity, signifies singular supernatural qualities. In the hunt that leads to the cave of love, the invocation of a white stag implies that greater forces direct Marke to what he finds.) In this huge, unfinished rendering of the tale, Tristan, the former master of the chase, becomes "the hunter hunted" – the stalked victim, first, of Minne, then of Marke and his minions, destined to be undone like the stag he has earlier broken. Müller, one remembers, read the tale of Tristan before the creation of the Stägemann *Liederspiel* and declared that Luise must read it as well.[41]

If the *chasse d'amour* is one thread, albeit an important one, among many in the huge tapestry of Gottfried's *Tristan*, it becomes the central organizing element of another medieval German romance written more than a century after Gottfried's death circa 1210. In 1335–40, the Bavarian knight Hadamar von Laber (*c.* 1300–1360) wrote the lengthy and elaborate *Die Jagd* (The Hunt), whose central protagonist, the *Minnejäger*, is accompanied by a pack of allegorical hounds, among them "Fröude, Trôst, Triuwe, Lust, Liebe, Leit" (Joy, Comfort, Faithfulness, Happiness, Love, Sorrow). The tale turns on a denied sexual relationship; unfulfilled, it makes of the woman a frivolous destroyer and harrows the man's soul. Even in Germany, where the *chasse d'amour* most often dramatizes unrequited yearning, Hadamar more than others recognized the sexual dissonances of the chase imagery; in this literary realm, the lover may hunt forever, to no avail, and love's harshness is everywhere regnant.[42] The same dark vision appears in smaller forms as well; in one of the oldest hunting songs, "Herzog Ulrichs Jagdlied" (Duke Ulrich's Hunting Song), which Müller would have known as the dialogue-poem "Aufgegebene Jagd," or "The Hunt Relinquished," from *Des Knaben Wunderhorn*, a nobleman sorrowfully bids farewell to the hunt – but what sort of hunt? The language of the poem, with its references to a "Tierlein gut" (good little animal), to "your snow-white breast," to "another man [who] must awaken you," suggests the unwilling abandonment of a *chasse d'amour* by a lover thwarted of his young prey and mournful over his loss.

Herzog Ulrichs Jagdlied	**Duke Ulrich's Hunting Song**
(stanza 2 of 3)	
Far hin, gewild in waldeslust!	Farewell, wild animal in forest happiness,
ich wil nit mer erschrekken	I will never again frighten you
Mit jagen dein schneweiße brust,	by hunting your snow-white breast;
ein ander muß dich wekken.	another man must waken you
Und jagen frei mit hundes krei,	and freely hunt with hounds' baying,
da du nit magst entrinnen,	since that you cannot escape.
halt dich in hut,	Take care,
mein tierlein gut,	my good little creature,
mit leid scheid ich von hinnen.[43]	I leave here in sorrow.

When Müller casts his monodrama of lovers who hunt one another as a tragedy, he may have taken his cue in part from the customarily unhappy ending of the medieval *Liebesjagd*.[44]

But most often, the folkloric legendary hunter is irresistible to women, as in Johann Gottlob Schulz's (1762–1810) "Jägerlied":

Jägerlied	**Hunter's Song**
Und immer hat er frisches Blut	And he is always lively,
Und freien, heitern Sinn,	with a free, merry mind,
Und alle Mädchen find ihm gut	and all the maidens find him pleasing
Und werben gern um ihn.	and gladly court him.
Gern hat mit ihm manch Jüngferlein	Many young maidens have gladly danced
Getanzet und gespielt;	and played with him;
Die Herzen zahm und wild sind sein,	tame and wild hearts are his
Sobald er nur drauf zielt.[45]	as soon as he takes aim at them.

In "Der blaue Storch" (The Blue Stork), reportedly "verboten" in Basel in 1509, a young maiden has fallen in love with a hunter, and her mother counsels her to stay home another year, but the age-old parental ploy to "wait a while" in hopes that a short-lived infatuation will pass is to no avail. The choice of a hunter as the archetypal seducer of maidens, the young man so compelling that a girl would abandon parents, home, and the precepts of her upbringing for him, was a calculated one.

Der blaue Storch	**The Blue Stork**
(stanzas 4–8 of 8)	
"Ei Mutter, liebe Mutter,	"Oh mother, dear mother,
Was gebt ihr mir für Rat?	what advice do you give me?
Es läuft mir alle Morgen	Every morning, a proud hunter
Ein stolzer Jäger nach."	runs after me."
"Ei Tochter, liebe Tochter,	"Oh daughter, dear daughter,
Den Rat, den geb ich dir:	the advice I give you is:
Laß du den Jäger laufen,	let the hunter go –
Bleib noch ein Jahr bei mir!"	stay another year with me!"
"Ei Mutter, liebe Mutter,	"Oh mother, dear mother,
Der Rat, der ist nicht gut:	that advice is no good:
Der Jäger ist mir lieber	the hunter is dearer to me
Als sie und all ihr Gut."	than it and all your goodness."
"Ach Tochter, liebe Tochter,	"Ah daughter, dear daughter,
Dein Rede ist mir hart,	your words are hard –
So lauf du denn zum Jäger,	run then to the hunter;
Du bist ja schier vernarrt."	you are an utter fool."
"Ach Mutter, liebe Mutter,	"Ah mother, dear mother,
Euer Rat gefällt mir wohl.	your advice pleases me well;
So muß ich's halt abwarten,	I must wait
Bis mich der Jäger hol'."[46]	until the hunter comes for me.

Could Müller have known this poem? He might well have taken his model for the miller lad's words "Ach, Bächlein, liebes Bächlein" in the seventh stanza of "Der Müller und der Bach" from the refrain-like verse openings in dialogue-poems such as this one.

The maypole dance-song "Jagdglück," with its refrain "Im Mayen, / Am Reihen / Sich freuen alle Knaben und Mägdelein" (In Maytime, at the dance, all youths and maidens rejoice) is typical in its hunter's assertion of dominance over all he encounters in his forest domain and his magnetism for beautiful women; when he crooks his finger, they all come (sexual pun intended). The maiden of this poem is described as well worth his while, a swift and lively creature; although she accedes power voluntarily to him at the end, she is no weakling but his match. It is typical of the genre that she is both a "wild animal" and virtuous ("von Tugend reich"), animal and human-feminine alike; if her snow-white hands are a typical emblem of female purity and sweetness, she is also a "Wild" (the type of wild animal is not even specified in this instance).[47] While so-called "animal-groom" stories abound in fairy tales and folklore, tales in which men transformed into beasts represent a young girl's fear of adult male sexuality,[48] there are fewer instances of symbolic equivalence between girls or women and animals, and yet, this is a leitmotif of hunting songs. Hunters seldom metamorphose into animals, whatever their totemic kinship with the beasts they hunt in shared wildness, freedom, and untrammeled sexuality; it is the women they desire who are animals, a fairy-tale element that embodies recognition of animal sexuality in women as well as men and the perception that Woman is an Other, that she is prey to be mastered and tamed. When Müller's miller in "Der Jäger" designates the miller maid as "ein Rehlein, ein zahmes, für mich" (a little doe, a tame one, for me), he is both mimicking the traditional language of hunting songs in which the object of sexual desire becomes a forest animal and contravening the tradition by insisting that she is not "wild" and is therefore unsuitable prey for hunters. In the emotional turbulence engendered by the discovery that he has a rival, he borrows the rival's metaphors, especially as they so often spell sexual success, and yet simultaneously asserts his (and her) difference from the rival's realm. The unspoken fear just beneath the words is that she is, in fact, "ein Wild."

Jagdglück	**Hunting Fortune**
(stanzas 3–5 of 5)	
Der Jäger sah ein edles Wild,	The hunter saw a noble wild animal,
Frisch, hurtig und geschwinde,	lively, nimble, and swift.
Es war ein schönes Frauenbild,	It was a beautiful woman
Das sich allda ließ finden;	that he found there.
Der Jäger dacht in seinem Sinn:	The hunter thought to himself,
Zu diesem Wilde jag ich hin.	I'll hunt this creature.
[refrain]	[refrain]
"Ich grüß euch Jungfrau, hübsch und fein,	"Greetings to you, fair, pretty maiden,
Von Tugend reich und schöne,	from virtue rich and beautiful,
Was ich in diesem Wald erschleich,	whatever I spy out in this forest,
Das mach ich mir zu eigen."	I make my own."
"Ach, edler Jäger, wohlgestalt,	"Ah, noble, handsome hunter,
Ich bin nunmehr in eurer Gewalt."	I am from henceforth in your power.
[refrain]	[refrain]
Er nahm sie bei ihrer schneeweißen Hand,	He took her by her snow-white hand,
Nach Jäger Manier und Weise,	after a hunter's way and manner;
Er schwang sie vorne auf sein Roß,	he swung her before him on his horse.
Glück zu! wohlauf die Reise.[49]	Good fortune on the journey!

In "Jagdglück," the attraction is mutual, and the hunter is not a brutal seducer; indeed, the couple exchange courtly compliments on the other's beauty, nobility, virtue (hers), and power (his). Likewise, the hunter of "Jäger Wohlgemuth" (Happy Hunter), who meets his beloved under the linden tree, courteously spreads out his cloak for her and declares "Gehab dich wohl, mein Trösterin, / Nach dir steht mein Verlangen" (Make yourself comfortable, my consolatrice, you are the one I desire).[50] If it is not the longest of preliminaries to sex (but then, ballads and folk songs often compress events), it is undoubtedly consensual.

Where hunters were successful in their conquests, supplanted suitors mourned. Müller probably knew the poem "Der Überläufer" (The Traitor) from *Des Knaben Wunderhorn* in which a bereft young man, his occupation unknown, laments the loss of his sweetheart Rose – shades of "Heidenröslein" and its sexualized imagery of plucking flowers – to a hunter.

Der Überläufer

In den Garten wollen wir gehen,
Wo die schönen Rosen stehen;
Da stehn der Rosen gar zu viel,
Brech ich mir eine wo ich will.

Wir haben gar öfter beisammen gesessen,
Wie ist mir mein Schatz so treu gewesen!
Das hätt' ich mir nicht gebildet ein,
Daß mein Schatz so falsch könnt' sein.

Hört ihr nicht den Jäger blasen
In dem Wald auf grünem Rasen,
Den Jäger mit dem grünen Hut,
Der mein' Schatz verführen tut?[51]

The Traitor

We want to go into the garden
where the beautiful roses grow.
There are far too many roses,
so I will pluck one wherever I wish.

We have often sat side by side.
How faithful my sweetheart was to me!
I never would have imagined,
that my darling could be so faithless.

Don't you hear the hunter blowing his
horn amid the green grass in the forest?
The hunter with the green hat
who has seduced my sweetheart?

The word "we" changes definition in the course of this poem, at once wistful and angry. At first, "wir" is "we men," all men newly dazzled by their discovery of sex, men who wish to go into the garden of women and take their pick (one remembers Luise Hensel's poem of women as roses condemned to one short, hot season in which to flourish). In stanza 2, "we" becomes "you [the sweetheart] and I," as the young man – experience and maturity would never speak thusly – remembers a brief season of togetherness before betrayal shattered his youthful illusions of love as eternal. Müller's miller lad and this poetic persona could be twins: for both, the sound of the hunter's horn is omnipresent in their minds, and both, with the self-centeredness of young love and loss, imagine that others must be able to hear it as well. "Hört ihr nicht den Jäger blasen?" asks the one; "Horch, wenn im Wald ein Jagdhorn ruft . . . ," says the other.[52] Did Brahms, one wonders, notice the resemblance to the scenario of *Die schöne Müllerin* when he set "Der Überläufer" to music as one of his *Sieben Lieder mit Begleitung des Pianoforte*, op. 48, no. 3?

That the music of horn fanfares is also emblematic of hunters' archetypal ravening sexual appetites is evident in example after example; to play an instrument, after all, especially when one blows into it, is a frequent metaphor for sexual acts. In a context considerably more comic than "Der Überläufer," the character Quecksilber (Quicksilver) in Ferdinand Raimund's play *Der Barometermacher* (The Barometer Maker) hears "unterirdische Musik" – the directional symbolism hints, however humorously, at the nether regions of death and sex – in which a "Stimme des Hornes" asks "Wer will auf

mir blasen?" ("Who will play on me?" or, in a lewder translation, "Who will blow me?").
One could hardly miss the association of horn-playing with sex, and with oral sex in particular. "A curious question!", replies Quicksilver, and then enthusiastically declares, "Ich blas' dich!" ("I'll blow you").[53] Müller's horn-playing, however, is altogether tragic. The miller lad in "Die böse Farbe" does more than watch, helplessly, an erotic theatre *à deux* in his tortured, voyeuristic imagination – he *listens* to sex as well; when he earlier condemns the "Saus und Braus" of the hunting horns in "Der Jäger," he wants more than noise to stop. Schubert understood and bids the horn fanfares in "Die böse Farbe" bray and blare, increasing speed and pounding away in a frenzied, orgasmic manner. In a Baroque engraving of a hunter after the manner of the sixteenth-century fantasist Giuseppe Arcimboldo, who devised images of "human" faces out of clustered animal, vegetable, and mineral attributes (for example, a fisherman concocted entirely of fish), the hunter's lips are composed of two hunting horns fixed in a suggestive, sexual leer (Fig. 9); certainly the phallic symbolism of the instrument is not far to seek. Guns too have obvious phallic overtones – when hunters plied their instruments, animals and women alike died, whether the "little death" of sex or the extinction of life itself.

Thus, the dark side of hunting mythology tells of the rape and murder of women, even where the woman is ostensibly loved. In "Der weiße Hirsch" (The White Stag) by August Mahlmann (1771–1826), a hunter who loves his sweetheart kills a white stag, only to discover upon returning home that he has killed his beloved.

Der weiße Hirsch

(stanzas 4–5 of 5)

Der Waidmann kehrt zum Hause sein,
Da stand kein Mahl bereit,
Da fand er keinen Becher Wein,
Kein Bett mit Blumen bestreut.
Ach, draußen im Garten, vom Taue naß,
Da lag unter Blumen Herzliebchen
  blaß.
O weh, o weh, o weh!
Trara, trara, trara,
Herzliebchen, sie war tot!

Da blies er irre, als wär es im
  Traum:
"Hirsch tot!" und "Jagdt vorbei."
Sein Horn, das hing er an einen Baum
Und schlug sein Büchse entzwei.
Von fernher da dröhnte der Hirsche Schrei'n,
Die Nebel die stiegen und hüllten ihn ein,
Da war's um ihn geschehn,
Trara, trara, trarara,
Man hat ihn nie mehr gesehn.[54]

The White Stag

The hunter returns to his house;
there is no meal prepared for him,
he found no glass of wine,
no bed strewn with flowers.
Alas, outside in the garden, wet with dew,
there under the flowers lay pale heart's
  beloved.
Oh woe, oh woe, oh woe!
Trara, trara, trara,
Heart's beloved, she was dead!

Then he blew his horn waveringly, as if in a
  dream:
"Dead stag!" and "The hunt's over."
He hung his horn in a tree
and broke his gun in two.
The stags' cries resounded in the distance;
the mist rose and veiled him –
it was all over for him,
Trara, trara, trarara,
No one has ever seen him again.

Is this among the legends where a human being marries someone from another species and hence the marriage is doomed to fail, despite the love between the couple, evident in the flower-strewn bed, the wine, the carefully prepared meal that the hunter expects to

Figure 9 Engraving of a hunter after the manner of Giuseppe Arcimboldo.

find? Or is another interpretation possible? Every aspect of the *mise-en-scène* in which the hunter finds his dead beloved is laden with sexual meaning: she is removed from the safe domestic interior, outside in the garden symbolic of female sexual organs, wet with semen-dew, and buried under the flowers of sex. When the hunter "shoots" the stag, "shooting" possibly emblematic of orgasmic violence, it dies. For post-Freudian readers long accustomed to decoding fairy tales as allegories of grossly dysfunctional families, Mahlmann's variation on a *Märchen* could be one of wife-rape and murder, ending with the transgressor's remorse; one can even imagine the other stags' cries as the lamentations of the dead woman's kin and friends.[55]

Elsewhere, rape is more frankly adumbrated. The "schwarzbraunes Mädel" of "Zwey Schelme" (Two Scoundrels), her swarthiness indicative of greater sensuality, does not wish to be "caught."

Zwey Schelme	**Two Scoundrels**
(stanzas 3–6 of 35)	
Der Jäger der jagt ein wildes Schwein	The hunter hunted a wild boar
Bey Nacht, bey Tag, bey Mondenschein:	by night, by day, by moonlight:
Juchhey, Rassey! Hesasa, Faldrida!	Juchhey, Rassey! Hesasa, Faldrida!
Bey Nacht, bey Tag, bey Mondenschein.	By night, by day, by moonlight.
Er jagt über Berg und tiefe Straus,	He hunted over the mountains and deep
Er jagt ein schwarzbraunes Mädel heraus:	thicket, he hunted out a black-brown maiden:
[refrain]	[refrain]
Wonaus, wohin, du wildes Thier,	Where are you going, thou wild animal,
Ich bin ein Jäger und fang dich schier?	I am a hunter and have nearly captured you.
[refrain]	[refrain]
Du bist ein Jäger und fängst mich nicht,	Thou art a hunter and will not capture me,
Du kennst meine krumme Sprünglein noch	you do not yet know my artful
nicht:	leaping:
[refrain][56]	[refrain]

But he *does* capture her and rape her, upon which she resorts to trickery to escape him. "Sprung," one notes, is a word with sexual connotations, meaning coition among animals; when the swarthy maiden speaks of her "artful leaping," she is referring with pride to her sexual prowess. Both she and her raptor are "Schelme," but whatever her artfulness, in whatever wild sphere, it does not stay the hunter's depredations. Rape or near-rape is once again the subject in "Der ernsthafte Jäger." The poetic persona seeks "ein Hirschlein oder ein Reh" (a little hart or a doe) in the dark "three hours before dawn"; the diminutives and the gender of the animals are common symbolic indications of women in hunting songs, and the hour designated is the time when rapes are commonly committed. The hunter is angered when the "doe" he finds invites him to sleep with her and wants to kill her; she is not supposed to desire what he desires, and the discovery that she does arouses murderous rage (see chapter 4 for the connection between this poem, Shakespeare's *Othello*, and *Die schöne Müllerin*). But when she pleads with him, "his heart breaks," and he bids her become a "jung Jägersfrau" (young hunter-wife); the would-be rapist somehow comprehends his victim's suffering and repents on the spot, asking for her hand in bourgeois marriage. Interestingly, the color symbolism of white-and-green one finds in *Die schöne Müllerin* appears here: the maiden asks the hunter if she should wear a green wreath in her hair when he is away at the hunt, and he replies that green wreaths are for unmarried women. She must wear the white cap ("Häublein") appropriate for a wife instead[57] – from near-rape to propriety, from the green of the forest and Nature to the white of feminine *Sittlichkeit*. In *Die schöne Müllerin*, however, it is the gentle, flour-covered miller lad who is white (civilized, gentle), not the miller maid.

In a variant of "Der ernsthafte Jäger" entitled "Es wollt sich ein Jägerlein jagen," there is no last-minute *lieto fine* in remorse and marriage. The hunter and the customary beautiful young maiden sleep together with her willing compliance, but at dawn, she mocks him, declaring herself still a virgin ("Ein Jungfrau bin ich gewesen, juchhe, / Und eine Jungfrau bin ich als noch"). When the infuriated hunter wishes to kill her, she barters for her life with her father's silver and gold.[58] The woman in "Der Jäger im Tannenholz" (The Hunter in the Pine Forest), its scenario similar to that of "Der ernsthafte Jäger" and "Es wollt sich ein Jägerlein jagen," is even less fortunate. The hunter who encounters her in the forest and asks her where the path goes is told that it leads to her father, but, unimpressed by the implied nearness of paternal authority, he nonetheless demands her virginity then and there. This time, she says no, with fatal consequences.

Der Jäger im Tannenholz	The Hunter in the Pine Forest
(stanzas 4–7 of 8)	
Meine Ehr tu ich nicht lassen	My honor I will not give
Bei einem Jäger stolz,	to a proud hunter;
Viel lieber will ich meiden	nor will I do it
fein Silber und rotes Gold.	for fine silver and red gold.
Was zog er aus seiner Tasche?	What did he draw from his knapsack?
Ein Messer, war scharf und spitz.	A knife, it was sharp and pointed.
Er stach's der Lieben ins Herz,	He struck the beloved in the heart;
Das rote Blut gegen ihn spritzt.	the red blood spurted on him.
Was zog er aus seinigem Finger?	What did he draw from his finger?
Ein Ringelein, fein von Gold.	A little ring, fine and gold,
Er wirft Goldringelein ins Wasser,	he threw Little Gold Ring in the water
Wo's Wasser am tiefsten war.	where the water was deepest.
Schwimm hin, schwimm her, du Goldringelein,	Swim here, swim there, Little Gold Ring,
Schwimm in das tiefe Meer.	swim in the deep sea.
Wir zwei, wir haben uns geliebet	We two, we have loved each other
Und lieben uns nimmermehr.[59]	and will nevermore love each other.

The little gold ring is the name ("du Goldringelein") and the symbol for the woman this hunter kills, the knife and the blood possibly indicative of the rape of a virgin as well as murder. Does the hunter then fantasize that Little Gold Ring (she is thus, the song hints, the archetypal pure blond of so many fairy tales and folk songs) loved him and that he loved her, before he stabbed her and disposed of the body? Odder things have happened in the geography of the human psyche; certainly, the same phenomenon can be documented in actual court cases and historical anecdotes. Or is the poem a violent concatenation of symbols for rape, followed by a love affair, abandonment, and the utter repudiation of a woman once loved, who must now swim alone in the deep sea, far from land?

One of the most macabre variants of the rapist-hunter motif is "Die schwarzbraune Hexe" (The Black-Brown Witch), a Renaissance-era poem Müller would have known from *Des Knaben Wunderhorn*. This is a bizarre, even surreal creation with at least one motif repeated directly in *Die schöne Müllerin*. We know that Müller owned a copy of the Arnim–Brentano anthology because he mentions lending it to someone in his diary for October 31, 1815;[60] given Müller's propensity for magpie borrowings and transformations, this poem could speculatively have found its way into the later work. "Die schwarzbraune Hexe" is a *Totenjagd* (death hunt) whose narrator begins by sounding deadly music: "Es blies ein Jäger wohl in sein Horn / Und alles, was er blies das war verlor'n" (A hunter blew his horn, and all he blew was lost). If blowing or playing the horn is, as we have seen in other examples, representative of sexual acts, one therefore understands the initial lines as indicative of serial rape and murder. When the "black-brown witch" appears, the hunter warns her away, saying that his dogs will spring on her and she will die. She replies:

Die schwarzbraune Hexe	**The Black-Brown Witch**
(stanzas 7–10 of 10)	
"Sterbe ich nun, so bin ich todt,	"If I die now, then I am dead,
So bin ich todt,	then I am dead,
Begräbt man mich unter die Röslein roth."	they should bury me beneath the little red rose."
Hop sa sa sa,	Hop sa sa sa,
Dra ra ra ra,	Dra ra ra ra,
Begräbt man mich unter die Röslein roth.	they should bury me beneath the little red rose.
"Wohl unter die Röslein, wohl unter den Klee,	"Deep beneath the little rose, deep beneath the clover,
Wohl unter den Klee,	deep beneath the clover,
Darunter verderb ich nimmermehr."	there I will nevermore decay."
[refrain]	[refrain]
Es wuchsen drey Lilien auf ihrem Grab,	Three lilies grew from her grave,
Auf ihrem Grab,	from her grave.
Die wollte ein Reuter wohl brechen ab.	A ploughman wished to pluck them.
[refrain]	[refrain]
"Ach Reuter, laß die drey Lilien stahn,	"Oh ploughman, let the three lilies stand,
Die Lilien stahn,	the lilies stand,
Es soll sie ein junger frischer Jäger han."	A young, bold hunter should have them."
[refrain][61]	[refrain]

One cannot help but notice the resemblances to "Der Müller und der Bach," although Müller makes different use of the flowery symbolism of life and death. The "black-brown witch" killed by the hunter's hounds (an oblique reference to rape?) bids the hunter bury her "beneath the little red rose," beneath the emblem of passionate love; in this burial-place, she will be forever preserved, and the three lilies which grow from her grave are destined only for a hunter – no one else. Is one to interpret this as a folk-fantasy about a rape victim who falls in love with her rapist? Müller borrows the same symbolic language of flowers when his suicidal miller lad declares that the lilies (symbolic of virginal chastity) wither when love dies and the brook counters with the assertion that three roses, half-red and half-white, bloom when love conquers sorrow. The red of passion and the white of purity are conjoined in perfected love.[62]

This eerie poem bore poetic progeny. Joseph von Eichendorff – of all the Romantic poets, the one most fascinated by hunters and the hunt[63] – read *Des Knaben Wunderhorn* and, like Müller, assimilated it to his own use. In "Jägerkatechismus," first published in 1815, Eichendorff's poetic hunter quotes the evocative refrain of "Die schwarzbraune Hexe" ("Und alles was er blies das war verlor'n") in order to vary it. His sweetheart, he declares, comes willingly at the sound of his horn-calls and is *not* "verloren," that is, raped or murdered; "to shoot rosy-red" in this context is perhaps indicative of the blood a virgin sheds upon deflowering.[64] Sex is "*merry* death," the age-old metaphor of orgasm as the "little death" readily decipherable.

Jägerkatechismus	Hunter's Catechism
(stanzas 5–8)	
Die Thierlein selber: Hirsch und Rehen,	The little animals themselves: stags and deer
Was lustig haust im grünen Haus,	that merrily live in the green house
Sie fliehn auf ihre freien Höhen,	flee to their free heights
Und lachen arme Wichte aus.	and laugh at poor wretches.
Doch kommt ein Jäger, wohlgeboren,	Then comes a well-born hunter;
Das Horn irrt, er blitzt rosenroth,	the horn strays, his gun flashes rosy-red –
Da ist das Hirschlein wohl verloren,	then is the little stag truly lost,
Stellt selber sich zum lust'gen Tod.	presents himself to merry death.
Vor Allen aber die Verliebten,	But above all it is lovers
Die lad' ich ein zur Jägerlust,	I invite to hunting happiness,
Nur nicht die weinerlich Betrübten;	but not the tearfully troubled,
Die recht von frisch' und starker Brust.	those rightly of fresh and strong heart.
Mein Schatz ist Königin im Walde,	My sweetheart is queen in the forest –
Ich stoß' in's Horn, in's Jägerhorn!	I blow my horn, my hunting horn!
Sie hört mich fern und naht wohl balde,	She hears me from afar and soon draws near,
Und was ich blas', ist nicht verlor'n! –	and what I play is not lost! –

The phrase "er blitzt rosenroth" comes from another poem in the same anthology: "Husarenglaube" (the parallel between "-glaube" and "Katechismus" is obvious), with its line "Wir schießen rosenrot." Lest anyone miss the source, the character Leontin who sings this song in Eichendorff's *Ahnung und Gegenwart* points out ironically, "Ich glaube, ich blase gar schon aus des Knaben Wunderhorn" (I believe I am already playing from *Des Knaben Wunderhorn*). Did Müller know "Jägerkatechismus"? – the cross-references from one nineteenth-century poet to another, from folk song to *Kunstgedichte*, form a fascinating web of connections.[65] Müller's "Jägers Lust," cited earlier in the chapter, would seem a close cousin to "Jägerkatechismus," similarly a statement of the "hunter's Credo"; the reference to "God's breath" could possibly be the younger poet's variation on the mystical meanings with which Eichendorff often imbues his poetic hunts. Müller's hunter, however, is not impelled by the *Sehnsucht* Eichendorff's hunter both experiences himself and awakens within others when he blows his horn ("Wenn's euch nicht selbst lockst in die Weite, / Wie ihr vom Berg früh Morgens blast?").

Müller was not the only one to see the boldness of the legendary hunter, his fascination with killing and with sensuality, with the laws of Nature, as incompatible with piety.[66] The cast of fools on Sebastian Brant's 1494 *Das Narren Schyff* (The Ship of Fools) includes "Der Jagdnarr" (The Hunting Fool): hunting, Brant scornfully declares in "Von vnnutzem jagen" (Of Useless Hunting), is a waste of time and a great expense, but his ultimate condemnation is that one cannot both hunt and serve God.

Von vnnutzem jagen	**Of Useless Hunting**
Nembroht zum erst fing jagen an	Nimrod first took up hunting
Dann er von gott was gantz verlan,	when he was completely forsaken by God.
Esau der jagt vmb das er was	Esau who hunted: was he not
Eyn sünder, vnd der gotts vergasz	a sinner who forgot his God?
Wenig jäger als humpertus	One finds few hunters now
Fynd man yetz, vnd Eustachius	like Hubertus and Eustachius
Die liessen doch den jäger stodt	who threw away the hunter's rod
Sust truwten sie nit dienen gott.[67]	else they could not have served their God.

St. Hubertus is invoked in many German hunting songs, a saint to whom another saint's legend was appended. The historical St. Hubertus (*c.* 655–727) may have been a son of the Duke of Aquitaine and related to the Merovingians; after the deaths of his father and his wife Floribana, daughter of the wonderfully named Graf von Löwen, he retired to a forest hermitage in the Ardennes for seven years and then made a pilgrimage to Rome in 702–03, thereafter becoming bishop, first of Maastricht and then of Lüttich. At some later date (the chronicles differ), the legend of the second-century saint Eustachius, one of the Emperor Trajan's generals in second-century Rome, was grafted onto Hubertus's life: Eustachius was obsessed with hunting until he saw a vision of a white stag[68] with a shining crucifix between its antlers and promptly converted to Christianity. Albrecht Dürer's woodcut engraving, *Der heilige Eustachius* (1500–02), is perhaps the most famous artistic depiction of the subject (Fig. 10). The legend may have been transposed to the life of Hubertus because he forbade erstwhile heathen hunters in the Ardennes to dedicate their first kill to the Celtic hunting goddess Arduinna. Whatever the reason for this saintly echo, Hubertus was worshipped in the medieval German-speaking world and elsewhere as a patron saint of hunters; he is depicted in art as a figure in bishop's robes and holding a book atop of which is a tiny stag with a crucifix between its antlers or, more rarely, a hunting horn.[69]

In most of the small repertoire of songs invoking or featuring the saint, the newly converted hunter renounces his former life in the forest, as in "Das St. Hubertuslied," (St. Hubert's Song). Since God's mercy has created all living creatures, the former hunter will forbear killing them, exchanging the vaunted freedom of forest life for the small enclosure of the cloister. "Now I will no longer shoot any stags," he declares,

Figure 10   Albrecht Dürer, *Der heilige Eustachius*, 1500–02.

"but will rather shut myself away in the cloister. To the green woods I say 'Good Night' – God's mercy has created everything."[70] But there are also songs in which God-loving hunters continue to hunt, if only allegorically, the *chasse* thus bent to sacred as well as secular symbolic purposes.[71] The minstrel-hunter of "Der fromme Jäger" (The Pious Hunter) tells the foxes, hares, and stags not to fear, that he has written this poem rather than kill them, but declares that he is still a hunter in pursuit of a more beautiful existence when life's hunt is over. "All pleasure and worldliness is noisy hunting, but I have striven to go beyond this life's hunt," he declares.[72] One finds many similar allegorical interpretations of the hunt in medieval theology, literature, and art, such as the exquisite late fifteenth- or early sixteenth-century tapestry from the Netherlands, now in the Metropolitan Museum, entitled *The Hunt of the Frail Stag*; the "frail stag" is humanity beset by the hounds of desire, rashness, anxiety, fear, age, and grief, with Lady Vanity the first hunter and Death the last.[73] Müller knew the tradition well: in his *Blumenlese aus den Minnesingern*, he translated a poem entitled "Swer Gotes minne wil bejagen, / Der mus ein jagendes herze tragen" (Whoever would pursue God's love must bear a hunter's heart) wrongly attributed to Gottfried von Strassburg in the Manesse manuscript, a poem in which the quest for God and love of the Virgin is compared elaborately and at length to a hunt. He who would win divine love must be "heldenstark," heroically strong, or else he is, in the poet's beautiful phrase, no more than "a shadow on the wall" (one thinks of Plato's myth of the cave, in which the shadows are the things of this world, as opposed to God or the Forms).[74] The tradition which joins together the words "Jäger" and "Held" here assumes a Godly cast.

Müller tried his own hand at an allegory of the hunt in which the medieval model and folk song are fused. His 1823 poem "Die Jäger" (The Hunters) begins as a typical folkloric celebration of the hunting life, with all the expected motifs of freedom, fresh air, and high spirits. Just as one is about to yawn and turn the page, the hunting rhapsody modulates in the next stanza into an allegory of the futile chase after love in youth, honor in manhood, possessions in old age – Müller thus invoking yet another medieval theme, "The Ages of Man" – even as we are hunted by Death into the grave. Ultimately, the poem is a *memento mori* on a venerable allegorical topos in which the things of this world prove to be illusory, without the value their greedy pursuers ascribe to them. Are Müller's "Nebelgestalten" (misty shapes) perhaps indebted to the "shadows on the wall" in "Swer Gottes minne wil bejagen"? Death, says the mordant Müller, is the only truly all-powerful "Jägerheld."

Die Jäger	**The Hunters**
(stanzas 1–6 of 8)	
Hussah! Hussah, zur Jagd!	Huzza! Huzza, to the hunt!
Wir suchen im grünen Horste,	We seek in the green shrubbery,
Wir jagen im freien Forste	we hunt in the free woods,
Das stolze, lustige Wild.	the proud, merry wild animals.
Wir fliegen durch frische Lüfte,	We fly through the brisk breezes,
Wir trinken des Waldes Düfte,	we drink in the forest's fragrances,
Und das Herz im Busen, es schwillt!	and the heart swells in our breast.

Hussah! Hussah, zur Jagd!	Huzza! Huzza, to the hunt!
Wir jagen doch Alle auf Erden,	All on earth hunt,
Und alle wir Jäger, wir werden	and all of us hunters will be
Gejagt in die Gruben hinein;	hunted into the grave;
Es jagen die Jungen, die Alten,	the young, the old, all hunt,
Sie jagen nach Nebelgestalten,	they hunt for misty shapes
Und fangen sich Sorgen und Pein.	and capture pain and sorrow.
Hussah! Hussah, zur Jagd!	Huzza! Huzza, to the hunt!
Es jaget der Knabe nach Liebe,	The youth hunts for love,
Er jaget mit seligem Triebe;	he hunts with blissful urging,
Und fängt er das lustige Wild,	and if he captures the merry prey,
So sieht er, er hat sich betrogen,	then he sees that he is deceived;
Es hat seine Augen belogen	his eyes have belied
Von ferne das gaukelnde Bild.	in the distance the illusory image.
Hussah! Hussah, zur Jagd!	Huzza! Huzza, to the hunt!
Die Männer, sie jagen nach Ehren,	Men hunt for glory,
Sie jagen mit scharfen Gewehren,	they hunt with sharp weapons,
Sie zielen und treffen den Stern;	they aim for and strike the star,
Doch über ihm leuchten noch immer	but above it many stars shine
Viel Sterne mit hellerem Schimmer –	with a brighter light –
Wer hätte den hellsten nicht gern?	who would not gladly have the brightest?
Hussah! Hussah, zur Jagd!	Huzza! Huzza, to the hunt!
Der Alte, er jaget auf Schätze,	The old man hunts for treasures,
Und ob ihm zerreißen die Netze,	and if the nets are torn,
Sie sind ihm doch immer zu leer.	he finds them ever too empty.
Und hinter ihm kommen gezogen	And behind him come
Viel Jäger mit Spießen und Bogen,	many hunters with spears and bows,
Der Erben schnellfüßiges Heer.	the fleetfooted horde of his heirs.
Hussah! Hussah, zur Jagd!	Huzza! Huzza, to the hunt!
Doch schneller und klüger als Alle,	But quicker and more clever than all
Mit heulendem Hörnerschalle,	is one who hunts the hunters of the world
Jagt Einer die Jäger der Welt.	with howling horn-calls.
Er schießt nach den Greisen und Kindern,	He aims at graybeards and children,
Er schießt nach den Frommen und Sündern,	he shoots at the pious and sinful,
Der knöcherne, klappernde Held.[75]	the bony, clattering hero.

Even in his urbanite's existence, Schubert would surely have encountered the negative side of the hunter-myth, the hunter legendarily possessed of "zernichtender Wuth" (annihilating frenzy). A Viennese *Volkstheater* Singspiel of 1798, *Das Donauweibchen* by Karl Friedrich Hensler, begins with a hunting chorus which epitomizes the bloody fury at the heart of hunting:

Das Riedhorn erschallt,	The horn plays,
Durchstreifet den Wald,	roaming throughout the forest,
Verfolget das Wild mit zernichtender	pursuing the wild animal with annihilating
Wuth.	frenzy.
Auf, rastet nur nicht,	Away, do not rest
Bis Beute verspricht	while there is promise of booty,
Der stürzende Bär sich wälzend im Blut.[76]	of the bear crashing down, rolling in blood.

In the second scene, we see the huntsmen return, proclaiming themselves sated by blood; however comic the context, the words hark back to the ancient north German tradition of the *berserkr* ("beri," or "bear," plus "serkr," or "hide"), the warriors who worked themselves into a state of murderous frenzy by thinking themselves to be bears (the totemic royal symbol of the Germanic West, evident to this day in the Brandenburg bear), hence, the etymology of our word "berserk."[77] Could Schubert have known Adolf Bäuerle's parodistic *Zauberspiel* (magic play), *Lindane oder Die Fee und der Haarbeutelschneider* (Lindane, or The Fairy and the Wigmaker) of 1824 – a wonderfully overripe specimen of the *Zauberspiel* in its last years – in which the fifteenth scene features "Jagd-Musik. Jägerchor"? The second stanza tells explicitly of hunting bloodlust, of a landscape nightmarishly noisy with shrieking and stamping and snorting, while the third stanza presents the rewards of bloodlust: the services of his sweetheart at evening in the form of food, drink, and sex, until the sound of the hunting horn once again impels him to the forest the next morning.

Jagdchor

Dort raget dem Hirsch sein zackig Geweih,
Dort schallet der Jäger wildes Geschrei,
Da stürzen die Hunde des Ebers Zahn,
Mit Blute bezeichnet er seine Bahn,
Es wiehern die schnaubenden Pferde,
Sie stampfen die zitternde Erde,
Und jubelnd das Jagdhorn fern hallt!
Das klinget so prächtig,
Da treibt es ihn mächtig
Zum dunkeln Wald,
Dorthin, wo das Jagdhorn
    erschallt.

Und Abends, da harret das Liebchen zu
    Haus,
Im Arme des Jägers fühlt sie kein Graus,
Da würzt sie das herrliche Jägermahl,
Und wie sie kredenzt ihm den Pokal,
Da mag ers mit keinem nicht theilen,
Die Stunden in Lust ihm enteilen,
Bis Morgens das Jagdhorn erschallt.
Das klinget so prächtig,
Da treibt es ihn mächtig
Zum dunkeln Wald,
Dorthin, wo das Jagdhorn
    erschallt.[78]

Hunting Chorus

There tower the stag's jagged antlers,
there resounds the hunters' wild cry,
there the hounds fall to the boar's tooth,
with blood he marks his path,
the snorting horses neigh,
they stamp the trembling earth,
and joyfully the hunting horn sounds afar!
It rings out so splendidly,
that it drives him mightily
to the dark forest,
there yonder, where the hunting horn
    resounds.

And evenings, his sweetheart awaits him at
    home,
in the hunter's arms, she feels no fear,
She spices the delicious hunting dinner
and how she serves him the goblet –
he wouldn't change places with anyone.
The hours hurry by in happiness
until the hunting horn resounds at morning.
It rings out so splendidly,
that it drives him mightily
to the dark forest,
there yonder, where the hunting horn
    resounds.

The context is hilarious: a Kasperl figure named Schmieramperl (the very name, with its echoes of "Schmierenschauspieler," or "strolling player," and "Schmiererei," or "daubs, scribbles, and scrawls," is funny), here clad in "comic hunting garb over his old-fashioned attire, with shield and spear in hand," is being instructed in aristocratic ways, including hunting, by the fairy of the title. She has her work cut out for her: when he exults that he killed a stag with one shot, she replies, "That was no stag, my dear, that was a fox." "Right, it was a fox – it's all one, an animal is an animal," he replies. Could Bäuerle have known *Die schöne Müllerin* and been influenced by it? He knew others in the Schubert circle – it is at least conceivable that he could have known Schubert as well. Certainly the chronological succession of D. 795 in 1823 and *Lindane oder Die Fee und der Haarbeutelschneider*, first performed in March 1824, would tempt anyone to indulge in speculation.

In his youth, Schubert might also have heard of a real, not play-acted, stomach-turning "show" hunt close to home. The medieval tradition of kings staging elaborate hunts at great diplomatic events (Lucas Cranach in 1529 imagined *A Stag Hunt* for Emperor Maximilian I in a canvas now in Vienna's Kunsthistorisches Museum[79]) was gorily re-enacted at the Congress of Vienna, with its elaborate entertainments for the visiting heads of state. Auguste Louis Charles, comte de La Garde-Chambonas' *Fêtes et souvenirs du Congrès de Vienne* includes a horrifying account of a massive hunt for which beaters rounded up scores of animals in the woods by Laxenburg Castle near Schönbrunn so that the crowned heads of Europe could then slaughter them at close range. "Every care had been taken to ensure the hunt's success," La Garde-Chambonas writes; the four pages provided for each guest were charged with loading the guns lest royalty suffer any fatigue in their violent diversion. The carnage only ceased when several thousand animals had been killed, and all sight of the ground had disappeared under the heaped-up game, its blood still trickling. The French nobleman clearly disapproved; the demonstration of the medieval art of falconry that preceded the hunt was one thing, such staged carnage quite another. "The amusements of our fathers were superior to ours," he drily concludes.[80]

Obsessed hunters who abjured all else in life remained stock characters in German life and literature alike until at least World War II. In Ludwig Ganghofer's late nineteenth-century novel *Schloß Hubertus* (Hubertus Castle), one of the principal characters is the rich and eccentric Graf Egge-Sennefeld, who has devoted his life to hunting and ignored all other obligations, including his children. His castle, festooned with hundreds of antlered trophies (a "Jägerchronik," Ganghofer dubs the fictional structure), will recall to some readers the former Schwarzenberg hunting lodge at Ohrada in Bohemia, its rooms filled to bursting with specimens of taxidermy and with antlered, furred furniture, or the Archduke Franz Ferdinand's Konopiste Castle some thirty miles south of Prague. The Archduke, an omnivorous collector of *objets d'art*, armory, *Kitsch*, and dead animals, is surely to be numbered among the most maniacal hunters in history; the severed heads of every conceivable form of wild prey "decorate" the castle inside and out. "One need not be a Freudian," observes Francine Prose in a travel-essay on Bohemian castles, "to wonder about the psychosexual origins of all this avidity and carnage, nor need one be religious to see a glimmer of retribution in the Archduke's violent death, nor a mystic to marvel at how a man so addicted to violence managed to incite so much, even from beyond the grave."[81] In *Schloß Hubertus*, Ganghofer distinguishes between what he and others such as Clewing call "edle Waidwerk" (the very term signals awareness of a "Waidwerk" that is not so "edel") and the psychotic frenzy of a man who neglects his children, ignores the social and religious obligations of his rank, and abuses others, all in the name of the hunt.

What flashed from this face was not bright, merry pleasure in hunting, not the proud, manly joy that noble forestry offers. It was a wild, all-consuming passion that in its desire knows neither moderation nor boundary, that grips the entire man, body and soul, as a flame consumes dry wood, in which the feeling for all other worthiness in life is smothered. He only sees and craves what bewitches him and never satisfies him, what destroys him and others with him![82]

Ganghofer concocts a suitably horrendous end for the Graf and his hunting mania: blinded by an eagle, the Graf goes on a final sightless hunt and then dies soon after. If it all seems, and is, *grand Guignol*-style melodrama of the claptrap variety, it is nonetheless modeled from life and literature alike, from the long tradition of men in song, story, and actuality who lived and died for the hunt.

If I have chosen to end this section with allegorical hunters and "bad" hunters – obsessed, powerful, and destructive, it is for the obvious reason of parallels with the hunter of *Die schöne Müllerin* as the miller lad sees him. In shamanistic fashion, the hunter takes on the qualities of the beasts he hunts; along the fluid boundary between what is human and what is animal, the hunter is a distinctive hybrid, himself a stalking animal who participates willingly in nature's "kill or be killed" savagery and yet is master of the beasts. In sexual matters too, he appears quasi-animalistic, driven by instinct and sudden, overwhelming urges, the violent virility of it all compelling to that which is most animal-sexual in women. When one adds defiance of bourgeois laws and hyper-freedom to the mixture, one has the *Jägerheld*, a creature both men and women were taught to admire and to fear – this "cultural work" is precisely what many of the songs and poems discussed here served to inculcate. For Müller's miller, the hunter is an unstoppable force, a creature of such mythic power that the lad in "Erster Schmerz, letzter Scherz" can only imagine a counter-magic to whisk so powerful a legendary being away, off to an island where no women dwell. Germanic sagas of the sort that Jakob and Wilhelm Grimm were investigating in Müller's own day are rife with "wilde Jäger," with ghostly huntsmen condemned to the chase forever and hunters who sell their souls to the devil for the ability to hit their target every time (*Der Freischütz* comes immediately to mind), creatures born of ancient Germanic forest cults and centuries of superstition; behind even the bluffest, blandest incarnation of the hunter is a faint supernatural aura of blasphemy, of trafficking in infernal realms.[83] It is no wonder that the miller lad feels himself ill-matched to combat a figure mantled in so much myth.

EPILOGUES FOR A MOURNFUL HUNTER

If Wilhelm Hensel's hunter in the Stägemann *Liederspiel* mourned the death of the miller maid, no poems remain to tell us of his sorrow, but grief-stricken hunters, their loves lost to them, inhabit other poems by other poets. In these works, the fearless hunter whose shots always find their mark is merged with the hunter-as-lover; Franz von Schober provided Schubert with just such a text for "Jägers Liebeslied" (Hunter's Love Song), D. 909, of February 1827, the poem beginning with the hunter's traditional assertions that he has shot everything everywhere ("I shoot the stag in the green forest, the doe in the quiet valley, the eagle on the rocky eyrie, the duck on the lake," etc.) and culminating in love-sick avowals to his sweetheart. Peter Lindpaintner's hunter in "Jägers Lust und Qual"

Example 2 Peter Josef Lindpaintner. "Jägers Lust und Qual," mm. 106–28, from the *Sechs Deutsche Lieder*, op. 127, no. 3. Stuttgart: Allgemeine Musikhandlung, n.d.

(Hunter's Joy and Sorrow), the third lied in his *Sechs Deutsche Lieder*, op. 127, follows the same model by which the hunter's customary boasts about his prowess, punctuated with calls of "Halloh! halloh! hallali hahoh!", modulate by evening to lamentation for the absent beloved (Ex. 2).[84] But one hunter's *Klagelied* in particular compels attention for its possible derivation from Müller's monodrama. In 1837, Joseph von Eichendorff included a poem entitled "Der traurige Jäger" (The Mournful Hunter), another of his many "Jagdlieder" and the most evocative of all for those interested in *Die schöne Müllerin*, in the first edition of his collected verse. No one knows when the poem was written or what the circumstances of its inception might have been, but it seems like a postscript to Müller's cycle, published more than a decade earlier. If so, this is not the only example of Eichendorff varying a theme borrowed from Müller. Although Eichendorff said little or nothing of Müller in his essays, diary, or letters, scholars have assumed Eichendorff's awareness of a critically acclaimed contemporary and have speculated about specific instances of influence: Müller's "Vineta" on Eichendorff's "Meeresstille," Müller's "Der Prager Musikant" on Eichendorff's "Wanderlied der Prager

Studenten," and – most telling of all within these covers – Müller's "Wohin?" ("Ich hört' ein Bächlein rauschen, / Wohl aus dem Felsenquell") on Eichendorff's "In der Fremde" ("Ich hör' die Bächlein rauschen / Im Walde her und hin"), Müller's poem in turn closely modeled, in all likelihood, on Clemens Brentano's "Ich hört' ein Sichlein rauschen, / Wohl rauschen durch das Korn" from *Des Knaben Wunderhorn* – which Eichendorff also knew well.[85] Did Schumann, one wonders, notice the concatenation of resemblances from poet to poet when he set "In der Fremde" (In a Strange Land) to music in the *Liederkreis*, op. 39?

In "Der traurige Jäger," an unnamed, unknown poetic narrator tells of the beautiful miller maid's burial, the hunter's inconsolable grief, his farewell to the hunt, and his mysterious disappearance, "nevermore to be seen again" (a leitmotif phrase in Eichendorff). There is no context, no pre-history, no word of how the miller maid died; the poem is enveloped in a haze of mystery. There is no mention of a miller lad, dead – if one postulates a connection to the earlier cycle – before this poem begins, but the invocation of "die schöne Müllerin," words which appear by themselves in the second line in a manner that suggests a title, brings Müller to mind immediately.

Der traurige Jäger

Zur ew'gen Ruh sie sangen
Die schöne Müllerin;
Die Sterbeglocken klangen
Noch über'n Waldgrund hin.

Da steht ein Fels so kühle,
Wo keine Wand'rer gehn,
Noch einmal nach der Mühle
Wollt' dort der Jäger sehn.

Die Wälder rauschten leise,
Sein Jagen war vorbei:
Er blies so irre Weise,
Als müsst' das Herz entzwei.

Und still dann in der Runde
Ward's über Thal und Höhn:
Man hat seit dieser Stunde
Ihn nimmermehr gesehn.[86]

The Mournful Hunter

To eternal rest they sang
the beautiful miller maid;
the death-knell resounded
over the forest floor.

There stands a rock so cold
where no wanderer goes,
yet once more the hunter
wished there to see the mill.

The forest softly rustled,
his hunting was over:
he blew such an errant melody
as if the heart must break.

And silence then all around
was over the valleys and heights:
one has since that hour,
never seen him again.

Every detail of the deceptively simple language echoes in the vast, indefinite symbolic spaces Eichendorff, as so often in his verse, conjures up. Among the runes of his poetic cryptograms, what is the "rock so cold" that wanderers shun it? Why does the hunter seek it as the place from which to see the mill for the last time? Its coldness is more than mere temperature; the austere finality of the moment, the chill of death, the *terribilità* of the Romantic "sublime," the starkness of the vantage point from which to view the past – all of these are suggested in a mere three monosyllabic words, the poetic inversion of noun and adjective ("Fels so kalt") making us understand that this is coldness to freeze the marrow and stop the heart. The "other wanderers" (other seekers on quests or on the journey through life) avoid this place of confrontation with the past and farewell;

Example 3   Robert Franz. "Romanze (Zur ew'gen Ruh' sie sangen)," from the *Zehn Gesänge für eine Singstimme mit Begleitung des Pianoforte*, op. 51, no. 9. Leipzig: F. E. C. Leuckart, 1879.

one thinks of Müller's wanderer in "Der Wegweiser" from *Die Winterreise* who asks himself angrily why he shuns the roads other people travel and instead takes rock-strewn, snowy paths through the heights. If ever there were a demonstration that land-scape in Eichendorff is a symbolic medium for the ontology of human existence, "Der traurige Jäger" is it; one reads this poem and thinks irresistibly of all the paintings by Caspar David Friedrich in which *Rückenfiguren*, people with their backs turned to the viewer, sit on a rock and look out at the ships sailing away into the distance, into unknown destinies or realms beyond life.

Eichendorff renews the repertoire of seemingly simple words on which he draws over and over again by rendering them mysterious and by enlarging their dimensions to cosmic proportions. There is, for example, no antecedent for "sie" in the first line: who sang the beautiful miller maid to eternal rest? Friends and family? The poets who have sung of her for so many years? Whoever they were, they disappear after the first stanza.

74

The hunter too vanishes at the end, a lost soul whose "irre Weise" is the symbol of life gone awry. The "errant melody" dies away in the silence "in der Runde" – those words evoke a magic circle, an immense circumference embracing heights and depths, past and present, the entire forest of memory and the unconscious. If it is not fully translatable, neither is "irre," its multiple connotations of delirium, wandering, wavering, going astray, error, sin, and insanity resonating from a mere four letters. Is it the forest whose rustlings tell the hunter that his hunting days – life? love? the soul's quest? – are over? Again, one thinks of Müller, of the winter wanderer in "Der Lindenbaum" who hears the linden leaves' whispering "Come here to me," to death. Müller's protagonist lives on in misery, while the hunter does not – or does he? Eichendorff does not say. That the animate and resounding world is silenced at the end, the music of life, however errant, stilled, implies death. Like the ending of a Jacobean tragedy, everyone in the *schöne Müllerin* tale dies.[87]

Composers flocked to Eichendorff, but, oddly, not to "Der traurige Jäger." Were *Lieder-Komponisten* post-Schubert perhaps intimidated by the kinship to *Die schöne Müllerin*? Did it prove impossible to banish the ghost of Schubert's cycle when confronted with this text? Only one composer, a redoubtable figure who stoutly denied any influence from Schubert, set this poem to music: Robert Franz, who entitled it simply "Romanze" and included it in his *Zehn Gesänge für eine Singstimme mit Begleitung des Pianoforte*, op. 51, published in Leipzig by Leuckart in 1879 and dedicated to Ludwig II of Bavaria. (The song, however, was surely composed earlier – Franz had ceased composing altogether in 1867.) The unharmonized first measure of the piano introduction can perhaps be understood in retrospect as evocative of the "homecoming" motif in the poem, a tragic version of the Romantic circular quest in which one comes back to the point from which the quest began – the repeated figure in m. 1, its tonal identity unclear (B flat? F? D minor?) and its rhythmic context equally mysterious, not only circles about repeatedly but begins with the topmost pitch B flat, a foreshadowing of the climactic B flat major harmonies in the setting of stanza 3, when the poet announces "Man hat seit dieser Stunde [ihn nimmermehr gesehn]." The hunter's fanfare motif, richly sonorous and drenched in nostalgic melancholy, reminds us who has vanished; if we cannot see him any longer, his presence lingers in song (Ex. 3).

One of Eichendorff's imitators (he had many) also envisioned a tragic ending for the love-affair of the beautiful miller maid and the hunter in a manner that suggests a variation on Eichendorff's theme. "Des Jägers Klage" (The Hunter's Lament) by "H. Schütz," about whom nothing is known, was set to music by Wilhelm Sommer and published before 1855.

Des Jägers Klage

Das Mühlrad brauset, das Wasser zerstiebt
Zu eitel Blasen und Schaum;
Dich, schöne Müllerin, hab' ich geliebt,
Das war ein seliger Traum.

Nun kehr' ich zurück in den wilden Hag
Zu meinen Hirschen und Reh'n,

The Hunter's Lament

The mill-wheel roars, the water sprays
in futile sound and foam;
you, beautiful miller maid, have I loved –
that was a blessed dream.

Now I return to the wild grove,
to my stags and deer;

Nun will ich auch wieder den ganzen Tag	now I will once again roam through the forest
Den Wald mit der Büchse durchspäh'n.	the entire day with my gun.

Doch sieht durch der Wipfel webende Nacht	Yet when the moon with its silvery gleam
Der Mond mit silbernem Schein,	looks through the waving treetops' night,
Dann blas' ich auf meinem Waldhorn sacht	then I blow softly on my horn
Und denke im Herzen dein.	and think of you in my heart.

Bald kommt auch die stille, die stille Zeit,	Soon also will come the still, still time
Da schlaf' ich im grünen Revier,	when I will sleep in the green hunting ground;
Der Wald nur rauschet noch weit und breit,	only the forest still rustles far and wide
Und niemand fraget nach mir.[88]	and no one asks about me.

Schütz's hunter leaves the mill in stanza 2 and returns to his own element (one remembers Müller's miller angrily bidding another hunter to do likewise in "Der Jäger"), only to discover that hunting no longer brings contentment. The forest that had been his life should now, he feels, become the site of his solitary death. Schütz fused Eichendorff's "Der traurige Jäger" with the same poet's "In der Fremde," in particular, the last four lines of the poem:

(Eichendorff)

Wie bald, wie bald kommt die stille Zeit,	How soon, how soon comes the still time
Da ruhe ich auch, und über mir	when I too will rest, and over me
Rauschet die schöne Waldeinsamkeit,	rustles the beautiful forest loneliness
Und keiner mehr kennt mich auch hier.	and no one even knows me here.

Eichendorff, however, was a genius, and Schütz was not; one cannot help but notice how much prosier the latter-day imitation is. Where a masterful poet bids "forest loneliness" rustle, the pallid copier settles for a mere "rustling forest." Nevertheless, the setting by Sommer, within its *Volkston* boundaries, is lovely (Ex. 4). Could Sommer have intended this lied in E minor as an epilogue to Schubert's "Des Baches Wiegenlied" in E major? Although the choice of key could be merely coincidental, the possibility is intriguing, all the more since it can perhaps serve to bolster the supposition – sufficiently airy and unfounded to be a ghost right out of Eichendorff – that "Der traurige Jäger" was a poetic epilogue to Müller's *Die schöne Müllerin*.

Not all hunters à la Eichendorff are bereft. The unknown poet who provided the *Kleinmeister* Gustav Sobirey with the text for "Der Jäger," op. 4, no. 1, published *circa* 1850 in Kassel by Hainauer, seems to have cobbled together his lovestruck hunter from Eichendorff's "Waldeinsamkeit" added to Müller's "Jägers Lust." As in Müller's poem, this hunter woos his sweetheart by contrasting the falsity of the outside world ("Die Welt hier draussen ist falsch und kalt") with the purity and beauty of life in Nature, where they will reign as king and queen of the forest. She is, one notes, "so rein, so treu, so fromm" (so pure, so faithful, so pious), the conventionally worshipful invocations of the beloved that Heine had made suspect in "Du bist wie eine Blume" – is there a leaven of irony in this seemingly sentimental poem? The amatory hunter of yore may have become more *schwärmerisch*, but playing the horn retains all of its traditional sexual connotations, however sugary-sweet the context.

Example 4 Wilhelm Sommer. "Des Jägers Klage," mm. 1–12, to a poem by H. Schütz, from Bernhard Pompecki, ed., *Hörnerschall und Lustgesang*. Neudamm: J. Neumann, n.d.

1. Das Mühl - rad brau - set, das Was - ser zer - stiebt zu ei - tel Bla - sen und
2. Nun kehr' ich zu - rück in den wil - den Hag zu mei - nen Hir - schen und
3. Doch sieht durch der Wip - fel we - ben - de Nacht der Mond mit sil - ber - nem
4. Bald kommt auch die stil - le, die stil - le Zeit, da schlaf' ich im grü - nen Re -

Schaum; dich, schö - ne Mül - le - rin, hab' ich ge - liebt, das war ein se - li - ger
Reh'n, nun will ich auch wie - der den gan - zen Tag den Wald mit der Büch - se durch -
Schein, dann blas' ich auf mei - nem Wald - horn sacht und den - ke im Her - zen
vier, der Wald nur rau - schet noch weit und breit, und nie - mand fra - get nach

Traum! Dich, schö - ne Mül - le - rin, hab' ich ge - liebt, das war ein se - li - ger Traum!
späh'n, nun will ich auch wie - der den gan - zen Tag den Wald mit der Büch - se durch - späh'n.
dein, dann blas' ich auf mei - nem Wald - horn sacht und den - ke im Her - zen dein.
mir, der Wald nur rau - schet noch weit und breit, und nie - mand fra - get nach mir.

H. Schütz.

Der Jäger

O Kind, zieh mit in den grünen Wald,
Die Welt hier draußen ist falsch und kalt.
Zieh mit, mein rosiges Jungfräulein,
Du sollst des Waldes Königin sein.

Eine Krone von dunklem Tannenreis
Wind' ich dir um die Stirne weiß,
Die Hirsche, die Rehe, die Waldvöglein,
Die sollen dein lustiger Hofstaat sein.

Die sind so rein, so treu, so fromm,
Fast so wie du, o komm, o komm,

The Hunter

O child, come with me in the green forest,
the world outside here is false and cold.
Come with me, my rosy-cheeked maiden,
you shall be queen of the forest.

A crown of dark-green fir
I shall wind about your white forehead;
the stag, the doe, the forest birds
shall be your merry courtiers.

They are almost as pure, as faithful, as pious
as you – oh come, oh come

Auf der blühendsten Wiese, im Waldrevier,	to the blossoming meadow in the hunting preserve.
Da stehet mein Häuschen, da wohn' ich mit dir.	There stands my little house; there I will live with you.
Da singt dich mein Waldhorn in Schlummer ein,	There, my hunting horn shall sing you to sleep
Wenn die Wälder rauschen in Mondenschein,	when the forest murmurs in the moonlight;
Da weckt dich Morgens der Vöglein Lied,	there, birdsong will awaken you in the morning
Wenn im Frührot der Tannen Wipfel glüht.	when the fir-tree branches glow in the red light of dawn.
Der Wald ist ewig jung und grün,	The forest is ever young and green;
So soll meine Liebe auch nimmer verblühn.	so too my love will never wither.
Was sinnst du? O komm, du liebliche Maid,	What are you thinking? Oh come, gentle maiden,
Kommt mit in die schönen Waldeinsamkeit.	come with me in the beautiful forest-loneliness

Sobirey took his cue appropriately enough from Schumann, the *Komponist par excellence* of Eichendorff's "schöne Waldeinsamkeit." The song falls into three sections A B A', but with B subdivided into two distinct sections by change of tonality and change of meter, the first especially reminiscent of Schumann. After an A section replete with horn-call motifs in E major, Sobirey pauses on the dominant (vitiated of its third and therefore evocative of a horn motif arrested in mid-course); after chanting the words "Die sind so — " on the dominant pitch B, the word "rein" impels a third-related harmonic shift to a G major harmony and a change in the piano figuration. The quieter, but more intense worshipfulness of this brief passage (ten bars) is similar in effect to what transpires at the B section of Schumann's "Widmung" from *Myrthen*, op. 25, where a submediant modulation and a change of figuration underscore the words "Du bist die Ruh'." The harmonic inflections of G major, A minor, E minor, C major, and finally, V/tonic E major give the hunter's seductive pleas ("O komm, o komm") their lyrical urgency, leading to the *pianissimo* evocation of a nocturnal *Waldhorn* serenade (Ex. 5). "Der Jäger" is a charming specimen of the Schumannian lied at mid-century — Sobirey took his cue from the very latest trend in song composition — and well worth revival, as is "Des Jägers Klage."

Müller too envisioned a lovesick marksman. Fond of antitheses, this poet paired "Jägers Lust" with another poem entitled "Jägers Leid" (Hunter's Sorrow).

Jägers Leid

Es hat so grün gesäuselt
Am Fenster die ganze Nacht,
Mein Schatz im Tannen Walde,
Hast wohl an mich gedacht?

Und wenn alle Bäume rauschen
Im weiten Jagdrevier,
Und weht kein Lüftchen am Himmel,
Herzliebste, dann sing ich von Dir.

Hunter's Sorrow

It rustled so greenly
at the window the whole night through,
my sweetheart in the pine forest,
did you think of me?

And when all the trees rustle
in the wide hunting preserve,
and no little breeze blows in the sky,
then, sweetheart, I sing of you.

Example 5   Gustav Sobirey. "Der Jäger," op. 4, no. 1, mm. 20–41. Kassel: Hainauer, *c.* 1850.

Wann alle Zweige sich neigen
Und nicken dir Grüße zu,
Herzliebste, das ist mein Sehnen
Hat nimmer Rast noch Ruh!

Ach Welt, ich muss dich fragen,
Warum du bist so weit?
Ach Liebe, ferne Liebe,
Warum nicht heisst du Leid?

When all the branches bow
and nod greetings to you,
sweetheart, my longing
has neither rest nor peace!

Oh world, I must ask you,
why are you so wide?
Oh love, distant love,
why are you not called sorrow?

Ich möchte die Büchse laden,	I wanted to load my musket,
Nicht laden mit Pulver und Schrot,	but not with powder and shot;
Ich möcht' in die Lüfte schießen	I wanted to fire into the air
All meine Liebesnoth.	all my love's care.
Und wenn von allen Bäumen	And when the forest birds
Stürzen die Waldvögelein,	fall from all the trees,
Dann ist der Schuss gefallen.	then the shot has found its mark . . .
Wer soll nun Sänger sein?[89]	who shall the singers be now?

Once again, one sees the direct line of influence from Müller to Heine – the poetic persona who wishes to bury his tragic love in the symbolic sea of "Die alten, bösen Lieder" has his predecessor in Müller's hunter. Heine is, of course, well known for the overtly sexual content of certain poems, but stanza 5 of Müller's "Jägers Leid" is enough to make anyone gasp. The sexual implications of loading a "musket" with something other than powder and shot, of firing it into the air and thereby killing the forest birds, does not require great leaps of the imagination to decode. Müller thus links poetic creation explicitly to sex; if the birds who are traditionally love's messengers in folk poems die as a result of one gigantic masturbatory shot from a poetic penis, thereby expending all sexual energy, how can there be poetry, he asks? Sex sings, and song is sex.

"Jägers Leid" was set to music as "Der Jäger" by Jeannette Bürde as the second of her *Vier Lieder von Wilhelm Müller* (Berlin: T. Trautwein, [1830?]), which also includes a setting of "Der Berghirt" – one of the two poems Schubert put together for "Der Hirt auf dem Felsen," composed for Anna Milder-Hauptmann, Jeannette Bürde's sister and one of the most lauded singers of the era. "Jägers Leid" is a skillfully designed and attractive song, especially in the contrast between the beginning and end. Stanzas 1–2 are set as a single musical strophe repeated literally for stanzas 3–4, the strophe inspired by the "grün-säuselndes" murmuring and forest rustling, which here becomes *sempre pianissimo* measured tremolando-style figuration in the right-hand part.[90] At the first mention of "mein Schatz," the singer dwells in palpable desire on words that invoke the absent sweetheart; the last two lines of the stanza occupy twice as much musical space as the previous two lines, and the melodic line broadens in compass as well, the largely stepwise motion and restricted compass of the first phrase no longer regnant. But this barcarolle-like lyricism in the 6/8 meter so frequent in love songs gives way to angry despair and swelling sexual tension at the end. In Bürde's conception, the hunter begins to sing "Ich möchte die Büchse laden, nicht laden mit Pulver und Schrot" to a repetition of the first phrase of the song, but the quickened motion and the accents in the third measure of the phrase already tell of rapidly building intensity, culminating in the overthrow of the "rauschendes" figuration and the barcarolle rhythms. Bristling, dotted-rhythm chords in a rapid ("Schnell") 4/4 meter, with the bass pounded out in octaves, replace the former songlike strains; Bürde's attention to nuances is evident in the *diminuendo* for the words "Und wenn von allen Bäumen," followed by yet another *sforzando* accent for the violent verb "stürzen." Did Bürde understand the sexual implications of the poem? Looking at this setting, with its macho-martial dotted rhythms and swelling chords at just the crucial spot, it seems likely (Ex. 6).

The fact that the composer of this song was a woman did not escape notice. "A woman!

Example 6   Jeannette Bürde. "Der Jäger," mm. 13–39, from the *Vier Lieder von Wilhelm Müller*, no. 2. Berlin: T. Trautwein, [1830?].

May she be pretty, charming, and polite, Herr Critic! . . . What does one make of it?", the sarcastically bemused critic of the *Allgemeine Musikalische Zeitung* asked at the beginning of his review in July 1830. That he did not make much of it is spelled out at length and in slighting tones in a review longer than those accorded most of the lieder critiqued in the *AMZ*, unless they were composed by the likes of Carl Loewe or other composers held in high esteem, but then, sarcasm requires elbow room for fullest effect.

I make no demand [of Bürde's songs] regarding the elements of setting poetry to music, only that the poem and the music have something of their sentiment in common, in the most general sense; I make no demand that the harmonies in the accompaniment be clean and flowing; that, where they stand out most conspicuously, whether through sudden modulations, figuration, leaps, whatever, they at least have some instigation from the poetry, if not exactly an open invitation – of all this, I make no demand, but will only praise what I can honestly commend.

Having thus damned the work with faint praise, and in syntax by far more torturous in the original than in translation, he goes on to praise the poetry ("folk-like and merry" – he missed the point of the poetry as well as that of the music), "the utterly simple, naive melody" of "Liebesgedanken," and what he wrongly identifies as the "through-composed" (it is not) setting of the fourth song, "Abschied" – the gem of the set. Even *this* reviewer had to admit that "Abschied" demonstrated talent, and he was right, but so too does "Der Jäger." It is a delicious irony that a woman composer found music for poetic meaning hidden from this arrogant reviewer, who could neither see nor hear nor understand.

MILLS, MILLERS, AND MILLER MAIDS IN SONG AND STORY

It is no coincidence that these legendary figures meet at a mill or that the beloved woman is a miller's daughter. The site is traditional, rich with past literary associations, and its young, beautiful inhabitant had a long and highly erotic pre-history before Müller's lad ever met her. Metamorphosis happens at mills, where water, stone, and wood come together to transform grain into flour and meal, the basic sustenance of life, and it was perhaps for this reason that mills became symbols for matters both sacred and secular, spiritual and erotic. There are Godly mills and un-Godly mills: when Eduard Mörike wrote his ballad "Der Feuerreiter," or "The Fire-Rider," with its refrain "Hinter'm Berg, hinter'm Berg, brennt es in der Mühle," he was trafficking in the so-called "Teufelsmühle" motif by which mills are sites for the supernatural.[91] It is, one recalls, at the mill of Life and Death that Hieronymous Bosch divides the pictorial realm in the central panel of his triptych *The Temptation of Saint Anthony,* now in Lisbon.

If there is nothing mystical or religious about the mill in *Die schöne Müllerin,* it is still the *mise-en-scène* for transformation; the miller lad undergoes a wrenching metamorphosis, an *éducation sentimentale* that carries him from immaturity to death, from innocence to experience, all against the backdrop of turning wheels, rushing waters, and the forest primeval. *This* mill, like so many of its literary predecessors, is the site for sex. "Mahlen," "to mill, to grind" is an antique metaphor for sexual intercourse, derived from an ancient tradition by which the miller's daughter was supposedly offered for sex to the men bringing corn or meal to grind at the mill. (One already finds the Latin verb "mollere" used in antiquity with the double meaning of "grinding grain" and "copulating."[92]) Later, bordellos were often located in the "Mühlenstraße," and mills as the milieu for sexual goings-on of all sorts are endemic in folk poetry, comic opera, operettas, *Liederspiele*, the pictorial arts, and elsewhere – one need only recall the name of the Moulin Rouge in Paris. In legends of the "Altweibermühle" (the old women's mill), old women enter a magic mill and emerge young and beautiful, once again ready, willing, and able for "milling" of the sexual variety (metamorphosis once again),[93] but Müller's "schöne Müllerin" has no need of such a mill.

The unmarried miller maid or young miller's wife whose beauty impels propositions, honorable and otherwise, from men of varying degrees, high and low, appears in the folk traditions of England, Europe, and Scandinavia. She is often portrayed as sexually available and sensual, a willing collaborator in rendez-vous, as in "Der Müller auf der Nidermül" (one notes the directional and sexual symbolism of "the mill down below"), which is included in the sixteenth-century Ambraser Liederbuch and is perhaps much older.[94] When the knight with whom a miller maid is in love stands outside her window and begs for entrance by night, she responds eagerly, telling him that her father is not at home and her mother is preoccupied with cradling a child; her younger brother, overhearing the assignation, grabs her by her hair and throws her to the ground, upon which she bribes him with the prospect of fine silken garments, presumably to be supplied by her wealthy lover. How the story ends, we are not told: the narrator says only that he heard the song from "ein freier Hofmann" who was in love with "ein feins brauns megdlein" (a fine brown maiden) – once again, the sun-browned index of female sensuality in the lower classes. We are led to infer that the knight of the tale has told the singer-narrator his own story in song, which the narrator then repeats – oral tradition records its own processes within the song itself.

But whenever anyone mentions the sexually greedy inhabitants of the medieval mill, it is Chaucer who comes to mind first and foremost. The Reeve Oswald, whose name accords suspiciously well with "cuckold" ("Osewold" and "cukewold"), is so angered by the churlish miller's tale of Nicholas the Handy and the elderly carpenter's wife Alison – all the more obscene in its effect because it follows the knight's tale – that he responds with his own dirty story, a variation on the theme of the miller doubly cuckolded. Two Cambridge students, angered by the braggart miller Simkin's habitual thefts of grain (millers are often portrayed as cheats, perhaps out of jealousy over their comparative wealth), manage by trickery to have lusty sex both with the miller's wife and his snub-nosed, broad-buttocked, well-developed daughter – hardly the most "schöne" of miller maids – right in the same bedroom with the cuckolded miller. Chaucer was not the only one to tell this tale, although other versions lack his wealth of detail and insight into human nature; the French fabliau "Le Meunier et les II. Clers" (The Miller and the Two Clerks) closely resembles the Reeve's Tale,[95] as does the medieval Danish ballad "Møllerens Datter" (The Miller's Daughter).

Møllerens Datter	**The Miller's Daughter**
(stanzas 1–4 and 7 of 10)	
Der stode to Skalke og taenkte Raad –	There stood two wags and hatched a plan –
Ja hvad skulde man taenke?	Oh, what should one think?
De vilde til Møllerens Datter gaae.	They wanted to go to the miller's daughter.

Foroventil var hun Mø forneden var hun Enke.	Above the waist she was a maid, below she was a widow.
O hvad har du i Saekken din? Ja hvad skulde man taenke?	"And what do you have in your sack?" Oh, what should one think?
Jeg haver Rug og hveden fin. Foroventil var hun Mø forneden var hun Enke.	"I have rye and wheat so fine." Above the waist she was a maid, below she was a widow.
Du saet din Saek hos min Datters Seng! Ja hvad skulde man taenke?	"Put down your sack by my daughter's bed!" Oh, what should one think?
Der kommer ingen Rotter til den. Foroventil var hun Mø forneden var hun Enke.	"There no rats will get at it!" Above the waist she was a maid, below she was a widow.
Og der blev mørk udi i hver en Vraa, Ja hvad skulde man taenke?	Darkness came to every corner, Oh, what should one think?
Den saek begyndte at krybe og gaa. Foroventil var hun Mø forneden var hun Enke.	The sack began to creep and walk. Above the waist she was a maid, below she was a widow.
O, min kjaer Fader! I slukker Ljus. Ja hvad skulde man taenke?	"Oh, father dear, put out the light," Oh, what should one think?
Det var den kat han tog en Mus. Foroventil var hun Mø forneden var hun Enke.[96]	"It was the cat; he caught a mouse." Above the waist she was a maid, below she was a widow.

The antique imputation of women's duality – external purity and inner vice – here becomes a refrain in which the miller maid is pure up above and impure down below (widows are, according to some traditions, sex-starved after their husbands' death). The language is wonderfully suggestive: it is the darkness of sin, of sex, of unreason, which spreads to every corner at nightfall, and the daughter's sly truth-telling – the "cat" indeed caught a "mouse" – heightens the erotic danger.[97]

Müller would surely have known one tale of a sexually "hot" young woman who seeks her partner at the mill because it is included in *Des Knaben Wunderhorn*: "Der Habersack" (The Bag of Oats), which dates back at least to the early sixteenth century in written tradition and almost certainly earlier in oral tradition. The dramatis personae of this little ballad are "ein feines Fräulein" (a fine young woman) with sex very much on her mind, a miller with whom she proposes to satisfy her desires, and a miller's apprentice who longs for her to look his way. The young woman, one notes, is not a miller's daughter or wife, but as a naturally lusty creature, she knows to come to a mill for the sexual services she craves, and craves early; the poet slyly tells us "wie bald" (how soon) this fine female creature takes her "bag of oats" (her sexual organs) to the mill to have their contents ground according to *her* wishes ("um den Willen mein"). The euphemisms in this poem – "bag of oats," mixing the oats ("Dein und mein und aber dein"), "the grinder" – are more salacious in their effect than direct speech; to be "clever with her words" means that "das Fräulein" knows how to speak the language of sexual innuendo, which always emphasizes that which it purports to conceal. The old theme of the miller duped is slyly hinted when the poet makes himself known in the refrain to stanzas 2 and 3; the miller, he infers, can try as much as he likes, but "I" have already ravished her this very night.

Although his bragging rights are dubious at best, the miller cannot resist boasting of his sexual "conquest," even when asked to keep it a secret – this is a song about a song in which the directive "Es soll verschwiegen sein" is broken.

Der Habersack	**The Bag of Oats**

(stanzas 2–5 of 5)

Das Fräulein, das war weise,
Mit seinen Worten klug,
Wie bald nahm sie den Habersack,
Ihn zu der Mühle trug.
Nun seh, du lieber Müller mein,
Den Haber sollst du mahlen wohl,
Wohl um den Willen mein,
   Dein und mein und aber dein,
   Es soll verschwiegen sein.

The young woman was wise,
clever with her words.
She very soon took the bag of oats
and bore it to the mill.
Now see, my beloved miller,
you should grind the oats well,
according to my will,
   Yours and mine and once again yours,
   it should be kept secret.

Der Müller nahm den Haber
Und schütt ihn auf die Well,
Er konnt ihn nie gemahlen,
Es war sein Ungefäll.
Er mahlt die Nacht, bis an den Tag,
Gott geb ihm einen guten Morgen,
Und einen guten Tag,
   Tag und Tag und aber Tag
   Mit der ich heut Nacht sprach.

The miller took the oats
and poured them on the grinder.
He was unable to grind it;
that was his great misfortune.
He milled all night, until the day,
May God give him a good morning
and a good day –
   Day after day after day yet again
   with her to whom I spoke just this night.

Der Müller nahm die Stiefel,
Streift sie an seine Bein,
Er gieng die Gassen auf und ab,
Und sang ein Liedlein klein.
Er sang ein Lied vom Habersack,
Gott geb ihr einen guten Morgen,
Und einen guten Tag,
   Tag und Tag und aber Tag
   Mit der ich heut Nacht sprach.

The miller took his boots,
put them on his legs.
He went up and down the streets
and sang a little song.
He sang a song of the bag of oats;
God give you a good morning
and a good day,
   Day and day and once again day
   with whom I spoke this night.

Das hört des Müllers Knechte
In seinem Kämmerlein,
Er dacht in seinem Sinne,
Es wär ein Fräulein fein,
Es wär ein Fräulein minniglich,
Wollt Gott sollt ich sie schauen,
Wohl durch den Willen mein,
   Dein und mein und aber dein,
   Es soll verschwiegen sein.[98]

The miller's apprentice heard it
in his little room.
He thought that in his opinion
she was a fine young woman,
she was a young woman worthy of love.
Would God I could see her,
according to my will,
   Yours and mine and once again yours,
   it should be kept secret.

One notes in particular the sexualized in-and-out rhythms of the refrain "Dein und mein und aber dein" and the appearance in the final stanza of the miller's apprentice, who longs for the miller's luck in lust. The scenario in *Die schöne Müllerin* by which a young man awakening to sex comes to a place traditionally saturated with sexual symbolism of the earthiest variety thus has a long pre-history in song, although Müller deliberately fashions his lad to be not at all "klug" in this sense. His youth has read all the wrong poems and does not know what the *literati* who watch him blunder blindly into sexual knowledge know.

According to some scholars, the *Urquell* of all subsequent erotic mill songs and *Mühlenschwänke*[99] was the dialogue-poem "Die stolze Müllerin" (The Proud Miller Maid), known since at least the beginning of the fifteenth century; some 270 variants under a variety of titles – "Es war einmal ein Müllerin," "Es war ein stolzes Müllerweib," "Ich weiß'ne schöne Müllerin, ein wunderschönes Weib," and so on (There once was a Miller Maid, There was a Proud Miller's Wife, I know of a Beautiful Miller Maid, a Wonderfully Beautiful Woman) – have been found in the German-speaking countries. The antique topos of the young wife and the old husband who cannot satisfy her sexually is the subject of many of these songs, although there are also versions lacking the May-December contrast in age and sexual capacity.

Die stolze Müllerin	**The Proud Milleress**
Ich weiß mir eine Müllerin,	I know of a milleress,
Ein wunderschönes Weib.	a wonderfully beautiful woman,
Wollt Gott, ich sollt bei ihr mahlen,	God willing, I'll do my milling with her,
Mein Körnlein zu ihr tragen,	bring my corn to her,
Das wär der Wille mein,	that would be my wish,
Das wär der Wille mein.	that would be my wish.
Der Müller aus dem Holze kam,	The miller came out of the woods,
Von Regen war er naß:	wet with rain:
"Steh auf, Frau Müllerin stolze,	"Arise, proud miller's wife,
Mach mir ein Feuer von Holze:	and make me a wood-fire –
Von Regen bin ich naß,	I am wet with rain,
Von Regen bin ich naß."	I am wet with rain."
"Ich kann dir nicht aufstehen,"	"I cannot get up for you,"
Sprach sie, des Müllers Weib,	said the miller's wife,
"Ich hab die Nacht gemahlen	"I have milled away the night
Mit einem Reutersknaben,	with a ploughman's knave,
Daß ich so müde bin,	and I am too tired,
Daß ich so müde bin."	I am too tired."
"Hast du die Nacht gemahlen,"	"Since you have milled this night,"
Sprach er, der Müller stolz,	said the proud miller,
"Die Mühle will ich dir verstellen,	"I will shut down the mill,
Das Kampfrad und die Wellen,	the wheel and the waves,
Daß du nicht mahlen kannst."	so that you can no longer grind."
"Wilt du mir die Mühle verstellen,"	"If you close down the mill,"
Sprach sie, des Müllers Weib,	said the miller's wife,
"Ein ander will ich mir bauen	"I'll build another
Auf einer grünen Auen,	in the green field,
Auf einen grünen Zweig,	on a green branch,
Auf meinen eignen Leib."[100]	on my own body."

"Lighting a fire" and "getting [it] up" have roughly the same sexual connotations as they do in present-day parlance, nor is it difficult to decode being "wet with rain." Given the green motif in *Die schöne Müllerin*, it is interesting to see that the adulterous milleress defiantly connects her sexuality with Nature and proclaims that green fields and branches shall be her bedchamber. One naturally (the *mot juste*) associates green with hunters, with Nature, but it is also the color of human sexual nature, of urges belonging to the laws of the natural world. Sex outside the bounds of society's strictures, amoral sex that pays no heed to vows, to promises, to conventions, takes to the meadows. When Hedwig's and Müller's miller maid declares that she loves green, she is announcing her own favored *mise-en-scène* as well as her attraction to the green-clad hunter.

In an unfinished poem from 1792, Gottfried August Bürger clearly had the same dramatis personae as that of *Die schöne Müllerin* in mind, but when and how the hunter comes onto the scene are mysteries and what he does is left unsaid, although one can guess. However comic the context, Eve and the apples of the Fall lurk behind the appletree image in line 1.

Schön, wie der Apfelbaum im Mai,	Beautiful, like the apple tree in May,
Schön blühte Müllers Liese.	the miller's daughter Liese blossomed beautifully.
Sie harkte, wandt' und häuft' ihr Heu	She raked, twined, and heaped the hay
Auf rundumbuschter Wiese.	in the field, encircled with bushes.
Und als das Heu gehäufelt war,	And when the hay was gathered,
Da sank sie, sicher vor Gefahr,	she sank down, safe from danger,
Zum Labsal matter Glieder	on the last stack to refresh
Aufs letzte Häuflein nieder.	her tired limbs.
Da kam des Müllers junger Knapp,	There came, with light steps,
Er kam mit leisen Tritten	the miller's young apprentice
Das stille Wiesenthal herab	down from the quiet meadow valley
Zur Schläferin geschritten.	to the sleeper.
Er warf ihr Blumen ins Gesicht;	He threw flowers in her face;
Die Schläferin erwachte nicht.	the sleeper did not awaken.
Es half kein Händeklappen,	Handclapping did not help,
Kein Tippen und kein Tappen.	no tapping or fumbling.
Der rege Fleiß in schwüler Luft,	The active work in humid air,
Ein Mosttrunk auf die Schwüle,	a drink of cider in the heat,
Der Wiesenkräuter Würzeduft,	the spicy scent of the meadow plants,
Des Pappelschattens Kühle	the coolness of the poplar's shadows
Berauschten Lieschen. Sie entschlief;	intoxicated Lieschen. She slept;
Sie schlief so süß, sie schlief so tief,	she slept so sweetly, so deeply,
Kein Necken und kein Schrecken	no teasing and no alarms
Vermochten sie zu wecken.	were able to awaken her.
Zu sagen, was der Jäger that,	To say what the hunter did
Wär' itzt ein alberner Verrat.	would now be an absurd betrayal.
Doch sollt' er nach zwei Jahren	But he should, after two years
Samt Lieschen es erfahren.[101]	tell Lieschen all of it.

Goethe's pert miller maid in the first of that poet's mill ballads is, one recalls, named Liese. Theodor Storm's miller maid who sneaks out to a rendez-vous with the miller's apprentice while her father snores of a hot "Sommermittag" (summer midday) – "'Nun küsse mich, verliebter Junge; / Doch sauber, sauber! nicht zu laut'" (Now kiss me, amorous youth, but nicely, nicely! not so loud) – also conforms to the stereotype of lusty miller maids with sex very much on their minds; the Chaucerian echo of the nearby father is a notable detail.[102]

Readers alive to literary tradition would therefore have known that miller maids were sexy sorts. Not surprisingly, the motif at its most sensational appears in *Hintertreppenliteratur* (pornography), including some extremely dirty verses by high-toned poets. Friedrich Schlegel has been identified in some sources as the author of a set of ten sonnets, each on a different sexual act or perversion (drinking the beloved's urine, masturbation, deflowering a virgin, homosexual penetration, and so on), the cycle circulated in private printings; the appropriation of the most elevated poetic form for subjects whose only elevation is physical is a calculated element of the shock-value of these poems. One of the sonnets tells of a miller lad who inserts his penis into a millstone to find relief; the blond miller maid who observes him comes out to feel whether the member is flesh and bone, then asks him whether this is a way of demonstrating his worthiness for her bed. He, however, shows her an inscription "um den Reif" with the name "Elisabeth" written therein – the sonneteer both spoofs the literary tradition by which young miller apprentices yearn for sex and lusty miller maids provide it and uses the motif for purposes of titillation at the far end of the sexual spectrum.[103] Such flagrantly sexual associations with mills and their inhabitants are perhaps why Müller's "Der Dichter" in the prologue hastens to reassure his audience that the work to come will be decent, presumably expunged of all such sexiness and suitable for the family circle. It is not, and he lies, but the audience cannot know that as yet (see chapter 4).

When the poor miller apprentice Konrad, in love with the pure and dutiful miller's daughter Marie in Ernst Raupach's tragedy *Der Müller und sein Kind* (The Miller and his Child) of 1835, leaves his prior employment because "Frau Meisterin," the miller's widow, wants to seduce him, one sees in the widow a latter-day reincarnation of "Die stolze Müllerin" and in Marie the kind of rustic saint Müller's miller believed he had found – he first thinks her pure and pious, then believes her to be a whore.[104] Elsewhere in song, "beautiful and good" maidens who are obviously ripe for their first affair suddenly manifest an interest in sex when the appropriate love-object comes along, and one such example is strikingly related to *Die schöne Müllerin* (although in Müller's cycle, we do not know whether the lad is the maiden's first sexual conquest or a later experience). Could Schubert, one wonders, have known a 1799 Viennese "Volksmärchen mit Gesang . . . nach einer Sage der Vorzeit" (a folk fairy tale with song . . . after a story from olden times) entitled *Die Teufelsmühle am Wienerberg* (The Devil's Mill on the Wienerberg) by Leopold Huber and Karl Friedrich Hensler, with music by Wenzel Müller? It is certainly within the realm of possibility, as all three collaborators were well known in the city's musical and dramatic circles. In act 1, scene xi of *Die Teufelsmühle*, a guardian spirit named Jeriel, who announces herself as "the daughter of a Minnesinger from Vienna" (Müller was not the only one to locate the roots of idealized love in medieval poetry), sings a "Romanze"; although the young people of this tiny tale are not a miller maid and miller lad, the scenario is otherwise just as Müller's lad might have wished "Tränenregen" to end.

Romanze	**Romance**
Einsam weinte am murmelnden Quell	Lonely there wept at the murmuring stream
Ein Mädchen so schön und so gut;	a maiden so beautiful and so good;
Schwellende Thränen flossen hinab,	swelling tears flowed down,
Blumen auf Blumen pflückte sie ab,	flower upon flower she picked
Und warf sie betrübt in die Fluth.	and threw them sadly in the waters.
Schnell ergriff sie die Harfe, und sang	Quickly she grasped the harp and sang
Ein Liedchen der Liebe so rein.	a little song of love so pure.
Leise und leiser rauschte der Bach,	Soft and softer rustled the brook,
Lispelnder sangen Bäume es nach:	whispering trees sang after:
Nur Liebe beglücket allein.	only love alone brings happiness.
Sieh! da schritte ein Jüngling herbey,	Look! there walks a youth
Von deutschem und freysamen Sinn.	of free German heart.
Pochend von Liebe schlug ihre Brust,	Her heart beat, throbbing with love;
Ihn nur zu lieben, war ihre Lust,	to love only him was her happiness:
Sie gab sich dem Jüngling dahin.	she gave herself thither to the youth.

For all the lyrical euphemisms (the "Schutzgeist" is actually advising Mathilde to act upon her love for Günther von Schwarzenau), the meaning is plain. One looks at the motifs of the murmuring brook, the love song, the tears shed and the flowers plucked by the banks of the stream, the maiden "so gut," the love "so rein," and the implications of sex "im Freien" and recalls the same motifs reincarnated (but with what a difference!) in Müller's monodrama.

One central fact of *Die schöne Müllerin* – that the miller is the loser in a contest for the miller maid – also comes from the folk-poetic tradition. In "Müllers Abschied" (Miller's Farewell), one of the most widely disseminated mill poems, the miller bids a sad leave-taking in song to the knight's daughter he loved; as so often, we are told from within the poem that this is a song.[105] One wonders whether Müller's miller, who cries, "Ade, Ade, und reiche mir / Zum Abschied Deine Hand" (Farewell, farewell, and give me your hand in parting) at the end of "Die böse Farbe," owes his ancestry to stanza 2 of the earlier poem, which Müller would have known from *Des Knaben Wunderhorn* and other sources.

Müllers Abschied	**Miller's Farewell**
Da droben auf jenem Berge,	Up yonder on that mountain,
Da steht ein goldnes Haus,	there stands a golden house;
Da schauen wohl alle Frühmorgen	there every morning early,
Drey schöne Jungfrauen heraus;	three beautiful young women come forth.
Die eine, die heißet Elisabeth,	One is named Elisabeth,
Die andre Bernharda mein,	the other my Bernharda;
Die dritte, die will ich nicht nennen,	I won't name the third –
Die sollt mein eigen seyn.	she shall be my own.
Da unten in jenem Thale,	Down below in yonder valley,
Da treibt das Wasser ein Rad,	a wheel turns the water,
Da treibet nichts als Liebe,	turns nothing but love
Vom Abend bis wieder an Tag;	from evening until dawn;
Das Rad das ist gebrochen,	the wheel is broken,
Die Liebe, die hat ein End,	the love is finished,

Und wenn zwey Liebende scheiden,	and when two lovers part,
Sie reichen einander die Hand [italics mine].	they give one another their hand.
Ach Scheiden, ach, ach!	Alas, parting, alas, alas!
Wer hat doch das Scheiden erdacht,	Who ever thought of parting?
Das hat mein jung frisch Herzelein	That has made my fresh, young heart
So frühzeitig traurig gemacht.	sorrowful so soon in life.
Dies Liedlein, ach, ach!	This little song, alas, alas!
Hat wohl ein Müller erdacht;	a miller has made,
Den hat des Ritters Töchterlein	a miller whom the knight's daughter
Vom Lieben zum Scheiden gebracht.[106]	brought from love to parting.

This miller, one notes, is "young and fresh," not the experienced, married, coarse character from other poems; Müller would subsequently echo the theme of youthful freshness cast down by erotic grief.[107]

"Müllers Abschied" has numerous Romantic descendants, including Eichendorff's "Das zerbrochene Ringlein,"[108] probably conceived for his novel *Ahnung und Gegenwart* as an interpolated song sung by the lost and ill Erwine by the mill where she had earlier met the Graf Friedrich, whom she loves. Thus, in its original context, this exquisite lament "in which darkness shines through the most moving simplicity and quietness,"[109] its poetic persona clearly a man, is sung by a female character who had masqueraded as a man (and is imagined by a male writer); a grieving woman assumes the voice of a grieving man, rather than the more customary opposite exercise. Beneath the bell-like surface simplicity of "Das zerbrochene Ringlein" are depths that defy translation: what, for example, is one to do with the beautiful first two lines, with all the symbolic resonance of "Grund" as fundament, essence, foundation, cause, and ground? What equivalent is there for Eichendorff's austere but massive use of the verb "gehen" in line 2, with its implication of things going on their mechanical, unknowing way when the heart's mainspring is broken?

Das zerbrochene Ringlein	**The Broken Little Ring**
In einem kühlen Grunde	In a cool valley,
Da geht ein Mühlenrad,	a mill-wheel turns;
Mein' Liebste ist verschwunden,	my beloved is gone,
Die dort gewohnet hat.	who once lived there.
Sie hat' mir Treu' versprochen,	She promised me fidelity,
Gab mir ein'n Ring dabei,	gave me a ring as a sign,
Sie hat die Treu' gebrochen,	she broke her faith,
Mein Ringlein sprang entzwei.	my little ring broke in two.
Ich möcht als Spielmann reisen	I would like to travel as a minstrel
Weit in die Welt hinaus,	out into the wide world,
Und singen meine Weisen,	and sing my melodies
Und gehn von Haus zu Haus.	and go from house to house.
Ich möcht' als Reiter fliegen	I would like to flee
Wohl in die blut'ge Schlacht,	into the bloody battle,
Um stille Feuer liegen	to lie by the quiet fire
Im Feld bei dunkler Nacht.	in the fields by dark of night.

Hör' ich das Mühlrad gehen:	When I hear the mill-wheels turn,
Ich weiß nicht, was ich will—	I don't know what I want –
Ich möcht' am liebsten sterben,	I would like best to die;
Da wär's auf einmal still![110]	then it would all of a sudden be quiet!

Implicit in the penultimate line is the desire to die at once, immediately. The bereaved lover of this poem is close kin to Eichendorff's "Der irre Spielmann" (The Straying Minstrel, "irre" once again with connotations of "lost, sinful, near-mad") who sings "Durch's Leben jag' ich manch trüg'risch Bild, / Wer ist der Jäger da? wer ist das Wild? . . . Ich möcht' in den tiefsten Wald wohl hinein, / Recht aus der Brust den Jammer zu schrein" (Through life I hunted many a deceptive image – who is the hunter? who the wild animal? . . . I would like to be in the deepest woods to shriek forth my sorrow right out of my heart) – again, the allegorical theme of the futile hunt.[111] The beautiful setting of "Der zerbrochene Ringlein" by Alexis Holländer, in his *Sechs Lieder im Volkston*, op. 6, no. 5 (Leipzig: Breitkopf & Härtel, [1864?]) – a sterling example of the nostalgic-*volkstümlich* strain of song composition after the mid-century mark – has recently been republished.[112]

In the nineteenth century, *Kunstdichter* and *Lieder-Komponisten* seem increasingly drawn to tragic versions of the mill myth;[113] poets and their protagonists bid farewell to realms by then increasingly nostalgic, paper evocations of idealized former ages. The fictive mills fall into ruin, inhabited only by ghosts and dwarves; hunters by the score bid farewell to the forest; and maidens and millers die, one by one, poem by poem. The French-born Adelbert (Louis Charles Adélaide) Chamisso was one of those poets most intrigued by the scenario of romance at the mill; he wrote several tragic mill songs and ballads in which each of the customary personae at the mill – the miller, his daughter, and the apprentice – take center stage in their turn. In "Der Müllergesell" (The Miller's Apprentice), a condensation of Hans Christian Andersen's 1833 drama *Agnete og Havmanden*, itself based on a folk song,[114] Chamisso tells of a miller lad devoted to a miller maid and unable either to confess his love or leave. In unspoken anguish, he attends her marriage; in even greater anguish, he wishes to leave the scene of his pain but is prevented from doing so by the now-married miller maid, who regards him as a friend and brother. At the end of the ballad, he contemplates suicide in the millstream:

Der Müllergesell

(stanzas 1–2, 5, 13)
Ich hab' in dieser Mühle gedienet schon als Kind;
Die Tage meiner Jugend mir hier entschwunden sind.
Wie war des Müllers Tochter so herzig und so traut;
Wie hat man zu den Augen ihr in das Herz geschaut!

Sie setzte sich vertraulich am Abend oft zu mir;

The Miller's Apprentice

I have served in this mill since I was a child;
it was here that I passed the days of my youth.
How dear and sweet the miller's daughter was!
How one could look into her eyes, to her very heart!

She often sat cosily by me of an evening;

Wir sprachen viel zusammen, und alles sagt' ich ihr;	we spoke of much together, and I told her everything.
Sie teilte meinen Kummer und teilte meine Lust, –	She shared my troubles and shared my joy.
Das eine nur verschwieg ich, die Lieb' in meiner Brust.	I only kept silent about one thing: the love in my heart.
Sie kam mir nachgesprungen einst bei der Felsenwand;	She came bounding up to me once by the rocky wall;
Ihr Auge strahlte heller; sie faßte meine Hand:	her eyes shone brightly – she pressed my hand.
"Nun mußt du Glück mir wünschen, du grüßest eine Braut,	"Now you must wish me happiness: you greet a bride,
Und du, du bist der erste, dem ich mein Glück vertraut."	and you, you are the first to whom I confide my good fortune."
Ich höre stumm dem Brausen des Wasserrades zu	I mutely hear the noise of the water-wheels
Und denke: Tief da unten, da fänd' ich erst die Ruh'!	and think: Deep below, there would I first find peace!
Dann wär' ich ohne Schmerzen und ledig aller Pein!	Then I would be without sorrow and free of all pain!
Das wollen ja die beiden: Ich soll zufrieden sein.[115]	They both wish for this: I shall be contented.

The word "ledig" in the penultimate line also, of course, means "unmarried," and the persona's anger at those who have caused him such pain, however innocently, is evident both in that word and in the last line. "They [the bridal couple] want me to be content – well, so I shall, in death," he bitterly concludes. In the *Schauerballade* (horror ballad) "Der alte Müller" (The Old Miller), an elderly, white-haired miller speaks to the storm winds on a rocky prominence; in judgment for some unknown, unnamed sin, they sweep him from the rocks to his death and shatter the mill. The eerie atmosphere of supernatural retribution is heightened by the refrain at the end of each three-line stanza: "Hilf, Himmel, erbarme dich unser!" (Help, heaven, have pity on us).[116] And finally, in "Die Müllerin," a forsaken miller maid weeps beneath the linden tree (the archetypal rendezvous for lovers) on the hill:

Die Müllerin

(stanzas 1–2 of 4)
Die Mühle, die dreht ihre Flügel,
Der Sturm, der sauset darin;
Und unter der Linde am Hügel,
Da weinet die Müllerin:

Laß sausen den Sturm und brausen,
Ich habe gebaut auf den Wind;
Ich habe gebaut auf Schwüre, –
Da war ich ein törichtes Kind.[117]

The Miller Maid

The mill that turns its wheels,
the storm that roars therein;
and under the linden tree on the hill,
there the miller maid weeps:

Let the storm rage and roar –
I have built on the wind,
I have built on promises . . .
then I was a foolish child.

Brahms set this poem to music (without its pendant-poem "Des Müllerin Nachbars") in 1853, but never completed it; the fragment, which strikingly foreshadows his later setting of Eduard Mörike's "Agnes" (another abandoned maiden who weeps at the linden tree on the hill) was completed for publication by Joachim Draheim in 1984.

Poets, perhaps struck by the increasing mechanization (very un-Romantic) of mills, often tell of deserted mills, abandoned by the folkloric characters who used to inhabit them. Justinus Kerner in particular seems to have been drawn repeatedly to the mill as a dying relic, the site of bygone tragedy and death. In "Der tote Müller" (The Dead Miller) of 1813, the old miller dies, and the mill ceases its motion when its master's heart stops:

Der tote Müller

(stanzas 1, 2, and 4 of 4)
Die Sterne überm Tale stehn,
Das Mühlrad nur man höret,
Zum kranken Müller muß ich gehn,
Er hat den Freund begehret.

Ich steig' hinab den Felsenstein,
Es donnert dumpf die Mühle,
Und eine Glocke tönt darein:
"Die Arbeit ist am Ziele!"

Die treuen Lieben weinen sehr,
Still bleibt sein Herz und kühle;
Die Wasser fließen wohl daher,
Still aber steht die Mühle.[118]

The Dead Miller

The stars stand over the valley;
one hears only the mill-wheel.
I must go to the sick miller –
he has asked for his friend.

I climb down the rocks;
the mill thunders dully,
and a bell resounds therein:
"Your work is at an end!"

The faithful lovers weep greatly;
his heart stays still and cold.
The water flows onward,
but the mill stands still.

Twenty-eight years later, in 1841, Kerner wrote a *Schauerballade* entitled "Elsbeths Gespenst" (Elsbeth's Ghost), each stanza ending with the refrain "Die Mühle steht stille" (The mill stands still),[119] while the wanderer of "Der Wanderer in der Sägemühle" (The Wanderer in the Sawmill) returns to the place where his coffin is milled and his journey destined to end. When the wheel stops, so does his life.

Der Wanderer in der Sägemühle

(stanzas 1 and 6 of 6)
Dort unten in der Mühle
Saß ich in süßer Ruh'
Und sah dem Räderspiele
Und sah den Wassern zu.

Vier Bretter sah ich fallen,
Mir ward's ums Herze schwer,
Ein Wörtlein wollt' ich lallen,
Da ging das Rad nicht mehr.[120]

The Wanderer in the Sawmill

There down below in the mill
I sat in sweet peace
and watched the play of the wheels
and watched the water.

I saw four planks fall –
my heart was heavy,
I wanted to stammer one little word –
the wheel stopped.

In such poems, Kerner was, typically for him, embroidering a folk tradition in which the death of a miller, whose work is to grind the grains of life's most basic sustenance, demonstrates Death's remorseless power; all living beings are ground in *his* mill. In the folk song "Der Tod und der Müller" (Death and the Miller), the miller pleads with Death to spare him lest his seven children become fatherless, but Death is obdurate – "Master Miller, thou must die! Lie down on your bier!"[121]

In an eerie chronological conjunction with the transformation of mills into unenchantable machines, increasingly situated in urban surroundings rather than the depths of romantic forests, poets already begin to sing sad songs of ruined, abandoned mills by the 1830s and 1840s. In the Viennese poet Johann Nepomuk Vogl's (1802–1866) ballad "Die verfallene Mühle" (The Ruined Mill), set to music by Carl Loewe in 1847 as op. 109, an elderly count rides to a deserted mill, with rubble and weeds everywhere, a hole in the roof, no people, no wheel turning; there, he falls asleep. In his dreams, the mill comes to life once more, complete with the miller, surging water and rumbling mill works, and, most important of all, the miller maid he once loved. As she offers him a glass of wine, he awakens to find nothing there; the dream has vanished.

Die verfallene Mühle	**The Ruined Mill**
(stanzas 10–11 of 11)	
Verschwunden ist so Glas als Wein,	The glass and the wine were gone,
Der Müller und sein Töchterlein.	the miller and his daughter.
Kein Mühlrad geht, kein Wasser braust,	No mill wheel turns, no water surges,
Der Wind nur durchs	only the wind howls through the empty
Gebälke saust.	frames.
Und wieder auf den Rappen dort	The count threw himself onto his horse
Wirft sich der Graf und reitet fort.	once again and rode away.
Er reitet stumm den Wald entlang	He rode silently through the woods
Und streift ein Tränlein von der Wang.	and wiped a little tear from his cheek.

Loewe's Count rides gloomily to the deserted mill over a passacaglia bass in a suitably weary clip-clopping configuration, the antiquity of the bass pattern symbolic of the character's age. At the end, Loewe creates a canon in which the bass follows the soprano voice, but never "catches up" with it; the canon, like the "Trugbild," vanishes (Ex. 7). Even these last vestiges of human presence eventually disappear, and Romantic mills lie in equally Romantic ruins, tended only by dwarves in August Schnezler's (1809–1853) "Die verlassene Mühle" (The Abandoned Mill):

Die verlassene Mühle	**The Abandoned Mill**
Das Wasser rauscht zum Wald hinein,	The water murmurs on its way into the forest,
Es rauscht im Wald so kühle;	it murmurs in the forest so cool.
Wie mag ich wohl gekommen sein	How is it that I have come
Vor die verlass'ne Mühle?	before the deserted mill?
Die Räder stille, morsch, bemoost,	The wheels – still, rotting, moss-covered –
Die sonst so fröhlich herumgetost,	that once so merrily roared around,
Dach, Gäng' und Fenster alle	the roof, walkways, and windows all
In drohendem Verfalle.	about to tumble down in ruin.
Allein bei Sonnenuntergang	Alone at sunset,
Da knisterten die Äste,	the branches rustle;
Da schlichen sich den Bach entlang	then truly peculiar visitors
Gar sonderbare Gäste,	creep along by the brook,
Viel Männlein grau, von Zwergenart,	many little gray men, dwarf-like,
Mit dickem Kopf und langem Bart,	with big heads and long beards.

Example 7 Carl Loewe. "Die verfallene Mühle," op. 109, mm. 231–40, to a poem by Johann Nepomuk Vogl. From Carl Loewe, *Werke. Gesamtausgabe der Balladen, Legenden, Lieder und Gesänge*, vol. 9: *Sagen, Märchen, Fabeln, Aus Thier- und Blumenwelt*, p. 76. Leipzig: Breitkopf & Härtel, 1900 [reprint ed., Westmead, England: Gregg International Publishers Limited, 1970].

| Sie schleppten Müllersäcke | They carry mill-sacks |
| Daher aus Busch und Hecke. | from the bushes and hedges. |

Und als ich kam am andern Tag
In trüber Ahnung Schauern,
Die Mühle ganz zerfallen lag
Bis auf die letzten Mauern;
Das Wasser rauschet neben mir hin,
Es weiß wohl, was ich fühle,
Und nimmermehr will aus dem Sinn
Mir die verlass'ne Mühle.

And when I came there the other day
in gloomy, fearful foreboding,
the mill lay utterly in ruins
down to the last stone.
The water rustled by me;
it knew well what I feel,
and never will the abandoned mill
vanish from my heart.

By the century's close, poets such as Detlev von Liliencron (1844–1909), surveying their industrialized surroundings, lamented "Vergiß die Mühle nicht" (Do not forget the mill); the "little mill," placed "fern, fern am Erdenrand" (far away, far away at the end of the world), on the edge of oblivion, is the only consoling sight the poetic speaker and his wife can find in the barren world around them.[122] The folkloric context Müller made fun of in his Prologue to *Die schöne Müllerin* had become, for a later generation, a *locus classicus* for *Heimweh* and a nostalgic symbol of a bygone past. What was once a living thing becomes the stuff of song and story, tended by "allerlei Geister" until they too disappear.

By the end, poets not only empty the mill but kill off its inhabitants once and for all. Isolde Kurz's (1853–1944) ballad "Die Hochzeit in der Mühle" (The Wedding in the Mill) seems a dark distillation of all the themes of sexual transgression, infidelity, masters and apprentices, and rose-women at the mills of yore, a fin-de-siècle farewell to an antique cast of characters. In best balladesque tradition (this poem belongs to the venerable genre of the *Schauerballade*), Kurz omits full contextual information; one can discern only the vague outlines of a wedding day gone horribly wrong, of "the right bride" drowning in the millstream (pushed in by her rival?), of someone in the crowd of wedding guests who truly loved the dead young woman, of the miller stabbing the wrong bride, the whole scene culminating in utter desolation. This is *Götterdämmerung* at the mill.

Die Hochzeit in der Mühle	**The Wedding in the Mill**
(stanzas 1–3 of 5)	
Der Mühlbach stürzt mit Brausen,	The mill brook tumbles noisily,
Er gibt nicht Rast noch Ruh,	without rest or peace,
Und alle Räder sausen	and all of the wheels rush
Im raschen Takt dazu.	in bold measure.
Mahle, wer da mahlen mag,	Grind away, whoever wishes to grind,
Diesem filzigen Geschlechte!	these filthy folk!
Heut ist Meisters Hochzeittag.	Today is the master's wedding day.
Stellt das Rad, ihr Müllerknechte!	Stop the wheel, you mill lads!
Aus blauer Höhe zittert	In the blue heights trembles
Der Hochzeitglocken Klang,	the sound of the wedding bells,
Und in der Tiefe schüttert	and in the depths the gear
Das Werk mit Donnergang.	rattles thunderously.
Seht, am Rad, daß Gott erbarm!	See, on the wheel, God help us!
Fängt sich langes Haargeflechte,	a long braid caught;
Aus dem Wasser taucht ein Arm!	an arm emerges from the water!
Stellt das Rad, ihr Müllerknechte!	Stop the wheel, you mill lads!
O Röslein schön vom Bühle,	O beautiful little red rose from yonder hill,
Wie hängt dein Haupt verblaßt!	how your pale head hangs!
Du kamst wohl nach der Mühle	You came to the mill
Als ungeladner Gast.	as an uninvited guest.
Nun zur Hochzeitkammer dort	Now to the bridal chamber there
Tragt die bleiche Braut, die rechte.	carry the pale bride, the right one.
Seht, so hält der Meister Wort!	See, the master keeps his word!
Stellt das Rad, ihr Müllerknechte![123]	Stop the wheel, you mill lads!

At the end, the miller stabs himself and the deserted mill falls into ruin, its silence broken only when the haunted machinery groans into a shrill simulacrum of its former activity by night.

IN CONCLUSION

If Müller read folk poetry and Goethe in order to revise them, to put new wine in the old bottles of legend, other poets subsequently read Müller and revised *him*. Johann Nepomuk Vogl borrowed the title of his cycle *Lieder eines Waldhornisten* (Songs of a Waldhorn-Player), published in the poet's *Lyrische Blätter* of 1836, from the title of

Müller's two anthologies: *Gedichte aus den hinterlassenen Papieren eines reisenden Waldhornisten*. Vogl, significantly, abbreviated and simplified the title, and he did the same to *Die schöne Müllerin*: the *Lieder eines Waldhornisten* is a shortened, simplified retelling of Müller's tale, unmistakable to anyone who knew the source. But while Vogl's poetry is sentimental, watered-down Romanticism of the simpler sort, what is not simple is the relationship of this cycle to Müller's. Because Vogl so thoroughly altered what he so obviously borrowed from Müller, one guesses that he might at some level have wished to restore the folk-archetypes to innocence, removing all of Müller's scarifying elements and reversing virtually every major aspect of the narrative. If Vogl's mill romance also ends in tragedy, it is tragedy painted in pastels, devoid of the wormwood-and-gall tincture of Müller's tale in its latter stages.

Like Müller, Vogl too writes monodrama, and his speaker is the hunter, precisely the character who does not speak at all in Müller's cycle, while Müller's monodramist vanishes altogether from Vogl's revisionary and regressive work. A traditional amatory hunter of the most lyrical and least violent variety, Vogl's hunter sees the miller maid in the first song of the cycle; afraid that he might be captivated by the "schönes Kind," he begs her to close her window (the window motif a borrowing from Müller, who himself borrowed it from others) so that he will not see her, but it is too late – he is already "Gefangen!" ("Captured!", the title of the second poem, reminiscent of Müller's "Halt!"). Although he mentions the brook in the fifth poem, "Die Mühle" (The Mill), it is not the hunter's confidant, nor does it speak. Rather, it is the Waldhorn and its music that takes the place of the brook in Vogl's tale; the hunter hopes that the sound of his hunting horn will be like the nightingale's song – love's music and, when his love is not reciprocated, his companion in suffering (the sixth poem, "Hornklang," or "Horn Sound," and the eighth poem, "Das Waldhorn"). The miller maid, who never speaks, is the traditional blue-eyed, angelic love-object, part young woman and part child, so the lovesick hunter writes in the tenth poem, "Das Waldhornblasen." It is in the depiction of her eyes as forget-me-nots in the ninth poem, "Des Müllermädchens Augen" (The Miller Maid's Eyes) that Vogl most clearly both apes and inverts his source:

Des Müllermädchens Augen

(4th and final stanza)
Wohl seid ihr, Augen, ach so mild und licht,
Für mich ein blühend Paar Vergißmeinnicht!
Vergäß' ich Alles auch was
   Gott verlieh,
Euch, blaue Augen, euch vergeß' ich nie![124]

The Miller Maid's Eyes

Truly, you gentle, bright eyes are to me
a blossoming pair of forget-me-nots!
Were I to forget everything else God has
   granted me,
I will never forget you, blue eyes!

There are no black forget-me flowers, one notices. Although Vogl's Waldhornist has no rival for the miller maid's affections, she does not "understand" the message of his nocturnal serenade ("Sie hat dich nicht verstanden!," the hunter tragically proclaims in the fifteenth poem); with all hope of reciprocated love gone, the hunter stands outside her house by night and bids her a final farewell: "D'rum, Liebe, gute Nacht!" (was Vogl also aping the first poem of Müller's *Die Winterreise?*). The bereaved hunter then becomes a wanderer whose songs "In der Fremde" and "Auf der Wanderung" echo Eichendorff, whom Müller too echoed – a veritable concatenation of cross-influences and songs which are *Nachklänge* of other songs. After many years, the vagabond musician returns to the old mill in the twentieth and last poem ("Vor'm alten Mühlenhause"). "Only she, the pretty little one, no longer dwells therein. She has gone away, but I do not ask: why?" Is there a hint of Heine's "Der Doppelgänger," but without the all-important *Doppelgänger*, in the recipe? Why Vogl rewrote Müller is a question with, at present, no answer,[125] but at least one composer was subsequently inspired by these poems to set them to music: in 1846, the *Kleinmeister* Anton Hackel published his *Jäger und Müllerin: Ein Cyclus lyrischer Gedichte von J. N. Vogel* [sic], op. 92 (Vienna: A. O. Witzendorf, 1846). It took a brave man to write a mill cycle after Schubert and publish the results in Schubert's own city; the critic who reviewed Hackel's opus in the *Allgemeine Wiener Musik-Zeitung* pointed out, with relative gentleness, that similar works were bound to suffer by comparison.[126]

But in the end, homage becomes pure nostalgia – not the active appropriation and re-working of a Vogl or a Julius Becker (see chapter 3), their powers already a diminution of what preceded them, but small songs to hymn what had long ceased to be. The moss-covered wheel of the weary, decaying mill in Rainer Maria Rilke's lovely, small poem "Die Mühle" is stilled and quiet.[127]

Die Mühle

Du müde, morsche Mühle,
dein Moosrad feiert Ruh, –
Aus der Olivenkühle
schaut dir der Abend zu.

Der Bach singt wie verloren
Menschenlieder nach,
tiefer über die Ohren
ziehst du dein trutziges Dach.

The Mill

You tired, decaying mill,
your mossy wheel celebrates peace –
from the olive tree's coolness
the evening watches you.

The brook imitates human songs
as if lost;
lower over your ears
you pull down your defiant roof.

For those who remember that Müller's brook begins to sing "Menschenlieder" at the end of *Die schöne Müllerin*, the lines have a special poignance. Deprived of its own music, devoid of any living presence, the brook can only sing as it did before, in human strains, of human affairs, but the still-anthropomorphized mill on its banks, perhaps weary of all the human symbolism heaped upon it in bygone days, refuses to listen, pulling its roof-hat down over its ears. In 1896, the publisher and amateur poet Carl Zuckmayr wrote a "Danksagung an den Bach" – the title, of course, is taken from Müller – in which the reader is invited to imagine himself or herself as the ghost of Müller's miller lad, nos-talgically hymning the brook-companion of his past. From birth to death, the "Bächlein" has accompanied him; its singing impelled his own, and its mills have haunted his sleep. Is their groaning a reminiscence of the agony Müller's lad endured at one of those mills?

Danksagung an den Bach

(stanzas 1–3 and 7 of 7)
Warst du nicht mein Gefährte
In jener frühen Zeit,

Song of Thanks to the Brook

Were you not my companion
in that earlier time,

Die vor meinem Hiersein währte	that before my being here – endured,
Von Traum und Vergessen beschneit?	snowy from dream and oblivion?
Rauschtest du nicht in den Gruben,	Did you not rustle in the graves
Darin man die Ahnen begrub –	wherein they buried the ancestors?
Flüstertest schon durch die Stuben,	Did you not whisper already through the rooms
Wo das Kind zum Lichte man hub?	where they raised the child to the light?
Immer umsang mich dein Singen,	Always your singing sang around me,
Immer dein Eilen mich traf –	always your haste bore me along –
Mühlen, die stöhnend gingen,	mills that groaned as they moved
Geisterten durch meinen Schlaf –.	spooked through my sleep –.
(final stanza)	
Enteile du wieder und wieder!	Hurry away again and again!
Verweile du immer und eh'	Ever tarry and, of old,
Vergeh. Vergeh und ersteh	vanish. Vanish and arise again
Im silbernen Spiegel der Lieder.[128]	in the silvery mirror of song.

The nostalgia is thick enough to cut with a knife. For Europe on the brink of modernism, the Biedermeier world seemed as distant and hence as subject to idealization as the Middle Ages were to writers of Müller's time. An amber patina of longing for lost "simplicity," however mythical, is draped over Müller's mill tale, blurring into invisibility everything that is poisonous about the monodrama and turning both the inhabitants and their milieu into ghosts.

Zuckmayr was not the first to ignore the wormwood-and-gall at the heart of *Die schöne Müllerin*. What is ultimately most remarkable about the sentimental effusion above is the way in which it mirrors a long history of misunderstanding Müller and, subsequently, misunderstanding Schubert's cycle. Müller's achievement in *Die schöne Müllerin* is, after all, quietly radical. He took one of the most well known of all Germanic literary scenarios, its schematic elements inherited from folk song and echoed by *Kunstdichter*, and modernized it, while cleverly preserving those features which identify the tale as something hallowed by tradition. Beneath the traditional appurtenances, however, Müller subtly dissected the scenario, making of it a psychodrama of bad faith, warped sexuality, and a skewed *Weltanschauung*; the deeper one goes into the cycle, the more sad, bad, and mad the songs become. What is so amazing about the afterlife of his early masterpiece is how few people have recognized the strategy, then or later. One might have expected modernists, especially with the advent of what Carl Schorske calls "psychological man" at the turn-of-century, to see the worm at the apple's core, the stage-by-stage analysis of sex gone very wrong, the roiling mixture of delusion, ignorance, and disappointed idealism that pervades matters of "love," but no – the sentimental glosses continued. Whether those who have looked at the cycle and failed to see it were blinded by the Biedermeier-*gemütlich* image of Schubert created in the nineteenth century or by the simple, bluff versions of the hunter–miller–miller maid archetypes or by the expectation that song should house lyrical, "pretty" unrealities or by the sheer weight of accumulated decades of misperception is hard to determine. After all,

Schubert himself could not accept the full extent of Müller's unsparing tale, although I believe he understood it as few others have. Did Müller's Berlin contemporaries, the general-cum-poet Karl Decker and the composer Adolph Baron von Lauer, also reject – far more so than Schubert – the remarkably bleak and black vision in Müller's cycle and consciously attempt to restore the folk characters to a happier fate in their Singspiel *Rose, die Müllerin?* Were the other nineteenth-century composers who set Müller's poems to music also blind to the dark side of this cycle? It is to their efforts that we turn next.

Chapter 3

Before and after Schubert: at the mill with other composers

If Schubert was the most famous composer ever to set foot in Müller's mill, he was not the only one. Müller was a magnet for some 250 composers throughout the nineteenth century, from Berger to Brahms and beyond, for a total of more than 500 works. The long list includes settings of many poems from *Die schöne Müllerin* (the mill cycle was always more popular with composers than *Die Winterreise*), both as short cycles and as single lieder.[1] Many of these songs are appealing and most have vanished from sight and sound; hence, what follows in this chapter is a small *Liederkranz* of music by so-called *Kleinmeister*, some of them highly esteemed in their own day – like Müller himself. Where it seemed appropriate, I have also included the occasional mill song or hunting song to texts by other poets who also took to the woods and the mill for their poetry; Ernst Challier needed three pages of minuscule print merely to list all of the lieder entitled "Der Jäger" in his *Grosser Lieder-Katalog* of 1885.[2] With such an embarrassment of riches, I have, of necessity, omitted many songs eligible for inclusion and can only cite brief passages from those that survived the winnowing process, but perhaps even so small a compendium as this can serve to whet the appetite for still more discoveries from the archives of forgotten Romantic lieder.

But this chapter has more than the archival function of dusting off and bringing to light long-buried music, as honorable as I believe that purpose to be. The principal reasons are contextual and threefold: to demonstrate how other composers responded to Schubert's *Die schöne Müllerin* and, subsequently, how still other composers responded to them; to meditate once more on the vexed question, "What constitutes a cycle?", with settings of *Die schöne Müllerin* as the specimens under the microscope; and to marvel anew at Schubert's achievement in light of other settings of this poetry. While there is much to admire in the Müller songs by these lesser lights, one looks in vain for the profundity of D. 795; other composers either failed to see what Müller had done with his folkish archetypes or lacked the musical creativity to do more than skim the surface or both. Although Schubert rejected outright certain aspects of Müller's cycle and revised others (see the next chapter), his music nevertheless testifies to a greater understanding of a complex enterprise than anyone else in the flock of composers attracted to this highly "komponabel" poet.

ANOTHER LOOK AT GOETHE AND REICHARDT: THE "INTERNATIONAL"
MILL BALLADS

If Müller and his Austrian "kindred spirit" inspired numerous compositions and imitations, the poet's text had earlier, as we have already seen, arisen in part from a similar exercise on a highly sophisticated level: the re-writing of a prior model, a "taking back" or negation of Goethe's mill poems. While there is no account of the genesis of *Die schöne Müllerin* that mentions Johann Friedrich Reichardt's settings of Goethe's four ballads, it is possible to speculate, given Elisabeth Stägemann's friendship with Reichardt and the musical talents of some in the youthful salon, that the Stägemann *Kreis* might have known the musical settings as well as the poetry, and therefore, it seems only logical to begin a brief survey of mill songs and hunting songs with these works. After all, what bolder exercise could there be for literati in 1816 Berlin than to take on Goethe himself, that largest of contemporary targets? For the Goethe-composer whose settings preceded the *Liederspiel*, there were other challenges, specifically musical, arising from the idiosyncratic nature of these ballads, from the literary exercise Goethe set for himself in writing them. Despite the attraction of Goethe's poetry for song composers, no one else but Reichardt, to my knowledge, set these poems to music.

Three of the four ballads ("Der Edelknabe und die Müllerin," "Der Junggesell und der Mühlbach," and "Der Müllerin Reue") date from the autumn of 1797, when Goethe was on a journey in Switzerland; the last to be written – the third in the narrative order – was "Der Müllerin Verrat" in 1798. On August 31, 1797, Goethe wrote to Schiller from Stuttgart, saying:

After all this, I must say that en route I have been pleased with a poetic genre which we must make more of in the future and that perhaps will be good to do for the following almanach. It is conversations in song [Gespräche in Liedern]. We have, from a certain old German era, quite artful things in this manner, and one can say much if one only first enters into it and in this way extract what is unique from it. I have begun just such a dialogue between a youth, who is in love with a miller maid, and the millbrook and hope to send it to you soon. The poetic-allegorical trope will, through this variation, be rendered newly alive . . . [3]

On September 12, he sent Schiller a copy of the first of his mill ballads ("Der Edelknabe und die Müllerin," or "The Aristocratic Youth and the Miller Maid"), calling it "a little jest" and telling his friend that three others would follow in German, French, and Spanish fashion, that together the set would comprise "a little novel." The dialogue between the aristocratic youth and the lower-class maiden is supposedly in the "old English" style, and the dialogue between the youth and the millbrook is in the "old German" manner, while the love-betrayal is the Frenchified episode and the gypsy disguise at the end "Spanish." The most blatant nationalistic clichés of gypsies as Spanish literary spice and bedroom farces emblematic of Frenchness are at work; to have Nature speak and mill lads in the throes of amorous desire is a somewhat less obvious register of *Deutschtum* at the mill. The set belongs with the other ballads Schiller and Goethe devised in the last years of the eighteenth century, the years that gave us the king of Thule, the pied piper of Hamelin, the bride of Corinth, the faithful Eckart, and the Erlking, but the characters at the millstream are not their match in power or beauty, nor were they meant to be; this is, as Goethe himself stated, a diversion, a "Scherz." It is an ironic truth that he was, in this instance, outstripped by a younger and lesser writer of the *Goethezeit* whose mill drama ends very differently.

Goethe begins with the medieval lyric premise of an aristocratic youth importuning a lower-class maiden, here structured as a dialogue. There is no narrator, no poetic voice to describe the *mise-en-scène* or the young people or the preliminaries, and therefore nothing to mitigate the brusqeness of the boy's importunities or the maiden's strong-minded responses. The dialogue is a skeletal distillation of the antique scenario: the youth asks, "Where are you going, beautiful miller maid?" . . . only then does he ask her name. The miller maid Liese, no fool she, states pointedly that they are "on my father's land, in my father's field," an announcement of patriarchal authority that the youth brushes aside without acknowledgment. When he announces his plan to come to her in the heat of midday in the grape arbor ("the green, cosy house"), she fobs him off, declaring that only those of the same social class ("gleich und gleich," Goethe thus fore-shadowing the famous poem he sent to Carl Friedrich Zelter in April 1814) belong together. She will love a miller lad, she declares, because then she need not fear betrayal.

But it is she who does the betraying. The miller lad shows up on cue in the next poem, similarly a dialogue but with the brook playing the role of masculine confidant, as much a sex-obsessed young man as the apprentice himself. He used to be a "Bächlein," but now he has swollen to a full-grown brook, titillated by the sight of the miller maid's full, white breasts as she comes to bathe. The water can cool itself off, the young man replies, but what is mere flesh-and-blood to do?

Der Junggesell und der Mühlbach

Bach:

Dann stürz' ich auf die Räder mich
Mit Brausen,
Und alle Schaufeln drehen sich
Im Sausen.
Seitdem das schöne Mädchen schaft,
Hat auch das Wasser bessre Kraft.

Gesell:

Du Armer, fühlst du nicht den Schmerz
Wie Andre?
Sie lacht dich an und sagt im Scherz:
Nun wandre![4]

The Apprentice and the Millstream

Brook:

Then I hurl myself at the wheels
with a roar,
and all of the blades turn
with a rushing noise.
Since the beautiful maiden was here,
the water too has greater strength.

Apprentice:

You poor thing, do you not feel sorrow
like others?
She laughs at you and says in jest:
Now wander!

Somewhere in the interval between "Der Junggesell und der Mühlbach" and "Der Müllerin Verrat," the brook's mission as go-between is successful, and the two young people stage a nocturnal rendez-vous, with comically disastrous consequences. This third poem is the only one with a single speaker: the miller, who emerges as the central character in a first night gone hilariously wrong. The miller maid's "fiery glances" have led to the illicit tryst, which, however, is interrupted by the maiden's mother and a dozen or so relatives, a veritable river of people bursting in on the lovers, according to the humiliated youth. One should, the newly misogynistic lad declares bitterly, flee from country girls as well as city women; no woman, from whatever class of society, can be trusted, Goethe thus elaborating on Paisiello's ironically developed theme about the superiority of rustic maidens over citified loves. At the end, the narrator, whose amused moralizing suggests an older, wiser observer, states that the youth has brought his misfortune upon himself by his lack of gallantry and his sneakiness. Love, he implies, should live in the sunshine.

Der Müllerin Verrat	**The Miller Maid's Treachery**
(final stanza)	
So singt er in der Winterstunde,	So he sings in wintertime
Wo nicht ein armes Hälmchen grünt.	when not a single poor little blade is greening;
Ich lache seiner tiefen Wunde;	I smile at his deep wound,
Denn wirklich ist sie wohlverdient.	for truly he is well served.
So geh' es jedem, der am Tage	So it goes with one who by day
Sein edles Liebchen frech betriegt,	behaves cheekily with his gentle love,
Und nachts mit allzukühner Wage	and by night with all-too-bold daring
Zu Amors falscher Mühle kriecht.	creeps to Love's false mill.

Was it perhaps from this passage that Müller derived the subtitle "Im Winter zu lesen" (To Read in the Wintertime) for his monodrama?

The physical and farcical elements of the mill ballads virtually demand a *lieto fine*, and Goethe duly supplies it. In the final scene of this song-playlet, the repentant miller maid has disguised herself as a gypsy girl, the archetypal black-brown witch emblematic of female duplicity, sorcery, and sexuality. In this guise, she pleads the miller maid's cause, as we learn from the miller's angry rejection in the first stanza of "Der Müllerin Reue" – Goethe begins the scene *in medias res*, thus heightening the dramatic immediacy of the confrontation. From within the work, the characters remind reader and listener alike of their designated medium of song: the infuriated lad asks, "What is this sham you are singing about love and a quiet maiden's fidelity? Who wants to hear that fairy tale?" "I sing of the maiden's penitence," the so-called gypsy woman replies, and the irate youth responds, "I sing of treachery and selfishness, of murder and thieving robbery" after he has peremptorily bidden the "brown witch" leave his "purified" house – purified by the absence of women. As the "gypsy" laments operatically, "Alas, alas, what have I done?", "The Poet," easily convertible into stage directions for a mini-*Liederspiel*, intervenes, narrating how the gypsy washes her face in the fountain, revealing her true identity as the miller maid – was it as an echo of Goethe that Müller devised his prologue and epilogue for "The Poet"? Lest one forget the beginnings of the tale amidst the high-minded invocations of love's all-conquering power at the end, the miller maid assures the youth that "This young, untouched body is now all yours," upon which the pair sings a closing duet, assuring one another that their love will last as long "as the waters flow." Waters flow for a different purpose at the end of *Die schöne Müllerin* after love has proven sadly ephemeral and a body temporarily "all yours" has unleashed monsters in the mind.

Goethe's finale, however, is purest late eighteenth-century comedic goings-on, and it was appropriately set to music in purest late eighteenth-century song style by Johann Friedrich Reichardt, who included the four ballads in the the third volume of his collection *Göthes Lieder, Oden, Balladen und Romanzen*, published in Leipzig by Breitkopf &

Härtel in 1809–11. Interestingly, they are not presented as a cycle (what Carl Loewe would later call a "Liederzyklus in Balladenform") or set, gathered together under some sort of all-encompassing title. Either Reichardt or the publisher even separates "Der Edelknabe und die Müllerin" from the other three, interpolating a setting of Goethe's "Das Blümlein Wunderschön - Lied des gefangenen Grafen" after the initial "conversation." And yet, the last three ballads are printed consecutively, in narrative order, and the three dialogue-poems, "Der Edelknabe und die Müllerin," "Der Junggesell und der Bach," and "Der Müllerin Reue," are in the same F major or F minor/F major tonality – a pastoral key for a pastoral comedy. Only the Frenchified-farcical lament "im Romanzenton" for the miller alone is in a different key, the distant key of E minor; this song too is the only one of the four with the vocal line notated in the bass clef, the change of register suggesting comically that the youth has become a man and metamorphosed from tenor to bass clef in the course of his tribulations.

The musical model is clearly simple, strophic song; it is not only that "Der Junggesell und der Mühlbach" and "Der Müllerin Verrath" are strophic settings and "Der Müllerin Reue" is partially strophic, but the style throughout has all the hallmarks of the song simplicities Reichardt deemed appropriate for *Liederspiele* (Reichardt would subsequently experiment with lengthy, dramatic monologues for solo voice and piano in a more "difficult" style). It was perhaps the emphasis on the conversational tone that dictated certain aspects of these ballads, including the purely accompanimental function of the piano. In the first of the dialogue-ballads, "Der Edelknabe und die Müllerin," Reichardt begins as abruptly as Goethe, without any piano introduction; indeed, none of the four has an introduction, and only the second ballad, "Der Junggesell und der Mühlbach," has a minimal (one measure) postlude. Above the simple broken-chordal patterns in the right hand and light bass tones at the beginning of "Der Edelknabe und die Müllerin" are conversational vocal phrases deftly calibrated somewhere between the symmetries of song melody and the rhythmic inflections of recitative – this is both and neither, a hybrid of the two. (The other three ballads are more songlike.) Reichardt even treats the rapid-fire dialogue at the start as genuine conversation by eliminating all but the sparsest instrumental interludes between the nobleman's impassioned urgencies and the maiden's responses, while the youth's phrases are broken by rests to lend added verisimilitude to an impulsive would-be seducer's gasping pleas (Ex. 8).

Whatever the commitment to certain simplicities of song style, this is not unsophisticated music. Reichardt had fun, one suspects, with many details of these settings, such as the erotic-chromatic descending bass line in mm. 26–29 of the first song at the Edelknabe's words "Ist nicht eine stille Laube dabei?", the comic dissonant harmonic tangle in m. 42 when the youth comes to the point and declares "Ruhst du in meinen Armen aus," and her emphatic leap of a tenth upward in the next bar, when she denies his importunities. "Mit nichten!", she proclaims, and the dramatic gesture is a small electric charge in mid-song. The miller maid's first words to the youth, after he has learned her name, are a pointed reminder to the lad, his intentions already obvious, that she has a father ("Auf des Vaters Land, auf des Vaters Wiese"); Reichardt, tongue firmly in cheek, sets those words to a lyrical, skipping phrase that borders on the parodistically "innocent" – Schubert does likewise in "Mit dem grünen Lautenbande" – and

Example 8 Johann Friedrich Reichardt. "Der Edelknabe und die Müllerin," mm. 1–14, from Reichardt, *Göthes Lieder, Oden, Balladen und Romanzen*, vol. 3. Leipzig: Breitkopf & Härtel, 1811.

culminates in a comically firm cadence. Miller maids, like the servant girls of eighteenth-century opera, are often knowing creatures who need, and use, every ounce of wit at their disposal for survival in a world where noblemen take advantage, and Reichardt ensures that we hear and recognize her knowingness. Like Hedwig von Stägemann's Rose, miller maids are also sexually aware; if Liese is not to be trifled with by any passing nobleman who takes a fancy to her, she is nevertheless more than a little interested in sex and says so. "Im Garten daran / fangen die Birn zu reifen an, / die will ich brechen," she proclaims, complete with a triumphal high A and mildly melismatic vocal cadence; the references to ripe pears ready for the picking do not require much effort to decode.

At the end, in the tradition of the comedic mill tale, love triumphs in the final ballad (the "Edelknabe" disappears, presumably with a flea in his ear, after the first ballad). The angry miller lad at the start of "Der Müllerin Reue" – he, one notices, is not called upon to repent – resorts to phrases or portions of phrases in unharmonized texture and minor mode, while the penitent miller maid resorts to cozening rising chromaticism at the words "Und will zu deinen Füssen hier nun leben oder auch sterben." She, one readily infers, would prefer "the little death" of eroticism renewed. As quickly as Masetto succumbs to Zerlina's blandishments in *Don Giovanni*, the miller discards his anger, the darkness of minor mode, and the severity of unharmonized melody to sing with her of their love as a force of nature, coeval with the rhythms of sun, moon, and stars. At the close, the principle of "gleich und gleich" triumphs, and life at the poetic mill is restored to harmony.

That Müller and his cohorts knew Goethe's ballads is evident in Müller's blatant appropriation of the older poet's "Der Junggesell und der Mühlbach" for the *Liederspiel*. But Müller revises Goethe massively, especially in the monodrama; the miller maid of the *Liederspiel* comes to regret her change of heart, but not the miller maid of the poetic cycle – nor, perhaps, would it matter if she had, since the gravest psychic wound of all is what the lad discovers about himself. The element of class conflict, of country and city, aristocrat and lower class, is not to be found in Müller, nor is his brook a leering, hormone-driven young man comically obsessed with erotic titillation, as in Goethe. Love and sex appear in entirely different guises in Müller's mill romance, where literary illusions/allusions of medievalizing troubadour-like idealization give way to the psychological hell sex can and does engender. "Betrayal" in Goethe is sex interrupted before it can happen, and his narrative ends with instant forgiveness of the sort only possible in fiction and with the promise of a sexual "happily ever after" in marriage, but "betrayal" in Müller's mono-drama *is* sex gone horribly wrong (see chapter 4). The eighteenth-century operatic model shows us miller maidens and their lovers "milling" in harmony by the end of the tale –

Paisiello: *Die schöne Müllerin*

(Schlußszene)

Pistofolus:

O du holdes Müller Mädchen,
Nimm mich auf in deine Mühle,
Lass mich dort mit Küßen spielen
Zärtlich dir die Zeit vertreiben,
Schwör mir ewig treu zu bleiben,
Froh und glücklich bin ich dann.

Paisiello: *The Beautiful Miller Maid*

(Final scene)

Pistofolus:

O you gentle miller maiden,
take me into your mill,
let me play there with kisses,
sweetly pass the time with you.
If you swear to stay eternally true to me,
then I will be happy and fortunate.

but Müller shows us the extremity of dissonance lurking in the wings. Like a latter-day Iago, Müller surveys Goethe's distillation of eighteenth-century opera buffa and, in his own way, "set[s] down the pegs that make[s] this music" and fashions new, discordant songs from them.

LUDWIG BERGER'S "SOCIABLE" SONGS

No nineteenth-century composer, Schubert included, set all twenty-three of Müller's poems in the body of the narrative – indeed, Schubert's cycle is the most comprehensive of the lot, typical of his ambitious nature. Despite the rise of the concert *Liederkreis*, it was a more common practice throughout much of the century for composers to pluck an individual poem, a few poems, or a small group from within a longer poetic work, the selected segments thus shorn of their larger context. Certain poems lent themselves more readily to this enterprise than others: this might explain why, for example, "Morgengruß" was a popular choice for extraction from *Die schöne Müllerin* and "Eifersucht und Stolz" was not, as the latter makes little sense removed from Müller's full narrative surroundings, while the former is a serenade, a subspecies of love song frequently found on its own and readily congruent either within the smaller song cycles carved from *Die schöne Müllerin* or on its own. With each composer who selected poems from Müller's work and re-ordered them into a new succession, a "new" cycle is created, none of which duplicates the order of any other and each differing in the degree of narrative coherence and the proportions of idyll to tragedy.

The history of *Die schöne Müllerin* in music begins with songs selected from the larger body of the Stägemann *Liederspiel* in all the newness of its first creation: Ludwig Berger's op. 11 *Gesänge aus einem gesellschaftlichen Liederspiele 'Die schöne Müllerin.'* In his pupil Ludwig Rellstab's opinion, Berger had a particular gift for lieder composition,[5] evident for the first time in these songs which preserve a fraction of what the other members of the Stägemann salon contributed to the *Liederspiel* and five of Müller's poems in an early incarnation. (Given Müller's customary tinkering, the poems also appear in contemporary literary periodicals with details altered from Berger's cycle.[6]) This set of mill songs, forged by a poet and composer in collaboration, was never intended to be a complete narrative but rather highlights selected episodes along the way; if it follows the order of events in the story, it does not tell the entirety of that story.

There *is* a purposeful ordering. Berger begins the *Gesänge* not with "Das Wandern"[7] but with Müller's "Wohin?", which introduces the listener to the miller lad and the brook, followed by the development of conflict in songs 2–6, the climax in nos. 7 and 8, resolution in no. 9, and a finale for the anthropomorphized brook in no. 10. As Ruth Bingham has observed, certain themes come to the fore in this selection and ordering, the recurrences linking successive lieder and threading throughout the cycle: the color symbolism of blue (the brook, the forget-me-not flowers, the miller maid's eyes – the brook's color), white (flour, paleness, death – the miller's color), and green (the woods, May, the evergreen trees, jealousy, nature in general – the hunter's color); the friendship between the brook and the miller lad; and the birdsong and hunting horn motifs.[8] In sum, these are songs *from* a *Liederspiel*, the result an intriguing hybrid between the dramatic genre of the *Liederspiel* (hence, the presence of multiple characters and indications of dramatic action) and what Bingham calls an "internal-plot cycle," in which dramatic relationships appear principally through juxtaposition and disjunction and the narrative is rendered lyrical rather than dramatic. The weight is more on song cycle than *Liederspiel* in this work, however.[9]

1 Des Müllers Wanderlied. ("Ich hört' ein Bächlein rauschen," later entitled "Wohin?") Text by Wilhelm Müller. Andante, F major, 6/8

2 Müllers Blumen. ("Am Bach viel kleine Blumen stehn," later entitled "Des Müllers Blumen.") Text by Wilhelm Müller. Dolce, C major, 6/8

3 Nachtlied. (Gärtnerknabe.) Text by Luise Hensel. Larghetto, B flat major, 2/4

4 Am Bach. (Gärtnerknabe.) Text by Luise Hensel. Andantino, A major, 6/8

5 Am Maienfeste. (Der Jäger an die Müllerin.) Text by Wilhelm Hensel. Molto vivo, E major, 6/8

6 Vogelgesang vor der Müllerin Fenster. Text by Hedwig Stägemann. Leggiermente, e scherzando, A major, 6/8

7 Der Müller. ("Ich möchte ziehn in die Welt hinaus," later entitled "Die böse Farbe.") Text by Wilhelm Müller. Agitato, E minor, 4/4

8 Rose, die Müllerin. Text by Hedwig Stägemann. Grazioso, E major, 6/8

9 Müllers trockne Blumen. ("Ihr Blümlein alle, die sie mir gab," later entitled "Trockne Blumen.") Text by Wilhelm Müller. A minor - C major, 2/4

10 Des Baches Lied. ("Gute Ruh', thu die Augen zu," later entitled "Des Baches Wiegenlied.") Andante, A minor - C major, 2/4

All of the songs are strophic, and most are quite brief, the diminutive scale evident from the beginning in "Des Müllers Wanderlied," a mere eleven measures long. Could Schubert have known these songs? – the four-measure piano postlude of "Nachtlied" (one-third of the tiny twelve-measure musical strophe) curiously resembles the piano introductions to Schubert's "Rast" and "Das Wirtshaus" from *Winterreise*, especially in the rhythmic-melodic pattern, the mid-measure accents, and the doubling in thirds. As one can tell from this passage, the size of these songs may be small, but they are in fact "künstelt," the plethora of artful details testifying to something other than fake folk song; in the body of the song proper, the "mezza voce" marking, the vocal line of mm. 1–6 poised in tense uncertainty above the tonic pitch (only at the designation "*Lie*-[be]" does one hear the root of the tonic chord in the voice), and the neighbor-note chromaticism evocative in equal measure of erotic feeling and anxiety, are still further specimens of compositional artfulness. Like the poems Müller would later disingenuously label as "kunstlos," "artless," in the prologue to the monodrama (see the next chapter), Berger's settings too are far from artless. There is no mention of Berger in the Schubert documentation, but given the fact that Berlin was a center for lied publication and that Schubert might have been curious about other settings of *Die schöne Müllerin*, it is enjoyable to speculate that he could possibly have encountered the work. Whether he did or not, later musicians have not had much opportunity to acquaint themselves with it. Max Friedländer included Berger's "Wanderlied," "Der Müller," "Müllers trockne Blumen," and "Des Baches Lied" in his 1922 edition of Schubert's *Die schöne Müllerin*, but that edition is long out-of-print. Revival seems overdue.

The vexed question whenever one considers the Romantic cycle is the means of unification. What justifies performing a group of songs as a centipede-like multipartite work, the parts of which belong to a larger whole and only thereby attain their fullest coherence, even given the common practice of extracting individual songs for performance? Berger did not designate op. 11 as a "Zyklus," a "Kreis," or a "Liederroman," but simply as "Gesänge," nor did he compose the songs in their narrative order; according to Rellstab, he was first drawn to Hedwig's "Rose, die Müllerin," with its refrain "Ich habe das Grün so gern."[10] And yet, the *Gesänge* evince certain linked tonal relationships, with the first three songs in the related keys of F major, C major, and B flat major and nos. 4–8 even more closely connected by tonality (A major, E major, A major, E minor, and E major); one notices particularly the tragic-ironic relationship between the miller lad's lament in E minor (no. 7) and the miller maid's E major song of attraction to the hunter immediately following. Furthermore, the ninth and tenth songs are both in the same progressive tonality, albeit modestly so; these two linked songs each begin in the lamentation key of A minor and close in C major, the latter a primordial "Nature key" in which the brook sings her charge to eternal sleep and a tonality foreshadowed in "Müllers Blumen" ("*Am Bach* viel kleine Blumen stehn"). But the relationship of tonality to text is not consistent or all-embracing: the jolt downwards from B flat major to A major in the third and fourth songs, both of them belonging to the gardener-suitor, serves no discernible dramatic purpose, as the tonal disjunctions in Schubert's cycles so often do.

Nor does Berger restrict musical bonds between songs to tonal relationships only. Nos. 5 and 6, Wilhelm Hensel's "Am Maienfeste" (At the May Festival) and Hedwig von Stägemann's "Vogelgesang vor der Müllerin Fenster" (Birdsong outside the Miller Maid's Window), are paired in a manner that seems like a simpler prototype of the way in which the first two songs of Schumann's *Dichterliebe* are joined. But where Schumann's famously open "ending" of "Im wunderschönen Monat Mai" makes audible all the ambiguity of love, even where avowed, the pairing of these two songs in Berger's set tells of seduction en route to accomplishment and of attraction signified in musical appropriation. In "Am Maienfeste," the huntsman appears – his sole appearance – and confidently asserts that he can outdo his rivals, that lowly flowers are no match for towering trees. Wilhelm Hensel's hunter conforms in every respect to the bluffest versions of the amatory Teutonic hunter; his privileged relationship to Nature, his confidence in his sexual appeal to women, his ardor, his boastfulness are all conventional attributes, traditionally adumbrated.

Am Maienfeste	At the May Festival
Gärtnerbursche hat gepflanzet	The gardener's apprentice has planted
Grüner Kräuter mannigfalt—	a variety of green plants –
Müllerbursche hält umschanzet	The miller's apprentice has surrounded you
Dich mit grünem Maienwald.	with a fortification of green may-wood.
Doch am grünen Maienfeste	But at the green May-fest
Bring vom Grünen ich das Beste!	I bring the best green!
Sieh wie an des Hauses Schwelle	See how the slender fir-trees here
Hier die schlanke Tanne lauscht.	nestle up to the door of the house
Und vor deiner trauten Zelle	and outside your cosy little cell,
Liebesmelodien rauscht:	love songs rustle:
Blume schweigt im Staube lebend,	the flowers living in the dust fall silent,
Tanne singt sich stolz erhebend.	the fir-tree sings, proudly elevated.
Und der hohen Tanne, Liebchen,	And the tall fir-tree, beloved,
Gleicht der grüne Waidgesell.	is like the green hunter.
Tritt heraus aus deinem Stübchen	Come out of your little room,
Dann die Zweige senkt sie schnell.	then its branches will quickly descend,
Mit der Arme grünen Ringen	with its arms' green circlets
Dich weiss Röslein zu umschlingen.	to embrace you, little white rose.

In Berger's setting, horn-call figures in E major dominate both the vocal line and the piano accompaniment, complete with *pianissimo* echo effects and a comic emphasis on the hunter's boastful designation of *his* green as "das Beste" in stanza 1. Berger directs that the song can be performed by a woman as well as a man and further states that the piano part from m. 15 to the end, in which both hands are in the treble register, can be taken an octave lower, thus reversing the registral contrast between the accompaniment and voice. Are the different registers to be construed in this instance as masculine and feminine symbols in a courtship song? One notes as well the languid, *dolce*, descending chromatic thirds in the piano interlude (m. 11) linking the first two vocal phrases – a foreshadowing of the miller lad invoked in the next breath? Nothing else in the song tells of eroticism, languor, or tenderness; despite the generally delicate texture of the horn-calls, the hunter tends to blow his one well-known figure over and over again. All he need do in folk song, after all, is announce who he is and the maiden (usually) capitulates; the musical proclamation of his presence should serve just as well. The song ends with a fragmentary horn-call figure, evocatively arrested on an incomplete tonic 6–3 chord, echoed softly in the piano; the "Vogelgesang vor der Müllerin Fenster" subsequently begins with the dominant seventh of the new tonic A major, the two songs thus linked harmonically. One is invited to imagine the hunter departing for his rendezvous during the postlude of "Am Maienfeste," its open ending signifying that the song will resume in another place, and sending the libidinous birds ahead as messengers.

The link is reinforced in the postlude to the "Vogelgesang vor der Müllerin Fenster" when Berger combines hunting horn figures in the left hand with continued offbeat (mimesis for the unpredictability of Nature's rhythms) chirping, hopping, and trilling "birdsong figures" in the right hand, the horn-calls placed in the treble register, as in "Am Maienfeste." Here, Berger abandons the quasi-*volkstümlich* style regnant elsewhere in the cycle and indulges in a riot of birdsong acrobatics for both the singer – clearly a coloratura soprano with a ready supply of high As – and the pianist, especially the latter, whose postlude pyrotechnics required, so Berger felt, indicated fingerings; this is a miniature étude in parallel chromatic thirds, the chromaticism both a standard feature of such technical exercises and an index of eroticism (Ex. 9). The old trope in Western music by which the natural virtuosity of birdsong becomes highly stylized virtuosity for voices and instruments reappears in Berger's mill songs, but – perhaps – with an added sexual twist; if birdsong symbolizes "vögeln," or intercourse, the coupling of the horn-calls and the birdlike figuration in the postlude could be either an announcement of the hunter's and miller maid's first sexual encounter or a foreshadowing of it. Could Berger the virtuoso pianist also have known Domenico Scarlatti's sonatas, with their Spanishy guitar-strumming effects? The accacciatura "crush" chords in the left hand at mm. 11 and 13 certainly seem like a borrowing from the eighteenth-century keyboard master and, given the commonplace association of Spanish sound effects with passion, could be another sign of erotic energies at work.

The only source of Hedwig's poem for the "Vogelgesang" is the printed score of the *Gesänge*. Since musical setting turns all poetry into prose, it is impossible to determine the poetic structure precisely, all the more so as we know that the *Liederspiel* group was, to a certain extent, experimentally inclined (Müller's "Ein ungereimtes Lied" is one example of their abjuration of conventional poetic parameters). Hedwig's stanzas begin with the same pseudo-avian warbling refrain, followed by a rhyming line ending with -a; with the exception of the last verse, each stanza features penultimate lines of brief rhyming sounds ("Blickt nicht, nickt nicht," "Grüße, küße," "Rose, Lose" – the sharp, pecking quality of the multiple ts in the first instance is notable). Was Hedwig perhaps attempting a kind of poetic-elemental "Nature" music, in which the syntax is primitive, truncated, as if creatures unused to human language were employing an unaccustomed medium? With the postlude to each stanza, the birds abandon unnatural speech

Example 9 Ludwig Berger. "Vogelgesang vor der Müllerin Fenster," mm. 15–26, from *Gesänge aus einem gesellschaftlichen Liederspiele 'Die schöne Müllerin,'* op. 11. Berlin: E. H. G. Christiani, 1818.

and revert to their "natural" state: music. The unpredictable rhythms and meters, making it difficult to determine division into lines in several instances, might also have been consciously deployed for the same reason.

The content is less problematic than the stanzaic form, its sexual entendres easy to decipher. The talking birds, borrowed from folk poetry where they so often convey messages of love or lust, tell the miller maid not to be so "proud" ("stolz") – a traditional euphemism for withholding sexual favors; by the fourth verse, they openly bid the miller be gone and make way for the green-clad forester waiting nearby. Since "vögeln" is at the heart of it all, the flying messengers are indeed suited to their task, nor does the miller maid miss their significance. She is, they tell her, a "Wiesenblümchen," a little flower of the field, that is, a village girl, not a standoffish aristocratic lady: what is the point of postponing sexual pleasure, they imply? Lower-class types can indulge their desires right away.

Vogelgesang vor der Müllerin Fenster	**Birdsong in front of the Miller Maid's Window**
(stanzas 1–4 of 5)	
Tirili tirili eya,	Tirili tirili eya,
Der Mai ist da!	there's May!
Wiesenblümchen müßt nicht so stolz seyn!	Little flowers of the field mustn't be so proud!
Blickt nicht,	Don't gaze,
nickt nicht	don't nod
So viel in die Quellen und Bächlein hinein.	so much in the streams and little brooks.
Tirili tirili eya,	Tirili tirili eya,
Boten sind da!	there are messages!
Fliegen vor dein blank Fensterlein hin;	Fly in front of your empty little window;
Grüße,	Greet,
küße,	kiss,
Verkünden die Vöglein aus lustigem Grün.	The little birds proclaim from the merry green.
Tirili tirili eya	Tirili tirili eya
Waidmann ist nah!	the hunter is nearby!
Hat uns zu dir herüber geschickt.	He has sent us over here to you.
Rose,	Rose,
Lose,	roguish girl,
Sahn wir nicht wie du jüngst noch ihm zugeknickt.	didn't we see how you recently curtsied to him?
Tirili tirili eya	Tirili tirili eya
Müller weg da!	miller, go away!
Sonst uns den Maien willst nicht grün seyn,	Or else May will not be green for us,
Harrt dein	don't wait
auch kein	any more
liebes Feinsliebchen am Fensterlein.	for your beloved sweetheart at the window.

Hedwig, one notices, echoes Müller's motifs of the empty window and looking into the brook, as the miller lad and miller maid do in "Tränenregen"; the *Liederspiel* poems function almost as a series of *répliques*, one poem responding to another in sequence.[11]

Similarly, the musical links between Berger's settings continue. Each stanza of Hedwig von Stägemann's "Rose, die Müllerin" (no. 8) or "Wies Vöglein möcht' ich ziehen – the bird motif continued – begins with an echo of the hunter's horn-calls; the feint is that she hears his horn-calls and then sings of her desire to be with him, even calling out "Horch!" on one occasion. Did Berger wish us to hear her exhilarated octave leaps upwards for the refrain "Ich hab das Grün so gern" as a tragic-ironic echo of the grief-stricken miller lad's gesture on the same pitches at the words "*weite* Welt," "*grüne* Band" in "Der Müller," the offbeat rhythmic placement a measure of desperation? – it seems likely. Berger, however, did not set Müller's "Die liebe Farbe," which is an echo of Hedwig's poem in the same sestet stanza and with the same refrain for lines 3 and 6 of each verse. Did the changes of tone in Müller's poem (changes

Schubert subsumes in strophic setting) seem to Berger incompatible with strict strophic form? Even the motif of hunting in Hedwig's second stanza recurs in Müller's poem, but with her *chasse d'amour* transformed into an angry, wrought-up, grief-filled *Totenjagd*.

Rose, die Müllerin

Wies Vöglein möcht' ich ziehen,
In grüne Wälder fliehen
Ich hab das Grün so gern!
Will grün verhängen mein Fensterlein,
Den Boden mit grünem Kalmus streun,
Ich hab das Grün so gern!

Horch! Hörst den Waidmann pfeifen?
O könnt' ich mit ihm schweifen
Ich hab das Jagen so gern!
Hinaus mit dem rufenden Hörnerklang
Durch sonnendurchflochtenen Fichtengang.
Ich hab das Jagen so gern!

Wies Knösplein will ich leben
Mit Grün mich dicht umweben
Ich hab das Grün so gern!
Nein, blick mich nicht so fragend an,
Sieh nicht so bleich, du Müllersmann.
Ich hab das Grün so gern!

Rose, the Miller Maid

I wish I could fly like a little bird
into the green forest,
I love green so much!
I'll deck my window in green,
I'll strew the ground with green branches,
I love green so much!

Listen! Do you hear the hunter piping?
Oh, if only I could go roving with him –
I love hunting so much!
Outside with the horn-calls resounding
through the sun-flecked spruce trees—
I love hunting so much!

Like a small branch, I'll live
with green thickly woven around me.
I love green so much!
Nay, don't look at me so questioningly,
don't look so pale, miller.
I love green so much!

In Hedwig's poem, the miller maid proclaims the sexual nature of her attraction to the hunter in the imagery at the beginning of the third stanza, delicate yet disarmingly frank. Berger varies the setting of the last three lines of each verse in accord with the text: garlands of scalar passaggi for stanza 1 ("Will grün verhangen mein Fensterlein"), horn-call figures for the "rufenden Hörnerklang" of stanza 2 (the repeated dissonant neighboring tones in the right-hand inner voice are a very effective, economical evocation of blaring brass), and affective use of the flatted-sixth degree, dissonance, and hand-crossing textures for the miller maid's words to the downcast miller at the end. It is her sympathy with his grief that impels the flatted-sixth degree at the word "bleich," or "pale" ("Sieh nicht so bleich, du Müllersmann" – Müller echoes her language in "Die böse Farbe" when his miller wants to weep until the green leaves are bleached the color of death, *his* color, "todtenbleich") in m. 47, the chromatically fraught descent in the piano accompaniment of mm. 50–53 beneath the erotically charged exuberant words "Ich hab' das Grün so gern," and the accented "sighing figures" in the piano in mm. 44–47. She cannot deny her attraction to the hunter and therefore continues to sing of it, the vocal line of the refrain little altered from the previous stanzas, but compunction for the lover she is leaving colors the words beneath the surface, the music thus divided between two emotional states (Ex. 10). In "Müllers trock'ne Blumen" just after, what had been the miller lad's sighs become a full-fledged stream of tears; the principal musical material of the song is an extension of the sighing figures into the melodic cliché

Example 10 Ludwig Berger. "Rose, die Müllerin," mm. 39–56, from *Gesänge aus einem gesellschaftlichen Liederspiele 'Die schöne Müllerin,'* op. 11 Berlin: E. H. G. Christiani, 1818.

of an appoggiatura-filled, descending line – Schubert uses similar figuration in his setting of Goethe's "Wonne der Wehmut," D. 260, beginning with the words, "Trocknet nicht, trocknet nicht, / Tränen der ewigen Liebe."

In fact, Berger's setting of "Müllers trock'ne Blumen" provides a fascinating comparison with Schubert's "Trockne Blumen" because neither composer missed the point; the difference is one of degree, and it is a significant difference. Müller, one remembers, was present on the spot to discuss the poem with Berger, and one can therefore speculate that the poet himself may have pointed out his persona's inability truly to believe in the vision of epiphany after death that the lad conjures up in an attempt to find redemptive beauty and meaning in his death. Schubert's miller struggles mightily, far more so than Berger's miller, to convince himself of love's fulfillment beyond death's boundaries (a Romantic credo), and, for a few seconds, succeeds; he even repeats the ecstatic-proclamatory setting of the last verse so that it might outweigh the grief of the poet's first three stanzas. He does not truly believe what he insists so emphatically, however, the very

Example 11 Ludwig Berger. "Müllers trockne Blumen," mm. 16–35, from *Gesänge aus einem gesellschaftlichen Liederspiele 'Die schöne Müllerin,'* op. 11. Berlin: E. H. G. Christiani, 1818.

emphasis revelatory of disbelief, and in the postlude, Schubert graphically depicts the loss of hope in the lowered register and returning minor mode as soon as the words cease. If the lad does not say it/sing it, he cannot believe it, and doubt floods back in the instrumental postlude. But Berger fills both the vocal line and the piano part throughout the song with "flowing tears" figures that persist to the end of the *perdendosi* piano postlude, even after the A minor tonality of stanzas 1–3 is ousted by C major. When Berger's miller sings "Der Mai ist kommen, der Winter ist aus," the soprano–bass dissonances and the *morendo* indication are hardly indicative of the singer's trust in his own words; disillusionment and grief already overwhelm the false vision of future epiphany (Ex. 11).

Berger's "Des Baches Lied," is even more dissimilar from Schubert's later conception of the same text. The greater composer avoids any watery figuration in the piano, but not so Berger: his brook speaks in muted arpeggiation, broken-chordal figuration, and *tremolandi* in the depths of the piano (the rising-and-falling figures and the rhythmic alternation between thirty-second note groups of four pitches and sixteenth-note groups of three pitches in the arpeggiated right-hand figures even mimic the lapping of waves), while the singer chants on repeated pitches in *marche funèbre* dotted rhythms. Berger, one notes, was quite finicking about the precise inflections – multiple *mfp*, *fp*, and pedal markings – for his water-music. The vocal line rises slowly by degrees throughout the stanza, such that the small leap to C, the topmost apex of the funereally restricted range, at the verb "trinken" has a greater impact than would seem possible for so economical a gesture; the diminished seventh harmony tells us that "trinken" is death in a special sense, dissolution into a timeless afterlife. The beautifully expressive mediant shift from the cadence on the dominant E major at m. 12 to G major and C major harmonies at the words "Die Treu ist hier, sollst liegen bei mir" (mm. 12–14) occurs at the same spot where Schubert too enacts a mediant progression to even more moving effect (Ex. 12).[12] At the end of each musical strophe, Berger bids the voice drop back down to the dominant pitch to intone the last words, chant-like, while the piano engulfs and overtops it. At the culmination of the cadence, the piano drops back down to the original tessitura, to begin the murmurous A minor water-music once more; this is, not an ending, but an elision so that the water which bears the lad and us to the final stanza can continue to flow. At the end of the song, Berger varies the musical strophe in a very moving manner, entirely different from Schubert's death-lullaby: the bass line in the accompaniment sinks to the bottom of the fortepiano register, while the vocal line also traces a descent to recitation on middle C, its lowest point. It is from this vantage point, from the depths of the brook-become-grave, that one can see how broad are the heavens overhead. The inflections on the flatted-sixth degree of C major tinge the postlude with the sadness of suicide, whatever the C major assertions of ultimate clarity and peace to come – and the C major at the end is hardly the most stable of tonalities, as Berger only turns to it at the last moment.

This is a more melancholy ending than Schubert's: despite tinges of lamentation and doubt, Schubert's setting points upwards more than downwards, the vocal line arching into the heavens in the last half of each musical strophe, there to float above the fullest, richest chords of the entire cycle. Here is indeed epiphany, but not so Berger. What, one wonders, might Müller have thought of Schubert's setting? Would he have recognized and responded to the strength of this ending, even though it countermands what he and his first composer created? This is not, as we shall see in the fourth chapter, the only instance in which Schubert contradicts one of his favorite poets.

THE *LIEDERSPIEL* REVISED?

After the *Liederspiel*, Müller's miller appears reincarnated, his fate altered for the better, in the rustic (Ländliches) Singspiel *Rose, die Müllerin*, with a text by Adalbert vom Thale (a pseudonym for General Karl von Decker, 1784–1844) and music by Baron Adolph von Lauer von Münchofen (born 1796?). Here, the *Liederspiel* is returned to the realm of comic-sentimental opera from whence it came (in part) and the traditions associated with romance at the mill – three suitors, matrimonial wagers and contests, miller lad and miller maid happily betrothed at the end – are restored. Perhaps, like magpies, Thale and Lauer merely feathered their nest with whatever was readily at hand, but it is a more

Example 12 Ludwig Berger. "Des Baches Lied," mm. 1–22, from *Gesänge aus einem gesellschaftlichen Liederspiele 'Die schöne Müllerin,'* op. 11. Berlin: E. H. G. Christiani, 1818.

interesting speculation that they were bothered by the tragic ending and decided to provide a version in which the late eighteenth-century tradition is upheld. In a lovely irony of chronology, the Thale/Lauer Singspiel was performed for the first time on April 16, 1820 at the Royal Opera in Berlin[13] perhaps at the same time that Müller, by then returned to his native Dessau, was engaged in finishing his revision of *Die schöne Müllerin* as a lyric monodrama by adding ten additional poems. If it is possible that Thale and Lauer wished to "revise" the *Liederspiel* by restoring both the traditional *lieto fine* and the theatrical milieu of the mill tale, then it is indeed a notable coincidence that Müller was busily deepening the tragedy as they were lightening it.

Both the composer and the librettist of *Rose, die Müllerin* were highly placed in Berlin society. Lauer, who was much the same age as the youthful artists of the *Liederspiel*, was the regimental commander of the Prussian cuirassiers and later a major-general, but music was clearly his principal avocation; he studied music with the organist-composer Wilhelm Schneider (1781–1811), and his other compositions now in the collection of the Staatsbibliothek zu Berlin include three piano quartets (in E minor, B major, and A major), settings of songs from Goethe's *Faust*, three songs to poetry by Ernst Konrad Friedrich Schulze (the poet of Schubert's "Im Frühling" and nine other songs),[14] and eight songs to poems by Friedrich Rückert. The elder of the two collaborators, Thale/Decker, was the author of numerous books on military matters, but also wrote plays when literarily on leave from more warlike subjects, including the text for this lighthearted, rustic Singspiel; his very pseudonym, from the word "Tal" or "valley," brings with it pastoral associations, and the overture his collaborator devised begins with an "Andante pastorale" in the horn-key of E flat.[15] Since the Allegro which follows is filled to the bursting point with horn fanfares, one expects, and receives, a tale in which a hunter is among the principal characters.

Like Paisiello's heroine, Lauer's Rose, whose father Erbin has died, will become a wealthy heiress when she marries, so we are told by the judge who acts as the narrator. Money is thus crucial to the decision between the various suitors: the miller's apprentice Liepold, the hunter Rudolph, who comes from the Black Forest (a realm where evil spirits legendarily roamed and hence, a clue to his wicked character), and an unnamed gardener. It is clear from the gardener's lack of a name that he is not truly in serious contention, just as in the Stägemann *Liederspiel*, but there, the lack of proper names points to an allegorical substratum of which the Singspiel is devoid. Here, everything is more straightforward than it is in Paisiello, without the sophisticated role-playing – the gardener and the hunter are "real" in *Rose, die Müllerin* – and the opposition of city-versus-country, noble-versus-peasant that are such enjoyable elements of the earlier opera. There is no class conflict, no tweaking of rusticity, in Thale and Lauer's venture.

The collaborators announce their debts to Goethe and the Stägemann *Kreis* immediately. The first character to be introduced musically is the forlorn miller Liepold, who summarizes much of the first half or so of the Stägemann *Liederspiel* in a strophic "Romanze," the designation reminiscent of Goethe's "Romanze" for his angry and bereft miller lad in the third of the four mill ballads. Liepold's "Bächlein hab' ich zwar gefunden, / Arbeit auch und Unterhalt" (I found the little brook, also work and conversation), compresses into one small song Müller's miller setting forth in "Das Wandern," following the brook in "Wohin?", stopping at the mill in "Halt!", thanking the brook for his first sight of the miller maid in "Danksagung an den Bach," and falling in love with none other than Röschen. Her black eyes recall Goethe's miller maid and all the "schwarzbraune" maidens with whom folkloric hunters are enamored, while her name recalls Paisiello's heroine in her Germanic manifestation. She and the miller lad have already, we are told straightaway, plighted their troth, but Röschen is now angry with him. Poor Liepold sits forlornly by the brook, but there is no danger of frenzied jealousy or suicide here, none of the darker emotions or psychological depths Müller plumbs in his completed cycle or even in the *Liederspiel*.

There are, however, more echoes of Müller to follow: Decker/Thale quotes from Müller's"Wohin?" in Liepold's second air in act 1:

No. IV. Arie (Müller)	No. 4. Aria (Miller)
Was plätschert und murmelt, und rieselt so kühl,	What splashes and murmurs and coolly ripples,
Von blumigen Ufern begleitet?	accompanied by flowering banks?
Ist das eines Mühlenbachs rauschendes Spiel,	Is that a mill-brook's rustling play
Das Freude und Glück dir bedeutet?	that signals happiness and joy for you?
Folg', Müllersmann, folge dem Rieseln nach,	Follow, miller, follow the rippling water onward,
Im hüpfenden, plätschernden Silberbach,	in the leaping, splashing, silvery brook,
Da drehen sich Mühlenräder.	Mill-wheels turn.
Es ziehet und dränget mit Riesengewalt,	With a giant's force, you draw me
Zu dir mich, du blauer Gefährte.	to you, compel me, my blue companion,
Als ob eine lockende Stimme erschallt,	as if a seductive voice were calling,
So süss wie noch nie ich sie hörte.	sweeter than anything I have ever heard.
Da zog's mich dem flüsternden Rufe nach,	Then the whispering calls drew me onward,
Es riss mich gewaltsam zum Silberbach,	pulled me powerfully to the silver brook,
Und hin zu den Mühlenrädern.	and onward to the mill-wheels.
Nun bin ich gebunden, gefesselt, gebannt,	Now I am bound, chained, enchanted,
Will fliehen und kann doch nicht weichen;	I want to flee and yet cannot leave;
Hab' endlich das Ziel meines Lebens erkannt,	now at last I have recognised my life's purpose,
Und seh' es und kann's nicht erreichen.	and see it and cannot attain it.
O folgt' ich doch nimmer dem Rufe nach,	Oh, if only I had never followed the calls onward –
In jedem hüpfenden klaren Bach,	in every clear, leaping brook,
Da gehen ja Mühlenräder.	Mill-wheels turn.

All of Müller's implications of magic in the stream, of compulsion to follow, of sirens singing in the waters, are present, indeed exaggerated beyond Müller's more subtly limned style, but without any consequences later in the drama (Ex. 13). In Müller, the images are premonitory of tragedy to come, when the miller heeds the deadly siren calls from within his own vanquished spirit and drowns himself in the brook. Not so in *Rose, die Müllerin*: the *Wasser-Mythos* of Teutonic lore becomes little more than momentary regret and a splash of local color, a vanishing echo of an earlier, more powerful work.

The hunter's appearance is preceded by the other suitors' fears of his folkloric sexual attraction; in the second number, the miller and gardener, both tenors, sing of their rival's green coat bedecked with gold, "alluring to every pretty maiden." The gardener comforts himself by declaring that green also signifies gardens and should therefore make gardeners attractive to maidens as well, while the miller sings that green is the color of hope: "Hoffnung ist Immergrün." The district judge (like most operatic judges, a bass) then follows with a strophic song in which he describes huntsmen and soldiers

Example 13   Adalbert vom Thale and Adolph Baron von Lauer. Liepold's air, act 1, no. 4: "Was plätschert und murmelt und rieselt so kühl," mm. 1–12, from the Singspiel *Rose, die Müllerin.*

alike as "truly rakes . . . devilish scamps" ("Ja, Jäger und Soldaten sind wahre Teufelsbraten") and warns bridegrooms to tremble when such wild men are about. "Sie schnappen nur nach Beute," he declares and ends by invoking God's protection against "Jagd und Kriegesnoth," after which the gardener and miller sing yet another duet. They represent, they declare, love without any thought for riches, and they lament the hunter's incursion on the scene, this before he even arrives. Not until all of the other singing characters in the small cast have appeared does the hunter – a bass and therefore a weightier, more masculine presence than the gardener and miller – first step on stage and sing "Das Jagdhorn schallt im grünen Wald" (The hunting horns resound in the green forest). In this typical huntsman's boasting song, he celebrates his own mythical nature; over and over in the first verse, he exclaims that the wild animals he shoots "sinkt tod es zu Füssen ihm nieder" (sink down dead at his feet) and in the second and third verses sings of going to the blue stream in which his sweetheart is bathing, of kissing his sweetheart's red mouth. Not surprisingly, his music is filled with the traditional hunting horn figures of an especially simple and unsubtle type – but then, subtlety is not called for when characterizing the likes of Rudolph.

The title character Rose or Röschen is a mixture of two traditional types: she has the

Example 14 Adalbert vom Thale and Adolph Baron von Lauer. Rose's air, act 1, no. 7: "Ach, ich beging ihn sonst so fröhlich," mm. 1–18, from *Rose, die Müllerin*.

saucy soubrette's capacity to recognize and castigate the failings of men, along with the sentimental heroine's soft-heartedness, both evident in her ariette "Ach, ich beging ihn sonst so fröhlich, war ein gar glückliches, harmloses Kind" (Ah, I used to go on my way so happily, was a happy, innocent child). It is the sentimental side we see first, the pathos of an orphan who must now make a decision about her fate and do so without the familial guidance she once knew; Thale and Lauer thus enlist the audience's sympathies for her plight (Paisiello's influence? his miller maid was also fatherless) before turning to comic matters. At the crossroads between childhood's last vestiges and adulthood, she sings a poignant F minor lament for bygone childhood happiness and for her dead father (Ex. 14), but because she is essentially a spunky character whose bravery we are invited to admire, the lament is followed by a change of meter (from 2/4 to 6/8) and tempo (from Adagio to Allegro), for a second section. There, she sings of the necessity to choose among her various suitors and does so to sparkling music whose uncomplicated energy tells of someone well able to decide for herself and even make a bit of mild mischief along the way. "My good father believed," she tells the audience, "that a husband would crown

Example 15   Adalbert vom Thale and Adolph Baron von Lauer. Rose's air, act 2, no. 11: "Bist du schlafen gangen, theurer Vater mein?," mm. 1–10, from *Rose, die Müllerin*.

Rose's good fortune, but I would rather ask if a man can do that. Alas, the best man is often a wife's torment." Whatever her proto-feminist bravado, the fermata-sustained high As on the verb "kann" have an underlying erotic suggestiveness no one could miss, and it is entirely in character that she then takes charge of the rivalry, announcing to her three suitors that she will marry the man who makes her happiest and that she will gauge their capacity to do so by the gifts they must bring her. In her insouciant little air, "Drei Freier werben zwar um mich, drei schmucke brave Freier" (Three handsome men are contesting for me), the hunter is clearly in the ascendant; the miller is someone I love and value, she declares in the second stanza, but the gardener seems more like her cousin than a prospective lover and she cannot deny her attraction to the hunter. In the quartet at the end, the miller maid bids them all farewell, and the stricken miller lad sorrowfully proclaims his hopelessness; he does not, he feels, have any gift to offer her.

The echoes of the Stägemann song-play do not end with the first act. The miller maid's sauciness and bravado waver; at the beginning of act 2, a perplexed and saddened Röschen sings a soliloquy to her dead father, a soliloquy that begins, "Bist du schlafen gangen, theurer Vater mein?" (Have you gone to sleep, my dear father?) in an obvious reminiscence of Luise Hensel's gardener-serenade, albeit in a very different context. The A minor air is evidence of Lauer's modest but real musical gifts (Ex. 15), in particular, the ascending leaps of a minor or a major sixth that define the beginnings of the vocal phrases (also the mid-phrase in mm. 7–8), the affective use of the Neapolitan sixth in mm. 9 and 16 (the Neapolitan to the dominant minor in the first instance and the Neapolitan to tonic in the latter), and the beautiful melodic ascent to a higher tessitura in the second vocal phrase, expressive of despair, at the words "liesst dein Kind allein" (left your child alone), culminating on the dominant minor. The whole is curiously premonitory of the songs of Robert Franz, in particular, the maiden's lament "Mutter, o sing' mich zur Ruh'!", op. 10, no. 3 in A minor; both little works are characterized by the kind of undiluted, all-out Romanticism that produces short-breathed pieces, the intensity of emotional expression exhausting itself quickly (true of Franz in general).

Still other reminiscences of the *Liederspiel* follow in *Rose, die Müllerin*. The three suitors engage in a minstrels' song-contest – Rudolph first, then the gardener, and finally, the disconsolate Liepold – whose musical differences underscore the differences between the rivals. The hunter's echo-filled strophic song "Was des Waldes grüne Weide" has little of love or tenderness in it; the hunter derides the gardener and miller as "beasts of burden" ("Lastenträger") while he is king of the forest and she his queen. The plethora of hunting fanfares once again makes the self-centeredness of his wooing apparent. The gardener chimes in with a "Lied mit Chor," a serenade whose indebtedness to Hedwig von Stägemann's "Vogelgesang vor der Müllerin Fenster" is obvious:

(From No. XIII. Lied mit Chor)	**(From No. 13. Song with Chorus)**
Duftet, ihr Blümlein,	Be fragrant, little flowers,
Zwitschert, ihr Vöglein	twitter, birds,
Vor dem Fenster der Holden.	in front of the gentle one's window.

Lauer's modest grace-noted twittering birds are less virtuosic than Berger's pianistic display, but then his birds are not bringing such a bold message. It is typical of Thale and Lauer that they thus appropriate themes, images, motifs, and phrases from Müller and his companions and then alter the context, turning the borrowed material in tamer, more conventional paths.

In fact, one might well ask whether Berger's *Lieder aus einem gesellschaftlichen Liederspiele* was not possibly the principal source for Thale and Lauer. When the Singspiel miller sings mournfully "Und zieht nun in die weite Welt" (words that recall Müller's "Die böse Farbe" and its opening lines "Ich möchte ziehen in die Welt hinaus, / Hinaus in die weite Welt"), he does so to an E minor melody perhaps stemming from Berger's E minor setting of "Die böse Farbe"; despite differences in tempi and the (minimal) working-out of musical ideas, the two songs seem related by more than tonality. And this is followed by yet another reminiscence of the Stägemann *Kreis* when, soon after the Singspiel miller's lament, Rose sings a Vivace air about her love of green and the huntsman who wears it, with a solo clarinet given the melodic line for the four-measure introduction (was this an idea borrowed from Mozart and his operatic associations of clarinet sound and eroticism? or from Carl Maria von Weber's *Der Freischütz*, also peopled by a plethora of hunters?). Her words recall Hedwig von Stägemann's and Wilhelm Müller's "Ich hab' das Grün so gern," with perhaps a spice of Hedwig's "Mein Sinn" thrown in for good measure. If there is a reference to a different suitor in each stanza – the gardener in stanza 1, the hunter in stanza 2, and the miller in stanza 3 – there is also no doubt whose star is in the ascendant.

No. XV. Lied (Rose)	**No. 15. Song (Rose)**
Das Grün, das Grün, das lust'ge Grün	Green, green, merry green,
Will von den Farben allen,	will, above all the other colors,
Am besten mir gefallen.	please me most.

Auf grüner Matte schläft sich's süss	In green meadows I sleep sweetly,
Grün ist des Gartens Paradies,	green is the garden's Paradise,
Drum will das Grün vor allen	therefore above all, green
Am besten mir gefallen.	pleases me best.
Ein Jägersmann grün angethan	A huntsman clad in green
Muss von den Männern allen,	must please maidens
Dem Mädchen wohl gefallen.	above all other men.
O könnt ich fröhlich mit ihm ziehn	Oh, if I could go merrily with him
Durch Tannenwald und Fichtengrün,	through the pine forest and the green firs –
Der grüne Wald vor allen,	the green woods above all
Will mir so wohl gefallen.	will please me so much.
Der Myrthenkranz im grünen Glanz,	The myrtle garland in green splendor
Will von den Kränzen allen,	will please maidens
Dem Mädchen wohlgefallen.	above all other garlands.
Schilt nicht, du wackrer Müllersmann,	Do not scold, gallant miller;
Das Grüne hat mir's angethan,	the green did it to me.
Warum muss auch vor allen,	That is also why green must above all
Das Grün mir so gefallen.	please me so much.

Nevertheless, just as in the *Liederspiel*, Röschen is aware of the miller lad even as she announces her attraction to the hunter. When she bids the miller not scold her, she betrays the fact that she cares what he thinks of her. If her compunction in the Stägemann song-play is not enough to deter tragedy, it is here an omen for the happy outcome to follow.

After the display of competing minstrelsy and Röschen's decision in favor of the hunter, the dénouement comes swiftly. (The gardener, one notices with amused pity, has mounted the lengthiest and most elaborate musical tribute – he engaged an entire chorus – but was not taken seriously.) The judge suddenly announces that Rose was a foundling, not Erbin's daughter at all, and is therefore not entitled to the mill and the money. When the sorrowful Rose, believing herself cast out, bids farewell to her home in the quartet "Leb' wohl, du theures, geliebtes Haus" (Farewell, you dear, beloved house), she sings lines lifted directly from Müller's "Trock'ne Blumen," the context of the borrowing once again altered:

(From No. XVII. Quartett)	**(From No. 17. Quartet)**
Leb' wohl du theures geliebtes Haus,	Farewell, you dear, beloved house,
Ich muss' nun fort in die Welt hinaus,	I must now go forth into the world,
Was siehst du Gärtchen mich an so weh,	why do you look at me so sadly, little garden,
Ob du wüsstest wie mir geschäh?	as if you knew what had happened to me?

The miller lad then offers to take her home to his mother, and she agrees, Lauer underscoring her resolution with a sudden mediant shift from the previous cadence on E major to a passage on C major, which then culminates in a short-lived emphasis on D minor; both the clarity of her new-found resolution, founded upon the realization of who really loves her, and her sadness at leaving home are given harmonic garb. "Home is there only where joy blossoms for us . . . Hope will lead us home," they sing in the traditional harmonic thirds that signify lovers' togetherness. With the fortune-hunting hunter's departure, the judge and the gardener reveal that they fabricated the announcement in order to test the hunter's constancy, and the traditional *lieto fine*, complete with wedding announcement, then follows.

There are no citations from the Stägemann *Liederspiel* for the conclusion of *Rose, die Müllerin*, which seems only appropriate. Thale and Lauer, after all, reverse the ending of the *Liederspiel*: in the Singspiel, the miller maid, as she did before, chooses the hunter, but she is deterred from her bad choice – it is not, one notes, the miller, passive here as he is in the song-play, who deters her – before anything untoward can happen. "Lieb' und Treue werden siegen" (Love and faithfulness will triumph), the happy couple and their supporters proclaim in the final ensemble, but when "Lieb' und Treue" fail in the *Liederspiel*, the aftermath is devastation and death, as it so often is in real life. Far from depicting the agonized mechanisms of jealousy on the miller's part, the operatic Röschen is instantly forgiven for her attraction to the hunter, so long as she chooses her true love in the end, and happiness is restored after the manner of a *deus ex machina* or tale of enchantment, the situation patently unreal. The borrowings from *Liederspiel* to Singspiel, however, are intriguing. The chain-link sequence of Paisiello, Goethe, *et alii*, the Stägemann parlor-game, and Lauer/Thale's comedy exemplifies to a nicety the way in which new works of art spring into being as responses to previous works, responses not hidden but displayed openly for the cognoscenti to enjoy, and the ways in which those responses are skewed to bring out now this, now that aspect of an archetypal tale. Rejecting (or so one can conjecture) the death and misery at the close of the song-play, Thale and Lauer bring the miller maid, hunter, and miller back to life in order to identify and then punish the villain and to restore life to those robbed of it by their predecesssors. What this composer and librettist cobbled together from their sources is a remarkably tidy moral universe and a reassuring one, but Müller had other, and deeper, concerns in mind when he returned to the *Liederspiel* poems that same year to augment them as "drama" of a different, more unsettling sort.

OTHER "CYCLES"? FRAGMENTS OF MONODRAMA

After Berger's *Gesänge*, the subsequent settings are based on Müller's final version of his mill tale in the *Waldhornisten-Gedichte I*. The next "cycle" to be carved from the complete poetic work was composed by one Otto Claudius, who published his *Neun Lieder von W[ilhelm]. Müller* with Breitkopf & Härtel in 1833. Although we know very little about this *Kleinmeister* now, he won favorable notice in his own day for his *Sechs Gesänge*, op. 6 (Leipzig: Hofmeister, 1828) in the *Allgemeine Musikalische Zeitung* for February 1828, the reviewer comparing him approvingly with the likes of Ludwig Spohr, Gottlob Wiedebein, and – one can only chuckle – Franz Schubert.[16] Claudius's mill songs were also reviewed favorably, although briefly and with greater attention to Müller's text than to the music, in the same periodical for September 1833:

These are the texts of the well-known mill songs, which are brought forth here in new tones. In succession, they create a little novel with a tragic ending. The wander-happy miller lad at the beginning sings simple wandering songs to the murmuring of a brook, which he follows. The pretty mill and the prettier miller maid make him sentimental. In a charming poem, he plants forget-me-nots under the window of his beloved, who loves the hunting horn and green garb [of the hunter] – this drives the "white man" [the floury miller] out into the wild. The more his heart laments, the more compelling are its tones, until finally the brook sings his lullaby. Friends of song-novels will find much pleasure therein.[17]

I find this capsule review fascinating because of the historical misreading of Müller's enterprise. The mill songs – perhaps Schubert's D. 795? – are, we are told, "well-known" (Schubert was dismayed by the critics' and buyers' lack of response after the publication of the cycle in 1824, but matters were clearly remedied by the time of this review nine years later), and their poetic content is summarized in the simplest, most dismissive tones. To this writer, Müller's mill is the milieu for mere sentimentality, not passion, not obsession, not frenzy; it is typical that he should single out "Des Müllers Blumen" as representative of the tone and tenor throughout, ignoring the poetic signs of disturbance even in this small, flowery effusion. Nor did the reviewer read very attentively: the miller lad might briefly long to escape into the wide world ("Ich möchte ziehen in die Welt hinaus, / Hinaus in die weite Welt," he sings at the beginning of "Die böse Farbe"), but he cannot really do so and denies the impulse in the next breath, unable, like most victims of erotic compulsion, to leave the site of his obsession. "Simple, pretty, sentimental, charming," the reviewer chimes: the long tradition of trivializing these texts began early.

Was it because Schubert's prior example was so daunting that later composers who carved mini-cycles from Müller's larger work restricted themselves to smaller groupings? What were the factors that might have influenced the choice of certain poems and the omission of others? Whatever his reasons, Claudius only selected poems from the beginning and end of Müller's cycle for his *Neun Lieder*, or less than half of the complete text, although the nine songs appear in the correct chronological order, apportioned approximately half-and-half between songs before the hunter's arrival (nos. 1–5) and the tragedy which unfolds afterward (nos. 6–9). But Claudius omits everything that happens between "Des Müllers Blumen" and "Die böse Farbe," eight poems in which the miller maid becomes "Mein!", the hunter appears, and the miller explodes in panic and rage, then slips into suicidal despair. At the midway point of the *Neun Lieder*, one leaps from a love only just announced in "Danksagung an den Bach" and serenaded in "Des Müllers Blumen" straight to the bitter-angry-heartbroken farewell in "Die böse Farbe" and the last songs for the brook and the young man – the brook is thus a more visible, more important character than the hunter. By any calculation, this is a wide rift in the plot.

The title of the set designates the work as "songs," not as a "Zyklus" or "Kreis" or "Liederroman," and yet, whatever the gaping holes occasioned by his selection of less than half of Müller's text, Claudius clearly fashioned the nine songs as connected entities within an integrally organized work. The connections consist both of tonal links between some – but not all – of the lieder, for example, the circle-of-fifths motion from C to G to D in songs 1–4, and the kinds of harmonic and motivic connectives one found in Berger's *Gesänge*. Curiously, the huge gap between idyll and despair, the break in the narrative which occurs between nos. 5 and 6, is bridged by the relative major and minor modes connecting those two songs; the *forte* D minor reserved for the end of the musical strophe in no. 5, "Des Müllers Blumen," then becomes the tonality of the next song, which in turn begins with a dramatic vocal leap to a downbeat high F, referring back to the previous song with which it is paired.

Wanderschaft - C major, 2/4, Allegro, con leggerezza

Wohin? - G major, 2/4, Allegro, piacevole

Halt! - D major, 2/4, Vivace

Danksagung an den Bach - D major, 3/8, Allegretto, con tenerezza

Des Müllers Blumen - F major , 3/4, Andante, con sentimento

Die böse Farbe - D minor, 3/4, Andante quasi Allegretto

Trockne Blumen - E minor, 3/4, Andante con duolo

Der Müller und der Bach - A minor, 6/8, Andantino lugubre

Des Baches Wiegenlied - B minor, 4/4, Andante sostenuto assai

The purposeful *Wanderung* partway through the circle-of-fifths (the lad, after all, knows what he is looking for – a mill – and therefore journeys with a goal in mind) then stops at the mill with a song in F major. Schubert too used the tonalities whose associations are notably light and bright for songs near the beginning of his tale, before tragedy clouds the narrative landscape, his "Wohin?" in G major, "Halt!" in C major, and "Danksagung an den Bach" in G major.[18] At the midway point, Claudius's cycle swerves into those minor keys related to the previous major tonalities (F major/D minor, C major/A minor, G major/E minor, D major/B minor); the grief-stricken lad of "Trockne Blumen," swaying irresolutely back and forth between cadences on tonic E minor and A minor, thereby anticipates the A minor tonality of "Der Müller und der Bach." Schubert's cycle too swerved into minor modes at the moment (the fourteenth song, "Der Jäger") the miller becomes aware of the hunter's threat to his (the miller lad's) dreams of love. And, like Schubert, Claudius's cycle is not a tonally closed work, beginning as it does in C major and ending in B minor (traditionally a mournful key); Schubert begins with B flat major hopefulness and ends with a death-lullaby in E major (Mahler's propensity for ending his cycles with death-lullabies has its ancestry in Schubert). If ultimate surcease is promised the miller lad at the end of time, beyond death, that surcease is not yet arrived, and the gulf between life and death itself seems symbolized in the tritone distance separating them. Müller, in other words, does not invite a closed, circular design in which one "comes home" at the end, and no composer, to my knowledge, has imposed such a design on his mill drama.

Like Berger, Claudius too took pains to link paired songs by means other than tonal relationships, taking his cue from Müller when he did so. For example, no. 2, "Wohin?" is set as pure Nature-music in the piano, with a low bass G pedal point, coupled with a D pedal in the right hand two-and-a-half octaves above it throughout all fourteen measures of the musical strophe; the prominent open fifths and dominant harmonies over a tonic bass bespeak stylized "elemental" sounds, above which the voice continues its *Schwung*-filled "hiking" ways from the first song. The miniature coda ends with the third degree of the tonic triad (B) in the topmost voice; when the initial anacrusis at the start of no. 3, "Halt!", leads to a downbeat appoggiatura pitch B in m. 1, it sounds as a continuation of the preceding song. An even stronger link is the return of the "brook-

Example 16 Otto Claudius. "Halt!", mm. 23–33, and "Danksagung an den Bach," mm. 1–7, from *Neun Lieder von W. Müller.* Leipzig: Breitkopf & Härtel, 1833.

N<u>o</u>. 4 Danksagung an den Bach

music" of no. 2 in mm. 11–18 of the accompaniment to no. 3, at the words "Ei willkommen, ei willkommen, süsser Mühlengesang! Und das Haus, wie so traulich! Und die Fenster, wie blank!" (Now welcome, welcome, sweet mill song! And how inviting the house is! How brightly the windows gleam!). Claudius brings the music to a fermata-sustained pause in m. 10 after the words "durch Rauschen und Singen / bricht Rädergebraus," his miller lad stopping in his tracks to listen to the murmuring, the singing, the sound of the wheels. The recurrence of the water-music not only identifies the "sweet mill song" as synonymous with the brook but signifies the miller lad's belief that he has been led to this place by the watery emissary of his destiny.

Nos. 3 and 4, "Halt!" and "Danksagung an den Bach" ("Stop!" and "Song of Thanks to the Brook") are also connected, the bonds still stronger yet. At the end of "Halt!", the miller lad asks "Ei, Bächlein, liebes Bächlein, war es also gemeint?" (Now brook, dear little brook, is this what you meant?), a question dramatized by the *rallentando*, prolonged augmented sixth chord and half-cadence at the end, which only resolves to the shared tonic at the beginning of no. 4, when the lad repeats, "War es also gemeint, mein rauschender Freund?" (Ex. 16). Schubert was not the only composer to make potent use of a measure of silence at crucial points in the architecture of a song; Claudius follows the question "War es also gemeint" in "Halt!", first, with a silence in which no answer is forthcoming, then an instrumental repetition of the question, its yearning upward extension of an octave a particularly poignant detail of this evocative passage. Persistent

129

in his query (for a time), Claudius's miller ends each of the first four stanzas of "Danksagung" with a half-questioning, half-exultant leap of a sixth from A to F sharp, precisely the pitches outlined in the first vocal phrase of "Halt!"; not until the words "vollauf genug" (fully enough) at the end of "Danksagung" is there tonic closure in the vocal part. In the cadences at mm. 21–23 ("wie's immer mag sein") and mm. 32–34 ("vollauf genug"), Claudius anticipates the F major tonality to follow in "Des Müllers Blumen" by means of the B flat chromatic passing tone in the vocal line, which also tinges the lilting acquiescence to contentment with a brief hint of minor-modal tragedy, and quietly but memorably marks the way in which the lad relinquishes the inquiry, surrendering happily to happiness – "Ich gebe mich *drein*" (I submit to my fate), the lad sings, the expected resolution to a G major chord instead turning deceptively to V7 of E major at the word "drein" (darein). In this one small detail is the suggestion that the lad actually surrenders to a fate far different than he imagines in this "song of thanksgiving."

In Müller's cycle, a young poet-singer half-encounters, half-creates an idealized love and is clawed to death by it. The heartsick creature who dies is not the same exuberant youth we meet at the beginning, and Claudius, in his own way, makes the transformation evident in the changed formal structures as one goes through the nine lieder. The first songs are tiny, simple, tuneful, strophic constructions, "Wanderschaft" (Journeying) the simplest of them all – a true "hiking song," full of *Schwung*, with an Alphorn-like emphasis on the refrain "das Wandern," or "To wander." From the moment he arrives at the mill, the lad's music becomes, by degrees, more and more complex, culminating in the penultimate song, "Der Müller und der Bach" (The Miller and the Brook), and yet even where Claudius is at his most "simple," one notes the clustering of artful details. The lad's avowal of love in "Des Müllers Blumen" is, for example, a trifle sentimental, appropriate to this stage of the plot, with the first three of its four phrases ending with a pause on a dominant seventh or dominant harmony. Müller's lad, having as yet no basis in actuality on which to stake his claim of possession, speaks in a notably circuitous manner in this poem, and Claudius's multiple hesitations on a dominant which does not resolve until the assertion "D'rum sind es meine Blumen" ("Therefore they are my flowers") are nicely apropos. The sixteenth-note rest before the hushed setting of the words "meine Blumen" at the end of the first stanza of "Des Müllers Blumen" is a charming detail, the mingled tenderness and awe of first love enacted in the musical equivalent of a "catch in the throat."

Both in "Die böse Farbe" and "Trockne Blumen,"[19] Claudius's miller either angrily (no. 6) or numbly (no. 7) repeats the same phrases over and over again. For each of Müller's six verses of "Die böse Farbe," we hear the same eight-measure passage, clearly devised with stanza 1 in mind, six times in a row, with only the most minimal variations to the melodic line for prosodic reasons. Like Schubert, Claudius endows the lad's resolution to go out into the wide world ("Ich möchte ziehn in die Welt hinaus, hinaus in die weite Welt") with fierce energy, the initial vault upwards of a minor sixth endowing the verb "möchte" with the desperation of futile desire, but what follows is a collapse into irresolution and depression at the words "if only it weren't so green" ("wenn's nur so grün, so grün nicht wär"), the fateful word "grün" laden with the de-stabilizing associa-

Example 17 Otto Claudius. "Die böse Farbe," mm. 1–8, from *Neun Lieder von W. Müller*. Leipzig: Breitkopf & Härtel, 1833.

tions of horror and grief a diminished seventh chord can bring. At the final line of stanza 1, "da draussen in Wald und Feld," Claudius brings back the weak-beat accent of "hinaus" once more for "draussen," but his miller lad cannot sustain the fierce energy of the beginning and chants the words "Wald und Feld" on the dominant pitch. It requires two *forzando* statements of the words "Ich möchte ziehn," varied but its origins plainly recognizable, in the piano alone before the lad can whip himself up into a repetition, over and over again, of the same emotional cycle of angry energy - depressive collapse - partial recovery - anger (Ex. 17). The effect is curious, not because the phrase is ineffective, but because repetitions of it constitute the entire formal structure, nothing else. His miller lad, fixated and obsessed, sings as if trapped in an unchanging tape-loop of misery, but Müller's protagonist ranges wildly through a larger panoply of emotions, the near-madness of his voyeuristic wish to spy on the miller maid ceding to a farewell at the end.

The same limitation is true of Claudius's setting of "Trockne Blumen," the repetition even more noticeable because there is less rhythmic variety in the recurring passage than there was in "Die böse Farbe." As in Berger's setting, Claudius's miller is too grief-stricken for alleviation even by epiphanic fantasies, although he *does* try, however briefly: the words "Und Lenz wird kommen, / und Winter wird gehn, / und Blümlein werden / Im Grase stehn" (And spring will come, and winter will pass, and flowers will grow in the grass) are set as a sequence inching upwards by degrees and culminating in a *forte* diminished seventh chord and a fermata-prolonged pause (mm. 16–21). With that tension-fraught and ambivalent phrase ending, Claudius returns to the music of the beginning for the words "Und Blümlein liegen / in meinem Grab'" (And flowers will lie on my grave), the lowered tessitura and *pianissimo* dynamics indicative of leaden sadness once again regnant. Claudius repeats this same pattern at the end of the song: an attempt to instill belief in epiphany merely by saying/singing it, followed by the immediate failure of that attempt. His lad proclaims, "Der Winter [B *minor* harmony] ist aus [B *major*]," but the softer-and-softer cadence on E minor/major – the same succession of minor chord color, followed by a Picardy third – is hardly indicative of surety. Schubert's love- and grief-stricken youth fights harder against death and despair in "Trock'ne Blumen" than the same youth as musically imagined by Schubert's contemporaries; the persona of D. 795 can and does envision a glorious apotheosis, although it is tellingly couched in the key of "Des Baches Wiegenlied" and drains away altogether in the postlude, but Claudius's youth is even more a doubting Thomas.

No. 8, "Der Müller und der Bach" is the gem of the cycle. Here, Claudius departs from strophic form to write a through-composed lied laden with more chromaticism than anywhere else in the cycle, as when the word "Dornenreis" (thorny stems) impels an especially thorny dissonance of F natural in an inner voice against the sustained F sharp in the bass (m. 37). The tonal symbolism is particularly striking: the miller's first three stanzas begin in A minor, but with the flatted second degree B flat emphasized in the piano introduction. That pitch is then enharmonically respelled as the leading-tone to the B minor/B major on which this first section of the dialogue ends – the tonality of peace-in-death and of the brook's lullaby to follow. The B minor harmonies of the angels' weeping conclude with a Picardy third and a descent to low B in the vocal line for the word "Ruh'"; one notices as well the bitter emphasis on the accented syllable of "*treu -* [es]" in the first vocal phrase and the brief patch of C major harmonies in mm. 12–15 for the invocation of the full moon – Nature music that becomes C minor in the miller's last two verses, chillingly abbreviated from the three stanzas at the start. With the brook's words in the middle of the poem, the tonality changes to E major, in opposition to the lamenting A minor, and the tempo to Andante, while the piano part grows more animated and richer, although the increased richness and brightness are to no avail; the lad no longer has the heart to respond to any consolation. The way in which Claudius effects the transition from the brook's attempted persuasion to the miller's heartsick last words is especially effective, as is the invocation of death in mm. 54–55 at the words "die kühle Ruh'" (cool rest), the enharmonically wrought harmonic shock emblematic of the transformation from life to death. The low bass at the end tells of the brook's depths, and a fermata over the final empty measure symbolizes the death-haunted silence after the miller's submergence within the waters (Ex. 18). If one cannot deny Claudius's weaknesses, his faulty prosody, his frequent awkwardness, and his dismayingly brief musical strophes repeated too many times for tolerance, songs like this one show him to best advantage.

Claudius was not the only composer to construct a mill cycle in which one leaps from the beginning to the end of the tale, like those people who read only the beginnings and conclusions of novels: Carl Friedrich Zöllner (1800–1860) did likewise in *Des Müllers Lust und Leid, 6 Gesänge aus dem Liedercyclus 'Die schönen Müllerin' von Wilhelm Müller für vier Männerstimmen*, op. 6 (Leipzig: Fiedlein, 1844), or *The Miller's Joy and Sorrow, Six Songs from the Song Cycle 'The Beautiful Miller Maid' by Wilhelm Müller for Four Male*

Example 18 Otto Claudius. "Der Müller und der Bach," mm. 24–61, from *Neun Lieder von W. Müller*. Leipzig: Breitkopf & Härtel, 1833.

Voices.[20] The set is symmetrically divided between "Des Müllers Lust" and "Des Müllers Leid" in a tonally unified sequence, with the brief, hearty settings of "Wanderschaft" in D flat major and "Wohin?" in A flat major, as well as a comparatively immense (seven pages) rendition of "Halt!" and "Danksagung an den Bach" as a single choral piece in E flat major comprising the first half. (Amusingly, Zöllner's miller is downright vehement about his gratitude at having found the mill, the chorus repeating the final stanza of "Danksagung an den Bach" over and over again, in excess of all other textual repetition in op. 6.) "Die böse Farbe" in C minor, "Trockne Blumen" in A flat major, and the paired settings of "Der Müller und der Bach" in C sharp minor and "Des Baches Wiegenlied" in D flat major – the tonal symbolism of life and its enharmonic transformation in death – constitute the tragic second half. Zöllner only sets the initial stanza of "Wanderschaft" and the first two stanzas of "Wohin?"; since he neither prints the remaining stanzas nor indicates their performance by means of a marginal note or directive, one infers that he wished them omitted. What he omits, however, is not incidental to the narrative: the

Example 18 (*cont.*)

lad's request to his present employers ("Herr Meister und Frau Meisterin") in the fifth and final stanza of "Wanderschaft" to leave them and go wandering makes it plain that he is not already a *viator* but feels he should become one, and the siren-song of the brook in stanzas 3–5 of "Wohin?" tells of the lad's belief in fatefulness, in destiny. Did Claudius and Zöllner alike rely on their audience's knowledge of these "well-known songs" to fill in the blanks? Certainly the critics made the inevitable comparisons with Schubert's settings, already established as a model for other composers of song cycles, especially when later composers chose the same texts; the critic August Schmidt, writing for the *Allgemeine Wiener Musik-Zeitung* in 1845, somewhat drily pointed out that Schubert had greater success with his solo lieder than Zöllner could enjoy with his choral settings.[21]

Whatever Schmidt's opinion, with whatever justification, Zöllner understood the conventions of his chosen genre to a nicety and capitalized on them in this un-*volkstümlich* set, filled with high Gs, A flats, and even proclamatory B flats for the first tenors and text-painting details galore. The first basses may have been tempted to sleep through their notably uninteresting part in "Wanderschaft," but the first tenors are bidden to leap about like mountain goats, their echoed *sforzando - pianissimo* octave figures subsequently reappearing at the "perdendosi" (dying-away) conclusion to "Wohin?". But it is at the end of his cycle that Zöllner is at his best, especially in his effective use of the contrast between a solo quartet and the full male chorus in the last two pieces. "Trockne Blumen" is set for a quartet of soloists until the words "Dann, Blümlein, alle, / Heraus, heraus! / Der Mai ist kommen, / Der Winter ist aus!" (Then all you flowers, come out, come out! May has come and winter is past), when the tutti joins in for the prophesied springtime resurrection. The line "wie seht ihr alle mich an so weh!" (Why do you look at me so sadly) in mm. 9–12 crescendos to a dramatic diminished seventh chord at the word "weh!", while the tears of "Ach Thränen machen nicht maiengrün" (Alas, tears do not create Maytime green) impel a *con dolore* harmonic darkening, the A flat minor harmonies followed by a jolt to E major harmonies. The polarity between "todte Liebe" and "wieder blühn," between death and resurrection, is rendered visible on the page as well as audible. Zöllner too, in company with most of the other composers drawn to this famous poem, recognized the lad's inability truly to believe in the vanquishment of winter; over and over, *forte* or *fortissimo* pronouncements "Der Mai ist kommen" are followed by *piano* or *pianissimo* statements of the final words, "Der Winter ist aus." The final yearning leap of a sixth upwards in the first tenors sounds more like wistful wish than certainty.

Similarly, "Der Müller und der Bach" is set for solo quartet, followed by "Des Baches Wiegenlied" for the entire chorus, the one melting indissolubly into the other. Zöllner takes advantage of the *Männerchor* forces to merge the brook's symbol-laden attempt in stanzas 4–6 of "Der Müller und der Bach" to dissuade the heartbroken lad from committing suicide and the lad's refusal to be comforted and his death (stanzas 7–9): *his* miller lad – the solo second bass at the depths of the texture – rejects the brook's comforting words even as the brook sings them. As the solo tenor "Bach" sings soothing sotto voce broken-chordal patterns to the words of stanza 6 ("Und die Englein schneiden / die Flügel sich ab, / und gehn alle Morgen / zur Erde herab"), the "Müller" sings his final two stanzas (not three, as before . . . the abbreviated proportions tell of abbreviated life) as he sinks closer to submersion on low C sharp tonic and the inner voices murmur watery measured trills in the final measures before the death-lullaby begins. At the end of the dialogue-poem, the upper voices are still sounding, but the bass quietly ceases; in an alternative version also included in the score, its symbolism even more apparent, the *morendo* bass breaks off on the dominant pitch, without ever reaching the tonic – the miller has died in the depths of the water as the brook heeds his broken-hearted last words, "Singe, singe nur zu," or "Sing on" (Ex. 19).

The return to D flat major for "Des Baches Wiegenlied" reinforces the hints of fatalism in the early poems, despite Zöllner's textual omissions in "Wohin?", and draws a straight line from the ebullient beginning of the journey to its watery culmination, unlike Schubert's differently calibrated tonal symbolism. Zöllner even links the first and last songs by means of a reminiscence motif, varied to accord with a different tone and context but still quite recognizable: the melismatic setting of the words "das Wandern" in mm. 16–20 of "Wanderschaft" returns at the words "[bis das] Meer will trinken" in "Des Baches Wiegenlied" – *this* is where his wandering has led him. (Instead of the ath-

Example 19   Carl Friedrich Zöllner. "Der Müller und der Bach," mm. 50–70, from *Des Müllers Lust und Leid, 6 Gesänge aus dem Liedercyclus 'Die schönen Müllerin' von Wilhelm Müller für vier Männerstimmen*, op. 6. Leipzig: Fiedlein, 1844.

letic, staccato octave leaps in the second bass part of "Wanderschaft," Zöllner devises murmurous "sea-sounds" for the corresponding passage in "Des Baches Wiegenlied," a double-dotted figure on the tonic and leading tone pitches in the low bass.) The signification of the C sharp (life and love's distress) and D flat enharmony (death) is re-enacted in the brook's lullaby when the *molto agitato* C sharp minor setting of stanza 3 ("Wenn ein Jagdhorn schallt," or "When a hunting horn sounds") is followed by ultimate consolation ("Gute Nacht, gute Nacht, bis alles wacht," or "Good night, good night! Until all awaken") in D flat. Zöllner thus makes of the "miller's joy and sorrow" a *Schicksalstragödie*, a tragedy of fate whose end is foretold in its beginning; that the tonal design was calculated in accord with this composer's reading of the poetry, and not solely because he chose closed tonal design as the model for song cycle, is apparent in the symbolic meanings assigned the C sharp minor/D flat enharmonic polarity. Schubert had earlier avoided all hint of reminiscence motifs and any suggestion of fatalism – if Müller's miller lad dabbles in questions of predestination when he believes that happiness is coming his way, it is not a credo he sustains when his house of cards collapses.

With the final two cycles to be considered briefly in this chapter, we leave Müller's poetry for lyrical mill tales by other poets who were almost certainly inspired by him – of all the "costume dramas" and genre-scenes endemic in the first half of the century, mill songs were among the most popular – and for other composers who followed in Schubert's wake. The music critic Ludwig Rellstab, who was, as we have seen in chapter 1, a friend of Ludwig Berger's and hence knew about the inception of the poetic text and the circumstances of the first musical settings, wrote a review of Carl Banck's (1809–1889) *Des Müllerburschen Liebesklage in Mond und Morgenliedern* (The Miller Lad's Love-Laments in Moon and Morning Songs), op. 18 (Leipzig: Fr. Hofmeister, 1837), in the musical periodical he (Rellstab) founded and named *Iris im Gebiete der Tonkunst* for 1837:

The poems [by Carl Alexander] form a cohesive chain; the thought is very similar to that worked out in Wilhelm Müller's poems of a certain time and genre, and to which, at that time, other talents contributed. Perhaps Goethe's beloved poems of the miller maid provided the first model. Music finds here, naturally, very grateful material.[22]

The poetic texts were the work of one Carl Alexander, about whom little is known except that he was Banck's favorite poet by far: there are at least forty-six other Banck–Alexander lieder beside the op. 18 cycle in the collection of the Staatsbibliothek zu Berlin.[23] I have not been able to find the morning songs (the copy formerly in Berlin was destroyed in World War II), but the moonlit lamentations are well worth reviving for Banck's plangent musical miniatures, whatever Rellstab's reservations – he objected to Banck's numerous dynamic markings, tempo changes, and expression marks as overly dramatic. In Alexander's poetic conceit, a miller lad named Lindore whose erstwhile sweetheart Lindora (this is the Pappageno–Pappagena school of nomenclature for lovers) no longer loves him laments aloud to the moon on each of five nights in succession. The moon shall be her lover now, not the moon-pale miller, whose "bride" is night and tears, who hangs a tear-drenched funeral wreath on a weeping willow, who carves her name in an elm tree's bark. There is only the sketchiest narrative implied in the span of five nights and in the concluding desire for death "until all the wheels stand still and everything goes to sleep" – the references to the mill-wheels of Müller's and Schubert's cycle and to the words of "Des Baches Wiegenlied" are obvious. No action ever occurs, no other character appears or speaks, no hope is even hinted, and we are left to imagine the archetypal grieving youth keeping futile vigil outside his bygone love's window night after night.

All five of the *Mondlieder* are strict strophic settings, and the first three are closely linked tonally (A minor, E major, A major). But what seems to be an intent to mimic Schumannesque cyclic unification breaks down conspicuously in the final two songs, which are set in G minor and A flat major respectively, as if the tonal atmosphere were darkening, becoming more disjunct, breaking down, along with the miller lad (if indeed Banck thought of it in that way). The "First Night" is a melancholy version of a lover's nocturnal serenade, here, a serenade to the moon rather than the beloved; lamentation and loss mimic the ceremonies of love and togetherness. Banck consequently sets this lament "alla Serenata," the barcarolle rhythms perhaps impelled by the stars' merry dances in stanza 1, dances that unfurl to even greater length and greater motion in the postlude (nine measures, or slightly less than one-third of the entire strophe). Typically for Banck, the melody, however conventional, simple, and singable, is lovely, borne aloft above subdominant progressions that imbue the song with its distinctive gentle melancholy (Ex. 20).

Was it in Banck's "Zweite Nacht" that Schumann found a prior model for "Die Stille," the fourth song in the Eichendorff *Liederkreis*, op. 39? The resemblances are striking, each song with rests interpolated into the poetic "sentence"/melodic phrase, although Banck abandons the device for the second half of his strophe. The poet implies a voyeuristic obsession with looking, with glances, and Banck, alive to the erotic implications, creates a drive-to-the-end-of-the-strophe, an ever more accented, ever faster crescendo as his miller lad repeats "Wohl blickst du her und sie blickt hin." There is a certain similarity between the conceptual frameworks of the second and third nights' songs: an even airier texture recurs at the beginning of "Third Night," when the despairing protagonist commands the moon and stars to cease shining, to veil their light. By the end of each stanza, he changes his mind and bids the celestial bodies sparkle, shine once again, and Banck accordingly conceives yet another crescendo and intensification in the middle of the musical strophe. "Go, sparkle, shine," the miller lad commands, the vocal line – pervaded with accents and energetic dotted patterns – and the upper voices of the piano rushing upwards and onwards in evident eagerness, but the increased motion is chained to a dominant pedal point in the bass. The commonplace, yet effective, means of underscoring anticipation in music in order to heighten the effect of resolution here leads to sad negation ("Doch Lindora liebt dich nicht") and a return both to the tonic key and the uncertain, fragmentary, symbolically incomplete textures of the beginning; Banck tells us exactly when the brief outburst of energy and assertiveness drains away swiftly in the cadence at mm. 12–13, followed by the telling little word "doch." And at crucial points throughout the song, Banck plays with yet another detail indicative of the alternation between light and dark, sadness and hopefulness: the interjection of A minor and D minor chords into the A major fabric, as in m. 6, where the invocation of

Example 20 Carl Banck. "Erste Nacht," mm. 1–18, from *Des Müllerburschen Liebesklage in Mond und Morgenliedern*, Heft 2: *Mondliedern*, op. 18. Leipzig: Friedrich Hofmeister, n.d.

weeping ("voll Weinen") darkens the song momentarily to minor coloration, reverting to major at the words "Liebchens Herz." Similarly, the sad conclusion to each stanza ("Doch Lindora liebt dich nicht") impels another such poignant lapse into darkness, as does the piano postlude, with its funereal drum-beat in the low bass (the level gradually sinks throughout the musical strophe). Ultimately, one hears the final tonic major chord as a reassertion of bravery and brightness, a sadly tenuous reassertion because minor lurks ever nearby.

Banck had a knack for varying the accompanimental figuration in fresh ways even in the smallest of small songs, such as "Vierte Nacht" (fifteen bars long, four of them consumed by the instrumental postlude); the changing pianistic patterns are perhaps especially a necessity where phrases are as symmetrical as they are here, two-measure unit following two-measure unit with no deviation into asymmetry. Nonetheless, the fourth-night lament is one of the loveliest songs in this compelling little cycle, Banck's melodic gift evident and in full force (Ex. 21). The lied is emblematic of what often happens when the *Volkston* becomes *Kunstlied* in the first half of the century, such that both worlds of song are evident on the page at one and the same time, but with art-song the dominating force; this song is filled with refinements of articulation – many little crescendi and decrescendi crammed into a small space, "stringendo" and "morendo" markings – and poetico-musical interpretation of the sort foreign to true folk song, and yet the *Volkston* is everywhere apparent. Despite the miniature dimensions of the lament, Banck heightens the relative major – briefly – and the subdominant harmony – even more briefly, so that this song "con moto ed afflizione" might have the appropriate restlessness of active grief. This composer knew the power of judiciously employed touches of chromaticism: in the fifth and final song, when the exhausted poetic protagonist longs for death, Banck underscores the tragic desire by means of the chord of the flatted seventh degree, virtually the only chromaticism in the song and all the more effective for it.

If *Des Müllerburschen Liebesklage* is a latter-day response to *Die schöne Müllerin*, Banck responded even more directly to *Winterreise*, D. 911, and not only because he set "Die Post" to music.[24] In a fascinating case-history of the Romantic song cycle, Banck's *Des Leiermanns Liederbuch*, or *The Hurdy-Gurdy Player's Songbook*, op. 21 (Leipzig: Peters, 1838 or 1839?), begins where *Winterreise* ends, both as a continuation of the tale and a revision of it. *Winterreise* and *Des Leiermanns Liederbuch* overlap: Banck begins his smaller cycle (six songs, to Schubert's twenty-four) with a dramatic, even feverish, setting of "Der Leiermann" (Ex. 22), followed by a setting of Friedrich Rückert's "Ruhe der Liebe," best known by Schubert's title "Du bist die Ruh'." None of the other four songs has attributions to an identified poet; as Banck was generally scrupulous about such matters, one wonders whether he himself supplied the texts for the remaining songs: "Ergebung" (Resignation), "Seelendrang" (Soul's Distress), "Der Verlassne" (The Forsaken Man), and "Die Umkehr" (The Return). If so, Gustav Mahler, whose *Lieder eines fahrenden Gesellen* begins with a poem from *Des Knaben Wunderhorn* followed by the composer's own texts, had a predecessor in the same practice. Mahler was, I believe, responding to *Winterreise* as well in that cycle – it is fascinating to trace the effect down the days and throughout the century of Schubert's songs. If there is not space here to discuss this work, in which neither millers nor hunters figure in the action, it nonetheless exempli-

Example 21 Carl Banck. "Vierte Nacht," mm. 1–15, from *Des Müllerburschen Liebesklage in Mond und Morgenliedern*, Heft 2: *Mondliedern*, op. 18. Leipzig: Friedrich Hofmeister, n.d.

fies the phenomenon with which most of this chapter is concerned: Schubert reception in the songs of later composers, a subject which deserves greater consideration.

The same phenomenon – a later "reply" to Müller and Schubert – is evident in yet another mill cycle to appear in 1837, clearly a banner year for mill songs. Along with Banck's lieder of idyll and loss (one supposes that the lost "morning songs" were happier creations than the moonlit laments), Constantin Julius Becker (1811–1859), who was a member of the staff of the *Neue Zeitschrift für Musik* and of the circle around Schumann, published his *Lieder für eine Singstimme*, op. 3 in two volumes (Leipzig: J. Wunder, 1837), with a mini-cycle of three songs –"Hedwigs Lied von der Mühle,"

Example 22 Carl Banck. "Der Leiermann," mm. 1–10, from *Des Leiermanns Liederbuch*, op. 21. Leipzig: C. F. Peters, n.d.

"Schön Hedwig am Ufer," and "Hedwigs Lied am Bächlein" (Hedwig's Song of the Mill, Beautiful Hedwig on the Bank, Hedwig's Song to the Little Brook), nos. 3–5, surrounded on either side by unrelated poems.[25] Becker himself wrote the mill texts and then added to them for his "musical novel" *Der Neuromantiker* (The New Romantic) of 1840, filled with discussions of new and "old" music; there is, for example, an enthusiastic description of a performance of Beethoven's Scottish folk songs and discussions of Mendelssohn's "A Midsummer Night's Dream" overture and Berlioz's overture to *Les francs-juges*, among much else. In the sixth chapter of Part I, the character Waldau (the fusion of "Wald," or "forest," and "Aue," or "meadow," in his name suggests the alliance between music and Nature) writes a letter to his friends, recounting his love for the beautiful miller maid Hedwig, who plays the harp – the group of friends were much taken with Goethe's Mignon and Harper – and sings in a deep, full alto voice.

The cycle of seven poems Waldau encloses at the end of his letter seems, fascinatingly, like both a homage to Müller's *Die schöne Müllerin* and a revision of it.[26] In Becker's scenario, the monologist is the miller maid in love, not the miller lad; it is she who ecstatically exclaims, "Mein Herz ist die Mühle, / Der Müller sey Du!" (My heart is the mill, the miller is you), in the first poem, "Die Mühle" (The Mill), recalling the lad's refrain "Dein ist mein Herz und soll es ewig bleiben" in Müller's "Ungeduld." But the miller maid "Hedwig" – could Becker have known that the miller maid of the Stägemann *Liederspiel* was played by *Hedwig* von Stägemann? – is actually quadruply a male creation: in the novel, her songs are devised by a male character (Waldau) via a male author (Becker) who borrows extensively, with little or no effort to hide his source, from another male author (Müller) whose personae (the miller lad and winter wanderer) are men. In the third poem, "Die Rose" (The Rose), Hedwig's love, like that of the earlier miller lad, is briefly returned, but her beloved miller is depicted as androgynously feminized, with "schüchternen Blicken" (bashful glances), while she sips his tears from the rose's "purple chalice." The hints of oral sex and intercourse, in which tears are a metaphor for semen and the purple chalice an image of the labia's flowerlike folds, betray the male voice; one thinks of Heinrich Heine's "Das Meer erglänzte weit hinaus" from the *Buch der Lieder* (the text for Schubert's "Am Meer" in *Schwanengesang*, D. 957, no. 12) and recognizes the same symbolism.

It is when the miller maid tells the millstream in the second poem "Das Bächlein" (The Little Stream) that the brook "ohne Rast und Ruh" (without rest and peace) is the image of her heart that the presence of *Die Winterreise*, albeit varied and diminished, becomes evident in Becker's cycle; the winter wanderer in "Auf dem Fluße" who looks upon the frozen stream and asks "Mein Herz, in diesem Bache / Erkennst du nun dein Bild?" (My heart, do you recognize your image in this brook?) has a latter-day echo in the trials and tribulations of Becker's Hedwig. Her love idyll is short-lived; by the fourth poem, she already pleads with the youth to stay ("Die Bitte," or "The Plea") and reproaches him for his "Drang ins Ferne," his desire to wander far away. But he leaves, and in the fifth song, "Einsamkeit" (Loneliness, the same title as one of Müller's winter journey poems), she mourns.

5. Einsamkeit

(stanzas 1 and 5 of 5)
Abgeblüht ist Lenz und Liebe,
   Rings ein ödes Haideland;
Und ich sitze stumm und trübe,
   Welke Blumen in der Hand.

Knabe, kehre gut und bieder,
   Wie die Schwalbe treu zurück!
Blumen harren Dein und Lieder
   Und der Liebe süßes Glück.

5. Loneliness

Faded is spring and love,
   All around a bleak moor;
And I sit mute and sad,
   withered flowers in my hands.

Boy, return good and proper,
   like the swallow faithfully back!
Flowers await you and songs
   and love's sweet fortune.

Becker's cycle modulates from *Die schöne Müllerin* to the winter journey en route to its own bleak ending. "Turn, mill, in the wind until you decay! Break, like my heart, and fall," she sings in the sixth song, "Untreue" (Infidelity), and then becomes a wandering minstrel – love's loss creates poets – who quotes from Müller's "Gute Nacht," in which another heartbroken poet-singer sets out on a long journey. In the seventh and last poem, "Resignation," Becker's miller maid bitterly declares, "Mein Liebster liebt das Wandern sehr / Von Einer zu der Andern" (My lover loves to wander from one to another), recalling the winter wanderer who declares, "Die Liebe liebt das Wandern – / Gott hat sie so gemacht – / Von Einem zu dem Andern" (stanza 3 of "Gute Nacht"). Those who knew their Müller-and-Schubert (and Becker's novel was clearly directed to a musical *cognoscenti* familiar with debates about program music, poetic meaning in lieder, and the like) would not miss the source, but Becker's transmogrification is a queasy, and ultimately unsettling, one. Abandonment and loss are seemingly transferred back to their more customary "female" recipient, but Müller's male personae lurk just behind the facade of a female voice, this odd *Mischung* of the sexes particularly jarring when Becker sends his miller maid out into the world as a wandering singer – an unlikely possibility even for fictional women. Müller's gentle young miller, who is miserably aware of his effeminacy by contrast with the hunter's hyper-masculinity and whose identity as a poet-singer already marks him as suspect in gender, becomes in Becker a woman who at the end goes forth into the world as a Romantic, more commonly male, minstrel. The confounding of roles is enough to make one's head spin.

Ultimately, what one carries away from a survey of these cycles is a heightened sense of the aftermath of a work such as D. 795, held up as a model for emulation and yet so strong in its impact that the latter-day echoes could hardly hope to compete with their source. Indeed, the composers of shorter cycles seem to have relied on their audience's familiarity with the outlines of the story, in particular as transmitted through Müller and Schubert, so that they might dispense with the interior of the tale and concentrate on its outer limits, the songs of newfound love in Nature and of death (but it is the roiling, psychological complexities in the middle that fascinate modern temperaments). The *Nachklänge* in Schubert's wake also provide additional confirmation by comparison of Schubert's wonderful predilection to richness on all fronts: more poems from the poetic source, more harmonic and tonal complexity, more intricate structures, more nuances of poetic reading – more, more, more.

NOT GARLANDS BUT INDIVIDUAL BLOSSOMS: SINGLE SONGS PLUCKED FROM THE CYCLE

Most composers treated Müller's *Die schöne Müllerin* as a source for even smaller extracts, for single songs or paired lieder. It is one experience to encounter a fraction of the larger cycle re-ordered as a different cycle, still another to find isolated moments from the tale divorced entirely from the plot to which they belong. Müller himself knew this practice and even praised the Berlin composer Bernhard Joseph Klein (Fig. 11) for his setting of "Trockne Blumen" in Klein's *Lieder und Gesänge*, published by E. H. G. Christiani in 1822 – Klein (1793–1832) evidently found the text hot off the presses.[27] Looking at this lied, one wonders whether Schubert knew and remembered in some subterranean fashion the repeated note ostinato in the inner voice of mm. 8–12, 19–24, and most of mm. 29–45 when he composed "Die liebe Farbe" (not, notably, Schubert's own setting of "Trock'ne Blumen") – there, a similar funeral knell tolls throughout, the

Figure 11 Pen-and-ink portrait of Bernhard Klein (1793–1832) by Wilhelm Hensel, 1825.

sounding symbol of obsession. The descending parallel first inversion chords that lead to the half-cadences at the end of Klein's piano introduction (mm. 3–4) and in mm. 7–8 also seem a foreshadowing of the similar passages that are a miniature link between "Der Jäger" (mm. 7, 11) and "Eifersucht und Stolz" (mm. 12–14, at the words "Kehr um, kehr um," or "Turn back, turn back"). Before Schubert, Klein too turns to the parallel major mode for the future springtime epiphany the miller briefly envisions and then darkens the piano postlude with the flatted-sixth degree belonging to minor mode, as if to imply that his miller cannot sustain belief in the imagined resurrection, that death and despair are still present. In Schubert's setting, composed only a year or so after Klein's, the same contrasts are more sharply drawn and heightened beyond Klein's (his name cruelly apt) smaller powers, the major-mode epiphany more triumphal and the descent to tonic minor in the postlude more definitive; in Klein's setting, the flatted-sixth degree sounds in the inner voice, and the postlude ends with a tonic major harmony. But these resemblances could be merely coincidental, the result of separate choices of common musical symbols for aspects of the poem that both men saw (Ex. 23).[28]

Only a few years after Schubert's cycle was published in 1824, the prolific song composer Carl Gottlieb Reissiger (1798–1859)[29] set "Der Neugierige" in his *Lieder und Gesänge für Bass (oder Bariton)*, op. 53, no. 3 (Dresden: Paul, [183–?]), followed thereafter by a setting of "Halt!" and "Danksagung an den Bach" as a single bipartite lied – Zöllner was not the only composer to link the two poems – in his *Sechs deutsche Lieder u[nd] Gesänge*, op. 76, no. 1 (Bonn: Simrock, [183–?]), which also includes "Die liebe Farbe" as the third song in the opus. Still later, Reissiger returned to the same poetic source to set "Des Baches Wiegenlied" in the *Gesänge und Lieder*, op. 84, no. 2 (Dresden: C. F. Meser, [183–?]), but the most interesting of the Reissiger-Müller songs are the op. 76 set, dedicated to the beautiful and notorious Charlotte Stieglitz, the minor poet Heinrich Stieglitz's wife who stabbed herself through the heart on December 29, 1834 in a *cause célèbre* that reverberated for decades; the publication of the *Sechs deutsche Lieder* thus surely precedes her death (one wonders whether Reissiger afterwards noted the tragic irony of dedicating songs from a cycle which culminates in suicide to a woman who thereafter killed herself, albeit by different means).[30]

The through-composed pairing of "Halt!" and "Danksagung an den Bach" begins with a passage of quasi-Schubertian drama in the piano introduction: twice, the softly striding, unharmonized, ascending figures pause on a fermata-sustained dominant chord before instrumental recitative in the treble leads to the body of the song, as if the miller lad en route glimpsed the mill, paused, resumed his journey, stopped again and began musing aloud, first wordlessly and then in words. Something of his youthful ebullience and his walking stride are evident in the *Schwung*-filled appoggiaturas in the melodic line at mm. 10–11 (and thereafter), in the turn from tonic A major to C major when he hails the mill ("Ei willkommen, ei willkommen, süsser Mühlengesang!"), in the excited leap upwards to high G sharp at the word "helle" ("und die Sonne, wie helle vom Himmel sie scheint," or "And how brightly the sun shines in the sky") – bright indeed. At the end of "Halt!", he again pauses questioningly on the dominant, as he had at the beginning, before once more asking "War es also gemeint" in Allegretto motion, quickened slightly in excitement from the relaxed Moderato that precedes it. Wanting to

Example 23 Bernhard Joseph Klein. "Trockne Blumen," mm. 41–64, from the *Lieder und Gesänge*. Berlin: E. H. G. Christiani, 1822.

believe that he was sent to the miller maid, Reissiger's miller declares "Zur Müllerin hin, so lautet der Sinn" (Go to the miller maid! This is your meaning), to horn-call fanfare-like figures in the vocal line – was Reissiger courting an ironic reference to the hunter, one wonders? Struck by uncertainty, his miller lad then asks "Hat sie dich geschickt? oder hast mich berückt?" (Did she send you? or did you enchant me?), each time pausing on the fermatas familiar from the introduction. Reissiger turns to the briefly tonicized mediant of C sharp major when the lad asks whether the brook has cast a spell on him, the heightened mediant the realm not only of speculative enchantment but uncertainty: when he sings "was ich such', hab' ich funden, wie's *immer mag seyn*" once more to III chords, the last words leap upwards questioningly and pause yet again, the song as riddled with fermatas as with doubts. At the end, rejecting further speculation, he shrugs off the hint of magic and returns to the A major contentment from the beginning, singing "Nach Arbeit ich frug, / nun hab' ich genug" to the same horn-call melody as that to which he sang, "Zur Müllerin hin" . . . "Work indeed," Reissiger suggests, tongue-in-cheek (Ex. 24).

Example 24 Carl Gottlieb Reissiger. "Halt! – Danksagung an den Bach," mm. 48–67, from *Sechs deutsche Lieder u[nd] Gesänge*, op. 76, no. 1. Bonn: Simrock, n.d.

Unlike Schubert, who subsumes the considerable differences in tone and temper between the three verses of "Die liebe Farbe" to an all-pervasive funereal atmosphere, Reissiger varies each strophe. His miller is not numbed and frozen in the face of impending suicide but imbues his lamentation with considerable passion, evident in the octave leap that emphasizes the word "grüne" at the start of the second line of verse ("in *grüne* Thränenweiden," or "in green weeping willows"), in the chanting on a repeated pitch within a simple but lovely melody, in the appoggiaturas and semitone sighing figures, and the *Terzensteigerung* in the piano at the end of the first strophe in A minor – this is Reissiger at his most eloquent. A friend of Robert Schumann's, he echoes in his own way the tempo fluctuations of his greater contemporary, investing the words "eine Haide von grünem Rosmarein" (reminiscences of Ophelia) with particular chromatic potency and then pausing at the apex of the phrase before proceeding to the cadence. For the second verse ("Wohlauf zum fröhlichen Jagen," or "Up and away to the merry hunt!"), Reissiger turns to parallel major mode, a *più vivo* tempo, and comically naive chordal pounding for the "wild beast Death," while the last verse ("Grabt mir ein Grab im Wasen," or "Dig my grave in the grass") is set to a variation of the music for stanza 1 in which the pseudo-Baroque walking bass of mm. 1–4 becomes sixteenth-note motion, culminating with this Pagliaccio-in-lied singing *con dolore* in *major* mode at the end, presumably reflecting the word "gern" and the miller maid's happiness. The final cadence this time is echoed in *Terzensteigerung* rather than repetition at the same level; Reissiger is overly given to piano echoes of vocal cadences, and one grows tired of the automatic mannerism by the end of the lied. Nonetheless, the A sections of this song are indeed attractive (Ex. 25), despite the simple bombast that was Reissiger's way – an unsatisfying one – of portraying a *Totenjagd* in the middle of his lied.[31] When one hears these songs, however, one is reminded of Hugo Wolf's comment in 1891 about Peter Cornelius's music: "What he would like to do outstrips his ability to do it."[32] Reissiger's desire to be a singing poet, to mirror in music the twists and turns in his chosen texts, is evident in many of his compositional decisions, but without the level of inspiration or skill one finds in a Schubert or Schumann.

Reissiger's mill songs betray no influence of Schubert's cycle, but Schubert's "Ungeduld" is an unbanished ghost within every bar of Louis Spohr's (1784–1859) setting of the same text, composed in late 1836 and published in the *Sechs deutsche Lieder* for alto or baritone and piano, op. 94, no. 4 (Bonn: N. Simrock, 1837).[33] Spohr's setting is also in A major, also in 3/4 meter, and begins with a figure whose opening leap of a sixth from E to C sharp and descending scalar motion are distantly reminiscent of the first vocal phrase of Schubert's song. However, despite Spohr's indication "Feurig" (Fiery) to the performers, the temper of his setting is altogether less impatient, less Angst-ridden than the thrumming triplets and restless motion of the seventh song in D. 795, chained, however, to tonic A major throughout – the tonal emblem of obsession. Spohr may have taken his cue from Schubert in this regard when he devised the pedal point A at the beginning of his setting, animated by clichés of linear chromaticism in the inner voices. Unlike Schubert, Spohr briefly invokes C major at the refrain "Dein ist mein Herz," setting it apart harmonically from the body of the strophe; when he bids his miller repeat the words of the refrain, he does so softly, unlike the intense, wrought-up creature Schubert depicts. The tension between similitude and difference from Schubert's model bespeaks the difficulty of setting texts already claimed by the great lieder composers.

One of Spohr's students, the Berlin song composer Carl Friedrich Curschmann (1805–1841), who died tragically young, set "Mein!" and "Ungeduld" as op. 3, nos. 4 and 6 respectively, and "Danksagung an den Bach" as op. 5, no. 1, the op. 3 set favorably reviewed in the *Allgemeine Musikalische Zeitung* for June 1832 and the op. 5 set

Example 25 Carl Gottlieb Reissiger. "Die liebe Farbe," mm. 38–57, from *Sechs deutsche Lieder u[nd] Gesänge*, op. 76, no. 3. Bonn: Simrock, n.d.

reviewed even more favorably in September 1833 –"Herr Curschmann belongs among the most beloved song composers of the day."[34] In his autobiography, Spohr tells of meeting Curschmann in the summer of 1825 when the young man came to Kassel to study music with him, having abandoned the legal studies in Berlin and Göttingen that his widowed mother and family had wished him to pursue;[35] in a letter to a friend, Curschmann amusingly writes of having left "Donna Justitia" for "Don Apoll," who will find him a more grateful subject. Spohr, recognizing that the young man's musical education had been deficient, sent him to Moritz Hauptmann to study theory and composition for four years, with Spohr instructing him in "the aesthetic part of composition," in the choice and ordering of texts, declamation, and expression.[36] An outstanding boy soprano in his youth, later a baritone whose vocal gifts Spohr praised, he had evidently sung too much and too unwisely by the time Rellstab came to know him in the early 1830s, but Rellstab nevertheless testifies to the effect of Curschmann's performances of his own compositions, performances "so sweet, so finely nuanced" that he had "an unbelievable influence on the hearers, especially the women of the audience."[37]

In a fascinating instance of influence extended from one generation to the next in a chain, Curschmann's setting of "Ungeduld" recalls Spohr's. The motivic resemblances – the rising scalewise motion in the body of the first vocal phrase and the downturned third with which that first phrase ends – are too close to be merely coincidental, and Curschmann's *sempre legato* flowing triplet figuration is, like Spohr's, less feverish by far than D. 795. But he was nevertheless a skillful song composer, and his attractive setting of "Danksagung an den Bach" has been recently republished in an anthology of *Famous Poets, Neglected Composers*.[38] One notices in particular the shift from tonic G major to B minor harmonies at the words "[ich gebe mich] drein: was ich such', ist gefunden, wie's immer mag sein" (I submit to my fate; I have found what I sought, however it may be) – Curschmann's miller lad not only surrenders to what he believes to be destiny's benevolence, but proclaims it aloud, *forte* and to the most colorful harmonies in the lied. That they are *minor* harmonies is Curschmann's hint from within the music that tragedy lurks in the offing.

A. F. Wustrow (*c.* 1786–1852) was a Berliner *Hofrat* and pianist who gave concerts of Mozart's and Beethoven's concerti and composed songs to texts by Heinrich Stieglitz and Müller.[39] His settings of "Wohin" and "Danksagung an den Bach" from the *Neun Gesänge*, op. 15, nos. 4 and 5 (Berlin: Moritz Westphal, [183–?]) have attractive features and deserve revival.[40] Wustrow set "Wohin" as a strophic song in three strophes (two stanzas of poetry for each strophe) in the tragic key of D minor, with a single cadence on the relative major tonality that first occurs at the words "so frisch und wunderhell" – a momentary lightening of the fateful, dissonance-laden stream that flows throughout the piano accompaniment. His miller is more oppressed by premonitions of fatality when he first sees the brook than Schubert's character, as if Wustrow wished to compress the beginning and ending of the tale into a single song. The echoes of Schubert in the piano accompaniment are striking: the pedal point, with its rocking motion, reminds one of "Wohin?", and the C sharp neighbor note on the second half of the first beat of mm. 1–5 and thereafter, which then becomes a chord tone in the right-hand part on the second beat, reminds one dimly of the "folkish" asperities – sarcasm and misery combined in a single figurational pattern – in "Eifersucht und Stolz" at the words "Er schnitzt bei mir sich eine Pfeif aus Rohr" (He is on my banks, carving a reed whistle).

In "Danksagung an den Bach," however, the Schubertian reminiscences are confined to a single instance, surely deliberately invoked, while the remainder of this through-composed lied differs in many respects from its famous predecessor. Wustrow sets the questions at the beginning of the poem, "War es also gemeint? . . . Dein Singen und Klingen, war es also gemeint?" (Is this what you meant? . . . Your singing, your murmuring, is this what you meant?), as a series of rising sequences on secondary dominants, the rising motion and non-tonic harmonies tonal emblems of questioning. In fact, it is not until the words "ich gebe mich drein" (I yield to my fate) that we hear the first resolution to a tonic E major chord – in m. 41! It is an apt conception thus to evade tonic until the precise moment when the miller abandons all questioning and tonal quests in order to surrender happily to fortuitous circumstance, no matter how it happened. The exultation is made overt when Wustrow sets the remaining six lines of the poem as a gradual crescendo and ascent to high A in the vocal line. Nor are these the only felicities in this latter-day "Danksagung." Wustrow acknowledges the inescapable presence of D. 795 when he sets the words "Zur Müllerin hin, zur Müllerin hin! so lautet dein Sinn" to an unmistakable reminiscence of Schubert's "Wohin?" in the same G major harmonies, slightly varied by a more active inner voice; even the harmonic relationship of the cadence on a B major chord at the end of the previous section (mm. 8–9) and the G major harmonies that follow echoes a Schubertian gesture (Ex. 26).

The indefatigable Wilhelm Karl Gottfried Taubert (1811–1891), who in his youth was a pupil both of Ludwig Berger and Bernhard Klein in Berlin, composed a veritable flood-tide of music in all genres during his long life, including over 200 sets of lieder in a conservative, diatonic style (he had a special penchant for children's songs), a continuation of an earlier ideal of lieder composition well into the last half of the century. His mammoth song *oeuvre* includes settings of "Wo ein treues Herze" in *Sechs deutsche Lieder*, op. 6, no. 2 (Berlin: Trautwein [before 1844]); "Morgengruss," op. 174, no. 5; and "Des Müllers Blumen" in *Sechs Lieder mit Begleitung des Pianoforte*, op. 22, no. 5 (Leipzig: Hofmeister, [184–?]).[41] Taubert was successful early: he became a director of the court concerts when he was only twenty years old, then in 1834 a member of the Akademie der Künste, in 1841 director of the Royal Opera (which he and fellow conservative Heinrich Dorn, also staunchly opposed to all new music, made their personal forum), and in 1845 court Kapellmeister for twenty-five years until Hans von Bülow's concerts aroused the opposition to demand a new director. For Taubert, music stopped with Mendelssohn, and he believed fervently that nineteenth-century composers should take Mozart as their model, not Liszt, and certainly not Wagner. Robert Eitner, in the *Allgemeine Deutsche Biographie*, declared that the term "Kapellmeistermusik" might have been invented with Taubert in mind, but the naive-childish tone of the Kapellmeister's *Kinderlieder* found such advocates as Jenny Lind, who sang them on her tours. His pleasant but pallid version of "Morgengruss" has its virtues – the dominant harmony sustained throughout the miller's anxious questions ("Verdriesst dich denn mein Gruss so schwer? Verstört dich denn mein Blick so sehr?", or "Does my greeting annoy you so much? Does my gaze upset you so much?") and the inflection of the submediant harmony at the words "wieder gehen" (go away again) – but it is difficult to imagine that matters of life or death might follow after *this* morning serenade.[42]

Leopold Lenz (1803–1862), a royal court and opera singer in Munich who also composed an interesting cycle to Goethe's *Wilhelm Meister* poems, set "Mein" as the fourth song in his *Fünf Gesänge*, op. 25 (Munich: J. Aibl, [182–? or 183–?]) – Müller's "Seefahrers Abschied" rounds out the opus.[43] Schubert's influence is readily detectable: like Schubert, Lenz repeats lines 1–10 of Müller's single fifteen-line stanza as the final section of an A B A song form, and, again like Schubert, the poet's wavering line lengths, indicative of delusion, are straightened out and converted into pure *Schwung*, with a vocal line that leaps for joy even more energetically than in his famous contemporary's lied to the same text and a piano part filled with *sforzando* accents and thrumming motion (Schubert's song is marked "Mäßig geschwind," Lenz's setting "Geschwind"). Measures 24–27 and 28–31 are additionally reminiscent of Schubert's setting of the

Example 26 A. F. Wustrow. "Danksagung an den Bach," mm. 1–26, from the *Neun Gesänge*, op. 15, no. 5. Berlin: Moritz Westphal, [183–?].

words "unter seinem trauten Dach / schläft mein liebster Freund" (Beneath its cosy roof sleeps my dearest friend) from the lovely "Im Freien," D. 880, op. 80, no. 3 (1826) to a text by Johann Gabriel Seidl, with the same melodic contour at the beginning and the same texture (the bass doubled in thirds and in turn doubling the voice), although the cadence is unlike Schubert's and the tempo and atmosphere more hectic; given the miller lad's assertion of reciprocated love, one can understand how the

Example 27a Leopold Lenz. "Mein," mm. 1–19, from the *Fünf Gesänge*, op. 25. Munich: J. Aibl, n.d.

musical recollection of this passage from another song altogether might have occurred (Exx. 27a and 27b). When Lenz's miller returns to the A section at the end, he becomes even more exultant; the mammoth, *fortissimo* Neapolitan harmony at the verb "erschalle"[44] in mm. 85–86 and the high As – even a high C sharp! – at the end are emphatic indeed.

Schubert's "Der Neugierige" is so exquisite that it is impossible to hear other settings without making invidious and involuntary mental comparisons, but other versions *do* exist, one of them rather successful on its own, very different terms: Louis Dames's sixth song in the *Lieder und Gesänge*, op. 3 (Berlin: Bote & Bock, [183–?]).[45] Dames's miller tunes his song from the beginning to the "flowing brook figuration" so readily suggested by sixteenth-note broken-chordal patterns, unlike the more halting phrases – broken by pauses – in which Schubert's miller muses on the matter before turning to the brook in stanza 3 ("O Bächlein meiner Liebe"). But Dames's lighter song nonetheless has many felicities, even a chain-of-thirds succession by which the A major of the beginning is fol-

Example 27b Franz Schubert, "Im Freien," D. 880, op. 80, no. 3, mm. 65–74, to a text by Johann Gabriel Seidl. From Franz Schubert, *Neue Schubert-Ausgabe*, Series IV: *Lieder*, vol. 4a, ed. Walther Dürr, p. 14. Kassel & Basel: Bärenreiter Verlag, 1979.

lowed, first, by a darkening to relative minor for the repeated lines "Will ja nur eines wissen, / Ein Wörtchen um und um" (I want to know just one thing, one little word, over and over again) and then by a passage in D major at "Ja heisst das eine Wörtchen, das and're heisset Nein" (One word is Yes, the other is No). The latter ends by merging into a chromatically dyed, passionate, eight-measure proclamation, "Die beiden Wörtchen schliessen die ganze Welt mir ein" (The two little words contain the whole world for me), filled with martellato repeated pitches and full-textured chords en route back to tonic A major and a variation of the music for stanzas 1 and 2 at the close – he even veers into borrowed C major chords for the "wunderlich" (odd) brook and the anxious assurance "Will's ja nicht weiter sagen" (I'll tell no one else). Dames, one notices, subdivides Müller's stanzas into musical sections differently from Schubert. At the end, Dames's miller sings "liebt sie mich" over and over again, pressing for an answer that does not come, no matter how he prolongs, twists, heightens, and colors the words; even the quasi-declarative statement to an authentic cadence at the close is tinged with chromatic doubt and unresolved longing (Ex. 28).

Of the generation of German opera composers after Carl Maria von Weber, Heinrich Marschner is among the most prominent, his *Hans Heiling* and *Der Vampyr* cited in all the history books. However, his sizeable lieder output is virtually unknown (singers, pianists, and dissertation students, take note), which seems a shame: he was a prolific and skillful song composer. His *Sechs Lieder*, op. 61, includes settings of "Wanderschaft" and "Morgengruß" (nos. 1 and 3 respectively) from *Die schöne Müllerin*, as well as settings of two other poems by Müller ("Abendreihn" and "Frühlingsgruß" – although "Abendreihn" is not from the mill songs, this charmingly pawkish dialogue between a

155

Example 28 Louis Dames. "Der Neugierige," mm. 56–84, from the *Lieder und Gesänge*, op. 3, no. 6. Berlin: Bote & Bock, n.d.

lover and the moon is the best song of the set). The strophic "Wanderschaft" is especially attractive, a seeming cross-fertilization of Schubert's G major brook-figuration in "Wohin?" with Marschner's own music, such as the chromatic impulsion beneath the words "dem niemals fiel das Wandern ein" in mm. 9–10, a compelling way to under-score the lad's sense of compulsion. For each of the refrains at the end of Müller's

Example 29 Heinrich Marschner. "Wanderschaft," mm. 1–18, from the *Sechs Lieder*, op. 61, no. 1. Halberstadt: C. Brüggemann, n.d.

stanzas, with their merrily ritualistic naming of the mill's elements framed on either side by the invocation of wandering ("Das Wandern . . . Das Wasser . . . Die Räder . . . Die Steine . . . und wandern"), Marschner devises a simple but lovely melisma, elongating the ritual words in a graphic demonstration of how wandering culminates in song (Ex. 29). Similarly, his setting of "Morgengruß" seems a cross-fertilization of Schubert's "Des Müllers Blumen" (how interesting that influence can thus play leap-frog in the unconscious, shifting from one song to another poetic text in the same cycle), the rising A major arpeggiation at the beginnings of these two songs closely akin.

CONCLUSION

This Whitman's Sampler of lieder from the first half of the nineteenth century represents only a minute fraction of the pool from which one could choose – there was not even room for the complete *Die schöne Müllerin* repertoire. While it is undeniable that none of the songs visited here could jostle for position in the same circle of Paradise as Schubert's D. 795, they nevertheless have much to tell latter-day listeners; they are a window onto poetic vogues in song composition (fashionable poets of one decade dethroned in favor of a younger generation and different styles), onto spheres of influence rippling outwards from one generation to the next or from teacher to student, onto critical reception, and changing aesthetics of song. And they are often charming or even beautiful; if some of these composers were respected in their day, it was with reason, and we can hear those reasons resonating in their best lieder.

But charm is not profundity. Müller wrote his share of sentimental effusions; when a conservative late-Romantic composer like Wilhelm Stade sets this poet's "Das Veilchen" (The Violet – Müller taking on Goethe once again?) in a full-blown Romantic style, one nods approval (this is a lovely song, with just the right amount of *Schwärmerei* and no more),[46] but *Die schöne Müllerin* is a different matter, and most composers simply "didn't get it." For example, the "Affettuoso" setting of "Trockne Blumen" from Carl Hering's *Vier Lieder*, op. 1 misses the point entirely; this overheated, under-inspired lied, with its chugging repeated chords, suggests nothing of the poem's strangeness, of the various neurotic ploys at work in the words. Müller, who was, I believe, quite cognizant of the mythic dimensions of his subject, gave them full reign in his version of an old tale; he might even have sought, in competition with Goethe, to restore older resonances to legends that had become the stuff of light opera in the previous century. What his story has to say about human nature, as with most myths about human existence, is deeply disturbing, but the other composers drawn to these mill poems to a man either did not see or expunged from their music all traces of the poetry's dark depths as the work plunges into tragedy. Only Schubert plumbed those depths, and even he shied away from the nethermost abysses. How and why he did so are the subjects of the final chapter.

Chapter 4

"Lilies that fester": sex and death in Müller's and Schubert's cycles

The cover artist for the April 1909 issue of a popular American music educators' journal entitled *The Etude* imagined the composer sitting on a rustic bench by a millstream, the mill itself visible in the background and the whole depicted in an appropriately aqueous gray-green (Fig. 12). The nattily attired composer is portrayed with pen and staff paper in hand, although he is not writing anything down but rather staring reflectively at something beyond the picture frame; lest we miss the all-too-obvious point, the caption tells us, "SCHUBERT composing 'The Maid of the Mill.'" The temptation to chuckle at the naive pairing of life and art – and people once looked for mills that Schubert might have visited – is mitigated at second glance by the perception that perhaps the composer really was inspired by personal experience, not of external objects and places but of the miller lad's inner world. Schubert, I would guess, saw in *Die schöne Müllerin* something he knew all too well, an experience whose molten core had recently engulfed him as well as the mythical character in his first cycle: the discovery that sex can bring death. The words of this cycle were not Schubert's words, and song cycle is far from autobiography; nonetheless, it is surely plausible that vicissitudes in a composer's own life might account in part for the attraction to a particular text – and these were the gravest of vicissitudes.

Most scholars now are rightly dissatisfied with attempts to account for art by means of biography; it is, they feel, an ideological offense to "explain" a complicated artistic phenomenon by reducing it to something in the artist's calendar of days. Minds can and do roam beyond the boundaries of their own time, place, and culture, whatever the indelible stamp of those unchosen, uncontrollable factors, and artists as a matter of their vocation must practice inhabiting other mentalities, other voices, other lives not their own. Where a composer chooses poetry by someone else, the matter would seem even more Byzantine and less amenable to biographical reductionism. But neither, I believe, is the choice of poetry-for-music entirely disinterested, founded solely upon aesthetic grounds and divorced entirely from the composer's life, loves, prejudices, beliefs, and experiences, however circuitous the connection might be. Although many details of the genesis and chronology of *Die schöne Müllerin* are shrouded in mystery, we know that the composition of this cycle coincides with Schubert's discovery that he had a sexually contracted fatal disease. Despite the burgeoning polemics about Schubert's sexual orientation, his preferences one way or another seem less important, certainly from

159

Figure 12 "SCHUBERT composing 'The Maid of the Mill'" from *The Etude*, April 1909.

1823 onward, than the fact of death lurking in the wings. That he was drawn at that very moment to a work in which Eros leads to death and near-madness looms as one goes deeper into the cycle seems hardly coincidental. If there is nothing in the poetic cycle that specifically invokes syphilis or the situation (whatever it was) that led to Schubert's infection, that is hardly necessary. The emotions aroused by the discovery that love unlocks monsters in the mind and that sex can be the cause of one's own death are surely akin whether that death is self-inflicted or the result of disease.

Whatever the Biedermeier *Gemütlichkeit* wrongly draped over Schubert's cycle, the poetic text is actually a horrifying exploration of erotic obsession not to be prettified or more than lightly veiled by the rustic guises Müller adopts; the sexual jealousy which pervades the last half of the cycle – voyeuristic impulses, rape fantasies, jealous rages, panic-stricken desperation – blots out the country costumes and lyrical landscape. (Such *Gemütlichkeit* was always largely a lie, a mask behind which the grim economic and social facts of life in *Vormärz* Austria were thinly concealed.) The discovery of Eros's treachery, the way it metes out betrayal and death, overwhelms the poetic protagonist, throwing him into a cauldron of uncontrollable, kaleidoscopic emotions welling up from depths hitherto unknown; from the little we know of the Schubert chronicle in early to mid-1823, we can sense that he too was overwhelmed by despair born of a kindred experience. If betrayal took the form of disease rather than abandonment, the root cause, in life as in literature, was sex, and the ultimate result would be the same: death. Of all the poetic material Schubert might have found at the time, this seems horribly germane.

Müller too knew the depths of delusory love and loss by heart; he may, again speaking speculatively, have woven some trace-elements of his own love for Luise Hensel, his own discoveries of what love can do, into the later revision of the *Liederspiel* as a monodrama. His silence on the subject of Luise after the last diary-entry suggests someone too hurt to continue a document dedicated to dreams of a life with her; since we know that she reproached Brentano for bruiting it about Berlin that his (Brentano's) love for her was reciprocated, one can imagine that Müller might have heard the rumors and felt betrayed. *Die schöne Müllerin* is, in one summation, the tale of a youth horrified to discover what abysmal creatures the heart can spawn; unable to silence the tape-loop of hideous images in the mind, he silences himself forever, his art no consolation, no escape from the mental turmoil engendered by eroticism gone wrong. At the end, the former songs of courtship and hope are no longer possible, and the "new songs" are unbearable; abdicating art and life altogether, the lad consigns singing to nature and dies. His creator was luckier: he may speculatively have found solace from his own disappointment in love by means of travel (he visited Austria in 1817 and then went to Italy for more than a year) and literary work, including a revision of the poetry he wrote when he too was under the spell of romantic-poetic fantasy. In that revision, Müller makes of the jealousy his fictive miller lad undergoes something far blacker and bleaker than before, its degrading invasion of the mind portrayed in full; he does not shrink from the depiction of a soul blasted by sexual furies born when illusions are destroyed. If the illusions are sketched through allusions taken from literature, from a skillful pot-au-feu of Goethe, Minnesong, folk song, myth, and much else, the disillusionment is true to life – perhaps his own in particular and human nature in general.

But if Müller did not back away from the abyss, the composer who understood him best does. It is, paradoxically, a healthier creature ("health" a relative term in this context) who kills himself at the end of D. 795. If Schubert's miller still succumbs to suicidal depression, he does not arrive at death's door by the same pitch-black path that Müller's miller travels, does not descend as far into the abysses of his own mind as his poetic counterpart. We have already seen in chapter 3 that the Berger–Müller collaboration resulted in a more melancholy ending to "Des Baches Wiegenlied" than the one Schubert devised some six years later – and the *Liederspiel* and *Gesänge* precede those poems that would render the monodrama even bleaker than the song-play. In order to emend the poet's final transmutation of the mill poems, to turn his music along gentler paths, Schubert resorted both to omission and to compositional decisions that subvert and even contradict the poet's meanings. The composer's first and most drastic emendation of the poetic source is his omission of three lengthy poems from the body of the narrative: Müller's seventh poem, "Das Mühlenleben" (Life at the Mill), which occurs between "Der Neugierige" and "Ungeduld"; the seventeenth poem "Erster Schmerz, letzter Scherz" (First Sorrow, Last Jest), which comes after "Eifersucht und Stolz" and is followed by "Die liebe Farbe"; and the twentieth poem, "Blümlein Vergißmein" (Little Forget-me Flower), placed between "Die böse Farbe" and "Trock'ne Blumen." One guesses that Müller perhaps did not expect composers to set the lengthy prologue and epilogue framing his lyrical cycle (would he have wanted them read aloud? or perhaps performed as melodramas, with spoken text and musical background?), but the omission of approximately one-sixth of the monodrama itself is another matter. Although Schubert had no compunctions about editing his chosen texts, it is one thing to alter words and phrases here and there, or even to delete stanzas, and quite another to consign entire poems to the cutting-room floor.

Why Schubert did so, we shall never know with any certainty, but it was not because they are superfluous to the narrative and could be excised with impunity, as some commentators have stated. On the contrary, these are three of the most important poems in the work, especially the last of them. "Das Mühlenleben," after all, is crucial to an understanding of the virgin-whore dichotomy that is a central theme in *Die schöne Müllerin*; it is in this poem that the miller lad describes his beloved at length as an almost saintly figure, a rustic version of a Beatrice-like *inspiratrice* who is a civilizing force in the mill's small society and the impetus for song. The increasing savagery with which he excoriates her later in the cycle depends for its full effect upon contrast with this Minnesong-inspired depiction of her as being "almost like the eye of God." The other two poems Schubert omitted likewise tell the reader of stages in this narrative of psychological breakdown and episodes of mental turbulence not found elsewhere: it is in "Erster Schmerz, letzter Scherz" that masochistic despair sets in, while "Blümlein Vergißmein" shows the lad on the verge of madness, lacerating himself in a frenzy of sexual rage that breaks him utterly – these two works are almost unbearable to read. In particular, "Blümlein Vergißmein" is the moment of peripeteia in the cycle, the culmination of a desperate crescendo and the poem which makes the lad's suicide explicable, even anti-climactic. And yet, Schubert omits it.

Previous scholars (including the present writer) have not perhaps indulged in sufficient speculation about the reason for these omissions and their effect on the cycle, nor have the potent absences been connected to compositional decisions Schubert made in the poems he *did* set to music. Because these are the three longest poems in the poetic cycle, Richard Capell speculated that length may have been a factor in Schubert's decision to leave them out, while Ruth Bingham has suggested that Schubert may simply have disliked the poems, without wondering why.[1] Both of these scholars may be right to a degree, although Schubert had set poems much longer than these and would do so again. Dislike of the cloying vision of idealized feminine saintliness in "Das Mühlenleben" and the self-flagellation of the latter two poems is understandable, but there should and must be reasons for dislike that leads to the excision of essential material (and I find it hard to believe that Schubert would not have recognized the purposes these three poems serve in the whole cycle). A composer's reasons would surely have to do with his reading of the work for musical setting; where the words are not congruent with his vision of the music, this would constitute more valid grounds for omission than length alone, grounds not necessarily for "dislike" – one can admire something and yet find it unusable – but for rejection. Earlier, I speculated that Schubert, by excising "Das Mühlenleben," limits the miller maid's appearances to a few brief lines and thereby suggests more strongly that the miller's love is "almost entirely the product of his own longing, with little nourishment in reality,"[2] but I now believe that at least two of the poems were omitted in order to mitigate the sexual ugliness of the final stages before death (reality indeed) and to endow the composer's protagonist with a greater measure of balance and beauty at the end than the poet's more tragic protagonist. Ultimately, poet and composer have different things to say about the twinship of Death and Eros.

Why Schubert excised these poems is anyone's guess. Could the censorship have affected, or even impelled, his decision in the matter? It was, after all, at this time that Schubert was working with Josef Kupelwieser on the composition of *Fierrabras* and would have had the censors much on his mind; both self-censorship on Kupelwieser's part and minor alterations commanded by the censors entered into play. Even if the censors either did not notice or did not object to Müller's sexual frankness in these poems, Schubert might have worried about the reception of his planned cycle, for which he clearly desired a great success, perhaps hoping that critics and musicians alike would notice the transformation of the earlier, simpler song cycle into a complex work of great length and profound substance. The fact that he composed *Die schöne Müllerin* in the early months after he had discovered the nature of his affliction and his abbreviated future also makes one wonder whether the revisions have their origins in a creator's first shocked responses to intimations of mortality, his world turned to gall in an instant: did he want his miller (like Schubert himself, a "singer of songs"), dying for love, to have a more beautiful death (Vienna and its "schöne Leiche" cult comes to mind) than the poet's miller? Perhaps, but I believe there was more at stake than the habiliments of death or even necessary and practical considerations of the censors' powers of obstruction. Before we can hazard a guess why, we must turn to Müller's poems and see just what it was that Schubert rejected.

THE POET SHOWS HIS HAND: MÜLLER'S PROLOGUE AND EPILOGUE

People had, of course, noticed that five of the poet's pieces were unaccounted for in Schubert's setting and, on occasion, put them back, either as musical interpolations in someone else's settings ("insertion arias" of a sort) or as recitations by actors. At a performance in Vienna of Schubert's complete song cycle with the great singer Julius Stockhausen in 1860, possibly the first public performance of the entire work, a well-known actress named Pauline Rettich declaimed the prologue and epilogue as part of the concert; interestingly, Eduard Hanslick, who reviewed the occasion, does not mention the other three omitted poems in his withering condemnation of Müller's "scarecrows in verse," possibly the first salvo in the war on Müller's reputation among musicians.[3] Did Rettich, one wonders, also declaim the three omitted poems (and if so, how interesting to observe that a *woman* was chosen to be the voice of "The Poet" and the miller lad at his most desperate)? If Stockhausen and Rettich confined their efforts at restoration to the prologue and epilogue only, had they balked at the awkwardness of interpolating readings between songs (it is far less awkward to "frame" the musical cycle in readings at the beginning and end), or did they perhaps quail at the content of "Erster Schmerz, letzter Scherz" and "Blümlein Vergißmein"? Stockhausen did not, it seems, consider that Schubert might have wished certain poems deleted because they were dissonant with his musical purposes; there is an admirable but skewed fidelity to both the composer and the poet evident in the famous singer's determination to perform the whole musical cycle and, perhaps, the whole poetic cycle as well. We know furthermore that the deleted poems were read elsewhere, for other performances of D. 795 in the nineteenth century: what, one wonders, was the audience's reaction?

To understand the difference between Müller's cycle and Schubert's, one must know these five poems, although few people nowadays would recommend their inclusion in Schubert's setting – they are not part of the *musical* cycle. In "Der Dichter, als Prolog" (The Poet, as Prologue), the poet reminds us of his control, his primacy; his badge of identification as "The Poet" precedes mention in the title of what kind of poem this is. Here, he seems to show his hand (the crucial word is "seems"), adopting an ironic, distanced stance from his own creation and "revealing" that this is art, not life – Müller, like his friend Ludwig Tieck, practices Romantic irony and meditates, with theatrical flare, on the paradoxical nature of reality and art. If the listeners are thus insulted by implication as too stupid to figure this out on their own, they are also thereby invited to wonder why such disingenuous disavowals are necessary and what purpose they serve. The sarcasm is laid on with a trowel: this master-of-ceremonies, who ostentatiously flatters his audience as "lovely" (the women) and "clever" (the men), derides his chosen subject matter as rustic stuff but congratulates himself at length on his skill in making something brand-new out of these country matters; the rhyming couplets in Shakespearean iambic pentameters are perfectly apropos for this demonstration of how artful he conceitedly considers himself to be. Like a combination of carnival huckster and egotistical author, he assures the "audience" that the "play" is in the very latest style; the repeated jawbreaker of an adjective "funkelnagelneu" is comic in its very sound. Listing all of the attractions of his new work in order to entice the playgoers/readers inside and keep them there, the poet cites its open-air *mise-en-scène* and *echt* Germanic nature, conceived, he says, as family entertainment; that this is a trap and a trick, a lure concocted by someone who knows that simplistic patriotism and the pablum deemed suitable for home and hearth sell well, is not yet apparent, although the very tone of the poem should be a warning that its speaker cannot be trusted.

In the midst of this introductory hucksterism, Müller, a political poet scathingly critical of the Metternich regime and its anti-liberal repression of writers, sneaks in what may well be a sly political reference. His 1816 anthology *Die Bundesblüthen* had come under fire from the censors because the authors (Müller had banded together with four friends, including Wilhelm Hensel, to write this volume) had used the word "Freiheit" in the dedicatory poem; here, Müller pointedly repeats "Im *Freien* . . . die *freie* Handlung" in a context to which no censor could reasonably object.

Der Dichter, als Prolog

Ich lad euch, schöne Damen, kluge Herrn,
Und die ihr hört und schaut was Gutes
    gern,
Zu einem funkelnagelneuen Spiel
Im allerfunkelnagelneusten Stil;
Schlicht ausgedrechselt, kunstlos
    zugestutzt,
Mit edler deutscher Roheit aufgeputzt,
Keck wie ein Bursch im Stadtsoldatenstrauß,
Dazu wohl auch ein wenig fromm für's
    Haus:
Das mag genug mir zur Empfehlung sein,
Wem die behagt, der trete nur herein.
Erhoffe, weil es grad ist Winterzeit,
Tut euch ein Stündlein hier im Grün nicht
    leid;
Denn wißt es nur, daß heut in meinem Lied
Der Lenz mit allen seinen Blumen blüht.
Im Freien geht die freie Handlung vor,
In reiner Luft, weit von der Städte Tor,
Durch Wald und Feld, in Gründen, auf dem
    Höhn;
Und was nur in vier Wänden darf
    geschehn,
Das schaut ihr halb durch's offne Fenster an,
So ist der Kunst und euch genug getan.

Doch wenn ihr nach des Spiels Personen
So kann ich euch, den Musen sei's geklagt,
Nur *eine* präsentieren recht und echt,
Das ist ein junger blonder Müllersknecht.
Denn, ob der Bach zuletzt ein Wort auch
    spricht,
So wird ein Bach deshalb Person noch nicht.
Drum nehmt nur heut das Monodram vorlieb:

The Poet, as Prologue

I invite you, lovely ladies, clever gentlemen,
and those who gladly hear and watch
    something good,
to a brand-new play
in the absolutely newest style:
unpretentiously shaped, artlessly adapted to
    the stage,
decked out with noble German roughness,
saucy as a militia man with his decorations
    and badges of rank,
but a bit pious too, as befits the family circle.
That is perhaps enough for me to recommend
to whomever it pleases to just come in.
I hope, since it is just now wintertime,
you won't regret spending a little time here in
    Nature.
Know that today in my song,
spring blooms in all its floral splendor.
The unfettered plot proceeds in the open air,
in the pure air, far from the cities' gates,
through forest and open country, in the fields,
    in the hills;
and what only dare take place within four
    walls,
you half see through the open window.
Thus, enough is done for art and you.

But if you ask about the characters of the play,
I can only – let the Muses be blamed for it –
present one to you fairly and honestly:
that is a young, blond miller's boy.
Even though the brook does finally say a word
    or two,
it does not therefore become a character.
Today just make do with monodrama:

Wer mehr gibt, als er hat, der heißt ein Dieb.
Auch ist dafür die Szene reich geziert,
Mit grünem Sammet unten tapeziert,
Der ist mit tausend Blumen bunt gestickt,
Und Weg und Steg darüber ausgedrückt.
Die Sonne strahlt von oben hell herein
Und bricht in Tau und Tränen ihren Schein,
Und auch der Mond blickt aus der Wolken
    Flor
Schwermütig, wie's die Mode will, hervor.
Den Hintergrund umkränzt ein hoher Wald,
Der Hund schlägt an, das muntre Jagdhorn
    schallt;
Hier stürzt vom schroffen Fels der junge
    Quell
Und fließt im Tal als Bächlein silberhell;
Das Mühlrad braust, die Werke klappern
    drein,
Man hört die Vöglein kaum im nahen Hain.
Drum denkt, wenn euch zu rauh manch
    Liedchen klingt,
Daß das Lokal es also mit sich bringt.
Doch, was das Schönste bei den Rädern ist,
Das wird euch sagen mein Monodramist;
Verriet' ich's euch, verdürb' ich ihm das
    Spiel:
Gehabt euch wohl und amüsiert euch viel![4]

he who gives more than he has is called a thief.
The scene is also richly adorned,
hung below with green velvet,
brightly embroidered with a thousand flowers,
and printed over with road and path.
Here, the sun shines brightly above,
her light refracted in dew and tears.
And the moon, too, peers out from behind a
    gauzy veil of clouds,
melancholy, as fashion demands.
A high forest encircles the background,
the dog barks, a cheerful hunting horn rings
    out;
here, the stream at its source plunges down
    from the steep cliff
and flows in the valley as a silvery-bright little
    brook;
the mill-wheels roar, the machinery clatters
    within.
One can scarcely hear the little birds in the
    nearby grove.
Consider, if many a little song sounds too
    rough and unpolished to you,
that it belongs to the locale.
Yet what is most beautiful about the mill-
    wheels,
my monodramist will tell you.
If I say any more, I would spoil the play for him:
make yourselves comfortable and amuse
    yourselves greatly!

All of the accoutrements of the Romantic landscape are present and accounted for: velvety grass, a *mille fleurs* dazzlement of flowers (Müller himself compares the "backdrop" to a tapestry), the sun seen through tears, the moon fashionably veiled in clouds, a waterfall, a single little bird in a nearby grove, the high forest, barking dog, and hunting horn necessary for the hunter's appearance, and the clattering mill. This is all, he insists over and over, the product of artistry, an assembled and perfected confabulation of words arranged in a style chosen for its suitability to the subject and its fashionable appeal. Even the limitation to a single speaking character is the fault of the Muses, he declares grandiloquently; he would be dishonest otherwise, a "thief" who stole from others. (This is Müller tweaking himself for what would have been obvious to the *literati*: that he was, in fact, an unabashed thief who had stolen his subject matter from none other than Goethe.) The speciousness of the excuse for his choice of mono-drama as a medium is obvious, the contempt for an audience that would "buy" the excuse palpable, but implicit in the statement that he can only present one character "fairly and honestly" is – perhaps – a hint of self-revelation. This, he seems to say by way of innuendo, is the only "slice of life" in this traditional subject that I know fully and completely; the "young, blond miller's boy" just might be, he hints, me in disguise.

Certainly the real-life poet plays on his own name over and over again in the body of the cycle, from the first line of the first song onward ("Das Wandern ist *des Müllers* Lust").

It would seem that the reader is directed to take none of this artifice seriously, but the irony is Janus-faced. The poet's pride in the virtuosity with which he has assembled all of the requisite elements – it takes him considerable time and space merely to enumerate them all – culminates in the statement that there is something even more beautiful "bei den Rädern" that will be the miller lad's prerogative to narrate. Like an earlier Pirandello, he both acknowledges that his creation is something other than himself, a "person" with his own rights and privileges, his own voice, his own "life," and yet states that it is he, the poet, who has supplied the properly rough, *echt Deutsch* folkloric style for the songs to follow. Furthermore, he claims credit for the monodramist as his creation: "*mein* Monodramist," he proudly proclaims. But, astute salesman that he is, he does not reveal the grim nature of the story to follow. He even lies, by implication, if not forthrightly: the cycle may be "a bit pious" in the miller lad's adoration of the maid as a "Herrin," a Virgin Mary-like goddess, but nothing else of piety is detectable. He even hints lubriciously that a certain spicy naughtiness is forthcoming when he promises that we can peek through a "half-open window" at what should normally take place only within four walls, a readily comprehensible leering innuendo. But the full truth is withheld; at the end of his peroration, he even bids the audience "make yourselves comfortable and amuse yourselves greatly!" "Amüsieren"? At a performance of *Die schöne Müllerin?* This is a poet with a sadistic streak who takes pleasure in luring readers into an idyllic milieu and a traditional scenario for the purpose of harrowing their feelings. If they are not prepared to be thus harrowed, all the better – and all the better, perhaps, to deceive the censors as well. Awareness of censorship, attempts at circumlocution around it, and defiance of it are perhaps a red thread throughout the genesis of both the poetic and the musical cycles, possibly prompting poet and composer to differing strategies in response to the same inescapable obstacle. Were this in fact one element of Müller's strategy in the prologue, that would only deepen enjoyment of the irony for those "in the know."

"Der Dichter" clearly enjoys being in charge, and it is inconceivable that he would not demand the last word as his prerogative. When the story is over, the poet returns to the "crowded room" (the implicit self-congratulation that he has kept everyone riveted to their chairs for the entire length of the cycle is comic) in "Der Dichter, als Epilog" (The Poet, as Epilogue), ostensibly for the sake of symmetry and round numbers, to complain that he has been upstaged by the brook, who is, of course, his own creation, as he is Müller's creation – authorial presences keep appearing one behind another like different images in a hall of mirrors. The pathos, beauty, and majestic vision of the rising moon in "Des Baches Wiegenlied" are indeed a hard act to follow, and the poet, pretending a fit of pique, does so by deriding the brook for its "funeral oration in damp tones" and its "hollow, water-organ sound," the organ music appropriate for a funeral service transferred to Nature. That such derision has the effect of spurring the reader to even greater awareness of the beauty of his ending is, of course, calculated: this poet makes a practice of displaying his manipulation of the audience openly. (The excuse of "round numbers" may be feeble, but it is also yet another display of the poet's consciousness of his job: it is his duty to be aware of such things as large-scale form. One notes that he resumes his characteristic iambic pentameters and rhyming couplets from the prologue, also the division into two long parts – no folk-like quatrains or stanzas for him, although the epilogue is shorter than the prologue, properly so: final summations should be pithy.)

Der Dichter, als Epilog

Weil gern man schließt mit einer runden Zahl,
Tret ich noch einmal in den vollen Saal,
Als letztes, fünfundzwanzigstes Gedicht,
Als Epilog, der gern das Klügste
   spricht.
Doch pfuschte mir der Bach ins Handwerk
   schon
Mit seiner Leichenred im nassen Ton.
Aus solchem hohlen Wasserorgelschall
Zieht jeder selbst sich besser die Moral;
Ich geb es auf, und lasse diesen Zwist,
Weil Widerspruch nicht meines Amtes ist.

So hab ich denn nichts lieber hier zu tun,
Als euch zum Schluß zu wünschen, wohl zu
   ruhn.
Wir blasen unsre Sonn und Sternlein aus –
Nun findet euch im Dunkel gut nach Haus,
Und wollt ihr träumen einen leichten Traum,
So denkt an Mühlenrad und Wasserschaum,
Wenn ihr die Augen schließt zu langer Nacht,
Bis es den Kopf zum Drehen euch gebracht.
Und wer ein Mädchen führt an seiner Hand,
Der bittet scheidend um ein Liebespfand,
Und gibt sie heute, was sie oft versagt,
So sei des treuen Müllers treu gedacht
Bei jedem Händedruck, bei jedem Kuß,
Bei jedem heißen Herzensüberfluß:
Geb' ihm die Liebe für sein kurzes Leid
In eurem Busen lange Seligkeit!

The Poet, as Epilogue

Because one likes to close on a round number,
I return once more to the crowded room
for the last and twenty-fifth poem
as epilogue, in which one wants to say the
   wisest things.
But the bungling brook has already meddled
   in my business
with its funeral oration in damp tones.
From such a hollow, water-organ sound,
each had best draw his own moral;
I give up and leave this dispute,
since conflict is not part of my office.

So now I have nothing better to do here
than to bid you, at the close, to rest
   well.
We blow out our sun and stars –
now find your way safely home in the dark.
And should you wish to dream a pleasant
   dream,
then think of the mill-wheel and the foaming
   waters
when you close your eyes for a long night,
until it makes your head swim.
And whoever leads a maiden by the hand
 and begs her in parting for a pledge of love,
and if she gives him today what she often
   denies him,
then faithfully remember the faithful miller
with each squeeze of the hand, with each kiss,
with each fervent heart's excess:
may love grant him, for his brief sorrow,
eternal bliss in your bosom!

One looks at the phrase "nicht meines *Amtes* [italics mine]" and sees Müller taking yet another potshot at the bureaucracy. The poet pretends to throw up his hands and retire *hors de combat*, but not without dismantling the stage; reminding us that all of the props are verbal and that he is the omnipotent word-master, he "blows out the sun and stars," the verb "blasen" a final faint echo of the hunter's horn fanfares. But, heavy-handed director that he is, he does not leave without instructing his audience about how they should receive his work, how they should be affected by it. Once again, he seems to deny that the cycle is a tragedy when he bids the audience think of the mill, should they wish to invite "pleasant dreams," but *these* dreams make one's head spin. ("Spinning," that is, while waltzing, was considered "subversive" by some authorities in Vienna.) The true ending of *Die schöne Müllerin* – a moral which extends the ending of the literary work to a continuation in real life – lies in the way it teaches young men (the "whoever" of stanza 2, line 9 can only be construed as men) to be grateful for reciprocated love, as Müller was doubtless grateful that Adelheid Basedow had returned his affection in 1820 (they were engaged in November and married the next year); Müller, one remembers, added ten poems to his earlier *Liederspiel* poems, including "Der Dichter, als Epilog," possibly in the spring or early summer of 1820. If young men are happy in love and reflect, in their contentment, on the miller's faithfulness, the miller lad too will know "lange Seligkeit" in the hearts of readers. A *lieto fine* is in the readers' power, women as well as men. Despite Müller's ostensible exclusion of women from the "audience" he addresses in the epilogue, they are covertly admonished thereby: *Die schöne Müllerin* belongs among the lengthy list of cautionary tales about the consequences, in death and in hell, when women refuse their lovers (this is a "Ballo delle Ingrate" in lieder). But despite the warmth that surfaces at the end of the Epilogue, the Poet's hopes that his creation will work for good in the world, his distanced, coolly observing stance is entirely unlike the roiling emotional chaos his miller lad undergoes. If Shakespeare explores sexual jealousy and its degrading effect upon the mind, the way in which it leads to suicide, at greater length and with greater power in *Othello*, Müller did not shy away from it, especially in the last of the poems Schubert excluded from the cycle.

REJECTED LOVERS, REJECTED POEMS: THE POETRY SCHUBERT OMITTED

Müller builds up to the shattering climax of the twentieth poem gradually, although premonitory signs of mental distress are evident earlier, as in the first of the song-poems from the body of the narrative that Schubert eliminated: the seventh poem, "Das Mühlenleben" (Life at the Mill). This could, so James Taft Hatfield speculates, belong to the oldest layer of the miller poems because it seems so evidently written under Luise Hensel's influence and, perhaps, modeled on a besotted young man's idealized image of her.[5] Like the fifth poem, "Am Feierabend," the miller maid is depicted amidst the social setting of the mill and all its workers; it is, so the poet implies, the lad's panic-stricken consciousness of rivals all around – if she makes nets, that brings her into contact with fishermen, while work in the fields and garden results in proximity to hunters and gardeners – that perhaps prompts the fit of frenzied impatience in "Ungeduld" just after "Das Mühlenleben."

Das Mühlenleben	**Life at the Mill**
Seh ich sie am Bache sitzen,	I see her sitting by the brook
Wenn sie Fliegennetze strickt	when she knits fly-nets,
Oder Sonntags für die Fenster	or on Sundays when she picks
Frische Wiesenblumen pflückt.	fresh flowers from the fields for the windows.
Seh ich sie zum Garten wandeln,	I see her strolling in the garden
Mit dem Körbchen in der Hand,	with the little basket in her hand,
Nach den ersten Beeren spähen	looking for the first berries
An der grünen Dornenwand:	on the green, thorny wall.

Dann wird mir die Mühle enge,	Then the mill becomes small to me;
Alle Mauern ziehn sich ein,	all the walls close in,
Und ich möchte flugs ein Fischer,	and I would sooner be a fisher,
Jäger oder Gärtner sein.	hunter or gardener.
Und der Steine lustig Pfeifen	And the merry piping of the stones
Und des Wasserrads Gebraus,	and the roaring of the water-wheels
Und der Werke emsig Klappern,	and the busy clattering of the mill-works
's jagt mich schier zum Tor hinaus.	almost drive me straight out to the gate.
Aber wenn in guter Stunde	But when in a pleasant hour,
Plaudernd sie zum Burschen tritt,	chatting, she approaches the lads,
Und als kluges Kind des Hauses	and as the clever child of the house, glances
Seitwärts nach dem Rechten sieht;	around to see that everything is in order;
Und verständig lobt den Einen,	And judiciously praises the one,
Daß der Andre merken mag,	so that the other may take notice
Wie er's besser treiben solle,	how he should strive to work better,
Geht er ihrem Danke nach –	he goes after her praise –
Keiner fühlt sich recht getroffen	No one feels truly hurt,
Und doch schießt sie nimmer fehl[t],	and she never misses.
Jeder muß von Schonung sagen,	Each must speak of her leniency,
Und doch hat sie keinen Hehl.	and yet, she holds nothing back.
Keiner wünscht, sie möchte gehen,	No one wishes that she would leave,
Steht sie auch als Herrin da,	she stands there also as our mistress,
Und fast wie das Auge Gottes	and almost like the eye of God,
Ist ihr Bild uns immer nah.	her image is always nearby us.
Ei, da mag das Mühlenleben,	Then may life at the mill
Wohl des Liedes würdig sein,	be well worthy of the song,
Und die Räder, Stein und Stampfen	and the wheels, stones, and pounding
Stimmen als Begleitung ein.	harmonize in accompaniment.
Alles geht in schönem Tanze	All goes in a beautiful dance,
Auf und ab, und ein und aus:	up and down, and in and out:
Gott gesegne mir das Handwerk	May God bless my handiwork
Und des guten Meisters Haus!	and the good master's house!

In the first edition of the *Waldhornisten-Gedichte*, Müller included as the eighth stanza the following verse:

Und so wer zum Fallen strauchelt	And so whoever stumbles and falls,
Hält es ihn im Sinken schier,	she keeps him from sinking,
Und wo ich die Hände falte,	and where I fold my hands in prayer,
Kniet es still zur Seite mir.	she kneels quietly at my side.

The "es" in line 2 is confusing in this context and without an antecedent. Müller was attempting to demonstrate further the miller's objectification of the miller maid as an icon, a Virgin Mary figure who intercedes for sinners, but he omitted the prayer scene from the second edition in 1826. Its awkwardness may have offended his fastidious craftsman's eye, but, more important, he may also have decided that the reference to "the eye of God" in the next stanza was sufficient religiosity. A lad who prays might be expected to seek religious consolation when secular love deserts him, and Müller perhaps preferred to keep any hint of piety focused on the miller maid, indeed, emanating from her.

Müller re-works chivalric love in costumes from a later day and has his miller lad worship the beloved as a quasi-divine medieval *Herrin*, a curious hybrid of rustic folk-archetype and lordly lady. In stanzas 1 and 2, Müller emphasizes the miller maid's industriousness: she knits fly-nets, picks flowers for the windows, looks for berries to pick (one notices that the tasks have to do with beautifying the home and gathering food, or properly feminine chores). She picks fresh meadow flowers (not hothouse blooms), one notes, on Sundays, the implications of piety unmistakable; in his *Blumenlese aus den Minnesingern*, Müller had translated a poem by one Kristan von Hamle which he (Müller) entitled "An eine Wiese, wo sein Fräulein Blumen gepflückt hatte" (To a Meadow where his Beloved had picked Flowers), and one can perhaps detect traces of this poem both in "Das Mühlenleben" and "Blümlein Vergißmein."[6] In the seventh poem of *Die schöne Müllerin*, the miller maid is a Madonna-of-the-fields who does not shun suitably feminine, light labor, thereby inspiring the men at their more strenuous work (the verb "spähen," "to look," in the second stanza emphasizes the delicacy of her search, as if the miller maid were peering carefully under leaves and thorny branches). The miller lad, one notices, watches her intently whenever she is in view from his station at the mill; her image, he feels, sees him at all times, and he looks at her whenever and wherever he can. This delineation of covert observation, charged with erotic feeling, is a crucial theme in the cycle, increasingly so in the latter stages of the tragedy. The poem is pervaded by sight, by eyes and the act of seeing, especially by the spying gaze: that same gaze will soon sour, becoming a voyeur's stare at images he would banish if he could, but cannot.

It is in "Das Mühlenleben" that one sees most clearly the influence of medieval lyric on this cycle. Müller, who advertised his membership in the Berlin Gesellschaft für Deutsche Sprache (Berlin Society for the German Language) on the title page of his *Blumenlese aus den Minnesingern*, had busied himself in 1815 and early 1816 with these translations of Minnesong verse into modern German: the foreword is dated "Dessau, September 1815," with a postscript to that foreword dated March 1, 1816. The lengthy prefatory remarks – forty-two pages, complete with properly scholarly footnotes – and the annotations at the end of the volume testify to considerable knowledge of Middle High German, albeit neither encyclopedic nor free of flaws, and of the courtly love ethic embodied in Minnesong verse. His interest was avowedly more poetic than philological: he sought, he tells the readers at the beginning of the preface, to make them understand and feel "the old spirit" ("um den alten Geist verstehen und fühlen zu können") and hence, he attempted to translate the inner spirit rather than mere words. Do not be surprised, he counsels, to find some poems in which scarcely a word of the original is to be found (he exaggerates) and others in which only the old orthography is changed.[7] "German women, to you above all I wish to make a not unwelcome gift of my little book," he wrote. "May it become a friendly tutor to acquaint you, in playful instruction, with the customs and speech of that beautiful time that was so full of honor and love for you, so that we might yet richly adorn our miserable world of fashion, with its withered flowers [trock'ne Blumen]," and he hopes to hear "the olden songs, olden melodies, and olden speech" blossom again "on your lips and your harps." That they might be encouraged to do so, he included a *Musikbeilage* at the end of the volume, fold-out folios with two settings of Minnesong poems by his Berlin contemporary Theodor Gäde (1787–1829), a justice minister and composer of songs and piano music:[8] a setting of König Konrad der Junge's "Liebes-Klage im Mai" (King Konrad the Young's "Love-Lament in May") (Müller's title) and der von Kürenberg's "Klage des verlaßnen Fräuleins" (Lament of an Abandoned Maiden). It was in part from Minnesong that Müller found a model for the laments he would soon write, not in the voice of an abandoned maiden but her male counterpart.

In the lyric poetry of the troubadours, trouvères, and Minnesingers, secular love is understood as good because it is involved in a larger life, the life of a society that had a certain ethical mandate; the virtues of steadfastness, restraint, concern for others, and so forth not only work for good within that society but realize a divine intention. The beloved plays a role (and courtly love is in fact a poetic drama played out between the poet-singer, representing a variety of parts, and his audience) in this civilizing ethos by embodying and rewarding the virtues of courtliness, high principles, gentleness, pride, justice, and goodness; she is the ideal, and her knightly servitors strive to attain her degree of goodness and thereby, her notice, her smile, her favors. (Müller carefully uses the verb "merken" in stanza 6 to indicate that all of the mill apprentices pay close heed to every word the maiden speaks.) The pride of the courtly lover lies in controlling lust by allowing it no other object than a lady who is too great for it; he chooses – a conscious decision – to see the lady as the worthiest possible goal of all his striving, although he could, if he wished, see her in a more ordinary light as a carnal creature with whom he desires lovemaking. That it is sexual desire being thus expressed, its molten metal poured into the mold of art and courtly ways, is never in doubt or out of sight for a second.

Like the idealized object of a Minnesinger's love, the miller's daughter is depicted in "Das Mühlenleben" as a civilizing force, and the sight of her as she moves about, praising and gently chastising the mill workers, has the effect of poeticizing the young miller's world, making it "worthy of song." This, Müller knew, was a love possible only in song, not in real experience; it is confined to the space occupied by the singer and the time occupied by the song. Müller's miller in this poem borrows the pose of courtliness (like a hall of mirrors, this is a song within a song within a song) and attempts to see his beloved in an aureole of saintliness, but his equilibrium fails in the attempt. The transforming power she exercises on the miller's emotions is evident in the contradictory ways in which he reacts to the sound of the mill-wheel. In stanzas 3 and 4, the sound is oppressive, and he wants to escape into the open air to be with her; the same claustrophobia, the same overwhelming desire to break his bounds all at once and escape into the open, that one finds earlier in "Am Feierabend" reappears here in even stronger form – this is a psychologically accurate depiction of panic-induced manic motion. Once he has seen her in the role he has assigned to her as Lady Justitia, goddess, beloved, and a muse all rolled into one, the same sounds become dance music, like the sound of the stones and the mill-wheels of "Das Wandern" – if the parallel phrases "auf und ab, und ein und aus" evoke the dance, they are also resonant with barely subsumed sexualized motion. And yet, even as the miller lad hymns the miller maid's praises, he admits that she treats everyone alike – the same admission that has already impelled the outburst of furious, pent-up energy in "Am Feierabend" – and accords him no special notice. He has seen her single out another lad for praise, the reference to "the one" in stanza 6 of "Das Mühlenleben" making it clear that it was not him, but he valiantly attempts to control his desire that she pay attention only to him and, like a true *preux chevalier*, praises her for her ethical effect on the entire little society in which he and she both live. After the claustrophobic fit of suffocating need earlier in the poem, he does in fact overcome, if only temporarily, his lover's wish for exclusivity and sings, as a Minnesinger would, of his lady-saint – a saint he desires to have in his bed. In a telling detail, revelatory of this poet's craftsmanship, Müller uses the language of the hunt, in particular, the verb "schießen," in stanza 7; the lad misinterprets the miller maid's calculated praise of the workers as the language of the hunt and therefore the pursuit of love.

Müller, one guesses, knew – perhaps from his youthful experiences, first with the unknown Thérèse (sex incarnate, one gathers), then with Luise Hensel (sublimated, troubadour-like passion) – that no one can really love in this way: that, in a nutshell, is what lies at the heart of *Die schöne Müllerin*.[9] No object of passion can survive this kind of exaltation, and no human being can thus spiritualize his or her daily desires, at least, not for long and not without a struggle. The medieval poets he read and studied knew it as well; in a poem by Hartmann von Aue which Müller entitled "Der Minnemüde" (One Weary of Love – *courtly* love), the singer declares that from now on, he will pass the time "mit armen wiben,"[10] with poor women rather than "ritterliche frowen," or knightly ladies, because then his heart will have free rein. "What use is too high a goal?" ("Was taugt ein allzuhohes Ziel?"), he asks in disgust. (Luise, one remembers, particularly liked Hartmann's *Der arme Heinrich*.) Even more telling, in Bernart de Ventadorn's famous poem "Can vei la lauzeta mover" (When I see the Lark moving), the lover-singer whose lady has proven herself to have a carnal side both excoriates her, declaring his fear and mistrust of all women, and yet admits his continuing desire for her. That, of course, is the trap: self-hatred and helpless fury come into being when desire is unmasked as having little or nothing to do with high-minded ideals and everything to do with sexual carnality.

Can vei la lauzeta mover	**When I see the Lark moving**
(stanzas 3–5)	
Anc non agui de me poder	I have never had the power of myself,
ni no fui meus de l'or' en sai	I have not been my own man since that
que·m laisset en sos olhs vezer	moment
en un miralh que mout me plai.	when she let me look into her eyes,
Miralhs, pus me mirei en te,	into a mirror that gives great pleasure, even
m'an mort li sospir de preon,	now.
c'aissi·m perdei com perdet se	Mirror, since I beheld myself in you,
lo bels Narcisus en la fon.	the sighs from my depths have slain me,
	and I have lost myself, as fair Narcissus
	lost himself in the fountain.
De las domnas me dezesper;	I give up all hope in women.
je mais en lor no·m fiarai;	I shall not put my faith in them again;
c'aissi com las solh chaptener,	as much as I used to hold them up,

173

enaissi las deschaptenrai.	now I shall let them fall,
Pois vei c'una pro no m'en te	because I do not see one who is of any use to me
vas leis que m destrui e·m cofon,	
totas las dopt' e las mescre,	with her, who destroys me and brings me down.
car be sai c'atretals se non.	I shall fear and distrust them all,
	because they are all alike, I know it well.
D'aisso's fa be femna parer	This is how she shows herself a woman indeed,
ma domna, per qu'e·lh o retrai,	
car no vol so c'om voler,	my lady, and I reproach her for it;
e so c'om li deveda, fai.[11]	she does not want what one ought to want,
	and what she is forbidden to do, she does.

Müller does something very interesting with his compound of *hôhe Minne* and *nidere Minne* à la Walther von der Vogelweide: in the Minnesong repertoire, it is only lordly ladies who have tutelary power, who attract fruitless devotion and voluntary anguish from their poet-minstrels, but Müller assigns the same educative, spiritual qualities, directed to the betterment of the social order, to a lower-class woman. In Walther's songs of *nidere Minne*, the "vrowelîn" (maiden) has no moral dimension, for all her unspoiled charm, and she is readily available for lovemaking, like some small, gentle animal in the field. The poet who leads his lower-class beloved to a bed of roses must thereafter wonder about the moral substance of his lovely girl. There are no ennobling obstacles to overcome in winning her, and she does not provide, by the example of her conduct, an ennobling ideal to impel transformation for the better in the knight who woos her. In fact, she (indeed, all such pure pleasure untempered by conscience) can only exist in song; this is yet another instance of the self-conscious artificiality and artistry of the secular lyric in the Middle Ages. The medieval poets remind one constantly that they are singers, that what they do is perform for an audience, that the love they hymn is unreal and belongs to the realm of music and verse – this is precisely the function of Müller's "Der Dichter" in the prologue and epilogue. Müller has his miller lad at first impose a courtly ethos on a rustic beloved and then, even more violently than Bernart, shows how bitter, how deep, how destructive the aftermath can be when the beloved does not play the role assigned to her by the singer-poet. The punishment for deviation from the mind's ideal is severe, not so much for the woman they lash with whips made out of words but for the singer-poet who made her up in the first place.

Just as Müller had connected the third and fourth poems in the narrative, "Halt!" and "Danksagung an den Bach," by the repeated question to the brook, "War es also gemeint?" (Is this what you meant?), so he links his sixteenth poem, "Eifersucht und Stolz," with its successor, "Erster Schmerz, letzter Scherz," by their shared images of a solitary miller sitting on the river bank, singing and playing a reed pipe for "the children." The "children" are those childish enough, as he once was, to place their credence in the myths of love one hears in songs, childish enough to believe that love lasts. The title bespeaks corrosive self-mockery even before the poem begins, an echo of the "Liederscherz" invoked in "Pause," but the mockery quickly modulates to misery.

174

Erster Schmerz, letzter Scherz	**First Sorrow, Last Joke**

Nun sitz am Bache nieder
Mit deinem hellen Rohr,
Und blas den lieben Kindern
Die schönen Lieder vor.

Die Lust ist ja verrauschet
Das Leid hat immer Zeit:
Nun singe neue Lieder
Von alter Seligkeit.

Noch blühn die alten Blumen,
Noch rauscht der alte Bach,
Es scheint die liebe Sonne
Noch wie am ersten Tag.

Die Fensterscheiben glänzen
Im klaren Morgenschein,
Und hinter den Fensterscheiben
Da sitzt die Liebste mein.

Ein Jäger, ein grüner Jäger,
Der liegt in ihrem Arm –
Ei, Bach, wie lustig du rauschest!
Ei, Sonne, wie scheinst du so warm!

Ich will einen Strauß dir pflücken,
Herzliebste, von buntem Klee,
Den sollst du mir stellen ans Fenster,
Damit ich den Jäger nicht seh.

Ich will mit Rosenblättern
Den Mühlensteg bestreun:
Der Steg hat mich getragen
Zu dir, Herzliebste mein!

Und wenn der stolze Jäger
Ein Blättchen mir zertritt,
Dann stürz, o Steg, zusammen
Und nimm den Grünen mit!

Und trag ihn auf dem Rücken
Ins Meer, mit gutem Wind,
Nach einer fernen Insel,
Wo keine Mädchen sind.

Herzliebste, das Vergessen,
Es kommt dir ja nicht schwer –
Willst du den Müller wieder?
Vergißt dich nimmermehr.

Now sit down below at the brook
with your bright reed pipe,
and play beautiful songs
for the dear children.

Joy has truly vanished;
sorrow always has time:
now sing new songs
of bygone happiness.

The same old flowers still bloom,
the same old brook still babbles,
the gentle sun still shines
as it did on the first day.

The window panes sparkle
in the bright morning light,
and behind the window panes
sits my dearest.

A hunter, a green-clad hunter
lies in her arms –
Ah, brook, how merrily you murmur!
Ah, sun, how warmly you shine!

I want to pick a bouquet for you,
beloved, a bouquet of bright clover,
which you should put in the window for me
so that I do not see the hunter.

I want to strew the mill-path
with rose petals:
the path led me to you,
my dearest!

And when the proud hunter
tramples on a single little petal of mine,
then, path, collapse
and take the Green One with you!

And carry him on your back
into the sea, with a strong wind,
to a far-away island
where there are no maidens.

Dearest, forgetting is
not hard for you –
do you want your miller back?
He will never forget you.

This is a song of divided consciousness in which the miller bids the tormented self within to join forces with his poetic self and sing, as poets do, of the past. He too, like the hunter, will be a "musician" and play (the verb "blasen" is the same as that for the

175

hunter's brass instrument), not the horn but the reed pipe, with its clustered classical undertones of satyr-like sex, of Pan, and the masturbatory playing of one's own flute. Despite the poignant tone of the second stanza, with its measured song-like parallelisms ("Die Lust ist ja verrauschet / Das Leid hat immer Zeit" – one notes the inner verb "rauschen" in the first line, with its reminiscence of the brook), the miller in this poem mocks the poet's enterprise of turning life's distress into song as something trite and useless, and yet he can do nothing else. "Aus meinen großen Schmerzen, mach' ich die kleinen Lieder" (From my great sorrows, I make small songs), Heine would sing only a few years later (was he perhaps inspired by this poem?); Müller had already, with ironic intent, entitled this "beautiful song" with the tritest of all rhymes in German ("Schmerz, Scherz" – at least, "Herz" does not appear). But for all his painful irony, he makes a wholly serious observation about the poetic art when he speaks of fashioning poems from the stuff of memories and marvels bitterly at the transformation time brings about without seeming to change anything on the surface. The *mise-en-scène* is just as it was in "Halt!" and in "Mein!" – the same bright sun, the same tableau with the miller maid at her window, but he sees it now with different eyes. "Erster Schmerz, letzter Scherz" is the first of the "neue Lieder" he so feared at the end of "Pause," and now he will sing them.

After stanza 2, the miller veers into near-incoherent distress and self-abasement. The verbal rhythms quicken in stanzas 4 and 5 when the miller first mentions the miller maid and hunter (Müller was adept at manipulating poetic rhythm in accord with the fluctuating emotional content of his verse); in line 3 of stanza 4, an interpolated anapaest among the iambs ("Und hin - *ter den Fen* - sterscheiben") forces anyone reading the poem aloud to go faster. As in "Halt!", the windows of the mill-house gleam in the sunshine, but now as a barrier separating him from the miller maid, whom he imagines in bed with the hunter. (Could Müller have borrowed the motif of the beloved in the window from the Minnesinger Heinrich von Morungen's poem "Sach jeman du frowen," with its initial question "Seht ihr die Fraue, / Nach der ich schaue, / Am Fenster stehn?" Müller also entitled his translation of Herr Walther von Klingen's "Ich sah blumen schone entspringen" as "Fensterklage," or "Lament at her Window."[12]) Unable to bear the pain of sexual jealousy, the miller breaks off in mid-sentence and cries out in torment at the brook's merriment and the sun's warmth – Nature does more than ignore his plight and go its own way, but seems rather a co-conspirator with the hunter and the maiden. (Those cries foreshadow a passage in "Einsamkeit" from *Die Winterreise*, when the wanderer laments that Nature's beauty is at odds with his own misery: "Ach, daß die Luft so ruhig! / Ach, daß die Welt so licht!", or "Oh, that the breeze is so peaceful! Oh, that the world is so bright!") Unable to banish his voyeuristic imaginings, the notably passive miller at first wants the miller maid to blot out the sight, not by ceasing her lovemaking with the hunter – this, he recognizes implicitly, is a fait accompli – but by putting a bouquet of clover in the window, an ironic reversal of the plant's traditional symbolism as a good-luck emblem and possibly yet another borrowing from yet another Minnesong: Herzog Heinrich von Breslau's "Ich clage dir, meie" (I complain to You, May), with its line "Ich klage dir, augenleuchtender Klee." Here, the miller maid's green good fortune is his misery, but in self-lacerating masochism, he still wishes to pay court to her, to give her a lover's bouquet in her new favorite color: green. As in "Der Jäger," the miller knows he cannot compete with this more sexually potent rival and, at first, can only imagine blotting out the sight of him – to the lad himself, not to her – and doing so in a way that will still please his beloved, that will not anger her. Trapped between fury at the hunter and continuing desire for the miller maid, worse yet, the desire that she should take him back, the miller lad concocts psychologically revealing but impossible scenarios in the mind.

If he cannot have what he most desires in actuality, he can write it into being in his song. Stanzas six through nine are a catalogue of desires along a crescendo of increasing violence; from masochistic attempts to ingratiate himself with the beloved who has discarded him, he next envisions magically transporting the hunter to an Elba-like island without women (did Müller possibly have echoes of Napoleon in mind when his miller wishes to exile the hunter to an island?), the only way to neutralize the anarchic sexual prowess of the folkloric Teutonic hunter short of the murder inadmissible to the miller except on the level of symbolic displacement. It is the "path," that transparent symbol for the miller's destiny in life, that will do the deed, not he himself, but one notices that the path is bidden to carry the hunter "ins Meer," not "to the ocean" but "*in the ocean*" – is the path analogous to the brook (brooks, after all, flow into oceans)? Although the lad follows the revealing choice of preposition with another prepositional phrase, "nach einer fernen Insel," making it clear that the hunter survives the imaginary trip to his place of exile, the detail nevertheless tells of murderous desires just barely suppressed. In his island-prison, the hunter cannot trample – the imagery reminiscent of the sexualized "treten" and "wühlen" (trample, root about) invoked at the end of "Der Jäger" – on a single rose petal ("Rose, die Müllerin"); one notices the jealous claim of possession in the word "mir" ("Und wenn der stolze Jäger / Ein Blättchen mir zertritt . . .") and winces. The full-blown rose, especially one with its petals scattered, often symbolizes sexual experience in art and literature (François Boucher, for example, makes frequent use of this imagery of rosebuds for inexperience and full-blown roses for the sexually practiced); when the miller wants to strew the path with petals, he proclaims symbolically his wish to sleep with her in the hunter's place – he knows that this Rose has already scattered her petals, a hint that she has done so with him as well as the hunter. Still miserably in love with her, the lad does not excoriate her for his pain, saying only that "Forgetting comes easily to you": if she forgot him, she can forget the hunter as well. The reproach is prefaced by an endearment and followed by a plea that she take him back, the ending all the more powerful because she is not there – he can only plead with a presence in his mind. As so often in reading Müller, one thinks of Heine, whose paired poems "An deine schneeweisse Schulter" (On your Snow-White Shoulders) and "Es blasen die blauen Husaren" (The Blue Hussars blow their Bugles) from *Die Heimkehr* in the *Buch der Lieder* tell a similar story in still darker shades of sexual humiliation. Heine would only acknowledge Müller's influence in matters of form and versification, although he did so warmly, but the more one delves into Müller's poetry, the more one realizes that the influence extends to Heine's poetic content as well.

The path and the window in this poem also call up images of a man's physical access to a woman. While looking through the window, the miller lad could also be thinking about that other window – a membrane separating one space from another and therefore analogous to the maidenhead – that he has perhaps seen, perhaps even been through, the "window" which is the cause of all his loathing in "Blümlein Vergißmein" to follow. There was a proverb at the time, often quoted in *Volkstheater* plays, to the effect that "If the door is closed, go in through the window," a proverb invoked when fathers bar the door to their daughters' lovers: *felix caeli porta*, indeed. John Sienicki has pointed out to me the existence of a 1981 rock song entitled "Jerkin' Back and Forth" by Devo with the lines:

There is a thought that keeps me thinking
Like a stone inside my shoe
It is a vision reoccurring
A dirty window I can see you through [italics mine], etc.

The similarity to the miller lad's obsessive imagery of windows, to the way the lad harps in grief and anger on the same "vision reoccurring," is haunting. Certainly the miller lad's experience of women is, *mutatis mutandis*, the subject of much of current popular music; Müller is a poet *par excellence* of youthful male experience, of adolescence in its latter stages, while rock music dwells on adolescent experience for much of its imagery and many of its themes. The mill path in "Erster Schmerz, letzter Scherz" is, furthermore, perhaps conflated with that path the miller lad will want to block by closing the garden gate in the next poem. He already attempts to bar the way with clover leaves (are there sexual connotations to the somewhat archaic English expression "to be in clover"?) – rather ineffective as a chastity belt, one notes sadly.

Müller, fond of poetic leitmotifs that chime throughout his cycles, at the end brings back a variant of the Freudian stammer "Vergiß, vergiß mein nicht," or "Forget, forget me not"(the truer verb "forget" appears first) in stanza 3 of "Des Müllers Blumen." In the language of flowers, cultivated both by the Elizabethans (and Müller, one remembers, was well versed in their literature) and by eighteenth- and nineteenth-century writers, *Myosotis scorpioides palustris*, to cite its botanical name, was used as a charm: "Think of the one you wish to be thinking of you when you pull a sprig of forget-me-not, and you will immediately have a place in his, or her, thoughts."[13] Müller probably knew the forget-me-not charm included in the third volume of *Des Knaben Wunderhorn*:

Vergiß mein nicht	**Forget-me-not**
Ist es nicht eine harte Pein,	Is it not a cruel pain
Wenn Liebende nicht beysammen seyn,	when lovers cannot be together.
Drück mich fest in dein Herz hinein,	Press me strongly within your heart;
Wachsen heraus Vergiß nicht mein.[14]	forget-me-nots will grow out from it.

Did he also know "Die Wiese" (The Meadow) in Johann Gottfried Herder's *Stimmen der Völker in Gesang*, in which a heartbroken young woman gathers an armful of forget-me-nots after her lover has deserted her and then dies of grief?[15] Or, even closer to home, could he have known a poem entitled "Der traurige Garten" (The Sorrowful Garden) whose motifs of a garden, clover (as in "Erster Schmerz, letzter Scherz"), forget-me-nots, and a flower-maiden – in the third stanza, the grief-stricken poetic persona defines the "Blümlein" as his beloved, with her "fine eyes" and "sweet mouth" – are all reminiscent of *Die schöne Müllerin*, and especially "Blümlein Vergißmein"? "Der traurige Garten," which seems a variant of the folk poem "Scheiden und Meiden," was published in Josef von Görres's *Altteutsche Volks- und Meisterlieder* of 1817 and again in Friedrich Karl von Erlach's *Die Volkslieder der Deutschen* of 1834; Erlach tells his readers that the poem was "newly composed by Joseph Klein," the same Bernhard Klein who had earlier set poems by Müller to music.

Der traurige Garten	**The Sorrowful Garden**
(stanza 2 of 5)	
Hätt mir ein Gärtlein koren,	I would have liked a little garden
Von Veil und grünem Klee;	of violet and green clover;
Ist mir zu früh erfroren,	it is frozen too early,
Thut meinem Herzen weh;	does my heart grief;
Ist mir erfror'n bei Sonnenschein	is frozen in the sunshine
Ein Kraut: Je länger je lieber,	a plant: honeysuckle [the longer, the more loved],
Ein Blümlein: Vergiß nicht mein.[16]	a little flower: forget-me-not.

Forget-me-nots are rife in the Schubert poets' verse and elsewhere (Challier's massive song catalogue includes two entire pages of songs with forget-me-nots in the title[17]): was Franz von Schober quoting Müller in his (Schober's) lengthy flower-ballad "Vergißmeinnicht," which Schubert set to music (D. 792) in May 1823 at the same time as the continuing work on *Die schöne Müllerin*? The conjunction is intriguing. Rita Steblin has suggested that Schober's "An die Musik" was influenced by Müller's fairy tale "Das Harfenreich," published in the *Wiener Theater-Zeitung* for September 20, 23, and 25, with the conclusion on October 2, 1817 at the time of Müller's visit to the city, and it is perhaps equally tenable that another work by Müller, one which Schubert was composing at the time, should inspire yet another echo from Schober.[18] The twentieth and last verse of this ballad – a curious retelling of the Narcissus myth with a female flower-symbol, awakened to erotic life by Spring's kiss, in place of the beautiful Greek male ephebe of the original tale – even ends with the same refrain (but in a very different context):

Und sie fühlt sich ganz genesen,	And she felt entirely healed
Wenn sie zu dem Wasser spricht,	as she spoke to the waters
Wie zu dem geahnten Wesen:	as if to that being envisioned in the mind:
O vergiß, vergiß mein nicht!	O forget, forget me not!

(This revision by one of Schubert's closest friends of one of the foremost myths of homosexuality as one of *hetero*sexuality surely has implications, albeit speculative ones only, for the current debates about Schubert's sexuality.) The fifth musical section of this episodic ballad (the text extends from line 2, stanza 13 through stanza 17) is a delineation of the flower's sorrow in strains that mingle reminiscences of the "Unfinished" Symphony, the B minor ostinato throughout "Die liebe Farbe," and the rhythmic "Fate" motif in his setting of Matthäus von Collin's ballad "Der Zwerg" – a potent combination of some of this composer's most powerful musical emblems for grief, death, ominous atmospheres, and sexuality-turned-poisonous. Stanzas thirteen and fourteen of

Example 30 Franz Schubert. "Vergißmeinnicht," D. 792, mm. 172–82, to a text by Franz von Schober. From Franz Schubert, *Neue Schubert-Ausgabe*, Series IV: *Lieder*, vol. 13, ed. Walther Dürr, pp. 114–15. Kassel & Basel: Bärenreiter Verlag, 1992.

Schober's "Vergißmeinnicht" tell of the same narcissistic love (here, literally so) one finds in *Die schöne Müllerin*, whose protagonist falls in love with his own "poem" of a woman, not a woman herself, and who suffers horribly for it when she turns out to be real and sexual.

Vergißmeinnicht	**Forget-me-not**
(stanzas 13–14)	
Ach, sie weiß es selbst nicht! – Tränen	Alas, she herself did not know! Her tears
Sprechen ihren Schmerz nur aus,	expressed only their own sorrow,
Und ein unergründlich Sehnen	and an unfathomable longing
Treibt sie aus sich selbst heraus;	drew her out of herself,
Treibt sie fort, das Bild zu finden,	drew her away to find the image
Das in ihrem Innern lebt,	that lived within her,
Das ihr Ahnungen verkünden,	that was conjured up by her imagination,
Das in Träumen sie umschwebt.	that hovered about her in dreams.

Although this may truly be stretching the bounds proper to speculation, the rhythmic echo of "Der Zwerg," which tells a tale of perverse desire leading to the wish both to kill and to be killed, and the tonal echo of "Die liebe Farbe" in this section of "Vergißmeinnicht," suggests to me that Schubert might well have understood "Blümlein Vergißmein" in all of its sexual overtones (Ex. 30). The resemblances are too close not to be connected by some common thread in the composer's mind.

Nor are these the only forget-me-nots in the Schubert- and Müller-*Kreise*. Luise Hensel and Hedwig von Stägemann reportedly collaborated on a poem entitled "Leidgesang der Vergißmeinnicht auf Th. Körner's Grabhügel" (The Forget-me-not's Song of Sorrow on Theodor Körner's Grave-Mound) after the young war-hero – the poet of the famous *Leyer und Schwert* collection of patriotic songs – died in August 1813; one wonders whether Müller knew the poem and perhaps associated forget-me-nots with Luise. Given the obvious influence of Goethe on the Stägemann poets and on the Schubert circle, one also wonders whether Müller, Schober, and Luise might all possibly have modeled their flowery poetic endeavors on Goethe's "Das Blümlein Wunderschön," or the "Lied des gefangenen Grafen" (The Wonderfully Beautiful Little Flower: Song of the Imprisoned Count), in which the rose, the carnation, and the violet all speak. The crucial stanzas, however, are nos. 11 and 12, in which the prisoner himself sings:

Lied des gefangenen Grafen	Song of the Imprisoned Count
(stanzas 11–12 of 12)	
Doch wandelt unten an dem Bach	For the truest wife on earth
Das treuste Weib der Erde,	wanders down below at the brook
Und seufzet leise manches Ach,	and sighs many a soft "Ah"
Bis ich erlöset werde.	that I will be rescued.
Wenn sie ein blaues Blümchen bricht	When she breaks off a little blue flower
Und immer sagt: Vergiß mein nicht!	and each time says: "Do not forget me!"
So fühl ich's in der Ferne.	I can feel it in the distance.
Ja in der Ferne fühlt sich die Macht	Yes, in the distance one can feel the power
Wenn zwei sich redlich lieben,	when two love one another truly;
D'rum bin ich in des Kerkers Nacht	therefore I have yet stayed alive
Auch noch lebendig geblieben,	in the dungeon's night.
Und wenn mir fast das Herze bricht,	And when my heart comes close to breaking,
So ruf' ich nur: Vergiß mein nicht!	I only call out: "Forget me not!"
Da komm' ich wieder ins Leben.	. . . then I come to life once again.

Schubert perhaps knew Johann Rudolf Zumsteeg's setting of this poem in his *Kleine Balladen und Lieder* of 1801, a dialogue-ballad which might, Richard Green speculates, have been performed by more than one singer as a miniature *Liederspiel*.[19] Might Schubert have recognized the ironic echoes of this poem in *Die schöne Müllerin*, whose miller lad goes to the brook with his beloved and hopes for just such a love as this? Perhaps it is on romances of dungeons, imprisoned noblemen, flowery speeches, and charms of true love such as this one that the lad has furnished the chambers of his imagination; what happens to him when he attempts to "live" the romance is something else altogether.

If Müller conforms to the traditional charm formula earlier in the cycle, he inverts it massively in "Blümlein Vergißmein" (Little Forget-me Flower), one of his most powerful and original works. Here, anguish and sexual humiliation mingle with rage and become frenzy – this poem is a rapid crescendo of fury. Müller, given to poetic polarities, contrasts the forget-me-not of romantic love with its opposite, the newly invented "forget-me flower," its symbolism applicable both to the miller lad and the miller maid: she has already forgotten him, and he wants desperately to forget her, but cannot. The charm has become a curse from which he cannot escape, with forget-me-nots metaphorically omnipresent; he can see nothing else. But the attempt to seek symbolic oblivion not only does not work, but actually intensifies his consciousness of her. Rage fills the mind and heart as completely as misery, is indeed its Siamese twin.

Blümlein Vergißmein	**Little Forget-me Flower**
Was treibt mich jeden Morgen	What drives me so deep
So tief ins Holz hinein?	into the woods every morning?
Was frommt mir, mich zu bergen	What good is it to hide
Im unbelauschten Hain?	in the unspied grove?
Es blüht auf allen Fluren	The little forget-me-not flower
Blümlein Vergiß-mein-nicht,	blooms in every field.
Es schaut vom heitern Himmel	It looks down from the clear skies
Herab in blauem Licht.	in blue light.
Und soll ich's niedertreten,	And if I should trample it down,
Bebt mir der Fuß zurück,	my foot recoils;
Es fleht aus jedem Kelche	a well-known gaze beseeches
Ein wohlbekannter Blick.	me from every calyx.
Weißt du, in welchem Garten	Do you know in which garden
Blümlein Vergißmein steht?	the forget-me-flower stands?
Das Blümlein muß ich suchen,	I must look for that little flower
Wie auch die Straße geht.	wherever the road leads.
's ist nicht für Mädchenbusen,	It is not for maidens' bosoms –
So schön sieht es nicht aus:	it does not look so lovely.
Schwarz, schwarz ist seine Farbe	Black, black is its color;
Es paßt in keinen Strauß.	it belongs in no bouquet.
Hat keine grüne Blätter,	It has no green leaves,
Hat keinen Blütenduft,	no flowery fragrance.
Es windet sich am Boden	It coils on the ground
In nächtig dumpfer Luft.	in the musty night air.
Wächst auch an einem Ufer,	It also grows along a riverbank,
Doch unten fließt kein Bach,	yet no brook flows below,
Und willst das Blümlein pflücken,	and if you want to pick the little flower,
Dich zieht der Abgrund nach.	the abyss draws you in after.
Das ist der rechte Garten,	That is the right garden,
Ein schwarzer, schwarzer Flor:	a black, black florescence.
Darauf magst du dich betten –	There you may bed down –
Schleuß zu das Gartentor!	Lock the garden gate!

There is a fascinating problem of address in this poem – to whom is the miller lad speaking? The youth at first seems to speak to himself, asking and attempting to answer questions in an internal dialogue; like the wanderer of *Die Winterreise*, he does not understand what impels him to act in certain ways contrary to reason, and therefore he probes his heart and powers of understanding for answers. In stanza 4, when he resolves to seek the "forget-me flower," there is an ostensible shift of focus, the lad speaking to an undetermined "you," but is that shift seeming or real? Is he still speaking to himself, the use of "du" in stanzas 4 and 8 (also implicit in stanza 7, line 3) signifying greater intensity of feeling in the resolve to find an answer? Or is he perhaps speaking to the omnipresent internal image of the miller maid, or even both to himself and to her simultaneously? Have he and maiden fused in the youth's mind like Edvard Munch's terrifying image of lovers whose faces have melded together in a single monstrous, indeterminate blob without features? If the ambiguity of address is striking in its psychological acuity (to whom are any of us speaking when we mentally excoriate those we feel have wronged us?), so too is the resolution stated in stanza 4 and emphasized by the turn to "du." The lad recognizes that the obliviousness he longs for can only be attained when he understands what compulsion possesses him and resolves to seek self-knowledge "wherever the road leads." What he finds – and finds with shocking speed – at the end of his journey to the inmost recesses of mind and heart horrifies him.

"Blümlein Vergißmein" is a vision of hell, sex, and death that Villiers de l'Isle-Adam would have been proud to claim – the poem is astonishingly premonitory of later Symbolist, even Surrealist, works. Confronted with its clustered imagery of eyes and vision, one recalls Odilon Redon's engravings *Il y eut peut-être une vision première essayée dans la fleur* (There was perhaps a first vision attempted in the flower) from the series entitled *Les Origines* (The Origins) or, even more apropos, *Vision* from the series *Dans le Rêve* (In Dream) (Fig. 13); Max Ernst's image of a gigantic, floating eye; and Gustav Mahler's "Die zwei blauen Augen von meinem Schatz" (My Sweetheart's Two Blue Eyes), with its blue eyes who pursue the wanderer of *Lieder eines fahrenden Gesellen* to his death. Müller carefully chooses his words to convey paranoia and painfully heightened erotic sensibility, voyeurism turned in upon itself and become utmost suffering. Eyes are everywhere: the lad believes himself spied upon by unknown and malign witnesses, and the omnipresent eye-flowers plead ("flehen") wordlessly with their gaze. ("Kelche" refers to the calyx of the flowers, but the word also has New Testament connotations of a "chalice" and of suffering beyond bearing, recalling Christ's plea in Matthew 26: 39: "Möge dieser Kelch an mir vorübergehen," or "May this cup pass from me.") The lad who is unable to put a halt to his panic-stricken inner pictures of rape in "Der Jäger" – it is not difficult to decode the boars who trample the kitchen-garden as the hunter trampling and despoiling the miller maid's body – or his visions in "Erster Schmerz, letzter Scherz" of the hunter and miller maid copulating in her room punishes himself for his errant sexual sight by imagining *himself* as spied upon by eyes who plead and condemn. "O, woe is me, / To have seen what I have seen, see what I see!", Ophelia laments in act 3, scene i of *Hamlet* (the so-called Nunnery scene), and Müller's lad, in his own way, echoes her.

Eyes kill as well, and they do so in an eerie poem written for Luise Hensel one year before the time of the Stägemann *Liederspiel*. In his diary for November 13, 1815, Müller tells of an evening with Luise in which he looked at the moon and fancied he saw her eyes in its face. "When I walked out from the garden into the street and Luise closed the gate behind me . . . it seemed to me as if her blue eyes looked out at me from the golden circle."[20] Three days later, on November 16, he began a song of the blue eyes in the moon, completed the next day. "I have named it 'Der blaue Mondenschein' [The Blue Moonlight]," he records. "It is a curious song, but Luise will surely be pleased with it."[21] He says nothing subsequently about her reaction, and one indeed wonders what she thought of this dialogue-poem between a mother and her son, especially if Müller had told her of his sentimental

Figure 13   Odilon Redon, *Vision* from the series *Dans le Rêve*, 1879.

fancy that it was her eyes looking at him from the moon's countenance. Here, Müller modernizes the *Schauerballade* in a proto-Symbolist fashion – Maeterlinck would later appropriate some of these same poetic strategies. The moon's blue eyes, we are told in balladesque meter, stanza, and rhythms, follow the boy everywhere, even shining through the walls and doors; he cannot flee from them. His frightened mother, who sees only moonlight, begs him to close his eyes and go to sleep, but in the morning, she finds him dead, his eyes wide open and his mouth rose-red – or so goes the literal surface of the balladesque poem. No one could mistake that this is a collocation of symbols operative on several different levels; the poem practically shouts "tiefere Bedeutung" throughout. Did Luise understand the sexual implications of the poem, one wonders? If so, what did she think of this literary love-offering?

Der blaue Mondenschein

Ach Söhnchen, liebes Söhnchen,
Was suchst du nur immer allein?
Du wirst dich schier verirren
Im trüglichen Mondenschein.

Ach Mutter, liebe Mutter,
Ich bitt' euch, laßt mich sein,
Ich werde mich nimmer verirren
Im treuen Mondenschein.

Ach Söhnchen, liebes Söhnchen,
Wie sind deine Wangen so blaß!
Du wirst dich schier verkälten
Im thauigen Wiesengras.

Ach Mutter, liebe Mutter,
Das mach' euch keinen Harm:
Wollt nur auf's Herz mir fühlen,
Bin viel, ach viel zu warm.

Ach Söhnchen, liebes Söhnchen,
Du treibst mit mir wohl Scherz?
Dir wären Puppen und Stecken
Viel besser als ein Herz.

Ach Mutter, liebe Mutter,
Wollt doch nur über euch sehn:
Die Augen, die blauen da droben,
Wie leuchten sie heute so schön!

Ach Söhnchen, liebes Söhnchen,
Laß solche Rede sein:
Ich sehe doch nur den Himmel
Und drin den Mondenschein.

Ach Mutter, liebe Mutter,
Ihr müßt geblendet sein,
Die Augen, die blauen, sie stehen
Ja mitten im Monde drein.

The Blue Moonlight

Oh, little son, dear little son,
what are you always seeking by yourself?
You will go completely astray
in the deceitful moonlight.

Oh mother, dear mother,
I beg of you, let me be,
I will never go astray
by the faithful light of the moon.

Oh, little son, dear little son,
how pale your cheeks are!
You will be entirely frozen
in the dewy meadow grass.

Oh mother, dear mother,
that does you no harm:
I only want to feel in my heart,
I am much, alas, much too warm.

Oh, little son, dear little son,
surely you are playing a joke on me?
Dolls and hide-and-seek would be much better
for you than a heart.

Oh mother, dear mother,
I only want to see above you:
the eyes, the blue ones, up above there,
how beautifully they shine today!

Oh, little son, dear little son,
don't say such things:
I see only the sky
and the moonlight within it.

Oh mother, dear mother,
you have been blinded;
the eyes, the blue ones, are
there in the middle of the moon.

Sie schauen so sehnlich hernieder,
Sie blinken und winken mir zu.
Ach Mutter, könnt' ich doch fliegen!
Hier hab' ich keine Ruh'.

Ach Söhnchen, armes Söhnchen,
Welch böser Narrenwahn!
Dir hat eine arge Hexe
Ein Leides angethan.

Komm laß uns gehn nach Hause
Und stell' dein Äugeln ein:
Es sind kein guten Geister,
Die schweben im Mondenschein.

Sie faßt den Knaben am Arme
Und zieht ihn fort und fort,
Da hilft kein Sträuben, kein Weinen,
Kein gutes, kein böses Wort.

Sie führt ihn in die Kammer,
Sie schließt die Laden zu:
Mein Söhnchen, hier lege dich nieder
Und schlaf' in guter Ruh'!

Ach Mutter, liebe Mutter,
Nie hab' ich Ruhe hier,
Die Augen, die blauen, sie scheinen
Ja hell durch Wand und Thür.

Der Knabe legt sich nieder
Und drückt die Äuglein zu,
Die Mutter weint und betet:
Gott geb' ihm sanfte Ruh'!

Und als der Morgen dämmert,
Da liegt der Knabe todt,
Die Äuglein stehn ihm offen,
Sein Mund ist rosenroth.

Und durch die Kammer flimmert
Ein wunderlicher Schein,
Es ist keine Morgenröthe,
Kann auch der Mond nicht sein.

Er schillert hell und trübe
In himmelblauem Licht,
Er kränzt mit Strahlenblumen
Des Kindleins Angesicht.

Und die den Schimmer sahen,
Die beklagen den Knaben nicht mehr,
Und der dies Lied gesungen,
Dem ward es gar nicht schwer.[22]

They look down at me so longingly,
they gaze and beckon to me.
Oh mother, if only I could fly to them!
Here I have no peace.

Oh my little son, poor little son,
what foolish craziness!
An evil witch has
done this sorrow to you.

Come, let us go in the house
and close your eyes:
these are not good spirits
that sway in the moonlight.

She took the lad by the arm
and drew him more and more strongly;
no resistance, no weeping,
no good, no evil word could help.

She led him to the room,
she closed his eyelids:
My little son, lie down here
and sleep in peace!

Oh mother, dear mother,
I will never rest here.
The eyes, the blue ones, they shine
brightly through wall and door.

The boy lay down
and closed his eyes.
His mother wept and prayed:
God give him gentle rest!

And when morning dawned,
there lay the boy dead,
his eyes are open,
his mouth is rose-red.

And through the room there shines
a curious light:
it is not dawn,
it cannot be the moon.

Its opalescence glittered
in the heavenly-blue light;
it wreathed the child's face
with flowery rays.

And those who saw its glow
did not mourn the youth any longer,
and those who sang this song,
it was not difficult for them.

If ever there was a poem written under the sign of "Der Erlkönig," this is it, but with the sexual implications and the gender of the protagonists changed. The older poet's dialogue between a boy, his father, and a male figure of Death here becomes a dialogue between a mother and son, with the unseen figure of a death-dealing "witch" – female, not male, and invested with all the eroticism which customarily drenches witchcraft – in the background. Again, Müller, barely emerged from adolescence himself, proves to be a masterful poet of adolescent experience. The son is on the cusp between childhood and puberty, to the alarm of his mother, who would clearly like to keep him a child; a son's struggle for independence from maternal solicitousness goes hand-in-hand with sexual awakening. "Hand" is perhaps indeed the relevant word: the line "Was suchst du nur immer allein?" in stanza 1 already suggests that the subjects are teenage masturbation and the onset in puberty of male sexual desire for a girl or woman. All of the moon's traditional associations with nocturnal magic, with female sexuality, are present; the mother, for all her incomprehension, dimly senses "an evil witch" as the cause, a witch-woman who wishes to take her son away from her. As in "Blümlein Vergißmein," the painterly Müller tints his poem with symbolic hues, the blue light of the Luise-moon's gaze additionally a recollection of Novalis's *Sehnsucht* flower, the famous "blaue Blume," while the rosy-red of the lad's mouth hints at an explicitly sexual "death." The quickened rhythms of the threefold line, "Die Augen, die blauen, da droben / sie stehen / sie scheinen" in stanzas 6, 8 and 14 – the only repeated phrase in the entire song – tell of quickened feeling, masterfully accentuated by the bright, piercing -ee sounds that chime throughout the line in the last two invocations. Müller beautifully captures the sense of irresistible compulsion as the novel sensations of newly roused sexuality flood the body and fill the mind. Are there in German culture the same injunctions of masturbation leading to blindness that one finds in English-speaking tradition? (If so, the lad telling his mother that she must be blind not to see the moon's blue eyes acquires an additional ironic connotation.) Is blueness endowed with the same sexualized melancholy that "the blues" so often have in present-day associations?[23]

The ending of "Der blaue Mondenschein" is wonderfully mysterious: "And through the room there shines a curious light," Müller writes in stanzas 17–19, "it is not dawn, it cannot be the moon," and it wreathes the boy's face with radiant flowers of light. Whoever saw the unearthly shimmering no longer mourned for the youth, and all went well for those who sang this song, we are told at the end, the verb tenses in the final stanza changing abruptly from present to past tense in a manner that provokes interpretation. Is the iridescent shimmer which fills the room and glows from the boy's face the aura of sexual experience, the mark of someone transformed into a fully sexual being? Has the lad "died" from one state of being (childhood) into another? Is the near-untranslatable last line (again, a line which impels decoding) meant to imply that only for those who leave childhood, despite their mothers' attempts to retain them in a childish state, do "things go well"? Do those who saw the former child not mourn him because he has metamorphosed from a child to a man, and this is not cause for mourning? (If Goethe was Müller's model, Müller was Heine's model: "Der blaue Mondenschein" was clearly the source for Heine's ballad "Die Wallfahrt nach Kevlaar," or "The Pilgrimage to Kevlaar," in the *Buch der Lieder*, the form, the poetic rhythms, and the tale itself all varied echoes of Müller. Typically, Heine intensifies what he borrows, piling still more Goethe references on top of Müller's Goethe references – it would not be possible in the 1820s to invoke "the dead Gretchen" without impelling thoughts of *Faust*, Part I – and a soupçon of near-blasphemy: a boy and his mother travel to a shrine for lepers to beg the Virgin Mary to grant surcease from the boy's anguished thoughts of dead Gretchen, and the Virgin does so, bringing him death in his sleep.)

To return briefly to "Der Jäger" and its voyeuristic imagery of rape, did Müller perhaps know the scene in Gottfried von Strassburg's *Tristan* in which the knight's erstwhile friend the Baron Marjodo dreams that a foaming, raging boar rushes from the forest into the palace, breaks into King Marke's bedchamber, and tramples on the bed, soiling it?[24] When Marjodo awakens, he wishes to tell Tristan of his strange dream, but Tristan is not there; the Baron, who is himself attracted to Isolde, follows his trail to the Queen's room, realizes for the first time the illicit love between the queen and the knight, and is aroused to furious jealousy. The parallels with "Der Jäger" seem uncannily exact, although Müller adapts the borrowed motif, if indeed it was borrowed, beautifully to the context of his mill tale (ironically, it is Tristan who is the hunter and hunted alike in the medieval romance). Both Müller and Gottfried were perhaps harking back to the legend, recounted in Herodotus, of Atys, son of Kroisos, who wished to hunt a wild boar of great size and strength living on the slopes of Mount Olympus. Kroisos dreamt that a wild boar would kill his son by means of an iron lance and forbade his son to take part in the hunt; Atys ignored the advice and was killed when one of his companions cast his lance at the boar and struck Atys after the boar dodged the weapon. Was Müller's miller hoping for a similar "accident" in which the hunter he detested might die? Schubert would have known Atys, if not elsewhere, from his friend Johann Mayrhofer's poem "Atys," which Schubert set to music in 1817.

Hairiness equals bestiality: Müller calls up associations of yet another venerable Teutonic archetype when his miller lad angrily cries "Und schere vom Kinne das strup-pige Haar" (and shave the bristling hair from your chin) to a hunter who is not even there, however much he fills the young man's entire alarmed consciousness at the moment. To him, the hunter is more Wild Man than *Jägerheld*, "der wilde Mann" an *alt-Deutsch* figure who appears in panel paintings, prints, tapestry, heraldry, and decorative arts since the late Middle Ages.[25] Almost naked but for the animal skins around the shoulders and loins, with unkempt hair, long, wild beard, and copious body hair, these creatures were emblematic, according to Joseph Koerner, of "primitive power, sexual lust, fallenness, and pugnacity."[26] When the miller lad bids the hunter become civilized in order best to woo the miller maid, we see Müller adapting an ancient theme (at least as old as Samson and Delilah and even going back to *Gilgamesh*, but no one knew that tale in Müller's time) by which a wild man is tamed by love, as in a fresco at Schloß Liebenfeld with the motto "Ich bin haarig und wild und Fuert mich ain wiplich bild" (I am hairy and wild and I am led by a damsel); the lad, attempting to deny that his blue-eyed beloved could be attracted to the hunter's hairy virility, tries to persuade himself that this particular wild man can become civilized by the power of *Minne*. The attempt does not work: by the end of the poem, a near-hysterical lad cannot keep fantasies of bestial sex in the miller maid's "Kohlgarten," or "kitchen garden," at bay – and the word

"Kohlgarten" is a treasure-trove of poetic associations and a testament to Müller's artistry as a word-smith, as someone who renews traditional images. As a symbol of the miller maid, the "Kohlgarten" is rustic kin to the medieval *hortus conclusus*, or a paradisaical garden of love which echoes the Garden of Eden, here varied as a properly *domestic* garden for the domestic saint of "Das Mühlenleben." (Müller's diary entries about the composition of "Der blaue Mondenschein" make it clear that the Hensel household in 1815 had a garden.) Gardens have furrows which are plowed and sown with seed, the sexual connotations of female genitalia obvious; "Kohl" – coal-black – can thus be understood in retrospect as a foreshadowing of the black garden to follow in "Blümlein Vergißmein." With this multivalent and wonderfully evocative word, we understand that the miller maid is on her way to conversion from saint to sinner in the miller lad's mind.

Paranoia breeds compulsion. Why, the lad asks at the beginning of "Blümlein Vergißmein," am I compelled to go deep into the woods? The forest, after all, is the hunter's territory, and, logically speaking, he would be expected to shun the place. Symbolically, however, the forest represents the depths of the mind, the dark, sunless, unexplored regions of the unconscious emotional world; those depths have engulfed the miller lad. The blue forget-me-not flowers (the blue of his sweetheart's eyes and of the flowers by the brook) emblematic both of faithful love and mistrust in that love, which must be bolstered by charms and is fraught with bad faith, supposedly bloom in the open air, but not so their antipode. The forget-me-nots are also associated with the girl's breasts ("'s ist nicht für Mädchenbusen," we are told of the black forget-me flowers, implying that the forget-me-nots are) – is anything being said here about the ambiguous nature of those "innocent" things that create a desire for things less innocent? In stanza 5, the blue flowers of love metamorphose into black flowers of lust growing, not on the banks of a stream but of a sexualized abyss.[27] This poem is almost as strong a noxious compound of sexual attraction/repulsion/misogyny/self-disgust as anything in Baudelaire, who unmasked Cythera as a place of death and whose "sunless caves" and "feverish miasmas . . . with their vile perfume" in "Delphine" garnered him prosecution for pornography. Like the half-serpentine, half-female Satans in an Altdorfer depiction of the Fall of Man, the forget-me flowers of Müller's imagination slither on the ground; where they cluster on a bank, no revivifying water (the element emblematic of life-giving femaleness) can flow. When the tormented lad tries to pluck the flower anyway, the proverbial "Heidenröslein" (meadow rose) sexual connotations of deflowering clear, a hellish abyss opens up, an abyss which both forcefully pulls ("ziehen") the lad to his doom but also attracts him so that he goes willingly; it "draws" him in both senses of the word. One thinks of Gustave Courbet's infamous painting for the Khalil Bey entitled *L'origine du monde* (The Origin of the World), its furred "gash" – everything about the woman but her sexual organs are excluded from the painting – the emblem above all of voyeuristic male fascination–repulsion with female genitalia, and realizes that Müller's musky-smelling cleft rimmed with clustered black flowers invokes precisely the same image. "That is the right garden!", the lad bitterly exclaims; the *mille fleurs*-bedecked *hortus conclusus* is a falsehood – this hellish place is the truth. (Hieronymous Bosch proclaims likewise in *The Garden of Earthly Delights*.) At the end, Müller refers obliquely to

Walther von der Vogelweide's famous Minnesong "Under der linden" (Under the Linden Tree), in which two lovers spend the night on a bed of "beautiful broken flowers and grass" beneath the linden tree (Müller, one recalls, had invoked the linden as the traditional lovers' meeting-place in "Ein ungereimtes Lied"), but he does so in order that his character might excoriate all such visions of "natural love." In Walther von der Vogelweide, lovemaking is Eden reborn; in *Die schöne Müllerin*, it is hell on earth.

Under der linden	Under the linden
an der heide,	on the open field,
dâ unser zweier bette was,	where we two had our bed,
dâ mugt ir vinden	you still can see
schône beide	lovely broken
gebrochen bluomen unde gras.	flowers and grass.

Lest anyone miss his meaning, Müller pointedly uses the verb "betten" in the final stanza of "Blümlein Vergißmein." "What's love got to do with it?", the lad implies; this is all about those "two unkind sisters" Debauch and Death, as Baudelaire dubbed them.

The verb "betten" triggers the sudden conclusion of the poem. As in "Erster Schmerz, letzter Scherz," which comes from the Stägemann *Liederspiel*, the miller lad is unable to bear any direct coupling (the *mot juste*) of the miller maid with sex and breaks off the poem abruptly. (In the earlier poem, Müller uses the slightly more euphemistic phrase "der [the hunter] liegt in ihrem Arm" in stanza 5. If the horizontal position implicit in the verb "liegen" bespeaks lovemaking, the phrase is less potent by far than the language of sex in "Blümlein Vergißmein," and hence, the lad turns away from the unbearable thought in mid-stanza, rather than putting a sudden close to the entire poem, as he does here.) The fever-pitch of rage and anguish building throughout stanzas 5–8 explodes in the final line. The terse imperative "Lock the garden gate!" is among the most masterful details of a masterful poem and at the same time, of all its wormwood-and-gall elements the most repugnant – deliberately so. There are multiple readings of this violent directive possible, but it seems most likely that the lad is savagely bidding the miller maid to close her legs, to bar any and all entry into the pestilent garden. Beyond the jealous assertion that if she will not sleep with him, she should not sleep with anyone is a profound disgust at the sight of the female sex organs and a graphic depiction of that sexuality, unmistakable to any but the most naive. Freud himself, in his essay on the Medusa-head, did not invoke any more powerfully than this the phenomenon of the male gaze upon the female genitals and the mingled castration anxiety and fury aroused by the sight.[28] Even for an early nineteenth-century readership that had already confronted such scandalously frank works as Friedrich Schlegel's *Lucinde*, this is a shocking poem.

If "Blümlein Vergißmein" is shocking for the reader, it is even more so for the character who experiences it. This moment is what breaks the miller lad: after this, he does not want to live. Whatever its power, Schubert would have none of it, and his omission of this poem, more than any of the others he omitted, makes of his cycle something fundamentally different from the poet's. If there is degradation and sexual misery aplenty in D. 795, there is nothing *this* corrosive, *this* sulphurous. Its removal means that the lad's suicide is less clearly motivated in Schubert's cycle, hazier around the edges. One reads "Blümlein Vergißmein" and understands fully why the lad rejects the brook's lyrically lovely symbolism of lilies and roses in "Der Müller und der Bach" – he knows, so he believes, the *real* language of flowers – and its platitudes about surmounting love's loss. His weary question, "Ach, Bächlein, aber weißt du, / Wie Liebe tut?" (But do you know, little brook, what love can do?) in the next-to-last stanza means something more precise and more horrible in Müller's cycle than in Schubert's. One can readily comprehend why Schubert might have shied away from the eruption of sexually charged anguish and hatred in "Blümlein Vergißmein" and yet understand that its omission diminishes the composer's *Die schöne Müllerin* by more than mere length. From "Der Jäger" through "Blümlein Vergißmein," Müller carefully constructed a crescendo of increasing tension leading to the climactic moment of peripeteia; at the culmination of the crescendo, the last veil of romantic illusion is ripped away, and psychological monsters appear from the depths, suddenly, shockingly. If one eliminates the instant of peripeteia, however, the crescendo which precedes it is thereby denuded of some, if not all, of its meaning.

But if Schubert undeniably omitted this poem, he might not have deleted all traces of it from his musical imagination. In "Trock'ne Blumen," which follows right after "Blümlein Vergißmein" in Müller's complete cycle, the lad brokenheartedly states at the beginning of the poem, "Ihr Blümlein alle, / die sie mir gab / Euch soll man legen / mit mir ins Grab" (You little flowers all that she gave to me, they must lay you in the grave with me). The word "Blümlein" is a leitmotif carried over from the preceding poem (Müller once again taking pains to create links between poems), the adjective "alle" implying that both the blue *and* the black flowers should be buried with him, that both should be dampened with the tears of sorrowful – and guilty – awareness of what she has done to him. Her wicked sexuality will be entombed with him, and after his death, she will realize what she has done and repent of it, so he imagines – or tries to. "When I'm dead, they'll be sorry," hurt children often say, and so in effect does the miller lad, thus reminding us of his youthfulness, but the wound from which he suffers – the bitter aftermath of shattered sexual illusions – belongs to blighted adulthood. (One hears "Ihr Blümlein alle" and thinks as well of Ophelia's rosemary, pansies, fennel, columbine, rue, daisy, and the absent violets, "withered all when my father died." Is this perhaps where Müller derived his title for this poem?) The effort to exorcise the demons of "Blümlein Vergißmein," to recapture a Minnesinger's proper worshipfulness of his lady, to find some meaning for good in the death he has resolved to seek, is tainted by lingering traces of hurt and anger and by the underlying realization, evident in "Der Müller und der Bach," that this will not work. When Schubert in mm. 3 and 7 emphasizes the accented syllable of "*al* - le" by ascending to the tonic E pitch at mid-measure, was he perhaps responding, however subliminally, to the heightened significance of the adjective "alle," significance which comes from "Blümlein Vergißmein"? He repeats the gesture twice, after all; the twofold melodic inflection acquires a different and darker meaning when heard in the knowledge of the omitted poem just before it. If this nugget of speculation is admittedly farfetched, it is nonetheless fascinating to realize that trace-elements of poems a composer decided *not* to set to music might still find their way into the musical work.

The sexual nightmare that is "Blümlein Vergißmein" strongly hints both that the lad has slept with the miller maid – between "Tränenregen" and "Mein!"? – and that he also fantasizes in voyeuristic fashion about her sexual involvement with the hunter. One can interpret "Mein!" as pure delusion (I did so in print only a few years ago), the miller lad so upset by the maiden's behavior in "Tränenregen" that he deludes himself into proclaiming that she is his, or as an unbalanced announcement of fact, its drunken-rhapsodic ecstasy belied by the desire to flee. "Das ist ein wahres Rasen" (This is truly insanity), the great singer Julius Stockhausen wrote of "Mein!" in his diary in 1862,[29] but such ravings can issue from someone thrown into chaos by an actual event as well as from someone feeding on pure fantasy.

Mein!	**Mine!**
Bächlein, laß dein Rauschen sein!	Brook, stop your babbling!
Räder, stellt eu'r Brausen ein!	Mill-wheels, cease your roaring!
All ihr muntern Waldvögelein,	All you merry little forest birds,
Groß und klein,	large and small,
Endet eure Melodein!	end your warbling!
Durch den Hain	Throughout the woods,
Aus und ein	within and beyond,
Schalle heut' *ein* Reim allein:	let one rhyme alone ring out today:
Die geliebte Müllerin ist *mein!*	the beloved miller maid is mine!
Mein!	Mine!
Frühling, sind das alle deine Blümelein?	Spring, are those all the flowers you have?
Sonne, hast du keinen hellern Schein?	Sun, have you no brighter light?
Ach, so muß ich ganz allein,	Ah, then I must remain all alone
Mit dem seligen Worte *mein,*	with this blissful word of mine,
Unverstanden in der weiten Schöpfung	uncomprehended anywhere in the wide
sein!	world!

The poem begins as if tightly under control, with the single rhyming sound -ein, the two initial imperatives constructed as parallelisms, and the heavily accented trochaic tetrameters in lines 1–3. But the feint of control disintegrates rapidly, and the lines thereafter veer unpredictably from dimeters to hexameters and everything in between. Even where symmetry is reasserted, as in the parallel prepositional clauses in dimeters at lines 6–7 ("Durch den Hain / Aus und ein") or the parallel questions to springtime and the sun in lines 11–12, these symmetrical elements occur within a wildly fluctuating form. The poem, one notices, is a single stanza, an uninterrupted gush of words in which the poetic persona is never able to "settle" on a particular meter or line length; he is too disordered by what has happened to him to devise an ordered form divided by pauses and spaces, although he attempts to do so, attempts to sing a proper song. (The same would later be true of "Täuschung," in which the winter wanderer of *Die Winterreise* is closer to insanity than at any other time in the cycle.) The single rhyme sounds, and is, obsessive, while the hysterical insistence on possession is unnerving to read – "Mine, all mine, only mine!", the lad repeats over and over. The insistence suggests sexual possession, but sadly, one notices that he does not say that she loves him or even that he loves her, nor does he turn the formula "She is mine" around and say that *he* is entirely *hers*. The unpleasant narcissism of "Mine, mine, mine" is all the more emphatic because she, one infers, does not do likewise; claims of possession are always louder and more fraught when tenuous. For all its overt frenzy, there is a kind of honesty in the lack of romantic idealization in this poem; if he rhapsodizes about spring and sunshine, he does not rhapsodize about reciprocated love. The omission is telling.

Earlier, in "Der Feierabend," near-frenzy in stanza 1 is followed by collapse in stanza 2, the collapse signalled by the exclamation "Ach" and a change of poetic meter. Here, there is no such formal differentiation between different emotional states; the lines blur, collapse hardly distinguishable from hysteria because both are pervaded by the same manic energy. The last three lines of "Mein!" do not, to put it politely, make *factual* sense, although they make a great deal of psychological sense when read between the lines. If it seems cogent to say that because nature in its strongest and most beautiful manifestations (springtime and the sun) cannot adequately reflect his joy, nothing else in all of creation can do so, this does not account for the telling words "ganz allein" and "unverstanden." It does not require much imagination to infer from the phrase "ganz allein" the aftermath of bad sex in a feeling of heightened solipsism, the manic tone of the poem once again evident in the adjective "ganz." This is a protagonist with little or no capacity for the golden mean; he is overwhelmed by what he experiences and sings in all-or-nothing terms of emotions that consume his entire horizon. And yet, he is emblematic of a real phenomenon: to assert simultaneously that someone belongs to you, is wholly yours, and yet that you are all alone is, sad to say, an experience many a reader can recognize. Comparing this final version of "Mein!" with the original *Liederspiel* version entitled "Das schönste Lied" (see chapter 1), one realizes that it is precisely the incursion of doubt, solitude, and suppressed despair that was added to the poem at a later stage, added for a monodrama whose exploration of dark psychological truths is far more intense than in the salon song-play.

It is the lad's own lack of understanding one sees mirrored in the word "unverstanden"; if he is not understood anywhere in all of creation, it is because he does not understand himself. Müller evidently knew that those vulnerable to suicidal impulses feel themselves to be beyond anyone else's comprehension; no one, the potential suicide thinks, can possibly understand the emotional turmoil he or she is enduring. What is so brilliant about this poem is that Müller locates the assertion of such utter aloneness at the moment of love's seeming vindication. If the beloved shares and reciprocates the lover's feelings, one need not look so frantically for affirmation in nature, but that is not the case here. On the contrary, physical possession only makes the lad aware, at some level below conscious admission, that he does not possess her heart and soul, and the underlying emptiness of his triumph engenders the emotional chaos of this poem. The form and language alike tell both of truth suppressed and truth that will "out" regardless, the latter becoming stronger as the poem hurtles to a close. By the end, one hears "Mein!" as replete with queasy, powerful, mixed messages, a compound of manic joy, hysterical insistence, overwhelming feelings of solitude, and awareness of incomprehension, while its formal structure embodies a telling struggle with song form. Try though the miller lad might to "sing a song" throughout this poem, to order and dispose such elements as *Kling-Klang* joyous refrains, rhyming couplets, rhythms within the poetic line, and so forth, the order of poetry and the disorder of his mind are at odds with one another. The poem's very brevity is an indication of his inability to continue the battle. (Müller's daring motif of the incompatibility of love and poetry is also the speculative reason for the abolition of rhyme in "Ein ungereimtes Lied," in which the poet sings about the banishment of song – here equated with poetry's most prominent identifying feature, or rhyme – and its replacement by the sensual delights of love-making (see chapter 1 for the text of the poem). Müller, I would guess, might have deleted the poem both because he wished to remove from the monodrama all trace of happily reciprocated physical love and because the desire to "sing" and the inability to do so in this instance are not fraught with any subterranean hints of anguish to come.)

Schubert could not omit "Mein!" and preserve the narrative of *Die schöne Müllerin*. It is crucial to the plot that the miller maid either sleeps with the lad – a reading that I believe is supported by the symbolic details of "Blümlein Vergißmein" to follow there-after – or else that he deludes himself with fantasies of possession (and how artful of Müller to make the matter so ambiguous). But if the composer could not eliminate this poem, he could and did refuse to accept it as given, rejecting both a reading of the poem as delusion or a reading as tainted "fact," that is, of "Mein!" as a betrayal willy-nilly of poisoned sex. Instead, he attempts a strategy of overwhelming the words with music that upholds only their topmost surface, only the joy that the lad wishes were his and tries to assert as his; the miller lad is, at Müller's clever behest, unsuccessful in the attempt, but Schubert countermands the failure entirely and alters the tale thereby. Virtually every detail of his setting contradicts what is wild, unbalanced, ambivalent, and desperate in Müller's poem, although the composer's energetic proclamations of a lover's exuberance and untainted joy crack on occasion and reveal, I believe, Schubert's awareness of the *poet's* poem.

Nevertheless, throughout most of the 103 measures of "Mein!", Schubert stands Müller's creation on its head. Where Müller overturns attempted songlike symmetry with asymmetry and imbalance, Schubert insists upon regularity and repetition; where Müller is feverish, the rhythmic pace driven and hectic, Schubert is calmer, more leisurely; where Müller's protagonist staggers to and fro, Schubert's protagonist dances for joy, the mildly bagpipe-like rusticity of the strains suggestive of a character at one with his surroundings, rather than at odds with them, as Müller's creation is. The tempo is "Mäßig geschwind" (Moderately fast) rather than the outright "Geschwind" of the panic-drenched "Der Jäger" and "Eifersucht und Stolz," and the principal tonalities are the *plein-air* keys of D major and its flatted-sixth B flat major (the key of "Das Wandern," with which "Mein!" shares the somewhat jaunty, rustic intervals of open fifths and octaves in the bass figuration). B flat major then becomes the principal key of the paired songs "Pause" and "Mit dem grünen Lautenbande" (nos. 12 and 13), when the miller lad still believes that she is "Mein!"; if the brief patch of G minor harmonies in mm. 47–50 is a premonition of "Eifersucht und Stolz," we cannot know that as yet. And certainly no one listening to the eight-measure piano introduction would suspect "wahres Rasen" to follow, nor does it: the four-plus-four phrase symmetry is balance incarnate, and the simple harmonies (I V V/IV IV V/ii ii V I) are sunny and obvious, with nothing out of the ordinary and no trace of Schubert's more radical tonal language. The texture is both full and yet clear, due to Schubert's use of broken-chordal figuration; in the last half of the introduction and beneath the body of the song, Schubert sinks the founda-tion bass tones deep in the fortepiano register, a solid and sure ground beneath his miller lad's feet. As in a dance song, Schubert marks the quarter-note tactus with accents on the downbeat or both on the downbeat and at mid-measure, the lied devoid of any rhythmic complexity; these are rhythms to sound the beat for country dancers to follow. The swinging motion in both the left and right hands is wide-spanning – just the kind of gently rollicking figuration one might find in one of Schubert's own "deutsche Tänze" – but not so much so as to indicate imbalance. On the contrary, rising-and-falling inflections are exquisitely calibrated, as when the ascending triadic motion in m. 9 of the vocal line (the first bar of the singer's part) is followed in m. 10 by scalewise descending motion; indeed, the vocal line is filled with similar instances. Furthermore, Schubert resorts to repetition, both literal and sequential, of small melodic units (one or two measures) in a manner merrily reminiscent of dance music; mm. 22–25 ("Durch den Hain, aus und ein, schalle heut' ein Reim allein"), with their "yodel melodics," their perfectly balanced rising and falling motion, and the literal repetition in the second measure of the first measure, is one example, and another is the repeated invocation "Endet eure Melodein!" (mm. 16–18, 19–21), its chromatic appoggiatura tone A sharp an enharmonic premonition of the B flat major tonality in the middle section. One hears this music and thinks of open-air song in the country, of rustic dance (albeit evoked by a sophisticated composer), of genuine rejoicing with nothing of immoderation or delusion about it. Not a cloud darkens the sky.

Until the midway point of the poet's strophe, Schubert had relatively little trouble adapting Müller's drunkenly uneven lines and obsessional -ein rhyme to his own very different purposes. When two lines in dimeters ("Durch den Hain / aus und ein") are followed by a line in tetrameters ("schalle heut' ein Reim allein"), the variation in line length actually lends itself to symmetrical phrase structure in music, while the regular tactus and perfect intervals in the bass seem to swallow up the one rhyme. Where a line is uneven, as in the climactic statement "Die geliebte Müllerin ist mein" in pentameters, Schubert simply resorts to repetition of the crucial words "ist mein" to complete the cadence and "round out" the phrase. One can even accept the poetic content and the music as congruent with one another. But with the last half of Müller's poem, Schubert ignores most of the disturbing aspects of the text. I would guess that he recognized the poetic swerve to partially revealed distress and knew that a shift in the musical wind was called for at the words "Frühling, sind das alle deine Blümelein?" hence, the sudden modulation to the key of the flatted sixth. The nature of the shift, however, is different in the poet and the composer; if that is to some degree inevitable, given the ineluctable differences between the two media, the composer's strategy must be understood as a disagreement with the poet and an attempt to cancel him out. Near the end of the poem, Müller's lad continues to proclaim "triumph" only in the assertion that he owns the "blessed word 'mine'" – the word, not what it symbolizes – while the phrases "ganz allein" and "unverstanden" erode any sense that she is truly his. If the youth stops short of any open admission that this might be so, he is nonetheless disturbed by dim inklings just below the surface, and his language reflects that disturbance. Schubert, however, may speculatively have decided that *his* lad would refuse to recognize any danger of loss whatever until forced to do so, until the appearance of "Der Jäger," and hence, his lad continues to dance for joy, albeit more quietly; the accompanimental figuration is just as before, carried over unbroken and without pause from the initial section of the song in D major.

The turn to B flat major has the effect of a sudden welling-up of warmth and tenderness, to be expected at times of love's vindication where real, but not so apropos here. Interestingly, Schubert acknowledges the greater darkness of the poetry at this point, the incursion of doubt and tension, by means of diminished seventh chords and relative minor (G minor) harmonies, but in each instance, his protagonist rejects the slightly darker strains and returns to clarity, major mode, and certitude. For example, the questions to spring and the sun in mm. 41–46 begin and end on the new tonic chord of B flat major, but the interior (mm. 43–45) consists of a reiterated diminished seventh chord on the leading tone A natural against the continued tonic pedal point in the low bass. (Schubert, one notices, treats the questions "naively" – just so would a young man suffused with happiness in love "speak" to inanimate phenomena around him. The things addressed are set apart in declamatory fashion from the continuation of the phrase by means of a rest, and each query ends with an upwards, questioning inflection.) Schubert's treatment of the word "unverstanden" is even more compelling as an example of the same strategy. The composer could not, or so it seems, ignore so lengthy and unexpected a word at the end of the poetic source, nor does he, but he makes of the two-measure elongation of "unverstanden" a vehicle for the return to B flat major chords and a completed cadence, expressive not of near-senseless ambiguity but of surety and clarity. In his reading, it is merely an expression of how great the lad's joy is that no one else could understand, without dire hints of distress, and its short-lived darkness is quickly overthrown. Rejecting the slight G minor shadow of "ganz allein," Schubert's miller embellishes the width of all creation with quickened motion and an ornamental turning figure (m. 59) that can only be heard as lightly, sweetly exuberant, as if he wanted to dance on his way into the wide world with the joyous news. The piano interlude in mm. 60–63, in particular, the rising motion in the right-hand part, seems as if ascending to lighter, brighter realms but not so high as to suggest ethereal fantasy; we return instead to solid ground in a mid-level tessitura, there to resume the dance. What, one wonders, would Müller have thought, had he heard this song?[30]

"Mein!" is not the only instance of Schubert repeating the poet's initial lines and his own initial section of music at the end of a song. He had done so in his 1817 setting of Johann Mayrhofer's "Fahrt zum Hades" (Journey to Hades), D. 526, I would guess, in order to end, not with the poet's anguished questions "Wann enden diese Qualen? Wann?" (When will these torments end? When?) but with the calm, dignified resignation – however fraught with undercurrents of dread – of the first stanza: a "better" death, if in song only, and one more amenable to closure in a song-form than Mayrhofer's unanswerable query. Nevertheless, for the composer to select a closure from *within* the poet's structure is to subvert the poem; how one understands a work is greatly affected by how it ends, and a different ending inevitably results in an altered notion of the poetic content. It matters, and matters greatly, that Müller's "Mein!" ends with the lad unable to go beyond the near-senseless ambiguity of the last line, a line one understands in retrospect as a foreshadowing of the expansion into the infinite in "Des Baches Wiegenlied," that exquisite vision of "weite Schöpfung" at the end of time. When

Schubert repeats his own A section of "Mein!", thus repeating Müller's first nine lines as the conclusion, he imposes a crystal-clear large-scale architecture on the poet's deliberately near-formless strophe and thereby rejects even more decisively the tell-tale hints of emotional distress at the close. To compound his rejection of Müller's ending, Schubert brings back not only the entire A section, altered only in order to provide an even more definitive vocal cadence in mm. 93–95, but the introduction as well. This introduction-become-postlude is likewise little changed, varied only by the addition of the final resonant, *fortissimo* chord in m. 103, the instrumental equivalent of a last jubilant repetition of the word "Mein!" Thus where Müller's miller undergoes an involuntary progression from seeming assuredness at the beginning of the poem to near-incoherent distress tarnishing the earlier assertions of joy, Schubert insists that there is really no change, that the lad's joy is uppermost throughout. The brief suggestions of heaviness, of darkness, in the B section are not allowed to develop, and the returning full-length A section thoroughly banishes whatever residue those faint hints of tragic meaning might have left behind; the end of the song is a club with which to beat any trace of doubt to a pulp. Interestingly, both the poet's and the composer's miller share a strategy of suppression, a refusal to allow subterranean disturbance to appear aboveground, but with such differing degrees of success as to be virtually different people at that crucial moment in the tale.

Even the composer's smallest emendations to the poetry tell of a desire to alter Müller's protagonist. In "Pause," which follows just after "Mein!", the lad wonders why he can no longer create, why the poetico-musical wellsprings have run dry and he has therefore "hung my lute on the wall." Is it, he wonders, paradoxically, because he is so happy? Are unrequited love and its attendant unhappiness the climate for creativity? Müller's musings on the emotional impetus for creative work include a leaven of sophisticated, self-conscious irony when his lad says "Meiner Sehnsucht allerheißesten Schmerz / durft' ich aushauchen in Liederscherz" (The hottest sorrow of my longing I could breathe forth in song-jest), the whiff of self-mockery especially apparent in the words "allerheißesten Schmerz." There is irony in the knowing conversion of anguished longing into "song-jests," irony and awareness of art's metamorphosis of experience into something else, something other. Suffering is one thing, song is another, and Müller's multiplication of poets (himself, "Der Dichter," and the lad) all know it. One remembers Laertes in act 4, scene v of *Hamlet* who, on hearing Ophelia's mad songs, says, "Thought and affliction, passion, hell itself, / She turns to favour and to prettiness." But Schubert would have none of it and insists upon closer equivalence, transforming Müller's "Liederscherz" into "Liederschmerz." I do not think that the emendation was a slip of the pen.

The decision to omit three poems and alter the miller's experiences as the cycle swiftly shades into tragedy had other consequences as well. Müller's "Die liebe Farbe" is shot through with masochistic anger; one could summarize it as an artful conflation of the statements "When I'm dead, she'll be sorry" and "Since she likes green so much, I will cover myself in it – I can be a hunter too," the (non-)rivalry with the hunter continuing. The placement of this poem along an emotional crescendo was carefully calculated: "Die liebe Farbe" repeats and amplifies both the masochism and the anger of "Erster Schmerz,

197

letzter Scherz" just before it, elements which are then even more strongly adumbrated in "Die böse Farbe" and "Blümlein Vergißmein" just after. The notably passive miller lad is nonetheless overwhelmed by anger pervaded by masochism; in this degrading *perpetuum mobile*, rage is fuelled by the humiliation of continuing desire for someone who no longer, or never, loved him. Vengeful anger is particularly evident in the second stanza:

Die liebe Farbe	**The Beloved Color**
(stanza 2)	
Wohlauf zum fröhlichen Jagen	Up and away to the merry hunt!
Wohlauf durch Heid und Hagen!	Away over heath and hedge!
Mein Schatz hat's Jagen so gern.	My love is so fond of hunting.
Das Wild, das ich jage, das ist der Tod,	The game that I hunt is Death;
Die Heide, die heiß ich die Liebesnot.	the heath I call Love's Suffering.
Mein Schatz hat's Jagen so gern.	My love is so fond of hunting.

The bitter echo of the hunter's archetypal cry in the first line and the angry statement that he too can hunt are given rhythmic impetus by the injection of more anapaests than anywhere else in the poem – a hunter's gallop. The tragic-ironic quickening of the pace created by the first anapaest at the word "fröhlichen" (merry) in line 1 and the pounding hooves of lines 4 and 5, with two anapaests in each line at precisely the same places, thus underscoring the syntactical-allegorical parallelisms, are a distinct variation from the slower, more even rhythms of stanzas 1 and 3. Even the refrain reflects the quickened anger: "Mein Schatz hat's Jagen so gern," with its internal anapaest, in place of the iambic trimeters of "Mein Schatz hat's Grün so gern." The breathiness of the accented *h*s in stanza 2, line 5 ("Die *Heide*, die *heiß* ich die Liebesnot") further accentuates the anger, a poetic technique Müller would shortly thereafter use again in the lines "Lass ihre Hunde heulen / vor ihres Herren Haus!" from "Gute Nacht," the first poem of *Die Winterreise*. Even the rhythmically interspersed, piercingly bright -ee sounds ("Die . . . die . . . die . . . Lie[besnot]" and "ihre . . . ihres") are similar. It is surely not coincidental that Müller uses the same iambic-anapaestic tetrameters for stanza 2, lines 4–5 that he used in "Der Jäger," its anger and panic palpable.

Müller's magpie borrowings are once again on display in a poem whose poetic persona reminds us from within the stanzas that he is a poet-singer. It is poets, after all, who engage in the didactic allegory of the second stanza, the lad telling us what the signs signify, while the groves and heaths he seeks are resonant with echoes from Shakespeare's tragedies – *Othello* and *Hamlet* – and the antique world, especially the former. No one could drape himself figuratively in willow branches without recalling Desdemona's "Willow Song" in act 4, scene iii of *Othello*; one remembers her lines "I call'd my love false love, but what said he then? / Sing willow, willow, willow: / If I court no women, you'll lie with no men" and shudders at Müller's variation on the theme. Othello, for all the gorgeous grandiloquence of his language (the "Othello-music"), his heroic character, and his age, so unlike the young and un-heroic miller lad, undergoes the same harrowing-from-within as Müller's later creation: both the Moor and the miller are done to death, not so much by the possibility of unfaithfulness, for all the anguish they suffer in the name of infidelity, as by the fact of physicality in love. In the romantic universe Othello inhabits, and after him, the Minnesong-spouting miller lad, virginity is a state of enormous symbolic significance, a powerful state which, once lost, renders the woman dispossessed of it vulnerable to murder by a man who considers himself contaminated by her, a man who has staked his life on her: "But I do love thee! and when I love thee not / Chaos is come again." If the woman proves herself to be a sexual being, who gladly gives herself in the physical communion of lovemaking, the romantic protagonist is scarified, brought to violence (against the woman and against himself) by the thickness of a membrane. There can be no doubt that the beloved women in *Othello* and *Die schöne Müllerin* know of sex; it is surely one purpose of what the philosopher Stanley Cavell calls "the difficult and dirty dialogue" between Iago and Desdemona in act 2, scene i to make this evident, while the miller lad's imaginings of sex between the hunter and the miller's daughter are hints of his own knowledge of her body. "If such a man as Othello is rendered impotent and murderous by aroused, or by having aroused, female sexuality . . . if this man is horrified by human sexuality, in himself and in others, then no human being is free of this possibility," Cavell writes.[31] For all the obvious differences of language, form, literary traditions, milieu, verbal trappings of many kinds, Shakespeare and Müller tell similar tales.

Likewise, what one might call the sex nausea afflicting Hamlet, the sickened belief that love is a lie to hide mere lust, is what also overwhelms the miller lad from "Der Jäger" on. When Hamlet's rage and disgust at Gertrude are transferred to Ophelia, whom he suddenly decides is also tainted, he mortally infects her with the filth corrupting his own imaginings; both then descend into a hell of madness and uncontrollable voyeuristic images in the mind. If Hamlet regains control of himself before the end, Ophelia, a broken reed, does not and sings herself to death. Like Hamlet, the miller lad becomes "passion's slave" – like Ophelia, he becomes at last pathetic, vulnerable, seeking a watery death like hers. But as always, Müller varies what he borrows, if indeed he took his cue from Shakespeare: his lad, however torn and tormented by sexual knowledge he cannot bear, dies in full possession of his wits and in tragic consciousness of what he does and why; it is women, not men, in Romantic and post-Romantic literature who tend to go mad for love. Unlike Ophelia, whose "melodious lays" continue until the water drags her under, the miller lad relinquishes all song to the brook as he dies. If the "tears seven times salt" Laertes invokes at the sight of the mad Ophelia belong to Müller's lad as well, it is for somewhat different cause and in a different context.

But what does Schubert do with the anger in "Die liebe Farbe," its bitter-tragic sarcasm evident in the title? He literally buries it in a dead march. If he has grounds to do so, if Müller invites funereal strains in stanza 3, that does not obviate the energy of the poet's stanza 2; we have already seen the *Kleinmeister* Reissiger respond to the electric charge of anger with new music at that point, but Schubert refuses to do so. (The lad who wishes to be buried with "Kein Kreuzlein schwarz, kein Blümlein bunt" is perhaps echoing Müller's own "Waldeskönig," discussed in chapter 2, a poem which ends with the line, "Kein Kreuz im Wege stehn." Just as the miller lad assumes the hunter's garb, so he assumes his rival's archetypal disdain for religious rites; the hunter's atheistic burial wishes become the miller lad's funeral directives. The word "Blümlein," one notices, will shortly recur with poisonous new significance in "Blümlein Vergißmein.")

Here is where the lad first contemplates suicide, more seriously at this point in Schubert than in Müller. It is not until after both "Blümlein Vergißmein" and "Trock'ne Blumen" that the poet's character is unwaveringly fixed in his resolve to kill himself, that the thoughts of suicide are translated into action. When Schubert sounds a haunting tocsin for the dead throughout "Die liebe Farbe," when he drenches the solo piano passages in appoggiaturas whose suggestions of longing are almost unbearably poignant (the fact that the appoggiatura on the downbeat of m. 3 does not resolve until the downbeat of m. 5, the cadence at the end of the piano introduction, is a breathtaking detail), when he entirely subverts the anger in the words "Mein Schatz hat's Grün so gern," he makes his miller lad more pitiable than the poet's and closer to death. Müller's lad still has a spark of angry energy commingled with the wistful despair, but there is no anger in Schubert's setting.

Schubert had reasons, even if we can only guess what they might be, for deleting "Das Mühlenleben," "Erster Schmerz, letzter Scherz," and "Blümlein Vergißmein." But fools rush in where angels fear to tread: almost forty years after the composition of Schubert's cycle, the vocal pedagogue and would-be composer Ludwig Stark (1831–1884), one of the founders of the Stuttgart Hochschule für Musik, would set the three omitted poems, plus Eichendorff's "Der traurige Jäger" (see chapter 2), as the *Nachtrag zu Franz Schubert's Liedercyklus 'Die schöne Müllerin'* (Supplement to Franz Schubert's Song Cycle 'The Fair Maid of the Mill'), op. 54, published circa 1880 by Stürmer in Stuttgart, and intended for interpolation into performances of Schubert's masterpiece.[32] In the preface, Stark at first apologizes for the "immodesty" of placing his compositions next to those of the "unerreichten Meister des deutschen Liedes" (the unrivalled master of German song), then explains that complete performances of the cycle had hitherto entailed spoken readings of the three poems from Müller's cycle that Schubert omitted, thus introducing a "foreign element" into a musical work.[33] How fascinating to discover that "Das Mühlenleben," "Erster Schmerz, letzter Scherz," and "Blümlein Vergißmein" were in fact read aloud at performances! How, one wonders, was the last of those poems received? Did no one notice what strong stuff this is? Certainly it burns holes through Müller's reputation as a lachrymose peddler of wishy-washy sentiment.

These Starkly awful interpolations do not do the poetry justice, however; Stark, a modernist prone to inept Lisztian gestures, flounders haplessly. One plays the first measures of "Das Mühlenleben," realizes that it would have been sandwiched between Schubert's "Der Neugierige" and "Ungeduld" in performance, and winces; even more shocking, Stark presumed to end Schubert's cycle with his (Stark's) music to Eichendorff. Whatever the ostensible pose of humility, this is chutzpah indeed. The rustic opening strains of "Das Mühlenleben" alternate with a faster section in 2/4, emblematic of the miller lad's outbursts of claustrophobic panic, followed by the return of relative calm – an admirable conception, one supposes, if only the level of musical invention were higher. When Stark quotes the hunter's fanfares from Schubert's "Die böse Farbe" as the introduction to "Der traurige Jäger" and then varies the passage at Eichendorff's words "Er blies so irre Weise," Schubert's music consumes Stark's flimsier stuff (the composer's name the ironic inverse of his compositional skills) altogether, and the latter-day school administrator seems not to have had a clue about what transpires in "Blümlein Vergißmein." Stark, fortunately, did not attempt to set the texts Schubert had composed so unforgettably over half-a-century earlier. In fact, Schubert was, to my knowledge, the only composer to set "Am Feierabend," "Tränenregen," "Pause," "Mit dem grünen Lautenbande," "Der Jäger," and "Eifersucht und Stolz" to music until Arnold Bredemeyer's settings in 1985 both of *Die Winterreise* and *Die schöne Müllerin* (many of the poems in *Die Winterreise* were also passed over by other composers), nor did any composer besides the inept Stark try his hand at the poems Schubert omitted. Did the poetic complexities, the emotional fluctuations and ambiguities Müller captures so vividly, the anger and self-abasement in poems such as "Der Jäger," frighten off everyone else? Or did Schubert himself and the achievement his cycle represents scare away those who came after him?

CONCLUSION: MEN AND WOMEN, LOVE AND DEATH

In *Die schöne Müllerin*, Müller availed himself of the long literary tradition by which women lament their abandonment, delve into tormented introspection, and kill themselves when all hope of love is lost – but it is a man, not a woman, who does so here. Men, as Lawrence Lipking has pointed out, often write poems in the assumed voice of the abandoned woman, to affirm their own maleness and their power over women, to learn how to feel and hence, how to be a poet at all, to see themselves mirrored in a woman's eyes and thereby discover who they are (this is what the miller lad wants), or to immerse themselves in the alien Other, even though the best such poets (Eduard Mörike comes to mind) still leave traces of themselves behind in the poem.[34] Müller turns the tables: it is the *male* lover who is innocent of sexual knowledge at the beginning, who is rejected and abandoned, who abases himself and begs for the beloved's return, and who kills himself in the end. These are all elements in a scenario not only traditionally associated with women but which often *defines* women, either as victims of abandonment or potential victims of abandonment; the man can leave at any time and frequently does. Here, those same elements become the properties of a male character, but this is not mere transposition – change the pronouns, nothing else, and all will still be applicable, for men as well as for women. Müller's enterprise was different and more complex.

Müller is not merely saying that men too suffer and die for loss of love, although that is one element of *Die schöne Müllerin*. Rather, he explores the *male* side of the equation of abandonment when the male persona is a poet-singer, someone committed to exploration of the life of feeling. When a man is abandoned, he feels like a woman, and those male poets who probe the sensations of abandonment are suspect in gender, vulnerable to the charge that they are effeminate beings. When Müller created a gentle, well-mannered miller lad who admits that he cuts no heroic figure and who, once abandoned, abases himself in pleading for the beloved's return, he was in effect saying, "Yes, poets necessarily stress that which is feminine in themselves," although the Poet's swaggering in the prologue and epilogue constitutes a counter-reply "No." The controlling voice, the rejection of feminine tears and feminine feeling in the poetic Foreword and Afterword, are defensive exaggerations of masculinity by one who perhaps feared that he had come

201

too close to the woman within him. But whatever the masculine posturing of the poet who speaks at the beginning and end, the story within those bookends is a narrative of love and loss, Müller even suggesting that abandonment is the very condition of song. The pleading, the abasement, the anger, the misery one finds from "Der Jäger" on are all addressed to a vanished object, are inspired by absence; when the miller lad believes himself happy, he cannot write, but the gigantic misery of love's loss, misery which tears the sinews and rends the breath, brings back the Muse. With the miller maid irretrievably gone, he can take the lute from the wall and retune its strings to sound "new songs."

Müller did not, of course, invent the literary depiction of young men destroyed by their first brush with love as it is rather than love on the printed page; Werther was only one of many such characters Müller might have known. But Müller *can* lay claim to startling originality in one aspect of *Die schöne Müllerin*, and that is the experience recounted in "Blümlein Vergißmein," an experience belonging only to men. In this harrowing poem, Müller brings to poetic life the phenomenon of male hostility to women, the fear and loathing that are engendered when a man's sexual innocence is lost. As the miller maid abandons the lad for the hunter, primal hatred for the sexual Other erupts into being, an unlooked-for volcano of anxiety and terror. Müller connects the experience to sight, specifically, to sight of the female body unveiled, and he does so in a remarkably imaginative and powerful way. The power is all the greater because Müller makes it clear that the lad does not suspect at the beginning of the poem that he will be overwhelmed by uncontrollable rage in a matter of minutes, rage pervaded by anguish beyond bearing. It is no wonder that the lad wants the angels to shut their eyes and the moon to veil itself in clouds in "Der Müller und der Bach," no wonder that the brook at the end tells him, "Close your eyes" ("Tu' die Augen zu"), and demands the miller maid's shawl "daß ich die Augen ihm halte bedeckt" (that I may keep his eyes covered).[35] The greatest comfort the brook-poet can offer at the end is the obliteration of earthly sight – "You do not have to see the abyss any longer," it says pityingly – and a vision of cosmic beauty to supersede the earlier vision of hell. When it tells of the full moon rising into the heavens and the dispelling of the mist symbolic of all that evades our understanding in this life, it insists upon the ultimate victory of harmony and beauty in the realm of the infinite.

One infers Schubert's strong reaction to "Blümlein Vergißmein" in his deletion of it from op. 25. Did he shy away from its sexual explicitness because of possible problems with censorship or because he found it objectionable? The flower imagery is, after all, no euphemistic veil for the radical frankness of this poem but rather a way of heightening the intensity poetically; the lad has seen that which shocks and wounds him to the core, and his creator paints shocking pictures of the sight in our minds, images that writhe and fester.[36] We will never know why Schubert acted as he did, but I doubt it was timidity which dictated his decision. He had, in May of 1823, set to music Schiller's "Der Pilgrim" (The Pilgrim), and that poem is the strongest of strong stuff, its subject an allegory of youthful religious fervor become nihilism in the course of life's journey; if Schubert rejected "Blümlein Vergißmein" and rewrote "Mein!", it was, I would like to believe, for other reasons. In his revisions of Müller, Schubert rescues the poet's character not from death but from "the Medusa experience," and he grants him an idyll of almost unalloyed happiness, brief though it is. If love ends in death, so be it, I can almost

202

imagine Schubert saying to himself, but it shall not be *this* death, nor shall he be deprived of all joy in his love. It was bold, even heroic, of Müller to find words for what one conjectures must have been an experience he himself knew, in imagination if not in actuality, and equally heroic of Schubert to turn it away. As I stated at the beginning, I do not mean to imply that supplying the right biographical item provides the key to a complex artistic event, either for Müller or for Schubert, but I *do* believe that neither man was in thralldom to an abstraction; works like these do not spring from such shadowy ground. Given what Schubert himself was confronting, his revisions (if these speculations have any validity) of Müller's *Die schöne Müllerin* are almost unbearably moving.

Notes

1 Behind the scenes: the genesis of Wilhelm Müller's cycle

1 Wilhelm Müller, *Sieben- und siebzig Gedichte aus den hinterlassenen Papieren eines reisenden Waldhornisten* (Dessau: Christian Georg Ackermann, 1821), pp. 3–48. Müller was fond of poetic antitheses: the cycle that follows *Die schöne Müllerin* in the anthology is entitled *Johannes und Esther.* (*Im Frühling zu lesen*). Madeleine Haefeli-Rasi, in *Wilhelm Müller. 'Die schöne Müllerin': Eine Interpretation als Beitrag zum Thema* STILWANDEL *im Übergang von der Spätromantik zum Realismus* (Zürich: Schippert & Co., 1970), suggests an additional significance for the subtitle "(Im Winter zu lesen)." Müller, in her opinion, looks back at the remembered springtime of Romantic unities from the disillusioned, wintry vantage point of one no longer able to subscribe to Romantic doctrine.

2 Max Friedländer, "Die Entstehung der Müllerlieder. Eine Erinnerung an Frau von Olfers" in *Deutsche Rundschau*, 19/2 (1892), 301–07. There have been many subsequent brief references to the Stägemann circle in the wake of Friedländer's essay; the most recent appears in Bernd Leistner's "Einleitung" to Wilhelm Müller, *Werke. Tagebücher. Briefe*, vol. 1: *Gedichte I*, ed. Maria-Verena Leistner (Berlin: Gatza, 1994), pp. xvi–xvii and xxii–xxv.

3 Periodically, scholars argue otherwise. See Alan Cottrell, *Wilhelm Müller's Lyrical Song-Cycles: Interpretations and Texts* (Chapel Hill, North Carolina: The University of North Carolina Press, 1970); Klaus Günther Just, "Wilhelm Müllers Liederzyklen 'Die schöne Müllerin' und 'Die Winterreise' in *Übergänge: Probleme und Gestalten der Literatur* (Bern and Munich: Francke, 1966), pp. 133–52; John Reed, in "'Die schöne Müllerin' Reconsidered," *Music and Letters* 59 (1978), 411–19; and the author's *Retracing a Winter's Journey: Schubert's Winterreise* (Ithaca, New York & London: Cornell University Press, 1991) and *Schubert: Die schöne Müllerin* (Cambridge, England: Cambridge University Press, 1992).

4 Friedrich August was studying law at the University at Halle in 1784 when he first saw Johanna Elisabeth Fischer Graun (born in 1761 to a Königsberg merchant Johann Jakob Fischer and his wife Regina née Hartung), unhappily married to the son of Carl Heinrich Graun (the composer of *Der Tod Jesu*); although Graun had abandoned his wife and their two children Antoinette and Ferdinand in 1787, Stägemann was not able to marry Elisabeth until 1796. See Margarete von Olfers, *Elisabeth v. Staegemann. Lebensbild einer deutschen Frau 1761–1835* (Leipzig: Koehler & Amelang, 1937); Erich Mayr, *Friedrich August von Stägemann* (Munich: Kastner & Callwey, 1913); Elisabeth von Stägemann, *Erinnerungen für edle Frauen. Nebst Lebensnachrichten über die Verfasserin und einem Anhange von Briefen*, ed. Wilhelm Dorow, 2 vols. (Leipzig: Hinrichs'che Buchhandlung, 1846) and "Briefe an Fr. Reichardt" in Karl von Holtei, ed., *Dreihundert Briefe aus zwei Jahrhunderten*, vol. 2 (Hannover: Karl Rumpler, 1872), pp. 155–66. As early as 1788, Elisabeth Graun's house in Königsberg had become a "bildungsbürgerlich" salon whose guests included the composers Franz Benda and Vincenzo Righini, the young E. T. A. Hoffmann, Immanuel Kant, Johann

Friedrich Reichardt, and Heinrich von Kleist. See Petra Wilhelmy, *Der Berliner Salon im 19. Jahrhundert (1780–1914)* (Berlin & New York: Walter de Gruyter, 1989), pp. 142–44 and 848–60, also Kurt Fervers, *Berliner Salons, die Geschichte einer grossen Verschwörung* (Munich: Deutscher Volksverlag, *c.* 1940).

5 See Hedwig Abeken, *Hedwig von Olfers geb. von Staegemann. Ein Lebenslauf,* 2 vols. (Berlin: Mittler & Sohn, 1908).

6 Friedrich Förster, ed., *Die Sängerfahrt. Eine Neujahrsgabe für Freunde der Dichtkunst und Mahlerey* (Berlin: Maurer, 1818, facsimile edition published in Heidelberg by Lambert Schneider, [1969?]).

7 Reichardt's letter-essay "Etwas über das Liederspiel" (On the Liederspiel) in the Leipzig *Allgemeine Musikalische Zeitung* 43 (July 22, 1801), 709–17, is reprinted and translated in Appendix I to Ruth Otto Bingham, "The Song Cycle in German-Speaking Countries 1790–1840: Approaches to a Changing Genre," Ph.D. diss., Cornell University, 1993, pp. 251–64; for her discussion of the *Liederspiel,* see pp. 69–85. Reichardt's *Lieder aus dem Liederspiel Lieb' und Treue* was published in Berlin by Johann Friedrich Unger in 1800; the first song in the work is a setting of Goethe's "Heidenröslein." For more on the *Liederspiel,* see Ludwig Kraus, "Das Liederspiel in den Jahren 1800 bis 1830: Ein Beitrag zur Geschichte des deutschen Singspiele," Ph.D. diss., Vereinigte Friedrichs-Universität Halle-Wittenberg, 1921; Susanne Johns, *Das szenische Liederspiel zwischen 1800 und 1830: Ein Beitrag zur Berliner Theatergeschichte,* 2 vols. (Frankfurt am Main: Peter Lang, 1988); and Luise Eitel Peake, "The Song Cycle: A Preliminary Inquiry into the Beginnings of the Romantic Song Cycle and the Nature of an Art Form," Ph.D. diss., Columbia University, 1968, although her account of the Stägemann circle's activities in ch. 4, "A Play with Songs" (pp. 177–83) should be taken with a grain of salt. Peake chose to flesh out the sparse documentation with a story of her own devising, difficult to disentangle from the facts of the matter. She also writes (p. 177) that the documents relating to the Stägemann meetings "do not, in themselves, contain anything . . . worth preserving," with which I do not agree.

8 See Johann Friedrich Reichardt, *Goethe's Lieder, Oden, Balladen und Romanzen - Dritte Abtheilung: Balladen und Romanzen* (Leipzig: Breitkopf & Härtel, 1809), facsimile edition (Wiesbaden: Breitkopf & Härtel, 1969). Both Hedwig and Müller were musically talented: in a letter to Antoinette Schwinck dated "Berlin, 30 November 1816," Hedwig writes, "Recently we had a concert at our house. Wild, Mlle Blanc, Herr Grell and others sang, and the Rosens, Pappenheims, etc. were the audience. I sang a duet with Grell in which the chorus enters at the last lines and repeats the stanza. It was the only German piece sung that evening, and the simple melody to quiet words, the bashful manner that sometimes escapes attention, was most effective." Müller sang in choral societies, married a gifted contralto named Adelheid Basedow in 1821, and became a friend of Carl Maria von Weber, to whom the second volume of *Waldhornisten-Gedichte* is dedicated.

9 Wilhelm Müller, *Blumenlese aus den Minnesingern,* vol. 1 (Berlin: Maurer, 1816). There was no volume two.

10 *Diary and Letters of Wilhelm Müller,* ed. Philip Schuyler Allen and James Taft Hatfield (Chicago, Illinois: The University of Chicago Press, 1903), p. 22. The diaries have recently reappeared in Wilhelm Müller, *Werke. Tagebücher. Briefe,* vol. 5: *Tagebücher,* ed. Maria-Verena Leistner (Berlin: Gatza, 1994).

11 Johann Wolfgang Goethe, *Briefwechsel mit Friedrich Schiller,* ed. Ernst Beutler (Zürich: Artemis Verlag, 1950), p. 906.

12 The opera was shortened and reorganized for export: in accord with the old-fashioned theatrical conventions still current in Naples in the late 1780s, Paisiello had divided his comic opera into three acts, the last containing only three scenes, while contemporary fashion elsewhere favored two acts. In order to achieve the reorganization into two acts, companies would either exclude the third act altogether, remove the second-act finale (no. 26) and substitute the last section of the third act, or retain only the last section of the third act and place

it just prior to the second-act finale, now become the finale to the entire opera. See Michael F. Robinson, *Giovanni Paisiello: A Thematic Catalogue of his Works*, vol. 1: *Dramatic Works* (Stuyvesant, New York: Pendragon Press, 1991), pp. 415–33. Vocal arrangements include a score consisting only of the overture and favorite arias arranged for keyboard by Beethoven's teacher Christian Gottlob Neefe (Bonn: Simrock, n.d.). The "complete" two-act score without the spoken dialogue was published in Berlin in 180–? by E. H. G. Christiani and in another two-act version with dialogue edited by Richard Kleinmichel and published in Vienna by Universal-Edition Aktien Gesellschaft and in Leipzig by Bartholf Senff.

13 The plaintive quality of "Nel cor più non mi sento," the pathos at which Paisiello excelled, made this air one of the great best-sellers of the era: Beethoven used it twice for theme-and-variation sets, for the *Neun Variationen* in A major for piano, WoO 69, and the *Sechs Variationen* in G major, WoO 70.

14 Did Beethoven know this opera and remember it at some level when he composed the beautiful canonic quartet "Mir ist so wunderbar" in *Fidelio?* The would-be lovers of *L'amor contrastato / Die schöne Müllerin* sing a canonic quartet, "Ansioso, curioso, pien di dubbio il cor mi sta," or "O wie sehnlich voll Verlangen," in act 1 about the mingled anxiety and longing with which they await the outcome of so many simultaneous suits. The contrapuntal intensification tells us that, whatever the comic surroundings, the characters are aware of the "chagrins d'amour" as well as its "plaisirs."

15 When Wilhelm Hensel went off to fight in the War of Liberation, Luise wrote a number of poems about the war ("Beim Einzug der Krieger," "Schlachtgesang der Frauen") and her anxious love for her brother; these poems were republished in 1917 with the ascription to "Luise Hensel, unser Vorbild in Kriegsnöten," or "Luise Hensel, our predecessor in wartime tribulations."

16 *Theodor Körner's Sämmtliche Werke*, ed. Karl Streckfuß (Berlin: Nicolai, 1835 and Vienna: Carl Gerold, 1835), p. 82 from the "Nachtrag, Ungedrucktes." Körner also wrote a German contrafactum to Paisiello's "Nel cor più non mi sento," beginning "Wie still mit Geisterbeben / Die Sehnsucht mich durchglüht."

17 Förster's works include *Friedrichs des Grossen Jugendjahre, Bildung und Geist* (Berlin: A. M. Schlesinger, 1823); *Neuere und neueste preussische Geschichte* (Berlin: G. Hempel, 1851–61); a continuation to Adalbert von Chamisso's *Peter Schlemihl's wundersame Geschichte* entitled *Peter Schlemihl's Heimkehr* (Leipzig: B. G. Teubner, 1849, 2nd ed.); a book of Italian travel lore entitled *Briefe eines lebenden* (Berlin: Duncker & Humblot, 1831); reminiscences of his youth; and a three-volume account of the War of Liberation.

18 *Diary and Letters of Wilhelm Müller*, p. 87. In the entry for November 10, 1816, Müller writes, "After a long interruption, I resume my diary. Time has lapsed in which I lived very frivolously, without thought. I have been in Dessau for over four weeks: when I am away from Luise, I am always a worse person."

19 According to Dieter Siebenkäs, *Ludwig Berger: Sein Leben und seine Werke unter besonderer Berücksichtigung seines Liedschaffens* (Berlin: Verlag Merseburger, 1963), p. 18, Berger's manuscript of "Rose, die Müllerin" is dated October 16, 1816. The chronology is foggy both for the Stägemann *Liederspiel* and Berger's involvement with the group.

20 Clemens Brentano's *Gesammelte Briefe von 1795 bis 1842*, vol. 8 of the *Gesammelte Schriften* (Frankfurt am Main: J. D. Sauerländer, 1855), p. 216.

21 Franz Binder, *Luise Hensel. Ein Lebensbild nach gedruckten und ungedruckten Quellen* (Freiburg im Breisgau: Herder, 1885), p. 37.

22 Ruth Otto Bingham, "The Song Cycle in German-Speaking Countries 1790–1840," p. 136.

23 Friedrich Förster, *Die Sängerfahrt*, p. 149.

24 Frank Spiecker, *Luise Hensel als Dichterin: Eine psychologische Studie ihres Werdens auf Grund des handschriftlichen Nachlasses* (Evanston, Illinois: Northwestern University, 1936), pp. 150–61. See also Bingham, "The Song Cycle in German-Speaking Countries," pp. 139–40.

25 The miller poems published in various anthologies between 1816 and 1818 include:

"Wanderschaft" (which also appeared under the titles "Wanderlust" and "Das Wandern"), "Wohin?" (also entitled "Müllers Wanderlied" and "Der Bach"), "Am Feierabend" (also "Feierabend"), "Der Neugierige" (also entitled "Am Bach"), "Das Mühlenleben," "Des Müllers Blumen" (also entitled "Meine Blumen"), "Thränenregen," "Mein!" (also entitled "Das schönste Lied"), "Ein ungereimtes Lied," "Der Jäger" (also entitled "Als er den Jäger sah"), "Eifersucht und Stolz" (also entitled "Trotzige Eifersucht"), "Erster Schmerz, letzter Scherz," "Die liebe Farbe" (also entitled "Das liebe Grün"), "Die böse Farbe" (also entitled "Der Müller"), "Trock'ne Blumen" (or "Müllers trockne Blumen"), "Der Müller und der Bach," and "Des Baches Wiegenlied" (or "Des Baches Lied" and "Wiegenlied des Baches"). James Taft Hatfield, who edited *Wilhelm Müller Gedichte: Vollständige kritische Ausgabe* (Berlin: B. Behr, 1906), p. 452, felt that "Das Mühlenleben" might be among the oldest of the miller poems because of Luise Hensel's possible influence. Between May 25 and June 8, 1818, *Der Gesellschafter* printed Müller's cycle *Müller-Lieder* in six issues, each containing two poems: (1) "Am Bach" and "Meine Blumen"; (2) "Das schönste Lied" and "Ein ungereimtes Lied"; (3) Als er den Jäger sah" and "Trotzige Eifersucht"; (4) "Erster Schmerz, letzter Scherz" and "Das liebe Grün"; (5) "Das böse Grün" and "Müllers trockne Blumen"; and (6) "Der Müller und der Bach" and "Wiegenlied des Baches." Bingham observes ("The Song Cycle in German-Speaking Countries 1790–1840," pp. 159–60) that although the resemblances to Ludwig Berger's song cycle op. 11 are quite striking (not surprising, as the two worked together closely), the differences are equally striking, in particular, Müller's omission of the gardener, the hunter, the messenger birds, and the miller maid. Furthermore, she notes Müller's addition of two tragic poems, thus altering Berger's emphasis on lighter songs appropriate to a *Liederspiel* (p. 162).

26 *Frauentaschenbuch für das Jahr 1820* (Nürnberg: Johann Leonhardt Schrag, 1820), p. 197. In the same issue, one also finds Wilhelm Hensel's "Sonett. An meine Schwester" (Sonnet to my Sister) on p. 330; the brother–sister pair were very close. One notes that Wilhelm Hensel eventually married a woman – Fanny Mendelssohn – who was also extremely close to her brother in complex ways.

27 Friedrich Förster, ed., *Die Sängerfahrt*, p. 97.

28 Ibid., pp. 201–02.

29 This poem was originally published in *Der Gesellschafter* for 1817 and then reprinted in Max Friedländer's 1922 edition of Schubert's cycle (Leipzig: C. F. Peters, 1922), p. 108.

30 The poem was originally published in Friedrich Wilhelm Gubitz's (1768–1870) *Der Gesellschafter* for May 30, 1818.

31 In the *Diary and Letters of Wilhelm Müller*, entry for October 8, 1815, p. 5, Müller writes as if speaking to E. T. A. Hoffmann's Kapellmeister Kreisler, saying "I closely resemble your Enemy of Music. I can neither play nor sing, but when I write poetry, then I both sing and play. If I could invent melodies, my poems would be more pleasing, but I trust I can find a kindred spirit [well-tuned soul] who can hear the melodies in the words and give them back to me." See Carl Koch, *Bernhard Klein (1793–1832). Sein Leben und seine Werke* (Leipzig: Oscar Brandstetter, 1902), pp. 34–35 for Müller's letter to Klein.

32 Ruth Otto Bingham, "The Song Cycle in German-Speaking Countries 1790–1840," p. 149.

33 *Diary and Letters of Wilhelm Müller*, p. 89.

34 Ludwig Rellstab, *Ludwig Berger, ein Denkmal* (Berlin: T. Trautwein, 1846), pp. 111–12.

35 Heinrich Lohre, ed., *Wilhelm Müller als Kritiker und Erzähler. Ein Lebensbild mit Briefen an F. A. Brockhaus und anderen Schriftstücken* (Leipzig: F. A. Brockhaus, 1927), p. 274, letter of February 19, 1827.

36 Cecilia Baumann, *Wilhelm Müller - The Poet of the Schubert Song Cycles: His Life and Works* (University Park, Pennsylvania: Pennsylvania State University Press, 1981).

37 Additional sources of biographical information about Luise Hensel include Ferdinand Bartscher, *Der innere Lebensgang der Dichterin Luise Hensel nach den Original-Aufzeichnungen in ihren Tagebüchern* (Paderborn: Schoningh, 1882); Hermann Cardauns, *Aufzeichnungen und*

Briefe von Luise Hensel (Hamm: Breer & Thiemann, 1916); Hermann Cardauns, *Aus Luise Hensels Jugendzeit: Neue Briefe und Gedichte zum Jahrhunderttag ihrer Konversion (8. Dezember 1818)* (Freiburg im Breisgau: Herder, 1918); Winfried Freund, *Müde bin ich, geh' zur Ruh: Leben und Werk der Luise Hensel* (Wiedenbruck: Guth & Etscheidt, 1984); Oskar Kohler, *Müde bin ich, geh' zur Ruh: Die hell-dunkle Lebensgeschichte Luise Hensels* (Paderborn: Schoningh, 1991); Joseph Hubert Reinkens, *Luise Hensel und ihre Lieder* (Bonn: P. Neusser, 1877); Hans Rupprich, *Brentano, Luise Hensel und Ludwig von Gerlach* (Vienna & Leipzig: Österreichischer Bundesverlag für Unterricht, Wissenschaft, und Kunst, 1927); and Hubert Schiel, *Clemens Brentano und Luise Hensel. Mit bisher ungedruckten Briefen* (Frankfurt am Main: Gesellschaft der Bibliophilen, 1956).

38 Ries's setting was his op. 8, no. 1 published by Sulzer, while Reinecke's op. 37, no. 3 was published by Breitkopf & Härtel. See Ernst Challier, *Grosser Lieder-Katalog* (Berlin: Published by the author, 1885), p. 604; see also *Lieder von Luise Hensel*, ed. Hermann Cardauns (Regensburg: Josef Habbel, 1923), p. 71.

39 *Die Sängerfahrt* ends with a section containing thirteen *Geistliche Lieder*, four of them ("Todtenfeier," "Gebet," "Trost," and "Ergebung" on pp. 264–67) by "Ludwiga."

40 Hedwig Abeken, *Hedwig von Olfers. Ein Lebenslauf*, vol. 1, p. 293.

41 *Lieder von Luise Hensel*, pp. 40–41, 60–61, 77–78, 72–73, and 67.

42 Ibid., p. 46.

43 *Diary and Letters of Wilhelm Müller*, the entry for November 30, 1815, p. 54.

44 *Lieder von Luise Hensel*, ed. Hermann Cardauns, p. 56.

45 Schiel, *Clemens Brentano und Luise Hensel*, p. 129. After reading this passage, it comes as no surprise that when Luise converted to Catholicism and made her first confession, she wrote a poem on December 7, 1818 entitled "An St. Maria Magdalena" (To Saint Mary Magdalen), the archetypal female sinner-turned-saint, the witness to Christ's resurrection, and the first person to be charged with proclaiming the Christian message. In the second stanza of three, Luise mourns her sinfulness: "Ich hab' ihn viel gekränkt / Und hab' es wohl gewußt; / Mein Herz hab' ich ertränkt / In Erdeschmerz und -lust. / Ich hab' ihn oft vergessen, / Den ich doch früh erkannt, / Und habe ganz vermessen / Von ihm mich abgewandt." See Winfried Freund, *Müde bin ich, geh' zur Ruh: Leben und Werk der Luise Hensel*, p. 108, also Susan Haskins, *Mary Magdalen: Myth and Metaphor* (New York: Riverhead Books, 1993), pp. 1–3.

46 Cited in Wilhelm Müller, *Vermischte Schriften*, ed. Gustav Schwab, vol. 1 (Leipzig: F. A. Brockhaus, 1830), p. xxvi, and in Madeleine Haefeli-Rasi, *Wilhelm Müller. Die schöne Müllerin*, p. 9.

47 Luise's attraction to Hartmann von Aue's *Der arme Heinrich* is unsurprising, given its theme of physical transformation – Heinrich becomes a leper – as the agency of spiritual growth. One of the principal characters is a maiden in early adolescence whose conflicts regarding sexuality, God, and death might well have spoken to Luise's own conflicts, all the more so because it has a fairy-tale ending after the harrowing of hell the maiden and Heinrich undergo. See Susan L. Clark, *Hartmann von Aue: Landscapes of Mind* (Houston, Texas: Rice University Press, 1989).

48 See *Diary and Letters of Wilhelm Müller*, entry for October 15, 1815, p. 10.

49 Ibid., entry for November 8, 1815, p. 38.

50 Ibid., p. 47.

51 Ibid., entry for October 23, 1815, pp. 19–20.

52 Ibid., entry for November 30, 1815, p. 55.

53 Ibid., entry for December 28, 1815, p. 70.

54 Ibid., entry for December 10, 1815, p. 59.

55 Ibid., entry for February 1–4, 1816, p. 85. See also Cardauns, ed., *Lieder von Luise Hensel*, p. 71.

56 *Diary and Letters of Wilhelm Müller*, entry for November 10, 1816, p. 87.

57 Ibid., entry for December 15, 1816, pp. 89–90.

58 Hedwig Abeken, *Hedwig von Olfers*, vol. 2, p. 3 and *Diary and Letters of Wilhelm Müller*, pp. 39–40. Lilies connote virginity: no wonder Müller was jealous.

59 Hedwig Abeken, *Hedwig von Olfers*, vol. 2, pp. 14–15, and Schiel, *Clemens Brentano und Luise Hensel*, pp. 15–16. See also Frank Spiecker, "Clemens Brentano und Luise Hensel: Eine Schicksalsstunde im Leben zweier Romantiker" in *Journal of English and Germanic Philology*, vol. 34 (1994): 59–73.

60 Luise's Hensel's "Bruchstücke aus dem äußern und innern Leben des seligen Clemens Brentano," was written for Emilie Brentano's preface to the *Gesammelte Schriften* and was later reproduced by Schiel in *Clemens Brentano und Luise Hensel*, pp. 60–66. In the "Bruchstücke," Luise writes of herself in the third person, and does not even identify the house as belonging to the Stägemanns – Clemens Brentano is one of the only people mentioned by name. It is Luise's account one finds in Johannes Baptist Diel and Wilhelm Kreiten, *Clemens Brentano: Ein Lebensbild nach gedruckten und ungedruckten Quellen*, vol. 2: *1814–1842* (Freiburg im Breisgau: Herder, 1878), although this source must be read with a grain of salt. The Catholic Diel devises an anti-Protestant account of Luise's conversion and thereby distorts the documentary record. For example, according to them (p. 66) Brentano poured out his distress to Luise on the second or third evening after their first meeting and then said, "Read the seventh chapter of the Letters to the Romans and you will understand my plight," to which Luise supposedly replied, "You mean the eighth chapter . . . What help is it to say all this to a young girl? You are so lucky as a Catholic to have confession: tell what troubles you to your priest." At these words, Brentano burst into loud weeping and declared "Nun soll mir das die lutherische Pfarrerstochter sagen!", at which Herr von Stägemann came running. But it was in Brentano's second letter to Luise, a letter dated December 1816, that he told her "Read the seventh and eighth chapters of Romans – therein is my situation and my longing." See Clemens Brentano, *Briefe*, ed. Friedrich Seebass, vol. 2: *1810–1824* (Nürnberg: Hans Carl, 1951), p. 185.

61 Brentano's mother, Maximiliane von La Roche, who he felt had neglected him, was the daughter of the famous eighteenth-century novelist Sophie von La Roche; that he himself later married a writer named Sophie and had a stormy marriage seems too neat a coincidence to be truly coincidental. Alfred Gerz, in *Wandel und Treue. Karoline von Günderode, Bettina von Arnim, Sophie Mereau, Luise Hensel* (Potsdam: Rütten & Loening, 1938), published poems by four women poets all connected in some way with Brentano, Achim von Arnim, and their circle. The letters of Brentano and his first wife, published in *Briefwechsel zwischen Clemens Brentano und Sophie Mereau*, 2 vols., ed. Heinz Amelung (Leipzig: Insel Verlag, 1908) and *Lebe der Liebe und Liebe das Leben: Der Briefwechsel von Clemens Brentano und Sophie Mereau*, ed. Dagmar von Gersdorff (Frankfurt am Main: Insel Verlag, 1981), are remarkable for the sharp antitheses of naiveté and perversity, blasphemy and religious ecstasy, sentimental longing and near-insanity – Sophie even told him at one time, "Clemens, you are a demon! You are an oddity, a spirit, not a man." Regarding the dissolution of Brentano's second marriage to Auguste Bussmann, see Heinz Rölleke, "Zu Brentanos Eheschließung mit Auguste Bussmann" in *Jahrbuch des Freien Deutschen Hochstifts 1978*, ed. Detlev Lüders (Tübingen: Max Niemeyer Verlag, 1978), pp. 291–97, and Hans Magnus Enzensberger, *Requiem für eine Romantische Frau: Die Geschichte von Auguste Bussmann und Clemens Brentano* (Berlin: Friedenauer Presse, 1988). Auguste Bussmann's mother, Maria Elisabeth Bussmann, married a Vicomte de Flavigny as her second husband; their daughter was Marie d'Agoult, Franz Liszt's mistress.

62 Brentano's other Luise-poems include "Weihelied zum Ziel und Ende," 1816; "An den Engel der Wüste," 1816; "Schweig', Herz! kein Schrei," 1816; "Einsam will ich untergeh'n," August 25, 1817; "An eine Jungfrau, welche das Kind ihrer verstorbenen Schwester erzog," 1817; "Wiegenlied eines jammernden Herzens," January 1817; "Es scheint ein Stern vom Himmel," 1817; "Wenn ich über die Flur hinschaue," 1817; "Beim Geschenk der Sakontala," 1817; "Zum Geburtstag, 30. März 1817" (Luise's birthday); "Nun soll ich in die

Fremde ziehen," summer 1818; "Pilger! all der Blumenschein," May 17, 1817; and "Die ummauerte Seele und der Epheu," 1817.

63 In response to Luise's gift to him on Christmas Day 1816 of a selection of her religious verse, Brentano dedicated his poems of 1817–1818 to her, collaborating with her on their composition and appropriating many of her turns of phrase. See Clemens Brentano, *Gedichte*, ed. Wolfgang Frühwald, Bernhard Gajek, and Friedhelm Kemp (Munich: Deutscher Taschenbuch Verlag, 1977), pp. 363–64. Lines 3–4 of stanza 1 ("Den ich in einer wunder-sel'gen Stunde, / An einer Wand empfand"), notably resistant to translation, imply that the poetic persona is looking over a wall at someone who does not yet see him.

64 Clemens Brentano, *Briefe*, ed. Friedrich Seebass, vol. 2 (Nürnberg: Verlag Hans Carl, 1851), p. 165.

65 Ibid., letter from "Berlin, December 1816," p. 179.

66 Ibid., pp. 140–41. At the end of 1815, Brentano wrote a similar letter to a Catholic priest named Sailer, who called it a "Buch de se ipso." See also Erika Tunner, *Clemens Brentano (1778–1842). Imagination et Sentiment Religieux*, Ph.D. diss., Université de Paris, 1976, published Lille and Paris, 1977. According to the young doctor Ringseis, Brentano oscillated between Christianity and pantheism at the time of their debates about religion in 1816.

67 Brentano, *Gedichte*, pp. 375–76. Brentano later altered the ending to give it a religious inflection: "Ich kann nichts anders singen, / Als, Jesus schau auf mich."

68 Brentano, *Briefe*, pp. 174–75. Köhler, in *Müde bin ich, geh' zur Ruh': Die hell-dunkle Lebensgeschichte Luise Hensels*, p. 21, movingly observes that Brentano's entire life was in a certain sense a repetition of a poem Brentano included in his 1800–02 novel, *Godwi oder das steinerne Bild der Mutter*: "Ich habe früh das Bein gebrochen, / Die Schwester trägt mich auf dem Arm, / Aufs Tambourin muß rasch ich pochen – / Sind wir nicht froh? / Das Gott erbarm." It is only given to a few who have felt themselves thus wounded when young to "play the tambourine" so beautifully.

69 Ibid., pp. 174–77. A portion of this letter hinges on the words "Vergeblich" and "vergebens" (in vain) and "vergeben" (forgive). "In vain! [Vergeblich!] – do you know this horrible word? It is the title of my entire life," he tells her (ibid., p. 175).

70 Ibid., p. 180.

71 Ibid., p. 187.

72 Brentano's poem "An eine Jungfrau, welche das Kind ihrer verstorbenen Schwester erzog," includes the lines "Sie ist ohn' Liebe, lauter Pflicht, / Sie geht mit mir nur in's Gericht; / Wie wär ich armer Mensch so rein, / Spräch sie: 'Lieb' mich zu Buß und Pein.'" The letter in which he enclosed the poem is largely a frantic plea that she should not banish him: "O thou good creature, grant me shelter, for I am homeless without you" (see *Briefe*, ed. Friedrich Seebass, vol. 2, p. 45). These letters were published without Luise Hensel's consent; she had given his letters back to him in March 1819, before she left Berlin, with the request that he copy the poems he had written for her and then burn the letters. He did not do so, and they were discovered among his *Nachlass*, gathered into a blue envelope with a large cross painted on each side. Emilie Brentano published them in shortened form, without notifying Luise, who related her distress in a letter to Marie von Radowitz on January 20, 1874 from Paderborn.

73 Luise wrote a poem "in den ersten Nächten des Jahres 1817" that begins with the lines, "Die Nacht ist schwarz und kalt und lang, / Der Tag noch – wie so fern . . . / Der Kummer mir zu Häupten steht, / Und bei mir liegt der Schmerz, / Die Sorge um mein Bette geht, / Die Angst fällt mir an's Herz / Und draußen steht der Tod, die Noth, / Der Jammer und der Harm." The "Nachtgebet" was written January 3,1817 in this time of crisis. At the end of February 1817, Hedwig von Stägemann told her older cousin Antoinette Schwinck that Luise's continued illness was the result of grief over the death of her sister. See Hedwig Abeken, *Hedwig von Olfers*, vol. 2, p. 18, and *Lieder von Luise Hensel*, pp. 18–19.

74 Brentano, *Briefe*, p. 194.

75 Brentano, *Werke*, vol. 1, p. 404.

76 Lujo Brentano, "Ein Brief Luise Hensels an Clemens Brentano" in *Hochland: Monatsschrift für alle Gebiete des Wissens der Literatur & Kunst*, ed. Karl Muth, vol. 14 (October 1916–March 1917): 345–46. Lujo Brentano was a nephew of the poet.

77 Schiel, *Clemens Brentano und Luise Hensel*, pp. 102–03.

78 Ibid., p. 104.

79 Ibid., pp. 105–06. In the same letter, she tells him "Oh, how often I have wavered, wondering if I should listen to the world or the Savior!" The notion of a Josephite marriage was recorded in a "letter" to Brentano written in Luise's diary for January 6, 1819. See Cardauns, *Aus Luise Hensels Jugendzeit*, pp. 32–33.

80 Ibid., p. 110. In this letter, she calls him, not "Brother" (her frequent mode of address) but "Sister": "Beloved soul, thou art my sister, my soul's sister."

81 Ibid., p. 111.

82 See Hans-Joachim Schoeps, "Clemens Brentano nach Ludwig von Gerlachs Tagebüchern und Briefwechsel" in *Jahrbuch des Freien Deutschen Hochstifts* 1970, ed. Detlev Lüders (Tübingen: Max Niemeyer Verlag, 1970), p. 291.

83 Luise Hensel's diaries are in the possession of the Franciscan convent in Münster and have never been published in full. Fragments are cited in Hermann Cardauns, *Aus Luise Hensels Jugendzeit* (see pp. 83–84 for the cited passage), and still more were edited by Ferdinand Bartscher in *Der innere Lebensgang der Dichterin Luise Hensel* (see note 37). In an appendix "Zu Luise Hensels Tagebuch 1818–1819," Bernhard Gajek, in his *Homo Poeta: Zur Kontinuität der Problematik bei Clemens Brentano* (Frankfurt am Main: Athenäum Verlag, 1971) pp. 463–70, criticizes Bartscher for various problems, including omissions, in this edition of the diaries.

84 Cardauns, *Aus Luise Hensels Jugendzeit*, p. 84. One of the diary passages which Bartscher omitted and Gajek restored is the following self-flagellation written on January 12, 1818: "Es ist immer das größte Elend in meiner Seele gewesen daß meine Phantasie so gern unreine, schändliche Bilder aufnahm und die Neugier darnach ausschickte. Gott, du Ewigreiner, weiß meine Abscheulichkeit genauer als ich – wie soll ich vor dir bestehn – ach, ach, wie groß ist meine Schuld!" See Gajek, *Homo Poeta*, p. 469.

85 Ibid., pp. 84–85.

86 Ibid., p. 85.

87 Hans Joachim Schoeps, *Aus den Jahren Preußischer Not und Erneuerung: Tagebücher und Briefe der Gebrüder Gerlach und ihres Kreises 1805–1820* (Berlin: Haude & Spenersche Verlagsbuchhandlung, 1963), p. 215.

88 Ibid., p. 214.

89 Schoeps, "Clemens Brentano nach Ludwig von Gerlachs Tagebüchern und Briefwechsel," p. 292. See also *Ernst Ludwig von Gerlach. Aufzeichnungen aus seinem Leben und Wirken 1795–1877*, ed. Jakob von Gerlach, vol. 1 (Schwerin: Fr. Bahn, 1903), p. 98. Following Ludwig Gerlach's citation of a diary entry for January 7, 1817, Gerlach's nephew (the editor) observed parenthetically that "Brentano's witty, fiery nature was often at odds with the thoroughly earnest manner of the Gerlach brothers." Brentano seems to have returned Ludwig Gerlach's antipathy, and told his friend Goetze in January 1817 that "Ludwig was a fearful apparition to me from the moment I first saw him."

90 Schoeps, "Clemens Brentano nach Ludwig von Gerlachs Tagebüchern und Briefwechsel," p. 284.

91 Ibid., p. 113, and Schoeps, *Aus den Jahren Preußischer Not und Erneuerung*, p. 290.

92 Ibid., p. 290.

93 Schoeps, "Clemens Brentano nach Ludwig von Gerlachs Tagebüchern und Briefwechsel," pp. 298–99, and Schoeps, *Aus den Jahren Preußischer Not und Erneuerung*, p. 291.

94 Cardauns, *Aus Luise Hensels Jugendzeit*, p. 86.

95 Ibid., p. 312. Köhler in *Müde bin ich, geh' zur Ruh': Die hell-dunkle Lebensgeschichte Luise Hensels*, pp. 19–20, briefly discusses the divergent opinions in the scholarly sources about Luise's conversion.

96 The letter is cited in *Luise Hensel und Christoph Bernhard Schlüter. Briefe aus dem deutschen Biedermeier 1832–1876*, ed. Josefine Nettesheim (Münster: Verlag Regensberg, 1962), pp. 43–44.

97 According to Ludwig Gerlach, in *Aufzeichnungen aus seinem Leben und Wirken*, p. 113, and Schoeps, *Aus den Jahren Preußischer Not*, p. 290, Brentano's campaign for conversion was already underway before he left Berlin for Dülmen.

98 See Jürg Mathes, "Ein Tagebuch Clemens Brentanos für Luise Hensel" in *Jahrbuch des Freien Deutschen Hochstifts 1971* (Tübingen: Max Niemeyer Verlag, 1971), pp. 198–310; see in particular pp. 234 and 238.

99 Cardauns, *Aufzeichnungen*, p. 20.

100 Schiel, *Clemens Brentano und Luise Hensel*, p. 129. She rejected Catholicism at first because it seemed to her too easy, too comfortable, a well-furnished chamber in comparison with the properly difficult, ascetic "desert" that is Protestantism, and because it requires an intermediary between the believer and God.

101 In Hartwig Schultz, "Brentanos 'Wiegenlied eines jammernden Herzen'" in *Jahrbuch des Freien Deutschen Hochstifts 1977*, ed. Detlev Lüders (Tübingen: Max Niemeyer Verlag, 1977), p. 362, Schultz points out that Brentano's letters to Emilie mimic those he had earlier written to Luise Hensel. See also Konrad Feilchenfeldt and Wolfgang Frühwald, "Clemens Brentano: Briefe und Gedichte an Emilie Linder. Ungedruckte Handschriften aus dem Nachlaß von Johannes Baptista Diel SJ" in *Jahrbuch des Freien Deutschen Hochstifts 1976*, ed. Detlev Lüders (Tübingen: Max Niemeyer Verlag, 1976), pp. 216–315.

102 Cardauns, *Aus Luise Hensels Jugendzeit*, pp. 34–35.

103 See John F. Fetzer, *Romantic Orpheus: Profiles of Clemens Brentano* (Berkeley, California: University of California Press, 1974) in which the author discusses the Melos–Eros alliance in Brentano's poems. In the Luise-poems, angelic or seraphic song is a recurring metaphor.

104 *Luise Hensel und Christoph Bernhard Schlüter*, p. 39.

105 Ibid., p. 38. See Clemens Brentano, *Gesammelte Schriften*, ed. Emilie Brentano, or the *Gesammelte Briefe von 1795 bis 1842* (Frankfurt am Main: J. D. Sauerländer, 1855).

106 Diel-Kreiten, *Clemens Brentano: Ein Lebensbild nach gedruckten und ungedruckten Quellen*, vol. 2, p. 109.

107 Förster, *Die Sängerfahrt*, pp. 196–97.

108 See *Luise Hensel und Christoph Bernhard Schlüter*, p. 113. Despite what she says about the poem, she encloses a copy of it in her letter to Schlüter.

109 Brentano made quite free to change her poetry, even telling her on one occasion that she had included elements unsuitable for a woman to say. In his preface to the *Lieder von Luise Hensel*, p. 8, Hermann Cardauns cites Brentano's letter of June 7, 1829, telling Luise that he was pleased that she did not mind the changes he made in her poems for Apollonia Diepenbrock's *Geistliche Blumenstrauß* published that year. There has been a continuing scholarly debate over their poetry because Brentano borrowed liberally from her verse, apparently considering much of the phraseology to be their common property, according to John Fetzer, in *Clemens Brentano* (Boston: Twayne Publishers, 1981), p. 23. See also Siegfried Sudhof, "Brentano oder Luise Hensel? Untersuchungen zu einem Gedicht aus dem Jahre 1817" in *Festschrift Gottfried Weber: Zu seinem 70. Geburtstag überreicht von Frankfurter Kollegen und Schülern*, ed. Heinz Otto Burger and Klaus von See (Bad Homburg: Gehlen, 1967), pp. 255–64; the section entitled "Luise Hensel oder Clemens Brentano?" in Cardauns, *Aus Luise Hensels Jugendzeit*, pp. 46–73; and Günther Müller, "Brentanos Luisengedichte" in *Jahrbuch des Freien Deutschen Hochstifts* (1928), 154–77.

110 *Luise Hensel und Christoph Bernhard Schlüter*, p. 53.

111 Schlüter was also a close friend and confidant to Annette von Droste-Hülshoff, whose poetry

he recommended to Luise. She evidently knew Droste-Hülshoff's poem "An die Blaustrümpfe in Deutschland und Frankreich" (To the Bluestockings in Germany and France); Luise once recommended a friend named Henriette Reusch to Schlüter as "a very nice young woman and, despite her books – God be praised! – no bluestocking; those always seem frightful to me" (*Luise Hensel und Christoph Bernhard Schlüter*, p. 330).

112 See Uta Treder, "Das verschüttete Erbe: Lyrikerinnen im 19. Jahrhundert" in *Deutsche Literatur von Frauen*, vol. 2, *19. und 20. Jahrhundert*, ed. Gisela Brinker-Gabler (Munich: C. H. Beck, 1988), pp. 27–28.

113 *Lieder von Luise Hensel*, p. 239.

114 Ibid., pp. 107 and 201.

115 Ludwig Rellstab, *Ludwig Berger, ein Denkmal*, pp. 140–43.

116 Joseph Reinkens, *Luise Hensel und ihre Lieder*, p. 93. See also Dieter Siebenkäs, *Ludwig Berger: Sein Leben und seine Werke unter besonderer Berücksichtigung seines Liedschaffens* (Berlin: Verlag Merseburger, 1963), p. 19.

117 Rellstab, *Ludwig Berger, ein Denkmal*, p. 142. Rellstab romantically attributes Berger's predilection for melancholy lieder to this disappointment in love. According to the "Nekrolog" in the *Allgemeine Musikalische Zeitung* for March 6, 1839, Berger died suddenly on the morning of February 16, 1839 while teaching a student; according to his eulogist, he was loudly counting the beats of a 4/4 measure and collapsed lifeless between the third and fourth beats. See *Allgemeine Musikalische Zeitung*, March 6, 1839 (Leipzig: Breitkopf & Härtel, 1839): 186–89.

2   Variations on a poetic theme: hunters, millers, and miller maids

1 Justinus Kerner, *Werke*, vol. 3: *Reiseschatten – Dramatische Dichtungen*, ed. Raimund Pissin (Berlin & Leipzig: Deutsches Verlagshaus Bong & Co., n.d.), p. 70. The playlet "Der Totengräber von Feldberg" (The Gravedigger from Feldberg) that follows the second "Schattenreihe" – the novel is divided into sections called "Schattenreihe" which are further divided into "Vorstellungen" – includes among the dramatis personae a hunter, a gardener who woos the gravedigger's daughter Elsbeth, an apprentice, a maiden, a poet, Death, and so on.

2 "Wenn ich ein Vöglein wär" appears in Achim von Arnim and Clemens Brentano, *Des Knaben Wunderhorn: Alte deutsche Lieder*, vol. 1 (Heidelberg: Mohr & Winter, 1819, reprinted Meersburg: F. W. Hendel, 1928), pp. 231–32. Friedrich Schlegel's "Der Knabe," which Schubert set to music (D. 692, 1820), might be a cheeky variation on this poem, as it begins with the line "Wenn ich nur ein Vöglein wäre." For the tune and text of "Der Jäger aus Kurpfalz," see Albert Träger, *Deutsche Lieder in Volkes Herz und Mund* (Leipzig: C. F. Amelang, 1864), p. 140.

3 The letter is dated October 5, 1808: "Bald werden wir alle Fürsten, Könige, Kaiser von Europa hier sehen. Morgen erwartet man sie alle zu einer Jagd in Eltersburg; da läßt man sie für Geld sehen, und werden Billets ausgeteilt. Wer pränumeriert, kriegt von den besten Plätzen. Ich bin eine zu gute Wirtin, . . . um für Etwas Geld zu haben, das mir keine Freude macht; denn die armen Hirsche, die man aus ihren Wäldern jagt, bin ich so albern, noch mehr zu bedauern als die Könige, die man aus ihren Ländern treibt." See Wilhelm Bode, *Charlotte von Stein* (Berlin: Siegfried Mittler und Sohn, 1917, 3rd ed.), p. 558.

4 La Motte-Fouqué, Friedrich Baron de. *Jäger und Jägerlieder. Ein kriegerisches Idyll* (Hamburg: Perthes & Besser, 1819). The play, which begins with everyone singing "Auf, auf zum fröhlichem Jagen!", is dedicated to Christian Gottfried Körner, the bereaved father of the Schubert poet Theodor Körner, the poet-martyr of the War of Liberation; one of the characters, allegorically dubbed Friedlieb Horn, appears late in the play to bring news of Theodor's death, and the drama ends with the singing of Körner's "Lützows wilde Jagd" (see ch. 2 of the author's *Schubert's Poets and the Making of Lieder* [Cambridge, England:

Cambridge University Press, 1996] for more on Körner and music). Schubert actually met Theodor, a rising star at the Burgtheater, before Körner volunteered for the Lützower Jägerkorps and left Vienna forever.

5 Bernhard Pompecki, *Hörnerschall und Lustgesang: Ernste und heitere Wald-, Jagd- und Jägerlieder mit leichter Klavierbegleitung* (Neudamm: J. Neumann, n.d., 2nd ed.), pp. 30–31.

6 In my handbook, *Schubert: Die schöne Müllerin* (Cambridge, England: Cambridge University Press, 1992), p. 58, I proposed another interpretation: in a vivid enactment of the wish-fulfillment by which one indulges murderous fantasies while exculpating oneself from blame, the miller is actually telling the hunter, whom he equates with the wild boars hunters kill, to shoot *himself*. Both readings, it seems to me, could be present simultaneously.

7 Carl Clewing, *Musik und Jägerei: Lieder, Reime und Geschichten vom Edlen Waidwerk*, 3 vols. (Neudamm: J. Neumann and Kassel & Wilhelmhöhe: Bärenreiter-Verlag, 1937–38). The second volume (1938) is entitled *Jägerlieder zum Singen beim Klavier* and includes songs from circa 1390 through Hugo Wolf's "Jägerlied"; the third volume (also 1938) contains *Jagdmadrigale*, or polyphonic vocal works.

8 Clewing's compendium was not the only hefty tome published during the 1930s to glorify the German tradition of hunting and forestry; a non-musical (except for an appendix with hunting-horn calls at the end of vol. 2) work from the same time was Richard Hilf and Fritz Röhrig, *Wald und Weidwerk in Geschichte und Gegenwart*, 2 vols. (Potsdam: Akademische Verlagsgesellschaft Athenaion, 1938). In the first volume of their scholarly work, Hilf and Röhrig recount the nineteenth-century treatment of forestry as a science, complete with professorships and institutes; the Nazis did not invent German interest in the hunt or in forestry, merely deployed it for their own ends. See also Ulrich Wendt, *Kultur und Jagd: Ein Birschgang durch die Geschichte*, 2 vols. (Berlin: Georg Reimer, 1907–08) and Kurt Lindner, *Deutsche Jagdtraktate des 15. und 16. Jahrhunderts*, 2 vols. (Berlin: Walter de Gruyter, 1959).

9 Simon Schama, *Landscape and Memory* (New York: Alfred A. Knopf, 1995), p. 68.

10 Josef Alois Gleich, "Der Hölle Zaubergaben: Allegorische Gemälde mit Gesang, Tänzen und Tableaux, Musik von Wenzel Müller" in Otto Rommel, ed., *Die romantisch-komischen Original-Zauberspiele* (Leipzig: Reclam, 1939).

11 Pompecki, in *Hörnerschall und Lustgesang*, includes his own settings of Müller's "Die liebe Farbe" (p. 228) and "Der Müller an den Jäger" (Müller's and Schubert's title is "Der Jäger," pp. 304–05), both in major mode (B flat major and E flat major, respectively). Schubert's settings are in no danger of being displaced by Pompecki's pedestrian music, influenced but not rescued by the ineradicable memory of Schubert's songs: the lack of rests and pauses between phrases in "Der Jäger" is something Pompecki most likely took from his predecessor, and the initial melodic gesture of "Die liebe Farbe" is a major mode variant of Schubert's poignant first phrase.

12 Friedrich von Wildungen, *Jägerlieder für Jagd- und Forstfreunde* (Quedlinburg & Leipzig: Gottfried Basse, 1823). In the first "Jägerlied" of the volume, Wildungen declares, "We hunters are the sons of free Nature – we do not know citified constraints" ("Wir kennen nicht städtischen Zwang," p. 3).

13 See Otto Lauffer, *Farbensymbolik im deutschen Volksbrauch* (Hamburg: Hansischer Gildenverlag, 1948), p. 23.

14 Joseph Bergmann, *Das Ambraser Liederbuch vom Jahre 1582* (Hildesheim & New York: Georg Olms Verlag, 1971, 2nd reprint of the Stuttgart 1845 ed.), pp. 51–52.

15 Lauffer, *Farbensymbolik im deutschen Volksbrauch*, pp. 33–34. See also "Die Farben" (The Colors) in Friedrich Karl Freiherrn von Erlach, *Die Volkslieder der Deutschen. Eine vollständige Sammlung der vorzüglichen deutschen Volkslieder von der Mitte des fünfzehnten bis in die erste Hälfte des neunzehnten Jahrhunderts*, vol. 1 (Mannheim: Heinrich Hoff, 1834), pp. 233–34.

16 Louis Pinck, ed., *Verklingende Weisen: Lothringer Volkslieder*, vol. 4 (Kassel: Bärenreiter Verlag, 1962), p. 104.

17 Ibid., pp. 229 and 227 respectively.

18 For Schubert and the Viennese, green may have had still another connotation, as the Hanswurst figure in *Volkstheater* plays customarily wears a green hat to designate that he is a fool.

19 It was not only in German-speaking countries that hunters wore green. In Angelo Dalmedico's *Canti del popolo Veneziano* (Venice: Andrea Santini e Figlio, 1848), p. 19, one finds the poem "Sia benedeto 'l verde e chi lo porta," with its lovely, chiming, repeated phrase "De verde va vestida." Paul Heyse, in his *Italienisches Liederbuch* (Berlin: Wilhelm Herz, 1860, the poems all reprinted in Paul Heyse, *Italienische Dichter seit der Mitte des 18ten Jahrhunderts*, vol. 4: *Lyriker und Volksgesang* [Berlin: Wilhelm Hertz, 1889], pp. 175–348) translated the poem into German as "Gesegnet sei das Grün und wer es trägt!" – was it perhaps the Germanic tradition of hunters and hunting that impelled Heyse to select this poem from Dalmedico's anthology? Hugo Wolf's exquisite setting, composed on April 13, 1896, is justly famous.

20 Franz Wilhelm Freiherr von Ditfurth, *Deutsche Volks- und Gesellschaftslieder des 17. und 18. Jahrhunderts* (Hildesheim: Georg Olms Verlag, 1956, reprint of the Nördlingen 1872 original edition), p. 208.

21 Ibid., p. 4.

22 This poem is the fourth in the poetic cycle *Ländliche Lieder* (Rustic Songs). See Wilhelm Müller, *Gedichte: Vollständige kritische Ausgabe*, ed. James Taft Hatfield (Berlin: B. Behr, 1906), p. 127. See also Ditfurth, *Deutsche Volks- und Gesellschaftslieder*, p. 183. This is Ditfurth's epigram at the start of the section devoted to "Jägerlieder" (pp. 183–214).

23 It is worth pointing out that hunters such as this one have little to do with the courtly hunts endemic in the sixteenth through the eighteenth centuries, when *Jagdschlößer* dotted the landscape, and large numbers of courtiers would participate in the *Jagdorden*, or rituals, associated with these expensive diversions. Lucas Cranach der Ältere's painting of *A Stag Hunt* (1529) in Vienna's Kunsthistorisches Museum, although an imaginary assemblage of royalty, gives an idea of the scale and richness of these hunts. See Werner Schade, *Cranach: A Family of Master Painters*, trans. Helen Sebba (New York: G. P. Putnam's Sons, 1980), plate 162.

24 This was not Kreutzer's only setting of Müller's poetry: his *Sechs ländliche Lieder von Wilhelm Müller*, op. 80 (Leipzig: H. A. Probst, 182–?) includes settings of "Der Berghirt," "Liebesaufruf," "Ergebung," "Der Lindenbaum" and "Frühlingstraum" extracted from *Die Winterreise*, and "Abrede."

25 Ditfurth, *Deutsche Volks- und Gesellschaftslieder*, p. 207.

26 Ibid., p. 185.

27 Other Schubert songs in which one finds extensive use of this figure are the setting of Johann Mayrhofer's "Der Alpenjäger," D. 524, and Zacharias Werner's "Jagdlied," D. 521. In a similar instance, perhaps most affecting of all, *pianississimo* hunting-horn fanfares in the piano can be heard as symbols of happy bygone memories, of the Romantic past, in "Der Lindenbaum" from *Winterreise*.

28 Ditfurth, *Deutsche Volks- und Gesellschaftslieder*, p. 212.

29 Ibid., p. 193. The verses of "Edles Jagen" are taken from a compendium with the delightful title *Ganz neue Lust-Rosen, worin die allerneusten und schönsten Arien und Lieder enthalten sind* (Entirely New Roses of Pleasure, in which the Newest and Most Beautiful Airs and Songs are included) of 1807.

30 Bellmann was both a poet and a musician (he was dubbed "the Swedish Anacreon") who took the melodies for his poems mostly from marches, *opéras-comiques*, folk songs, and dances.

31 Clewing, *Musik und Jägerei*, vol. 1, p. 219.

32 Ditfurth, *Deutsche Volks- und Gesellschaftslieder*, p. 190.

33 Clewing, *Musik und Jägerei*, vol. 1, p. 17. Clewing sets Karl Bunsen's words to the folk song "Auf, ihr Brüder, und seid stark."

34 Pinck, *Verklingende Weisen*, vol. 2, p. 191; see also Franz M. Böhme, *Altdeutsches Liederbuch. Volkslieder der Deutschen nach Wort und Weise aus dem 12. bis zum 17. Jahrhundert* (Leipzig: Breitkopf & Härtel, 1877), no. 438, pp. 544–45. Immediately following "Jäger und Graserin" in Böhme's *Altdeutsches Liederbuch* is a song entitled "Liebesjagd (Jäger und Nonne)," in which a hunter's seduced sweetheart is led to the cloister (pp. 545–46) – an interesting conflation of the topos known as "nun's lament" (*Nonnenklage*) and that of the amorous hunter.

35 Bergmann, *Das Ambraser Liederbuch vom Jahre 1582*, pp. 124–25.

36 In "Ein neues Lied von einem Jäger" (A New Song of a Hunter), one encounters a maiden seduced by a hunter who tells her angry mother, "Ich weiß ein freien Jäger / Erfreut mich mit sein Horn" (I know a free hunter who makes me happy with his horn) – explicit enough for anyone. See Friedrich Karl von Erlach, *Die Volkslieder der Deutschen*, vol. 1, pp. 43–45.

37 Pinck, *Verklingende Weisen*, vol. 3, pp. 157–59.

38 Ibid., vol. 1, p. 183.

39 See Marcelle Thiebaux, *The Stag of Love: The Chase in Medieval Literature* (Ithaca, New York: Cornell University Press, 1974); David Dalby, *Lexicon of the Medieval German Hunt* (Berlin: W. de Gruyter, 1965); and Gregson David, *The Death of Procris: "Amor" and the Hunt in Ovid's Metamorphoses* (Rome: Edizioni dell'Ateneo, 1983).

40 The youthful Tristan's breaking of the stag is in lines 2,759 through 3,376 of the romance. See Gottfried von Strassburg, *Tristan*, ed. Peter Ganz after the edition by Reinhold Bechstein, 2 vols. (Wiesbaden: F. A. Brockhaus, 1978), vol. 1, pp. 107–27, or the edition of *Tristan*, eds. Gottfried Weber, Gertrud Utzmann, and Werner Hoffmann (Darmstadt: Wissenschaftliche Buchgesellschaft, 1967), pp. 77–94. The hunt scene in which Marke, to forget his cares, goes hunting and is led by a strange stag near the grotto of love where Tristan and Isolde are dwelling occurs in lines 17,279 through 17,346. See the Ganz edition cited above, pp. 234–36, and the Weber, Utzmann, and Hoffmann edition, pp. 481–83.

41 Wilhelm Müller, *Diary and Letters of Wilhelm Müller*, ed. Philip Schuyler Allen and James Taft Hatfield (Chicago, Illinois: The University of Chicago Press, 1903), entry for October 25, 1815, p. 22. "Nachmittags las ich auf der Bibliothek in Hagens und Büschings Buch der Liebe. Die Geschichte Tristans zog mich sehr an und das alte Gewand derselben machte sie mir noch lieber. Das muß Luise lesen! dachte ich." In Wilhelm Müller, *Blumenlese aus den Minnesingern* (Berlin: Maurer, 1816), pp. 44–45, Müller translated Heinrich von Veldeke's poem in praise of Minne, a poem which begins by citing Tristan as a counter-example of true *Minnedienst* (the service of love):

(Middle High German)	(Müller's translation)	
Tristan muse sunder sinen dane	Tristan mußte liebeskrank must	Sick with love, Tristan must
Stete sin der kuniginne,	Stete sein der Königinne,	always be with the queen,
Wan in der poysun darzu twane	Weil ein Zaubergift ihn zwang	because a magic poison compels him
Mere dan du kraft der minne.	Stärker als die Kraft der Minne.	more strongly than the power of love.

42 See Hadamar von Laber, *Die Jagd*, ed. Karl Stejskal (Vienna: Alfred Hölder, 1860). This work was not edited and published until after Müller's death.

43 In Arnim and Brentano, *Des Knaben Wunderhorn*, vol. 1, pp. 162–63, the farewell is spoken by "Erster Jäger" to which is appended a stanza for a "Zweyter Jäger": "Kein Hochgewild ich sehen kann, / Das muß ich oft entgelten; / Noch halt ich stets auf Jägers-Bahn, / Wiewohl mir Glück kommt selten: / Mag ich nicht han ein Hochwild schön, / So laß ich mich begnügen, / Am Hasenfleisch, nichts mehr ich weiß, / Das mag mich nicht betrügen." See also another version of this song in Franz Böhme, *Altdeutsches Liederbuch*, no. 443, p. 549. Clewing, *Jägerlied zum Singen beim Klavier*, pp. 8–9, arranges both Arnt von Aich's and

Ludwig Senfl's sixteenth-century settings of this poem to lush, quasi-modal accompaniments in thickly plush Romantic textures. Brahms included a setting of this text in his *Vier Gesänge für eine Singstimme mit Begleitung des Pianoforte*, op. 43, no. 2, published in 1868; in Brahms's textual source, as in many others, the first line of the poem appears as "Ich schnell mein Horn in Jammers*tal*" instead of the correct word "Jammers*ton*."

44 The motif is actually of even greater antiquity: "Have you never seen the ways lovers hunt each other?", the questioners ask in Plato's *Sophist*, and the hunting-party of Dido and Aeneas in book 4 of the *Aeneid*, in which Dido is both huntress and smitten prey, is among the most famous examples of all. Ovid's tales of the Calydonian boar-hunt and the hunt of Procris and Cephalus in the *Metamorphoses* are still other examples; the latter tale – the source for numerous works thereafter – culminates in the hunter Cephalus mistakenly killing his beloved wife Procris with his javelin. Gottfried knew and acknowledged the influence of Heinrich von Veldeke's *Eneit*, a retelling of the Aeneas legends.

45 Clewing, *Musik und Jägerei*, vol. 1, p. 20.

46 Ibid., vol. 1, p. 149. There is an extended variant of this poem entitled "Die Grasmagd und der Jäger" in Ernst Meier, *Schwäbische Volkslieder mit ausgewählten Melodien* (Berlin: George Reimer, 1855), pp. 332–34, in which the maiden asks her mother for one hundred thalers, the mother replies that the father has gambled away most of their money, and the girl laments that she was not born a boy; she could then have earned money as a drummer in the regiment.

47 See "Jägers Fund" in Franz Böhme, *Altdeutsches Liederbuch*, no. 444, pp. 550–51.

48 Maria Tatar, *The Hard Facts of the Grimms' Fairy Tales* (Princeton, New Jersey: Princeton University Press, 1987), ch. 7, "Taming the Beast: Bluebeard and Other Monsters," pp. 156–78.

49 Arnim and Brentano, *Des Knaben Wunderhorn*, vol. 1, pp. 316–18.

50 Bergmann, *Das Ambraser Liederbuch vom Jahre 1582*, pp. 125–26. See also "Der wolgemute Jäger" in Franz Böhme, *Altdeutsches Liederbuch*, no. 441, pp. 547–48, and Friedrich Karl von Erlach, *Die Volkslieder der Deutschen*, vol. 1, pp. 309–10.

51 Arnim and Brentano, *Des Knaben Wunderhorn*, vol. 2, pp. 21–22.

52 It is possible to speculate that Schubert might have eliminated Müller's imperative "Horch" and changed it to "und" because his anacrusis to the succeeding phrase required a less prominent, less intense part of speech, and changed the verb to "schallt," its -a vowel and liquid *l*s more singable, more "musical," in conjunction with the words "Da klingt" just after.

53 Ferdinand Raimund, *Dramatische Werke in drei Bänden*, vol. 1 (Berlin & Leipzig: Th. Knaur Nachf., n.d.), pp. 6–7. I am grateful to John Sienicki for pointing out this example.

54 August Mahlmann, *Gesammelte Gedichte* (Halle: Renger, 1837). See also Clewing, *Musik und Jägerei*, vol. 1, pp. 190–91. The poem was set to music by Johann Friedrich Reichardt.

55 There is an added *frisson* to the tale in that a *Hirsch*, or stag, is a *male* animal, not the usual unspecified *Tierlein*, *Wild*, or shy, feminine *Reh*, although one can also translate "Hirsch" generically as "deer."

56 Arnim and Brentano, *Des Knaben Wunderhorn*, vol. 2, pp. 154–57.

57 Ibid., vol. 1, p. 303; see also Erlach, *Die Volkslieder der Deutschen*, vol. 2, p. 109.

58 Pinck, *Verklingende Weisen*, vol. 3, pp. 161–62. This same volume includes a modern woodcut engraving of a grave monument topped by a hunter on horseback and blowing his horn, a monument with the name "SHVBERTVS."

59 Ibid., vol. 2, pp. 188–89. In Meier, *Schwäbische Volkslieder mit ausgewählten Melodien*, pp. 305–06, one finds a conflation of "Der ernsthafte Jäger" and "Es wollt sich ein Jägerlein jagen" entitled "Des Jägers Verdruß." Here, the maiden proclaims herself still a virgin, and the hunter threatens to shoot her and then decides to make her a "Waldfräulein." She, however, still rejects him: "Jetzt lass ich mein Härelein fliegen, / Ein anders schöns Schätzle zu kriegen, / Dem Jäger zur Schand und zum Spott, ja Spott, / Dem Jäger zur Schand und zum Spott." This is, Meier states (p. 306), "a very old song."

60 Müller, *Diary and Letters of Wilhelm Müller*, p. 28.
61 Arnim and Brentano, *Des Knaben Wunderhorn*, vol. 1, pp. 34–35. The poem "Der Nachtjäger" (The Nocturnal Hunter) in Pinck, *Verklingende Weisen*, vol. 1, pp. 186–88, seems a conflation of "Zwey Schelme" and "Die schwarzbraune Hexe": the second and third stanzas ("Bist du der Jäger, grad kreisjt mich nit / Und allemal und alle Tag, / Denn meine Spring, und die weisst du gar nit / Und allemal bei der Nacht. / / Und deine Spring, o die weiss ich schon / Und allemal und alle Tag," etc.) are reminiscent of "Zwey Schelme," the remainder of "Die schwarzbraune Hexe." Here, the hunter threatens death by degrees – "I will throw a noose around your head . . . around your arm . . . around your body . . . around your feet," the sexual nature of the threat explicit when he declares "Ich werf dir ein Schlupf um deinen Leib / So bist du gefangen als ein Jägersweib." "If you bury me at the churchyard door, my sweetheart will come to me every day . . . if you bury me on the high street, I will hear all the carters talking . . . if you bury me in the green woods, I will hear all of the birds singing . . . if you bury me in the open field, the priest won't demand any money," she declares as the poem and her life end.
62 One thinks inevitably of the Grimm Brothers' famous tale "Schneeweißchen und Rosenrot" in this connection. See also Erlach, *Die Volkslieder der Deutschen*, vol. 2, pp. 530–31.
63 It should be pointed out that many of his hunting songs were published after Müller's tragically early death; the line of influence runs from Müller to Eichendorff rather than in the other direction. In Eichendorff's inimitable poetic landscape, its dimensions high, deep, and wide, his poetic personae are lured into adventure, into realms of sorcery or salvation, out into "die weite Welt" – the phrase above all that evokes Eichendorff's poetic cosmos – by music, including the sound of hunting horns. In this cosmos, hunters inhabit a symbol-laden realm of the forest, of night, of the polarities between "Heimat" and "Fremde" so characteristic of Eichendorff; wanderers by trade, they dwell amidst a pure and beautiful Nature where, nonetheless, mysterious dangers lurk. See Hermann Kunisch, "Freiheit und Bann - Heimat und Fremde," in *Eichendorff Heute: Stimmen der Forschung mit einer Bibliographie*, ed. Paul Stöcklein (Munich: Bayerischer Schulbuch-Verlag, 1960), pp. 131–64.
64 The sexual attraction of folkloric hunters is repeated in their more artful descendants: the proud maiden in Eichendorff's "Die Stolze" hymns the "Waldkönig" (forest king) who roams the woods and blows his horn for sheer pleasure and declares that whoever would win her must be a hunter. See Joseph von Eichendorff, *Werke und Schriften*, vol. 1: *Gedichte, Epen, Dramen*, ed. Gerhard Baumann and Siegfried Grosse (Stuttgart: J. G. Cotta, 1957), pp. 205–06. In the enchained dialogue-poem "Jäger und Jägerin" (the last line of each quatrain becomes the first line of the next), the hunter's sweetheart is compared to a female hart; where the hunter would capture and confine it, the "Jägerin" would have it escape, "free and wild," to the forest, there to laugh at fools in love. Ibid., pp. 207–08.
65 For example, the third and last of the small set entitled *Anklänge* first published in 1837 (the title is multivalent, meaning both "Harmonies" and "Reminiscences") is a "Jagdlied"; here, the horn-calls tell of "Ferne" (distance), luring the poetic persona away from bounded earthly love ("O Lieb', o Liebe, / So laß mich los!") into the night, a time and a place either of mystical purity or of soulless sorcery. See Eichendorff, *Gedichte*, p. 182. The 1829 "Jagdlied" was composed in the same rapid-rattling, anapaest-laden tetrameter lines as Müller's "Der Jäger" and with the same emphatic, accented "end-stop" to each line. More than rhythm and meter, however, one finds in both poems, albeit differently expressed and for very different ends, a conception of hunting as a force of nature, something pagan, uncivilized, unstoppable, and allied with death. The hunter's horn-calls awaken all the gods – Aurora, Venus, Diana above all – while both the wild animals and the hunter are "drunk on death, sunk in the depths of the green night . . . o thou beautiful hunter's joy!" See ibid., pp. 193–94.
66 The decidedly secular song "Der Jäger im Tannenholz" already cited (one version begins "Es wollt ein Jäger jagen / Wohl in das hohe Holz / Was begegnet ihm auf der Reise? / Ein Mädchen und das war stolz") became a famous contrafactum "Der englische Gruss" (The

Angelic Greeting), dating back to at least the early seventeenth century: "Es wollt ein Jäger jagen, / Wollte jagen an dem Himmelsthron; / Was begegnet ihm auf der Reise? / Maria, die Jungfrau schön." See Pinck, *Verklingende Weisen*, vol. 4, p. 4; Arnim and Brentano, *Des Knaben Wunderhorn*, vol. 1, pp. 140–41; Böhme, "Vom geistlichen Jäger" in *Altdeutsches Liederbuch*, no. 598, pp. 707–08; and Erlach, *Die Volkslieder der Deutschen*, vol. 2, pp. 539–40.

67 *Sebastian Brants Narrenschiff*, ed. Friedrich Zarnecke (Hildesheim: Georg Olms Verlag, 1961), p. 73. See also Sebastian Brant, *The Ship of Fools*, trans. Edwin H. Zeydel (New York: Columbia University Press, 1944), pp. 246–47.

68 In a haunting variant of the white stag-motif, the three hunters in Ludwig Uhland's ballad "Der weiße Hirsch" each dream that they have captured and shot a white stag, only to see it run by them the next moment. The pure and miraculous cannot be killed; in his compressed, compelling dream sequence, Uhland hints that hunters, symbolic of humanity, endlessly seek to vanquish a mysterious magic force, something totemic and immortal. See Harald Haselbach, ed., *Deutsche Balladen* (Klagenfurt: Neue Kaiser Verlag, 1978), p. 143.

69 See Otto Wimmer and Hartmann Melzer, *Lexikon der Namen und Heiligen*, 4th ed. (Innsbruck & Vienna: Tyrolia Verlag, 1982), pp. 379–80, and Joseph Braun, *Tracht und Attribute der Heiligen in der Deutschen Kunst*, 3rd ed. (Berlin: Mann, 1988), pp. 338–41. Plate 178 on pp. 339–40 of Braun shows Stephan Lochner's fifteenth-century depiction of Saints Catherine, Hubertus, and Quirinus now in the Alte Pinakothek in Munich. See also L. Huyghebaert, *Sint Hubertus: Patroon van de jagers in woord en beeld* (Antwerp: De Sikkel, 1949). The motif of the stag that leads its pursuer to the Christian faith is widespread in hagiographic literature; see C. Pschmadt, "Sage von der verfolgten Hinde," Ph.D. diss., University of Bonn, 1911.

70 Träger, *Deutsche Lieder in Volkes Herz und Mund*, p. 136. See also Arnim and Brentano, *Des Knaben Wunderhorn*, vol. 3, pp. 110–11.

71 One thinks of the early sixteenth-century artist Rueland Freuauf the Younger, whose altar-piece of the Legend of Saint Leopold at the monastery of Klosterneuburg depicts a boar-hunt. See Jacqueline and Maurice Guillaud, eds., *Altdorfer and Fantastic Realism in German Art* (Paris: Guillaud Editions, 1985), p. 153.

72 Ditfurth, *Deutsche Volks- und Gesellschaftslieder*, pp. 213–14.

73 Adolfo Salvatore Cavallo, *Medieval Tapestries in The Metropolitan Museum of Art* (New York: The Metropolitan Museum of Art, 1993), pp. 347–58 and 458–62.

74 Wilhelm Müller, *Blumenlese aus den Minnesingern*, pp. 120–29. See Ludwig Wolff, *Der Gottfried von Strassburg zugeschriebene Marienpreis und Lobgesang auf Christus* (Jena: Frommann, 1924); Friedrich Heer, in *Die Tragödie des heiligen Reichs* (Stuttgart: Kohlhammer, 1952–53), tried to re-establish this work as being by Gottfried, but the attempt is not generally accepted.

75 Müller, *Gedichte*, pp. 397–99.

76 Otto Rommel, ed., *Die Romantisch-Komischen Volksmärchen* (Darmstadt: Wissenschaftliche Buchgesellschaft, 1964), p. 99. I am grateful to John Sienicki for pointing this passage out to me.

77 The bear was the king of the beasts in early medieval lore, as Marina Warner points out in *From the Beast to the Blonde: On Fairy Tales and their Tellers* (New York: Farrar, Straus & Giroux, 1995), p. 300. See also Otto Höfler, "Über germanische Verwandlungskulten" in *Zeitschrift für deutsches Altertum* 75 (1938): 109–15 and the same author's *Verwandlungskulten: Volkssagen und Mythen* (Vienna: Österreichische Akademie der Wissenschaften, 1973).

78 See Otto Rommel, *Das parodistische Zauberspiel* (Leipzig: Philipp Reclam jun., 1937), pp. 248–49.

79 Hunting has long provided artists with imagery. In the Metropolitan Museum in New York, one can see a magnificent Meissen porcelain hunting cup fashioned by Johann Joachim Kändler for Augustus III of Saxony circa 1741, a cup with the figure of a hunter playing the hunting horn at the base; it is not difficult to imagine its use during the costly hunts staged

by royalty and the nobility in the eighteenth century. Lest one forget that hunting existed elsewhere than the German-speaking world, the Metropolitan also owns a powerful *Hunting Scene* by Piero di Cosimo, a scene pervaded by violence and dark allegorical symbolism, and a cabinet in dazzling pietra dura which was perhaps made for a Barberini cardinal and depicts hunting scenes and images from Aesop's fables. Furthermore, no one who reads Shakespeare's *As You Like It* can escape awareness of the English hunting tradition. There are, of course, thousands of other examples one could cite.

80 See Auguste Louis Charles, comte de La Garde-Chambonas, *Fêtes et souvenirs du Congrès de Vienne; tableaux des salons, scènes anecdotiques et portraits, 1814–1815* (Paris: Librairie Historique et Militaire Henri Vivien, 1901, 1st ed. Paris: A. Appert, 1843), pp. 103–04. La Garde-Chambonas' reminiscences were translated into English as *Anecdotal Recollections of the Congress of Vienna*, trans. Albert Vandam (London: Chapman & Hall, Ltd., 1902) and into German as *Gemälde des Wiener Kongresses, 1814–1815: Erinnerungen, Feste, Sittenschilderungen, Anekdoten*, ed. Gustav Gugitz (Munich: G. Müller, 1912).

81 Francine Prose, "Bohemia, where fairy tales might be true" in *New York Sunday Times Magazine*, part 2: *The Sophisticated Traveller*" (March 5, 1995), p. 52.

82 Ludwig Ganghofer, *Schloss Hubertus* (Berlin: Deutsche Buch-Gemeinschaft, n.d. [original copyright, Stuttgart: Adolf Bonz & Comp., 1917]), pp. 66–67.

83 The bibliography on the subject of Germanic myth and folklore is too vast for more than the sketchiest references here. The 1816 *Deutsche Sagen* (German Legends) of Jakob Ludwig Karl Grimm and Wilhelm Karl Grimm include numerous legends of supernatural hunts; in one legend of particular interest in this context, a miller who possesses magic bullets is outdone and killed by a hunter whose magic is stronger. See *The German Legends of the Brothers Grimm*, 2 vols., trans. Donald Ward (Philadelphia, Pennsylvania: The Institute for the Study of Human Issues, 1981), vol. 1, legend no. 258. See also Arno Beurmann, *Der Aberglaube der Jäger: Von der beseelten Magie, von Mystik und Mythen und allerlei Zauberwahn der Jäger* (Hamburg & Berlin: Verlag Paul Parey, 1961); G. Jungwirth, "Jagd, Jäger" in Eduard Hoffmann-Krayer and Hanns Bächtold-Stäubli, eds., *Handwörterbuch des deutschen Aberglaubens*, vol. 4 (Berlin & Leipzig: Walter de Gruyter, 1927–42), pp. 575–93; Karl Meisen, *Die Sagen vom Wütenden Heer und Wilden Jäger* (Münster: Aschendorff, 1935); Wilhelm Mannhardt, *Wald- und Feldkulte*, 2 vols. (Berlin: Gebrüder Bornträger, 1975); and Hans Weininger, *Das wilde Heer oder die Nachtjagd* (Landshut: The Historical Society for Lower Bavaria, 1863).

84 Peter Josef Lindpaintner (1791–1856) was Hofkapellmeister and a prolific opera composer in Stuttgart from 1819 on. His operas included *Der Vampyr* of 1828, *Die Amazone oder Der Frauen und der Liebe Sieg* of 1831, *Die Macht des Liedes* of 1836, and *Libella* of 1855.

85 See Joseph von Eichendorff, *Gedichte: Kommentar*, vol. 1/2 of *Sämtliche Werke des Freiherrn Joseph von Eichendorff*, eds. Harry Fröhlich and Wolfgang Kron (Stuttgart & Berlin: Verlag W. Kohlhammer, 1994), pp. 24, 71, and 106.

86 Before he discovered Müller's cycle in late 1822 or early 1823, Schubert would set to music Mayrhofer's "Trost" (Consolation) in 1819 (D. 671), a poem in which horn-calls in the depths of the forest are associated with love: (stanza 1 of 2) "Hörnerklänge rufen klagend / Aus des Forstes grüner Nacht, / In das Land der Liebe tragend, / Waltet ihre Zaubermacht, / Selig, wer ein Herz gefunden, / Das sich liebend ihm ergab, / Mir ist jedes Glück entschwunden, / Denn die Teure deckt das Grab." (Lamenting horn-calls sound from the green night of the forest; their magic power is at work, bearing us to the land of love. Happy he who has found a heart that gave itself to him lovingly; for me, all happiness is gone, for my beloved is buried in her grave.) The text is not to be found in either of Mayrhofer's published collections. The second stanza is probably not by Mayrhofer, and the subsequent stanzas, their existence evident in the repetition sign at the end of Schubert's musical strophe, are not extant.

87 For those who know Eichendorff's *Aus dem Leben eines Taugenichts*, the motifs and images in "Der traurige Jäger" will seem familiar, especially the mill. Mention of the Taugenicht's

father's mill recurs throughout the novel; when, at the end, Friedrich sees it once again, sees it truly, he cries out, "Was ich sehe, hier und in der Runde, alles gemahnt mich wie ein Zauberspiegel an den Ort, wo ich als Kind aufwuchs! Derselbe Wald, dieselben Gänge . . ."

88 Pompecki, *Hörnerschall und Lustgesang,* p. 306.

89 Müller, *Gedichte,* ed. Hatfield, p. 128. "Jägers Lust" was originally published in the *Taschenbuch Urania für 1823* (Leipzig: F. A. Brockhaus, 1823), p. 377, and "Jägers Leid" appeared a year earlier, in *Urania für 1822,* p. 421, with the title "Der Jäger."

90 Schubert varies his "rauschendes" figures in "Wohin?" – also in G major – such that we hear a premonition of the mill-wheels in their circling motion. In Adolph Hofmeister, *Achter Nachtrag* to the *Handbuch der musikalischen Literatur* (Leipzig: Friedrich Hofmeister, 1825), p. 59, one finds a listing for Bürde's *Zwei Gedichte,* consisting of "Das Mädchen und der Mond" and "Das Heidenröslein" (Berlin: Trautwein, [1824?]) and, decades later, in Hofmeister, *Handbuch der musikalischen Literatur 1852–1859* (Leipzig: Friedrich Hofmeister, 1860), p. 384, a listing for the single song "Der Schiffer: Ich stand gelehnet" (Magdeburg: Heinrichshofen, n.d.).

91 See Alois Brandstetter and Gerhard Trumler, *Das Buch der alten Mühlen* (Vienna: C. Brandstetter, 1984); Richard Wittich, *Romantik und Wirklichkeit der alten Mühlen* (Kassel: Roth, 1976); and Ernst Wilhelm Neumann, *Mühlenspuk. Sagen von Mühlen und Müllern* (Leipzig: Moritz Schäfer, 1939).

92 See Siegfried Grosse, "Die Mühle und der Müller im deutschen Volkslied" in *Jahrbuch des Österreichischen Volksliedwerkes,* vol. 11 (1962): 8–35.

93 Lucas Cranach the Elder's painting *Der Jungbrunnen,* now in the collection of the Gemäldegalerie in Berlin, depicts a variation of this legend in which elderly, naked women, stooped and with sagging breasts, enter a gigantic tub-like well from the left and emerge on the other side with flowing golden hair and youthful bodies.

94 Joseph Bergmann, *Das Ambraser Liederbuch vom Jahre 1582,* pp. 128–29. See also Ludwig Uhland, *Alte hoch- und niederdeutsche Volkslieder,* 5 vols. (Hildesheim: Georg Olms Verlag, 1969, reprint of 1st ed., Stuttgart & Tübingen: J. G. Cotta, 1844), pp. 393–94.

95 See W. F. Bryan and Germaine Dempster, *Sources and Analogues of Chaucer's Canterbury Tales* (New York: Humanities Press, 1941, 2nd ed. 1958), pp. 124–47; the tale is also translated in Larry D. Benson and Theodore M. Andersson, *The Literary Context of Chaucer's Fabliaux: Texts and Translations* (Indianapolis & New York: The Bobbs-Merrill Co., Inc., 1971), pp. 100–15.

96 Rasmus Nyerup, *Udvalg af danske viser fra midten af det 16de aarhundrede til henimod midten af det 18de,* 2 vols. (Copenhagen: Schultz, 1821), vol. 2, pp. 154–56. See also Benson and Andersson, *The Literary Context of Chaucer's Fabliaux,* pp. 198–201.

97 From the fourteenth century on, for every *Schwank* ballad featuring a miller as adulterer, there are three referring to millers who lose their wives or pretty daughters to the advances of strangers. See Klaus Roth, *Ehebruchschwänke in Liedform: Eine Untersuchung zur deutsch- und englischsprachigen Schwankballade* (Munich: Fink, 1977). A similar scenario but with a different ending is found in the folk song "Des Müllers Tochter" in Meier, *Schwäbische Volkslieder mit ausgewählten Melodien,* pp. 315–16; a nobleman in love with the miller's daughter is brought to the mill in a grain sack, but she will have none of him, proclaiming instead "Einen braven Burschen muß ich haben."

98 Arnim and Brentano, *Des Knaben Wunderhorn,* vol. 2, pp. 392–93, and Erlach, *Die Volkslieder der Deutschen,* vol. 1, pp. 491–92.

99 Roth, *Ehebruchschwänke in Liedform,* pp. 46–47. See also Johannes Mager, Günter Meißner, and Wolfgang Orf, *Die Kulturgeschichte der Mühlen* (Tübingen: Ernst Wasmuth, 1989), p. 151. One of the subsequent *Mühlenschwänke,* enormously popular despite, or because of, being placed on the index of prohibited books, was the satire *Die Mülle von Schwyndelßheim und Gredt Müllerin Jarzit* of 1515 by Thomas Murner, subsequently edited by Gustav Bebermeyer (Berlin: Vereinigung Wissenschaftlicher Verleger, 1923).

100 John Meier, ed., *Das deutsche Volkslied: Balladen*, vol. 2 (Leipzig: Philipp Reclam, 1936), pp. 281–82. This version comes from the *Bergliederbüchlein*, *c.* 1700; see also Böhme, *Altdeutsches Liederbuch*, no. 43, pp. 121–23. See also Roth, *Ehebruchschwänke in Liedform*, pp. 46 and 279–81. In one of two versions cited in Roth, promiscuity and avarice are allied – "Es war einmal eine Müllerin, ein wunderschönes Weib, / sie tät so gerne mahlen, sich Geldchen zu ersparen, / das war ihre einz'ge Freud" (p. 279) – and the miller ends by pleading for his wife's forgiveness. In Pinck, *Verklingende Weisen*, vol. 2, pp. 132–33, the beautiful miller's wife "wollt selbst der Müller sein"; when her husband threatens to sell the mill and spend all of the money on red wine "wo schöne Mädchen sein," she threatens to build another mill. Here, the miller's traditional unscrupulousness in folklore is attributed to his wife as well.

101 Gottfried August Bürger, *Bürgers Gedichte*, ed. Arnold Berger (Leipzig: Bibliographisches Institut, n.d.), p. 330.

102 Theodor Storm, *Gedichte, Novellen 1848–1867*, ed. Dieter Lohmeier (Frankfurt am Main: Deutscher Klassiker Verlag, 1987), p. 13. See also Wilhelm Schott, *In einem kühlen Grunde*: *Bilder verschwundener Mühlen* (Munich: Winkler Verlag, n.d.), p. 34.

103 I shall consign the sonnet to the "plain brown wrapper" of a footnote: "Der Müllerbube schiebt hinauf zur Mühle / Auf seinem Karren einen Mühlenstein, / Und in die Öffnung schob er glatt hinein / Sein steifes Glied und schaffte so sich Kühle. / / Die blonde Müll'rin sieht's im Sonnenschein, / Und trotz der unerträglich dumpfen Schwüle / Läuft sie hinab, daß prüfend sie's befühle. / Sie faßt und fühlt, es ist von Fleisch und Bein. / / 'Na hör mein Junge' ruft sie sehr brutal, / Was soll die Schweinerei mit deinem Schweif? / Ist das die Prüfung, die ich dir befahl, / / Ob du auch würdig wärest für mein Bett?' / Doch er zeigt nur die Inschrift um den Reif, / Und ach! sie liest gerührt: 'Elisabeth.'" See Heinz Ludwig Arnold, ed., *Dein Leib ist mein Gedicht: Deutsche erotische Lyrik aus fünf Jahrhunderten* (Bern: Rüttert Loening in der Scherz-Gruppe, 1970), p. 161. In the *Mühlenschwank* ballad "Die Beichte des Müllerpaares" (The Miller Couple's Confession), the miller's wife tells the priest that she has slept with the schoolmaster and with three miller's apprentices – again, the motif of the apprentice and the miller maid or miller's wife (stanza 7, "Der ist gewest mein bule / so lange zeit wider recht / der schulmeister in der Schule / und auch drey Mülners knecht/ noch mer die ich nicht nennen kan / darüber beger ich busse / die Fraw sprach lieber Mann"). See Roth, *Ehebruchschwänke in Liedform*, pp. 281–82.

104 Ernst Raupach, *Der Müller und sein Kind* (Hamburg: Hofmann und Campe, 1835). The cast of characters in this "Volksdrama" – a lengthy farrago of superstition, melodrama, love, and death – does not include a hunter, but does have a rich and tyrannical miller, his impossibly pure daughter, and a miller apprentice. Raupach's Konrad is a rustic musician who plays Lutheran hymns on the flute for his God-fearing beloved. For more about the medieval origins of the virgin–whore dichotomy, see Howard R. Bloch, *Medieval Misogyny and the Invention of Western Romantic Love* (Chicago, Illinois: The University of Chicago Press, 1991).

105 See Wolfgang Pfeiffer-Belli, "'Müllers Abschied.' J. F. Böhmer und das deutsche Volkslied" in *Jahrbuch für Volksliedforschung*, ed. John Meier, vol. 8 (Berlin: Walter de Gruyter & Co., 1951), pp. 221–23.

106 Arnim and Brentano, *Des Knaben Wunderhorn*, vol. 1, pp. 102–03.

107 In a review of the Arnim–Brentano anthology in which Goethe briefly characterized many of the individual poems in the anthology, the great writer described "Müllers Abschied" as "Für den, der die Lage fassen kann, unschätzbar" (priceless, for those who can comprehend the circumstances). See Johann Wolfgang von Goethe, *Schriften zur Literatur* from the *Gedenkausgabe der Werke, Briefe und Gespräche*, ed. Ernst Beutel, vol. 14 (Zürich: Artemis, 1950), p. 448.

108 See Jacob Harold Heinzelmann, *The Influence of the German Volkslied on Eichendorff's Lyric* (Leipzig: Gustav Fock, 1910), pp. 40–41.

109 Hermann Kunisch, "Freiheit und Bann - Heimat und Fremde" in *Eichendorff Heute*, p. 152.

110 Eichendorff, *Gedichte*, pp. 346–47.

111 Ibid., pp. 52–53.

112 J. W. Smeed, ed., *Famous Poets, Neglected Composers: Songs to Lyrics by Goethe, Heine, Mörike and Others* (Madison, Wisconsin: A-R Editions, 1992), pp. 63–65. Holländer was not the only composer drawn to this beautiful poem: Carl Banck, in his op. 20, Heft 2, no. 12, and Ludwig Berger were among the twenty-six composers in addition to Holländer who set "Das zerbrochene Ringelein" to music. See Ernst Challier, *Grosser Lieder-Katalog* (Berlin: Ernst Challier's Selbstverlag, 1885), pp. 1003–04.

113 Challier's catalogue includes five settings of a poem entitled "Müllers Klage" ("Dort tief im Erlenthale"), three settings of "Müllers Abschied," a song by Karl Gottlieb Reissiger entitled "Müllers Liebesnoth," and more. If there are not as many mill songs as there are hunting songs, it is nonetheless a frequent and familiar theme. See Challier, *Grosser Lieder-Katalog*, pp. 604–05.

114 See Hans Christian Andersen, *Agnete og Havmanden* (Copenhagen: B. Luno & Schneider, 1834).

115 Adelbert von Chamisso, *Sämtliche Werke*, vol. 1 (Berlin & Leipzig: Th. Knaur, n.d.), pp. 112–13.

116 Schott, *In einem kühlen Grunde*, p. 30.

117 Chamisso, *Sämtliche Werke*, vol. 1, p. 101.

118 Kerner, *Werke*, vol. 2, p. 28.

119 Ibid., pp. 43–45.

120 Ibid., p. 219.

121 Ditfurth, *Deutsche Volks- und Gesellschaftslieder*, pp. 15–16.

122 Cited in Johannes Mager, Günter Meißner, and Wolfgang Orf, *Die Kulturgeschichte der Mühlen*, p. 200.

123 Isolde Kurz, *Gedichte*, 2nd ed. (Stuttgart: G. J. Göschen, 1891), pp. 111–12, and Harald Haselbach, ed., *Deutsche Balladen* (Klagenfurt: Neuer Kaiser Verlag, 1978), pp. 325–26. The words "Bühle, bühlen, Bühlerin, bühlerisch" all have connotations of illicit intercourse, of wantonness.

124 Johann Nepomuk Vogl, *Lyrische Gedichte* (Vienna: Peter Rohrmann, 1844, 2nd augmented edition), p. 9. The first edition was entitled *Lyrische Blätter* (Vienna: Rohrmann & Schweigerd, 1836).

125 Vogl might also have taken his cue from Müller's "Die Post" from *Die Winterreise* when he (Vogl) wrote his "Liederkranz" entitled *Posthornklänge*, published in *Orpheus: Musikalisches Taschenbuch für das Jahr 1840*, vol. 1 (Vienna: Franz Riedl's Witwe & Sohn/Leipzig: Liebeskind, 1840), pp. 49–54. The *Taschenbuch* also includes Johann Gabriel Seidl's poem "Jägers Qual (Mit Hornbegleitung)," pp. 126–27, in which an amatory hunter blows his horn and listens for his beloved's reply. She does not hear at first, and the hunter, who grows more anguished with each stanza, fantasizes drowning himself in a lake deep within the forest – and then she answers. Redeemed from death, he cries at the end, "Mein Horn, stimm' ein! / Nie riefst du umsonst in den Wald hinein!"

126 *Allgemeine Wiener Musik-Zeitung*, vol. 6 (1846), pp. 251–52.

127 Schott, *In einem kühlen Grunde*, p. 50.

128 Ibid., p. 39.

3   Before and after Schubert: at the mill with other composers

1 See Richard Paul Koepke, "Wilhelm Müllers Dichtung und ihre musikalische Komposition," Ph.D. diss., Northwestern University, 1924, and Günther Eisenhardt, "Wilhelm Müllers Komponisten" in *Vom Pasqualatihaus: Musikwissenschaftliche Perspektiven aus Wien*, vol. 4 (Autumn 1994): 27–38. Other *Die schöne Müllerin* songs not discussed in this chapter – this is an incomplete list – include Heinrich Dorn (1804–1892), "Müllerburschen Abschied.

Wandern ist des Müllers Lust," op. 76, no. 3 (Berlin: Schlesinger, [1851?]); Julius Stern (1820–1883), "Das Wandern" in *Deutsche Gesänge für eine Singstimme mit Begleitung des Pianoforte*, op. 13, no. 5 (Berlin: Bote & Bock, [185-?]); and Heinrich Marschner (1795–1861), *Sechs Gesänge von Wilhelm Müller für eine Bariton-Stimme mit Pianoforte-Begleitung*, op. 68 (Leipzig: Fr. Kistner, [183-?]), dedicated to Ludwig Rellstab and including "Fastnachtslied von den goldnen Zöpfen," "Des Finken Gruss," "Wanderlied eines Rheinischen Handwerksburschen," "Entschuldigung," "Brüderschaft," and "Doppelte Gefahr." Still more mill songs are: (1) settings of "Des Müllers Blumen" by Karl Engel in the *Drei Lieder*, op. 5, no. 2 (Berlin: Bote & Bock, [183-?]), and Johann Stuckenschmidt, *Vier Lieder*, op. 5, no. 3 (Breslau: Leuckart, [185-?]); (2) settings of "Mein" by Alfred Brüggemann, *Drei Lieder*, op. 2, no. 2 (Leipzig: Breitkopf & Härtel, 1902) and Leopold Lenz, *Fünf Gesänge*, op. 25, no. 4 (Munich: Aibl, [183-?]); (3) settings of "Das Wandern" by Rudolf von Hertzberg, *Sechs Gesänge für Alt*, op. 4, no. 1 (Leipzig: Klemm, 1839); Otto Nicolai, *Drei Lieder*, op. 3 (Berlin: Trautwein, [183-?]); and Wilhelm Taubert, *Stimmen der Völker in 10 Gesängen*, op. 46, Heft 1, no. 9 (Berlin: Bote & Bock, [184-?]); (4) "Halt!" by Karl Engel, *Drei Lieder*, op. 5, no. 3 (Berlin: Bote & Bock, [183-?]); (5) settings of "Der Neugierige [Il curioso]"" by Johannes Dürrner, *Sechs Lieder*, op. 14, no. 4 (Leipzig: Peters, [184-?]) and Carl Gottlob Reissiger, *Lieder und Gesänge für 1 Bass-oder Bariton*, op. 53, no. 3 (Dresden: Wilhelm Paul, [183-? or 184-?]); (6) "Wohin?" by Julius Stern, *Sechs Lieder*, op. 6, no. 2 (Berlin: Schlesinger, [183-? or 184-?]); and (7) "Die böse Farbe" by Moritz Ernemann, *Acht deutsche Lieder*, op. 10, no. 6 (Breslau: Förster, [1844?]). The *Allgemeine Musikalische Zeitung* for November 13, 1839 includes a brief mention of Hertzberg's op. 4 *Sechs Gesänge*, as does the *Neue Zeitschrift für Musik* for March 19, 1839; the latter review is disapproving, the writer criticizing "Wandern von Wilhelm Müller" as the weakest song in the set, lacking the brisk, merry "Handwerksburschenton" that Marschner so ably gave to this text. Marschner, not Schubert!

2 Ernst Challier, *Grosser Lieder-Katalog* (Berlin: Ernst Challier's Selbstverlag, 1885), pp. 379–81.

3 Johann Wolfgang Goethe, *Briefwechsel mit Friedrich Schiller* from *Gedenkausgabe der Werke, Briefe und Gespräche*, ed. Ernst Beutler, vol. 20 (Zürich: Artemis-Verlag, 1950), p. 412. By "artful things . . . from a certain old German era," was Goethe referring to *Wechselgesang*? He would later employ dialogue-poetry in his own *West-östlicher Divan*. See Meredith Lee, *Goethe's Lyric Cycles* (Chapel Hill, North Carolina: The University of North Carolina Press, 1978); Lee (p. 84) observes that "Der Müllerin Verrath" is an adaptation of a French romance which Goethe first read and attempted to translate in 1789.

4 Goethe's "Der Junggesell und der Mühlbach" was probably also one model for Eichendorff's "Trost," which begins with the stanza: "Sag an, du helles Bächlein du, / Von Felsen eingeschlossen, / Du rauschet so munter immerzu, / Wo kommst du hergeflossen?" Eichendorff may also have taken a cue from Karoline Rudolphi's "Das Bächlein," with its first stanza: "Du Bächlein silberhell und klar, / Du eilst vorüber immerdar; / Am Ufer steh' ich, sinn' und sinn': / Wo kommst du her? Wo gehst du hin?" See Jacob Harold Heinzelmann, *The Influence of the German Volkslied on Eichendorff's Lyric*, p. 17.

5 See Rellstab, *Ludwig Berger*, pp. 110–23. In his lifetime, Berger published only a few sets of songs and several single songs. Adolph Hofmeister's *Siebenter Nachtrag* to the *Handbuch der musikalischen Literatur* (Leipzig: Friedrich Hofmeister, 1824), p. 78, lists a set of *Deutsche Lieder* (Carlsruhe: Velten, [1823 or 1824?]) and another set of *Sechs deutsche Lieder* published by the same firm, neither with opus number. In the *Neunter Nachtrag* to the Hofmeister *Handbuch* (Leipzig: Friedrich Hofmeister, 1826), p. 56, one finds a listing for Berger's *Neun deutsche Lieder*, op. 17 (Berlin: Laue, [1825?]) and the *Acht deutsche Lieder*, op. 19 (Berlin: Laue, [1825 or 1826?]). In Hofmeister's *Handbuch der musikalischen Literatur 1844–1845* (Leipzig: Friedrich Hofmeister, 1845), p. 108, one finds a listing for the posthumous publication of Berger's collected songs in eight *Lieferungen* (Leipzig: Hofmeister, 1841), beginning with the *Zehn Lieder* of op. 27 in vol. 1 and including scenes from Berger's opera *Sappho* in vol. 2, the

schöne Müllerin songs in vol. 3, the *Zwölf Lieder* of op. 33 in vol. 4, the *Zehn Lieder* of op. 55 and the *Drei Lieder* of op. 13 in vol. 5, the *Fünfzehn Lieder* of opp. 17 and 37 by Bernhard Klein and Berger in vol. 6, the *Zwölf Lieder* of op. 42 in vol. 7, and a reprint of the eight op. 19 songs and the op. 2, no. 1 "Lied zu Blücher's Gedächtniss" in the final group (one notes that the multi-volume set ends with a patriotic song).

6 For example, in Berger's text for stanza 4 (stanza 5 in the *Waldhornisten-Gedichte* and Schubert) of "Des Müllers Wanderlied / Wohin?", the miller *questions* "Ob wohl die Nixen singen / Da unten ihren Reihn?" (Do the nixies sing down below at their round-dances?), while Schubert's miller sings a declarative statement from the *Waldhornisten I* ("Es singen wohl die Nixen / tief unten ihren Reihn"), the depths of the waters emphasized by the added word "tief" (deep). What is now the third verse ("Hinunter und immer weiter / Und immer dem Bache nach, / Und immer heller rauschte / Und immer heller der Bach") appears neither in Berger's setting nor in the 1818 *Taschenbuch Gaben der Milde*, ed. F. W. Gubitz in Berlin; in the added verse, the incantatory siren-song of the water is suggested by the multiple liquid *l*s and murmurous *m*s, and the compulsion to continue onward resounds in the repetition of the words "und immer" at the beginning of lines two through four, telling us as well that the tale which has just begun is eternal. Nature has always and will always "speak" to youth in an incomprehensible language, luring it onwards to adventure, fortune or misfortune, and ultimately, death. The stream mysteriously swells from a cosy "Bächlein" to a "Bach," while the word "Hinunter," emphasized at the beginning of the initial line, is the first faint hint of the attraction of a watery death – it is here that Schubert would later couple the vocal line and the low bass in an audible symbol of that attraction. In another example, Berger's text for "Der Müller" ("Ich möchte zieh'n in die Welt hinaus") also differs from Müller's later versions, both in the periodical *Der Gesellschafter* for June 6, 1818, where the poem was entitled "Das böse Grün" (Wicked Green) and later in the *Waldhornisten-Gedichte*. The line "weinen so bleich, so bleich" became "Wohl weinen zerstört und bleich" in 1818, then "weinen *ganz todtenbleich*" in the final version, while the words "und singen leise" in Berger became "und singen *ganz* leise" in the final version, in both instances, revisions for greater emphasis. The most striking textual change, however, is the addition of another verse (stanza 3) in *Der Gesellschafter* ("Ach Grün, du lust'ge Farbe du, / Was siehst du mich immer an / So stolz, so keck, so schadenfroh, / Mich düsteren, weißen Mann?"), subsequently revised for the *Waldhornisten-Gedichte*.

7 "Das Wandern" was first published in the literary periodical *Gaben der Milde*, ed. Friedrich Wilhelm Gubitz, vol. 4 (Berlin: Für die Bücher-Verloosung "zum Vortheil hülfloser Krieger," 1818), pp. 214–15, along with two other "Müllerlieder" ("Der Bach," later entitled "Wohin?", and "Am Feierabend"). Here, the first poem of the complete cycle is entitled "Wanderlust," but otherwise, the poem is as we know it today.

8 Ruth Otto Bingham, "The Song Cycle in German-Speaking Countries 1790–1840: Approaches to a Changing Genre," Ph.D. diss., Cornell University (1993), p. 146.

9 Ibid., pp. 38–39.

10 Rellstab, *Ludwig Berger, ein Denkmal*, p. 111.

11 In Hofmeister, *Handbuch der musikalischen Literatur 1844–1851* (Leipzig: Friedrich Hofmeister, 1852), p. 311, one finds a listing for another setting of the "Vogelgesang vor der Müllerin Fenster" by Moritz Ernemann, *Fünf Lieder*, op. 22, no. 5 (Breslau: Scheffler, [184–?]).

12 Leon Plantinga, in *Romantic Music: A History of Musical Style in Nineteenth-Century Europe* (New York: W. W. Norton, 1984), pp. 112–13, briefly discusses Berger's cycle.

13 See Carl Freiherr von Ledebur, *Tonkünstler-Lexicon Berlin's von den ältesten Zeiten bis auf die Gegenwart* (Berlin: Ludwig Rauh, 1861), pp. 315–16 for the entry on Lauer. A tentative birth-day of May 16, 1796 (?) is given for him and no death-date, although it is recorded that he commanded a cavalry brigade in Brandenburg from 1854–56 and returned to Berlin when he retired. His other compositions include *Sechs deutsche Lieder von [Friedrich] Rückert*, op. 5 (Berlin: Trautwein, 1838); *Sechs Lieder von [Heinrich] Heine*, op. 6 (Berlin: Trautwein, 1838);

and *Sechs deutsche Lieder von Wilhelm Müller* (Berlin: Bethge, n.d.). "Rose, die Müllerin" is not one of the principal works investigated in Susanne Johns, *Das szenische Liederspiel zwischen 1800 und 1830: Ein Beitrag zur Berliner Theatergeschichte*, 2 vols. (Frankfurt am Main: Verlag Peter Lang, 1988), although it is mentioned.

14 Lauer's *Sechs deutsche Lieder* (Berlin: E. H. G. Christiani, n.d.), published without opus number, begins with three songs to texts taken from Ernst Schulze's romance *Caecilie* ("Flüchtig wehn die Kläng'," "Die wilde Jagd," and "Wehe nur, du Geist des Lebens").

15 Decker's military publications include *Der kleine Krieg, im Geiste der neueren Kriegführung* (Berlin: E. S. Mittler, 1822, 2nd ed.); *Der preussische Taschen-Artillerist* (Berlin, 1828); *Praktische Generalstabswissenschaft* (Berlin: F. A. Herbig, 1836); *Die Taktik der drei Waffen: Infanterie, Kavallerie und Artillerie* (Berlin: E. S. Mittler, 1828); and *Die Shrapnels: Einrichtung und Theorie der Wirkung dieses Geschosses* (Berlin: E. S. Mittler, 1842). His fictional *oeuvre* includes the four-act drama "Margot Stofflet. Ein historisch romantisches Gemälde aus dem Vendeekriege" (Berlin: E. S. Mittler, 1828).

16 *Allgemeine Musikalische Zeitung* for February 1828, no. 6, pp. 95–96.

17 Ibid., for September 1833, no. 38, p. 631.

18 Vivian Ramalingam, in "Schubart, Tonality, and *Die schöne Müllerin*" from *Studies in the History of Music*, vol. 3: *The Creative Process* (New York: Broude Brothers Ltd., 1993), pp. 201–16, believes that Schubert may have selected keys for the individual songs of *Die schöne Müllerin* based on Christian Friedrich Daniel Schubart's *Ideen zu einer Ästhetik der Tonkunst* of circa 1784, in particular, the "Charakteristik der Töne." See the edition edited by Ludwig Schubart (Vienna: J. V. Degen, 1806) or by Fritz & Margrit Kaiser (Hildesheim & New York: Georg Olms, 1990). See also Rita Steblin, *A History of Key Characteristics in the Eighteenth and Early Nineteenth Centuries* (Ann Arbor, Michigan: UMI Research Press, 1983), p. 211, and David Ossenkopf, "Christian Friedrich Daniel Schubart's Writings on Music," M.A. thesis (Columbia University, 1960).

19 Did he know Bernhard Klein's setting? He duplicates the same rhythmic patterns as at the beginning of Klein's version, and there are muted melodic resemblances as well.

20 See Alfred Heuss, "Franz Schuberts und Friedrich Zöllners 'Das Wandern ist des Müllers Lust'" in *Zeitschrift für Musik* 96 (1929), 5–10 and 65–70. Zöllner seems to have specialized in male-voice composition and to have had an affinity for Müller, witness his op. 14 *Wanderlieder von Wilhelm Müller*.

21 *Allgemeine Wiener Musik-Zeitung*, vol. 5 (1845), p. 13, also cited in Barbara Turchin, "Robert Schumann's Song Cycles in the Context of the Early Nineteenth-Century *Liederkreis*," Ph.D. diss. (Columbia University, 1981), p. 191.

22 *Iris im Gebiete der Tonkunst*, vol. 8 (1837), p. 25, cited also in Turchin, "Robert Schumann's Song Cycles in the Context of the Early Nineteenth-Century *Liederkreis*," p. 185.

23 Banck's copious song production (Hofmeister, *Handbuch der musikalischen Literatur 1844–1845*, pp. 104–105, cites a long list of songs, from op. 1 to op. 52, plus others published without opus number) includes a set entitled *Getrennte Liebe. Sechs deutsche Lieder für eine Singstimme mit Begleitung des Pianoforte*, op. 2 (Leipzig: C. F. Peters, c. 1837), including "Sehnsucht" (to a poem by "Caroline"), Müller's "Gute Nacht aus der Ferne," Hoffmann von Fallersleben's "Warum?", Müller's "Vom Berge" (Schubert used three verses of the same poem, whose title is "Der Berghirt," for the first section of "Der Hirt auf dem Felsen," D. 965, omitting the poet's last verse: "O süßes Liebchen, nimm mich bald! / Es ist so öd, es ist so kalt / Hier oben"), "Die Verlassne," and "Endliche Fahrt." Banck's *Sechs Gesänge*, op. 23 (Magdeburg: Wagner & Richter, [1838?]), includes settings of Adelbert von Chamisso's "Verrathene Liebe" and "Lustiges Lied im Mai" to a text from *Des Knaben Wunderhorn*. The reviews of op. 23 in the *Neue Zeitschrift für Musik* for March 23, 1838 (vol. 8, no. 24, p. 94) and in the *Allgemeine Musikalische Zeitung* for July 3, 1839 attest to recognition of Banck as one of the leading young song composers; the reviewer for the *Neue Zeitschrift für Musik* states that "a characteristic hallmark of Banck's songs is their predominating imagination [vor-

waltende Geist]; if they are not all equal in strength and freshness of inspiration, none is without imagination," while the redoubtable Gottfried Wilhelm Fink of the *Allgemeine Musikalische Zeitung* objected to details he considered "zu gesucht." This, as readers of the Schubert documentation will doubtless remember, is the same Fink who took aim at Schubert for wild, disordered, purposeless modulations.

24 "Die Post" was published (in the 1830s?) in Leipzig by Fr. Hofmeister. In my *Retracing a Winter's Journey: Schubert's Winterreise* (Ithaca, New York: Cornell University Press, 1991), I have speculated that "Die Post" tells of the power of music, even such humble music as posthorn fanfares, to move the heart of a poet-singer. Banck concludes his F major setting, replete with horn fanfares and clearly modeled after Schubert, by repeating the setting of Müller's stanza 2 ("Die Post bringt keinen Brief für dich. / Was pochst du denn so wunderlich, / mein Herz, mein Herz?"), as if he too thought that this was the central question of the poem.

25 Becker's *Lieder*, op. 3 were reviewed in the *Allgemeine Musikalische Zeitung* for March 1838 (no. 11): 172. The unidentified reviewer found both the text and music to "Hedwigs Lied von der Mühle" "sehr hübsch," criticized "Schön Hedwig am Ufer" for having a melody less compelling than the accompaniment, and dubbed "Hedwigs Lied am Bächlein" "ein zärtliches Spiel für zärtliche Seelen."

26 Julius Becker, *Der Neuromantiker: Musikalischer Roman* (Leipzig: J. J. Weber, 1840). The mill cycle is in vol. 1, pp. 60–69.

27 See Carl Koch, *Bernhard Klein*, also Carl Freiherrn von Ledebur, *Tonkünstler-Lexicon Berlin's*, pp. 287–89. Klein, whose father was a bassist and whose mother Marie Schwindl was the daughter of a composer and violinist, studied in Paris with Cherubini and was, for a time, associated with Zelter until that composer's authoritarianism ran afoul of Klein's refusal to be a disciple. He was famous as a teacher, and his list of accomplished students includes Heinrich Dorn, Wilhelm Taubert, Otto Nicolai, Julius Schneider, Friedrich Truhn, and others.

28 Klein also set "Der Neugierige" and "Wo ein treues Herze" ("Der Müller und der Bach") as nos. 1 and 8 respectively of the set of eight songs to texts by Müller (Berlin: Christiani, 1822) and listed in Hofmeister, *Sechster Nachtrag* to the *Handbuch der musikalischen Literatur* (Leipzig: Friedrich Hofmeister, 1823), p. 74. Klein evidently found Müller's verse "komponabel" on several occasions: Klein's *Trinklieder von Wilhelm Müller, mit Chor* (Berlin: Christiani, [1823?]) are listed in Hofmeister, *Siebenter Nachtrag* to the *Handbuch der musikalischen Literatur 1824*, p. 79, and his *Neugriechische Volkslieder übersetzt von W[ilhelm] Müller* (Berlin: Reimer, [1826?]) are listed in the *Zehnter Nachtrag* to the Hofmeister *Handbuch* of 1827, p. 61.

29 Reissiger was born January 31, 1798 in Belzig bei Wittenberg and went to Leipzig in 1811 at age thirteen to study at the Thomasschule. Seven years later, in 1818, he began his studies at the University of Leipzig, where he taught piano and organ, sang bass solos with the Gewandhaus, and played violin and viola in the orchestra. In 1821, he went to Vienna to pursue his musical studies and there composed his first opera (the censors did not permit its performance, however), an overture to Heinrich Kleist's "Käthchen von Heilbronn," and piano music. After a "Bildungsreise" to France and Italy in 1824–25, he settled in Berlin, where he found a position with the Royal Institute for Sacred Music, along with Carl Friedrich Zelter and Bernhard Klein. In October 1826, he was offered a post in Dresden as the royal music director in Heinrich Marschner's place; his success was such that Friedrich August made him Kapellmeister in 1827 in the wake of Carl Maria von Weber. He excelled in song composition, and his seventy-six opuses of lieder, ballads, duets, *Liedertafel* pieces, etc., were well respected in their day.

30 Reissiger's op. 76 songs, which include the lied "Jägers Lieb" (Hunter's Love) to a poem by Friedrich Kind, are listed in Hofmeister, *Handbuch der musikalischen Literatur 1844–1845*, p. 164, also his op. 53 setting of "Der Neugierige" and his op. 84 setting of "Des Baches Wiegenlied."

31 Schubert uses walking basses with similar associations in his settings of Franz von Schober's "Schatzgräbers Begehr" (The Treasure-Hunter's Desire), D. 761, Johann Mayrhofer's "An die

Freunde" (To my Friends), D. 654, and Jacob Nicolaus Craigher's "Totengräbers Heimweh" (Gravedigger's Homesickness), D. 842 (1825).

32 Hugo Wolf, *Briefe an Melanie Köchert*, ed. Franz Grasberger (Tutzing: Hans Schneider, 1964), letter of April 14, 1891, p. 37.

33 The song has been published in Louis Spohr, *The Complete Lieder Sets*, from *Selected Works of Louis Spohr 1784–1859*, 10 vols., ed. Clive Brown (New York & London: Garland Publishing, Inc., 1988), pp. 89–91.

34 In the Hofmeister *Handbuch der musikalischen Literatur* for 1844–45, Curschmann's op. 3 *Gesänge* are cited on p. 114. The review of op. 3 appears in the *Allgemeine Musikalische Zeitung* for June 1832, no. 25, pp. 419–20, and the review of op. 5 in the *AMZ* for September 1833, no. 37, pp. 622–23.

35 Ludwig Spohr, *Selbstbiographie*, 2 vols. (Kassel & Göttingen: G. H. Wigand, 1860–61), vol. 2, p. 169.

36 Georg Meissner, *Karl Friedrich Curschmann. Ein Beitrag zur Geschichte des Deutschen Liedes zu Anfang des XIX. Jahrhunderts* (Bautzen: E. M. Monse, 1899), p. 6.

37 Ibid., p. 9.

38 J. W. Smeed, *Famous Poets, Neglected Composers: Songs to Lyrics by Goethe, Heine, Mörike, and Others* (Madison, Wisconsin: A-R Editions, Inc., 1993), pp. 17–19.

39 Ledebur, *Tonkünstler-Lexicon Berlin's*, p. 657.

40 See the Hofmeister *Handbuch der musikalischen Literatur* for 1844–45, p. 189.

41 Ibid., p. 180. Taubert's setting of "Die Post" from Müller's *Die Winterreise* in his *Zwölf Lieder*, op. 9, no. 5 (Berlin: Schlesinger, [1833 or 1834?]) was reviewed in the *Allgemeine Musikalische Zeitung* for July 1834, no. 30, p. 498 as "Unruhig, eigen und treu durchgeführt; verlangt geschickten Vortrag"; the opus includes settings of Goethe's "Rastlose Liebe," Ludwig von Uhland's "Jägerlied" and "Frühlingsglaube," Ludwig Rellstab's "Bewusstseyn" and "Herbst," and Heine's "Wenn ich auf dem Lager liege."

42 But Taubert had his moments, and one of them is included in Smeed, *Famous Poets, Neglected Composers*: a setting of Hoffmann von Fallersleben's "In der Fremde," op. 67, no. 2 (pp. 46–47).

43 Hofmeister, *Handbuch der musikalischen Literatur* for 1844–45, p. 142. Lenz composed a song to "Maximilian Joseph, König von Baiern, an seinem Namenstag den 12. Oktober 1825," op. 23, which leads me to speculate that his op. 25 might have followed shortly thereafter.

44 Schubert has "schalle," not "erschalle." Lenz's miller also asks "Sonne, hast du keinen wärmern Schein?" rather than "helleren Schein" and sings "O so muß ich ganz allein" rather than "Ach, so muß ich ganz allein."

45 Hofmeister, *Handbuch der musikalischen Literatur* for 1844–45, p. 115. Dames's *Sechs Lieder*, op. 1 (Berlin: Bote & Bock, [183-?]) includes a setting of "Des Müllers Blumen" as no. 5.

46 "Das Veilchen" is the second of Wilhelm Stade's *Zwei Lieder* (Leipzig: C. F. Kahnt, n.d.); interestingly, the first song, "Vergeb'ne Treu" (Betrayed Fidelity), is a setting of an "Altdeutsches Minnelied a.d. 13. Jahrhundert." Müller, one imagines, would have approved of the conjunction.

4   "Lilies that fester": sex and death in Müller's and Schubert's cycles

1 Richard Capell, *Schubert Songs* (London: Duckworth, 1973, 3rd ed. [1st ed. 1925]), pp. 191–92, and Ruth Otto Bingham, "The Song Cycle in German-Speaking Countries 1790–1840," pp. 183–84.

2 Youens, *Schubert: Die schöne Müllerin* (Cambridge, England: Cambridge University Press, 1992), p. 43.

3 See Eduard Hanslick, *Aus dem Concert-Saal: Kritiken und Schilderungen aus 20 Jahren des Wiener Musiklebens 1848–1868*, 2nd rev. ed. (Vienna & Leipzig: Wilhelm Braumüller, 1897), p. 106, and the author's *Schubert: Die schöne Müllerin*, p. 27.

4 The complete text of the cycle, including prologue and epilogue, is published in Wilhelm

Müller, *Die Winterreise und andere Gedichte*, ed. Hans-Rüdiger Schwab (Frankfurt am Main: Insel Verlag, 1986), pp. 11–40, and in Alan P. Cottrell, *Wilhelm Müller's Lyrical Song-Cycles: Interpretations and Texts* (Chapel Hill, North Carolina: The University of North Carolina Press, 1970), pp. 117–34.

5 Wilhelm Müller, *Gedichte: Vollständige kritische Ausgabe*, ed. James Taft Hatfield (Berlin: B. Behr, 1906), p. 452.

6 Wilhelm Müller, *Blumenlese aus den Minnesingern* (Berlin: Maurer, 1816), pp. 60–61. In a lovely chronological coincidence, Müller entitles the first translated poem of the volume "An die ferne Geliebte" (To the Distant Beloved), a translation of Kaiser Heinrich's "Ich gruesse mit gesange" possibly written at the same time that Beethoven was working on the composition of his song cycle *An die ferne Geliebte*, op. 98. It is, furthermore, important to realize that the *Blumenlese* was a manifestation of Müller's "Germanomanie," a short-lived but crucial attempt to become one of the *Vaterlandsromantiker* in the wake of the War of Liberation, perhaps at least in part to compensate for his prior involvement, both military and erotic, with the French. Müller even wore "altdeutsch" garb on occasion, as when Luise told him on December 10, 1815 that the costume was becoming; see Müller, *Werke. Tagebücher. Briefe*, vol. 5: *Tagebücher*, ed. Maria-Verena Leistner (Berlin: Gatza, 1994), p. 47. It is thus his own bygone "echt Deutsch" sentiments that Müller mocks in the Prologue to the cycle.

7 Wilhelm Müller, *Blumenlese aus den Minnesingern*, p. ii. Müller also acknowledges his predecessors in the preface, including Johann Wilhelm Ludwig Gleim's *Gedichte nach den Minnesingern* (Berlin: Zum Besten zweyer armen Magdchen, 1773), which Müller both praises and criticizes as "ganz frei" (utterly free) paraphrases, with entire newly composed stanzas added (p. v).

8 Carl Freiherrn von Ledebur, *Tonkünstler-Lexicon Berlin's von den ältesten Zeiten bis auf die Gegenwart* (Berlin: Ludwig Rauh, 1861), pp. 177–78. Gäde's songs include the "Komisches Ständchen eines Gärtners" and his op. 10 settings of poems carved from Ernst Schulze's *Cäcilie*.

9 Müller reveals in his diary for the year before the Stägemann song-play that he was finding the attempt to suppress sexual impulses difficult indeed. On December 28, 1815, he wrote, "Heute Morgen hatte ich wieder einen Kampf mit der bösen Erdenlust in mir, den ich nicht ohne Wunden bestand' (This morning, I once again fought a battle with my wicked sensuality, which I did not overcome unwounded). See Müller, *Werke*, vol. 5: *Tagebücher*, p. 55.

10 Müller, *Blumenlese aus den Minnesingern*, pp. 86–87.

11 Frederick Goldin, *Lyrics of the Troubadours and Trouvères* (Garden City, New York: Anchor Press/Doubleday, 1973), pp. 146–47.

12 Wilhelm Müller, *Blumenlese aus den Minnesingern*, pp. 54–57 and 64–65 respectively.

13 The information about the forget-me-not charm comes from Graham Johnson, "Schubert in Full Flower," the booklet accompanying *The Hyperion Schubert Edition*, vol. 19, with Felicity Lott, soprano, and Graham Johnson, piano (Hyperion CDJ33019, 1993).

14 Achim von Arnim and Clemens Brentano, *Des Knaben Wunderhorn*, vol. 3, p. 341. In Ludwig Erk, *Deutscher Liederhort. Auswahl der vorzüglicheren Deutschen Volkslieder aus der Vorzeit und der Gegenwart mit ihren eigenthümlichen Melodien* (Leipzig: Breitkopf & Härtel, 1890, reprint of 1st ed. 1856), pp. 347–48, the male poetic persona of "Vergißmeinnicht" hears the nightingale speaking to him in a dream, telling him that his sweetheart will go with someone else if he does not declare his love. Hotheadedly assuming this to be an imputation of infidelity, he rides back to her and accuses her, upon which she assures him of her love and gives him a garland of forget-me-nots in pledge. This song, according to Erk (p. 348), was found in a manuscript dated 1603 in a library in Breslau and was subsequently disseminated to the melody of another folk song, "Es steht ein Lindlein in diesem Thal, ach Gott! was thut sie da!" (musicians are no doubt familiar with Brahms's arrangement, "Es steht ein Lind in jenem Tal" from the *Deutsche Volkslieder* [Berlin: Simrock, 1894]).

15 Johann Gottfried Herder, *Werke*, vol. 1, ed. Karl-Gustav Gerold (Munich: Carl Hanser, 1953), pp. 110–11.

16 Friedrich Karl von Erlach, *Die Volkslieder der Deutschen. Eine vollständige Sammlung der vorzüglichen deutschen Volkslieder von der Mitte des fünfzehnten bis in die erste Hälfte des neunzehnten Jahrhunderts*, vol. 1 (Mannheim: Heinrich Hoff, 1834), p. 308. See also Joseph von Görres, *Altteutsche Volks- und Meisterlieder aus den Handschriften der Heidelberger Bibliothek* (Frankfurt am Main: Gebrüder Wilmans, 1817), p. 43. Fascinatingly, Erlach also states that the poem can be found in "Sophie Brentano bunte Reihe kleiner Schriften" – Sophie Mereau-Brentano, or Clemens Brentano's first wife?

17 Ernst Challier, *Grosser Lieder-Katalog* (Berlin: Ernst Challier's Selbstverlag, 1885), pp. 871–72.

18 Rita Steblin, "Wilhelm Müllers Aufenthalt in Wien im Jahre 1817: Eine Verbindung zu Schubert durch Schlechta" in *Vom Pasqualatihaus: Musikwissenschaftliche Perspektiven aus Wien*, vol. 4 (Autumn 1994): 19–26. Steblin observes that Müller and Schubert might have been in the same place at the same time on at least one occasion: a performance of Müller's poem "Der Glockenguß zu Breslau" on December 22, 1817 at the Leopoldstadt theatre along with the tale "Der Gang zum Hochgerichte" by Schubert's friend Franz von Schlechta, whose "Auf einen Kirchhof," D. 151, Schubert had already set to music.

19 Zumsteeg's setting of the "Lied des gefangenen Grafen" has been reprinted in Richard D. Green, ed., *Anthology of Goethe Songs* (Madison, Wisconsin: A-R Editions, Inc., 1994), pp. 4–7.

20 Wilhelm Müller, *The Diary and Letters of Wilhelm Müller*, ed. James Taft Hatfield (Chicago, Illinois: The University of Chicago Press, 1903), p. 43.

21 Ibid., pp. 45–46.

22 Wilhelm Müller, *Gedichte: Vollständige kritische Ausgabe*, pp. 369–71.

23 The "temperature" of "Der blaue Mondenschein" is curiously similar – although there is little likelihood of influence – to an Irish folk tale about the "Banshee," or "bean-sidhe," a beautiful fairy woman who is an apparition of death. As the doomed male character approaches the banshee by a frozen marsh, he is engulfed in searing heat, although his death is attributed to cold. See Michael Scott, ed., *Irish Folk and Fairy Tales* (London: Penguin Books, 1989, first ed. 1983), vol. 2, pp. 90–97.

24 The account of the Baron Marjodo (or Meriadoc in modern German) and his dream occurs in lines 13,511 through 13,636. See Gottfried von Strassburg, *Tristan*, ed. Peter Ganz after the edition by Reinhold Bechstein (Wiesbaden: F. A. Brockhaus, 1978), vol. 2, pp. 115–19, and the edition of *Tristan*, eds. Gottfried Weber, Gertrud Utzmann and Werner Hoffmann (Darmstadt: Wissenschaftliche Buchgesellschaft, 1967), pp. 376–80. While many critics have identified the boar as Tristan, others feel that the raging boar who wounds the king is a symbol of Marjodo's own lust. See Hugo Bekker, *Gottfried von Strassburg's Tristan: Journey through the Realm of Eros* (Columbia, South Carolina: Camden House, Inc., 1987), pp. 196–203.

25 See Richard Bernheimer, *Wild Men in the Middle Ages: A Study in Art, Sentiment, and Demonology* (Cambridge, Massachusetts: Harvard University Press, 1952).

26 Joseph Leo Koerner, *The Moment of Self-Portraiture in German Renaissance Art* (Chicago: The University of Chicago Press, 1993), p. 170.

27 Could Müller have known the *Mailied* (May song) below? The anonymous poem begins as follows:

Das schwarz blümlein das bringet mir die klag;
Wann ich der allerliebsten nit enhab
Und ich mich von ihr scheid,
So truret min herz und fürt groß heimlich leid.

The little black flower brings me sorrow
when I no longer have my best-beloved
and I part from her,
thus my heart grieves and suffers greatly
in secret.

See Walther Gloth, *Das Spiel von den sieben Farben* (Königsberg: Grafe & Unzer, 1902), p. 72, and Otto Lauffer, *Farbensymbolik im deutschen Volksbrauch* (Hamburg: Hansischer Gildenverlag, 1948), p. 56.

28 Sigmund Freud, "Das Medusenhaupt," or "Medusa's Head," in *The Standard Edition of the*

Complete Psychological Works of Sigmund Freud, trans. James Strachey in collaboration with Anna Freud, assisted by Alix Strachey and Alan Tyson, vol. 18 (London: The Hogarth Press, 1955, reprinted 1957), pp. 273–74; this tiny essay (probably a sketch for a more extensive work), was written in 1922 and published posthumously in 1940.

29 Julia Wirth, *Julius Stockhausen: Der Sänger des deutschen Liedes nach Dokumenten seiner Zeit* (Frankfurt am Main: Englert & Schlösser, 1927), p. 229.

30 Could Müller have known about the existence of D. 795? It is intriguing to speculate because Schubert and Carl Maria von Weber knew one another and had a conversation in October 1823, that is, while Schubert was possibly finishing up his work on *Die schöne Müllerin*. Carl Maria von Weber and Müller were friends; the second volume of Müller's *Waldhornisten-Gedichte*, which begins with *Die Winterreise*, is dedicated to Weber. Whether Schubert in the autumn of 1823 knew of Weber's and Müller's friendship or whether mention of the song cycle ever came up is not known.

31 Stanley Cavell, *Disowning Knowledge in Six Plays of Shakespeare* (Cambridge, England: Cambridge University Press, 1987), p. 137.

32 Stark's published works include the *Deutsche Liederschule. Eine leichtfassliche systematische nach künstlerischen Principien eingerichtete Anleitung zum Sologesang* (Stuttgart: J. G. Cotta, 1861), filled with examples of lieder, duets, trios, and quartets by contemporary composers such as Immanuel Faisst, Ferdinand Hiller, Heinrich Marschner, Carl Reinecke, Anton Rubinstein, Franz Lachner, and others.

33 Ironically, it was in the 1880s that musicians and scholars began objecting to then-current editions of the cycle, based on Anton Diabelli's 1830 second edition and reflecting the great singer Johann Michael Vogl's emendations in performance. A combination of Schubert-veneration and the advent of historicist approaches to editing music produced calls for pur-ification of the Schubert canon. The winds had shifted, and the climate was not favorable for those wishing to attach their own afterthoughts to so famous a work.

34 Lawrence Lipking, *Abandoned Women and Poetic Tradition* (Chicago, Illinois: The University of Chicago Press, 1988), pp. xv–xxvii.

35 Is there a faint reminiscence of "Der blaue Mondenschein" in this poem, the broken youth no longer able to bear the moon's gaze? Perhaps the moon, which shimmers with Diana-like associations of chastity and purity in "Des Baches Wiegenlied," should veil its sight, lest it see what lovers really do by moonlight.

36 Several of Müller's most distinguished interpreters and biographers found "Blümlein Vergißmein" incomprehensible. Alan Cottrell, in *Wilhelm Müller's Lyrical Song-Cycles: Interpretations and Texts* (Chapel Hill, North Carolina: The University of North Carolina Press, 1970), p. 25, interprets the black flower as death and the quest for it as a path to suicide and says that "Trockne Blumen" is entirely devoid of the "weirdly demonic" atmosphere of the poem immediately preceding it. Klaus Günther Just, in "Wilhelm Müllers Liederzyklen 'Die schöne Müllerin' und 'Die Winterreise'" in *Zeitschrift für deutsche Philologie*, vol. 83 (1964): 425–71, reprinted in the same author's *Übergänge: Probleme und Gestalten der Literatur* (Bern & Munich: Francke, 1966), pp. 133–52, similarly finds death in "Blümlein Vergißmein," but says nothing of sexual content.

Select bibliography

Abeken, Hedwig. *Hedwig von Olfers geb. von Staegemann. Ein Lebenslauf*, 2 vols. Berlin: Mittler & Sohn, 1908.

Allen, Philip Schuyler. "Wilhelm Müller and the German Volkslied." Ph.D. diss., University of Chicago, 1899. Reprinted in the *Journal of English and Germanic Philology*, vol. 2, no. 3 (1901).

Arnim, Achim von and Brentano, Clemens. *Des Knaben Wunderhorn: Alte deutsche Lieder*, 3 vols. Heidelberg: Mohr & Winter, 1819, reprinted Meersburg: F. W. Hendel, 1928.

Bagge, Selmar. "Der Streit über Schuberts Müllerlieder" in *Allgemeine Musikalische Zeitung*, vol. 3, no. 5 (29 January 1868): 36–37, 44–46.

Bartscher, Ferdinand. *Der innere Lebensgang der Dichterin Luise Hensel nach der Original-Aufzeichnungen in ihren Tagebüchern*. Paderborn: Schoningh, 1882.

Baumann, Cecilia. *Wilhelm Müller. The Poet of the Schubert Song Cycles: His Life and Works*. University Park, Pennsylvania: Pennsylvania State University Press, 1981.

Baumgart, Wolfgang. *Der Wald in der deutschen Dichtung*. Berlin & Leipzig: Walter de Gruyter, 1936.

Becker, Julius. *Der Neuromantiker: Musikalischer Roman*, 2 vols. Leipzig: J. J. Weber, 1840.

Beifus, Joseph, ed. *Die bunte Garbe: Deutsche Volkslieder der Gegenwart*. Munich: M. Mörike, 1912.

Beurmann, Arno. *Der Aberglaube der Jäger: Von der beseelten Magie, von Mystik und Mythen und allerlei Zauberwahn der Jäger*. Hamburg & Berlin: Verlag Paul Parey, 1961.

Binder, Franz. *Luise Hensel. Ein Lebensbild nach gedruckten und ungedruckten Quellen*. Freiburg im Breisgau: Herder, 1885.

Bingham, Ruth Otto. "The Song Cycle in German-Speaking Countries 1790–1840: Approaches to a Changing Genre," Ph.D. diss., Cornell University, 1993.

Böhme, Franz Magnus. *Altdeutsches Liederbuch*. Leipzig: Breitkopf & Härtel, 1877.

Brentano, Clemens. *Gedichte*, eds. Wolfgang Frühwald, Bernhard Gajek, and Friedhelm Kemp. Munich: Deutscher Taschenbuch Verlag, 1977.

   Gesammelte Schriften, vol. 8: *Gesammelte Briefe von 1795 bis 1842*. Frankfurt am Main: J. D. Sauerländer, 1855.

Brentano, Lujo. "Ein Brief Luise Hensels an Clemens Brentano" in *Hochland: Monatsschrift für alle Gebiete des Wissens der Literatur & Kunst*, ed. Karl Muth, vol. 14 (October 1916–March 1917): 345–46.

Budde, Elmar. "'Die schöne Müllerin' in Berlin" in *Preussen, Dein Spree-Athen: Beiträge zu Literatur, Theater und Musik in Berlin*, ed. Hellmut Kühn, pp. 162–72. Berlin: Rowohlt, 1981.

Bürger, Gottfried August. *Bürgers Gedichte*, ed. Arnold Berger. Leipzig: Bibliographisches Institut, n.d.

Capell, Richard. *Schubert Songs*. London: Duckworth, 1973, 3rd ed. (1st ed. 1925).

Cardauns, Hermann. *Aufzeichnungen und Briefe von Luise Hensel*. Hamm: Breer & Thiemann, 1916.

   Aus Luise Hensels Jugendzeit: Neue Briefe und Gedichte zum Jahrhunderttag ihrer Konversion (8. Dezember 1818). Freiburg im Breisgau: Herder, 1918.

Chamisso, Adelbert von. *Sämtliche Werke*. Berlin & Leipzig: Th. Knaur, n.d.

Clewing, Carl. *Musik und Jägerei: Lieder, Reime und Geschichten vom Edlen Waidwerk*, 3 vols. Neudamm: J. Neumann and Kassel & Wilhelmhöhe: Bärenreiter-Verlag, 1937–38.

Cottrell, Alan. *Wilhelm Müller's Lyrical Song-Cycles: Interpretations and Texts*. Chapel Hill, North Carolina: The University of North Carolina Press, 1970.

Damian, Franz Valentin. "Über das Lied 'Pause' aus Schuberts Liederkreis *Die schöne Müllerin*" in *Schubert-Gabe der Oesterreichischen Gitarre-Zeitschrift*, pp. 35–43. Vienna, 1928.

Davis, Gregson. *The Death of Procris: "Amor" and the Hunt in Ovid's Metamorphoses*. Rome: Edizioni dell'Ateneo, 1983.

Diel, Johannes Baptist and Kreiten, Wilhelm. *Clemens Brentano: Ein Lebensbild nach gedruckten und ungedruckten Quellen*, vol. 2: *1814–1842*. Freiburg im Breisgau: Herder, 1878.

Ditfurth, Franz Wilhelm Freiherr von. *Deutsche Volks- und Gesellschaftslieder des 17. und 18. Jahrhunderts*. Hildesheim: Georg Olms Verlag, 1956 (reprint of 1st ed. Nördlingen: C. H. Beck, 1872).

Dürr, Walther. "'Manier' und 'Veränderung' in Kompositionen Franz Schuberts" in *Zur Aufführungspraxis der Werke Franz Schuberts*, ed. Roswitha Karpf, pp. 124–39. Munich & Salzburg: Musikverlag Emil Katzbichler, 1981.

"Schubert and Johann Michael Vogl: A Reappraisal" in *19th-Century Music*, vol. 3 (November 1979): 126–40.

Eichendorff, Joseph von. *Gedichte: Kommentar*, vol. 1/2 of *Sämtliche Werke des Freiherrn Joseph von Eichendorff*, eds. Harry Fröhlich and Wolfgang Kron. Stuttgart & Berlin: Verlag W. Kohlhammer, 1994.

Werke und Schriften, vol. 1: *Gedichte, Epen, Dramen*, eds. Gerhard Baumann and Siegfried Grosse. Stuttgart: J. G. Cotta, 1957.

Eisenhardt, Günther. "Wilhelm Müllers Komponisten" in *Vom Pasqualatihaus: Musikwissenschaftliche Perspektiven aus Wien*, vol. 4 (Autumn 1994): 27–38.

Erk, Ludwig. *Deutscher Liederschatz. Eine Auswahl der beliebtesten Volkslieder*. Leipzig: C. F. Peters, [between 1870 and 1890?].

Die deutschen Volkslieder mit ihren Singweisen. Leipzig: B. Hermann, 1843, modern reprint Potsdam: L. Voggenreiter, 1938.

Erk, Ludwig and Böhme, Franz Magnus. *Deutscher Liederhort. Auswahl der vorzüglicheren deutschen Volkslieder*, 3 vols. Leipzig: Breitkopf & Härtel, 1893–94.

Erlach, Friedrich Karl Freiherr von. *Die Volkslieder der Deutschen. Eine vollständige Sammlung der vorzüglichen Deutschen Volkslieder von der Mitte des fünfzehnten bis in die erste Hälfte des neunzehnten Jahrhunderts*. Mannheim: H. Hoff, 1834–36.

Feilchenfeldt, Konrad and Frühwald, Wolfgang. "Clemens Brentano: Briefe und Gedichte an Emilie Linder. Ungedruckte Handschriften aus dem Nachlaß von Johannes Baptista Diel SJ" in *Jahrbuch des Freien Deutschen Hochstifts 1976*, ed. Detlev Lüders, pp. 216–315. Tübingen: Max Niemeyer Verlag, 1976.

Fetzer, John. *Romantic Orpheus: Profiles of Clemens Brentano*. Berkeley, California: University of California Press, 1974.

Förster, Friedrich. *Die Sängerfahrt. Eine Neujahrsgabe für Freunde der Dichtkunst und Mahlerey*. Berlin: Maurer, 1818, facsimile ed. published Heidelberg: Lambert Schneider, 1969.

Freund, Winfried. *Müde bin ich, geh' zur Ruh: Leben und Werk der Luise Hensel*. Wiedenbruck: Guth & Etscheidt, 1984.

Friedländer, Max. "Die Entstehung der Müllerlieder. Eine Erinnerung an Frau von Olfers" in *Deutsche Rundschau*, vol. 19, no. 2 (1892): 301–07.

Gajek, Bernhard. *Homo Poeta: Zur Kontinuität der Problematik bei Clemens Brentano*. Frankfurt am Main: Athenäum Verlag, 1971.

Ganghofer, Ludwig. *Schloss Hubertus*. Stuttgart: Adolf Bonz, 1917.

Gerlach, Jakob von, ed. *Ernst Ludwig von Gerlach. Aufzeichnungen aus seinem Leben und Wirken 1795–1877*, 2 vols. Schwerin: Fr. Bahn, 1903.

Gleisberg, Hermann. *Das kleine Mühlenbuch*. Dresden: Sachsen–Verlag, 1956.

Gradenwitz, Peter. *Literatur und Musik in geselligem Kreise: Geschmacksbildung, Gesprächsstoff und musikalische Unterhaltung in der bürgerlichen Salongesellschaft*. Stuttgart: Franz Steiner, 1991.

Grosse, Siegfried. "Die Mühle und der Müller im deutschen Volkslied" in *Jahrbuch des Österreichischen Volksliedwerkes*, vol. 11 (1962): 8–35.

Hadamar von Laber. *Die Jagd*, ed. Karl Stejskal. Vienna: Alfred Hölder, 1860.

Haefeli-Rasi, Madeleine. *Wilhelm Müller. 'Die schöne Müllerin:' Eine Interpretation als Beitrag zum Thema STILWANDEL im Übergang von der Spätromantik zum Realismus*. Zürich: Schippert & Co., 1970.

Hake, Bruno. *Wilhelm Müller: Sein Leben und Dichten, Kapitel IV: Die schöne Müllerin*. Berlin: Mayer & Müller, 1908.

Heinzelmann, Jacob Harold. *The Influence of the German Volkslied on Eichendorff's Lyrik*. Leipzig: Gustav Fock, 1910.

Hensel, Luise. *Lieder von Luise Hensel*, ed. Hermann Cardauns. Regensburg: Josef Habbel, 1923.

Heuss, Alfred. "Eine Schubert-Liedstudie: Das Lied 'Pause' aus dem Zyklus *Die schöne Müllerin*" in *Zeitschrift für Musik*, vol. 91 (1924): 617–26.

"Franz Schuberts und Friedrich Zöllners 'Das Wandern ist des Müllers Lust'" in *Zeitschrift für Musik*, vol. 96 (1929): 5–10 and 65–70.

Hilf, Richard and Röhrig, Fritz. *Wald und Weidwerk in Geschichte und Gegenwart*, 2 vols. Potsdam: Akademische Verlagsgesellschaft Athenaion, 1938.

Hilmar, Ernst. "Ein 'geheimes Programm' in den drei wiederentdeckten Manuskripten zum Zyklus 'Die schöne Müllerin'" in *Schubert durch die Brille* 11 (June 1993): 35–47.

Johns, Susanne. *Das szenische Liederspiel zwischen 1800 und 1830: Ein Beitrag zur Berliner Theatergeschichte*, 2 vols. Frankfurt am Main: Peter Lang, 1988.

Jungwirth, G. "Jagd, Jäger" in Eduard Hoffmann-Krayer and Hanns Bächtold-Stäubli, eds., *Handwörterbuch des deutschen Aberglaubens*, vol. 4, pp. 575–93. Berlin and Leipzig, 1927–42.

Just, Klaus Günther. "Wilhelm Müllers Liederzyklen 'Die schöne Müllerin' und 'Die Winterreise'" in *Übergänge: Probleme und Gestalten der Literatur*. Bern and Munich: Francke, 1966.

Kerner, Justinus. *Werke*, vol. 3: *Reiseschatten – Dramatische Dichtungen*, ed. Raimund Pissin. Berlin & Leipzig: Deutsches Verlagshaus Bong & Co., n.d.

Koch, Carl. *Bernhard Klein (1793–1832). Sein Leben und seine Werke*. Leipzig: Oscar Brandstetter, 1902.

Koepke, Richard Paul. "Wilhelm Müllers Dichtung und ihre musikalische Komposition." Ph.D. diss., Northwestern University, 1924.

Köhler, Reinhold. "Aus Lorbers Gedichte 'Die edle Jägerei'" in Reinhold Köhler, *Kleinere Schriften zur neueren Literaturgeschichte, Volkskunde und Wortforschung*, vol. 3, ed. Johannes Bolte, pp. 484–91. Berlin: Emil Felber, 1900.

"Über Grässes Jägerbrevier" in Reinhold Köhler, *Kleinere Schriften zur neueren Literaturgeschichte, Volkskunde und Wortforschung*, vol. 3, ed. Johannes Bolte, pp. 491–94. Berlin: Emil Felber, 1900.

"Weidsprüche und Jägerschreie" in Reinhold Köhler, *Kleinere Schriften zur neueren Literaturgeschichte, Volkskunde und Wortforschung*, vol. 3, ed. Johannes Bolte, pp. 452–84. Berlin: Emil Felber, 1900.

Kohler, Oskar. *Müde bin ich, geh' zur Ruh: Die hell-dunkle Lebensgeschichte Luise Hensels*. Paderborn: Schoningh, 1991.

Kramer, Lawrence. "The Schubert Lied: Romantic Form and Romantic Consciousness" in *Schubert: Critical and Analytical Studies*, ed. Walter Frisch, pp. 200–36. Lincoln, Nebraska: University of Nebraska Press, 1986.

Kraus, Ludwig. "Das Liederspiel in den Jahren 1800 bis 1830: Ein Beitrag zur Geschichte des deutschen Singspiele." Ph.D. diss., Vereinigte Friedrichs-Universität Halle-Wittenberg, 1921.

Kreißle von Hellborn, Heinrich. *Franz Schubert*. Vienna: Carl Gerold's Sohn, 1865.

Kreutzer, Hans Joachim. "Schubert und die literarische Situation seiner Zeit" in *Franz Schubert:*

Jahre der Krise 1818–1823: Arnold Feil zum 60. Geburtstag am 2. Oktober 1985, ed. Werner Aderhold, Walther Dürr, and Walburga Litschauer, pp. 29–38. Kassel & Basel: Bärenreiter, 1985.

Laber, Hadamar von. *Die Jagd,* ed. Karl Stejskal. Vienna: Alfred Hölder, 1860.

La Garde-Chambonas, Auguste Louis Charles, comte de. *Fêtes et souvenirs du Congrès de Vienne; tableaux des salons, scènes anecdotiques et portraits, 1814–1815.* Paris: Librairie Historique et Militaire Henri Vivien, 1901, 1st ed. Paris: A. Appert, 1843.

La Motte-Fouqué, Friedrich, Baron de. *Jäger und Jägerlieder. Ein kriegerisches Idyll.* Hamburg: Perthes & Besser, 1819.

Lauffer, Otto. *Farbensymbolik im deutschen Volksbrauch.* Hamburg: Hansischer Gildenverlag, 1948.

Ledebur, Carl Freiherrn von. *Tonkünstler-Lexicon Berlin's von den ältesten Zeiten bis auf die Gegenwart.* Berlin: Ludwig Rauh, 1861.

Liess, Andreas. *Johann Michael Vogl, Hofoperist und Schubertsänger.* Graz & Cologne: Hermann Böhlhaus, 1954.

Lipking, Lawrence. *Abandoned Women and Poetic Tradition.* Chicago, Illinois: The University of Chicago Press, 1988.

Lohre, Heinrich. *Wilhelm Müller als Kritiker und Erzähler. Ein Lebensbild mit Briefen an F. A. Brockhaus und anderen Schriftstücken.* Leipzig: F. A. Brockhaus, 1927.

Mager, Johannes, Meißner, Günter, and Orf, Wolfgang. *Die Kulturgeschichte der Mühlen.* Tübingen: Ernst Wasmuth, 1989.

Mahlmann, August. *Gesammelte Gedichte.* Halle: Renger, 1837.

Mathes, Jürg. "Ein Tagebuch Clemens Brentanos für Luise Hensel" in *Jahrbuch des Freien Deutschen Hochstifts 1971,* pp. 198–310. Tübingen: Max Niemeyer Verlag, 1971.

Mayr, Erich. *Friedrich August von Stägemann.* Munich: Kastner & Callwey, 1913.

Meier, John, ed. *Das deutsche Volkslied: Balladen,* vol. 2. Leipzig: Philipp Reclam, 1936.

Meinecke, Friedrich. *The Age of German Liberation, 1789–1815.* Berkeley, California: University of California Press, 1977.

Meissner, Georg. *Karl Friedrich Curschmann. Ein Beitrag zur Geschichte des Deutschen Liedes zu Anfang des XIX. Jahrhunderts.* Bautzen: E. M. Monse, 1899.

Moore, Gerald. *The Schubert Song Cycles.* London: Hamilton, 1975.

Müller, Wilhelm. *Blumenlese aus den Minnesingern.* Berlin: Maurer, 1816.

　Diary and Letters of Wilhelm Müller, ed. Philip Schuyler Allen and James Taft Hatfield. Chicago, Illinois: The University of Chicago Press, 1903.

　Die Winterreise und andere Gedichte, ed. Hans-Rüdiger Schwab. Frankfurt am Main: Insel Verlag, 1986.

　Gedichte: Vollständige kritische Ausgabe, ed. James Taft Hatfield. Berlin: B. Behr, 1906.

　Sieben- und siebzig Gedichte aus den hinterlassenen Papieren eines reisenden Waldhornisten. Dessau: Christian Georg Ackermann, 1821.

　Vermischte Schriften, 5 vols., ed. Gustav Schwab. Leipzig: F. A. Brockhaus, 1830.

　Werke. Tagebücher. Briefe, 6 vols., ed. Maria-Verena Leistner. Berlin: Verlag Mathias Gatza, 1994.

　Wilhelm Müllers Rheinreise von 1827 sowie Gedichte und Briefe, ed. Paul Wahl. Dessau: Walther Schwalbe, 1931.

Murner, Thomas. *Die Mülle von Schwyndelßheim und Gredt Müllerin Jarzeit,* ed. Gustav Bebermeyer. Berlin: Vereinigung Wissenschaftlicher Verleger, 1923.

Mustard, Helen Meredith. *The Lyric Cycle in German Literature.* New York: King's Crown Press, 1946.

Nettesheim, Josefine, ed. *Luise Hensel und Christoph Bernhard Schlüter. Briefe aus dem deutschen Biedermeier 1832–1876.* Münster: Verlag Regensberg, 1962.

Neubauer, Friedrich. *Preußens Fall und Erhebung 1806–1815.* Berlin: Ernst Siegfried Mittler und Sohn, 1908.

Olfers, Margarete von. *Elisabeth v. Staegemann. Lebensbild einer deutschen Frau 1761–1835.* Leipzig: Koehler & Amelang, 1937.

Peake, Luise Eitel. "The Song Cycle: A Preliminary Inquiry into the Beginnings of the Romantic Song Cycle and the Nature of an Art Form," Ph.D. diss., Columbia University, 1968.

Pfeiffer-Belli, Wolfgang. "'Müllers Abschied.' J. F. Böhmer und das deutsche Volkslied" in *Jahrbuch für Volksliedforschung*, ed. John Meier, pp. 221–23. Berlin: Walter de Gruyter, 1951.

Pinck, Louis. *Verklingende Weisen: Lothringer Volkslieder*, 4 vols. Kassel: Bärenreiter Verlag, 1962–63.

Pompecki, Bernhard. *Hörnerschall und Lustgesang: Ernste und heitere Wald-, Jagd- und Jägerlieder mit leichter Klavierbegleitung*. Neudamm: J. Neumann, n.d., 2nd ed.

Ramalingam, Vivian. "Schubart, Tonality, and *Die schöne Müllerin*" in *Studies in the History of Music*, vol. 3: *The Creative Process*, pp. 201–16. New York: Broude Brothers Ltd., 1993.

Raupach, Ernst. *Der Müller und sein Kind*. Hamburg: Hofmann & Campe, 1835.

Reed, John. "'Die schöne Müllerin' Reconsidered" in *Music & Letters*, vol. 59 (1978): 411–19.
  The Schubert Song Companion. Manchester, England: Manchester University Press, 1985.

Reeves, Nigel. "The Art of Simplicity: Heinrich Heine and Wilhelm Müller" in *Oxford German Studies*, vol. 5 (1970): 48–66.

Reichardt, Johann Friedrich. *Göthe's Lieder, Oden, Balladen und Romanzen - Dritte Abtheilung: Balladen und Romanzen*. Leipzig: Breitkopf & Härtel, 1809, facsimile ed. Wiesbaden: Breitkopf & Härtel, 1969.

Reinkens, Joseph Hubert. *Luise Hensel und ihre Lieder*. Bonn: P. Neusser, 1877.

Rellstab, Ludwig. *Ludwig Berger, ein Denkmal*. Berlin: T. Trautwein, 1846.

Robinson, Paul. *Opera and Ideas: From Mozart to Strauss*, ch. 2: "The Self and Nature: Franz Schubert's *Die schöne Müllerin* and *Winterreise*," pp. 58–102. New York: Harper and Row, 1985.

Rommel, Otto, ed. *Die Romantisch-Komischen Volksmärchen*. Darmstadt: Wissenschaftliche Buchgesellschaft, 1964.

Roth, Klaus. *Ehebruchschwänke in Liedform: Eine Untersuchung zur deutsch- und englischsprachigen Schwank*. Munich: Fink, 1977.

Rowland, Beryl. *Animals with Human Faces: A Guide to Animal Symbolism*. Knoxville, Tennessee: The University of Tennessee Press, 1973.

Rupprich, Hans. *Brentano, Luise Hensel und Ludwig von Gerlach*. Vienna & Leipzig: Österreichischer Bundesverlag für Unterricht, Wissenschaft und Kunst, 1927.

Schiel, Hubert. *Clemens Brentano und Luise Hensel. Mit bisher ungedruckten Briefen*. Frankfurt am Main: Gesellschaft der Bibliophilen, 1956.

Schoeps, Hans Joachim. *Aus den Jahren Preussischer Not und Erneuerung: Tagebücher und Briefe der Gebrüder Gerlach und ihres Kreises 1805–1820*. Berlin: Haude & Spener, 1963.

Schollum, Robert. "Die Diabelli-Ausgabe der 'Schönen Müllerin'" in *Zur Aufführungspraxis der Werke Franz Schubert*, ed. Roswitha Karpf, pp. 140–61. Munich & Salzburg: Musikverlag Emil Katzbichler, 1981.

Schott, Wilhelm. *In einem kühlen Grunde: Bilder verschwundener Mühlen*. Munich: Winkler Verlag, n.d.

Schultz, Hartwig. "Brentanos 'Wiegenlied eines jammernden Herzen'" in *Jahrbuch des Freien Deutschen Hochstifts 1977*, ed. Detlev Lüders. Tübingen: Max Niemeyer Verlag, 1977.

Siebenkäs, Dieter. *Ludwig Berger: Sein Leben und seine Werke unter besonderer Berücksichtigung seines Liedschaffens*. Berlin: Verlag Merseburger, 1963.

Spiecker, Frank. "Clemens Brentano und Luise Hensel: Eine Schicksalsstunde im Leben zweier Romantiker" in *Journal of English and Germanic Philology*, vol. 34 (1935): 59–73.
  Luise Hensel als Dichterin: Eine psychologische Studie ihres Werdens auf Grund des handschriftlichen Nachlases. Evanston, Illinois: Northwestern University Press, 1936.

Steblin, Rita. "Wilhelm Müllers Aufenthalt in Wien im Jahre 1817: Eine Verbindung zu Schubert durch Schlechta" in *Vom Pasqualatihaus: Musikwissenschaftliche Perspektiven aus Wien*, vol. 4 (Autumn 1994): 19–26.

Stöcklein, Paul, ed. *Eichendorff Heute: Stimmen der Forschung mit einer Bibliographie*. Munich: Bayerischer Schulbuch-Verlag, 1960.

Sudhof, Siegfried. "Brentano oder Luise Hensel? Untersuchungen zu einem Gedicht aus dem Jahre 1817" in *Festschrift Gottfried Weber: Zu seinem 70. Geburtstag überreicht von Frankfurter Kollegen und Schülern*, ed. Heinz Otto Burger and Klaus von See, pp. 255–64. Bad Homburg: Gehlen, 1967.

Tatar, Maria. *The Hard Facts of the Grimms' Fairy Tales*. Princeton, New Jersey: Princeton University Press, 1987.

Thiebaux, Marcelle. "The Mouth of the Boar as Symbol in Medieval Literature" in *Romance Philology*, vol. 22 (1969): 281–99.

    The Stag of Love: The Chase in Medieval Literature. Ithaca, New York: Cornell University Press, 1974.

Träger, Albert. *Deutsche Lieder in Volkes Herz und Mund*. Leipzig: C. F. Amelang, 1864.

Treder, Uta. "Der verschüttete Erbe: Lyrikerinnen im 19. Jahrhundert" in *Deutsche Literatur von Frauen*, vol. 2: *19. und 20. Jahrhundert*, ed. Gisela Brinker-Gabler. Munich: C. H. Beck, 1988.

Tunner, Erika. *Clemens Brentano (1778–1842). Imagination et Sentiment Religieux*. Ph.D. diss., Université de Paris, 1976, published Lille and Paris, 1977.

Uhland, Ludwig. *Alte hoch- und niederdeutsche Volkslieder*, 5 vols. Hildesheim: Georg Olms, 1969 (reprint of 1st ed., Stuttgart & Tübingen: J. G. Cotta, 1844).

Vogl, Johann Nepomuk. *Lyrische Gedichte*. Vienna: Peter Rohrmann, 1844.

Warner, Marina. *From the Beast to the Blonde: On Fairy Tales and their Tellers*. New York: Farrar, Straus & Giroux, 1995.

Wildungen, Friedrich von. *Jägerlieder für Jagd- und Forstfreunde*. Quedlinburg & Leipzig: Gottfried Basse, 1823.

Wilhelmy, Petra. *Der Berliner Salon im 19. Jahrhundert (1780–1914)*. Berlin & New York: Walter de Gruyter, 1989.

Wirth, Julia. *Julius Stockhausen. Der Sänger des deutschen Liedes nach Dokumenten seiner Zeit*. Frankfurt am Main: Englert & Schlosser, 1927.

Wollny, Ute. "'Die schöne Müllerin' in der Berliner Jägerstraße" in *Wissenschaftliche Zeitschrift der Martin-Luther-Universität Halle-Wittenberg*, vol. 4 (1992).

Youens, Susan. "Behind the Scenes: *Die schöne Müllerin* before Schubert" in *19th-Century Music*, vol. 15, no. 1 (Summer 1991): 3–22.

    Schubert: Die schöne Müllerin. Cambridge, England: Cambridge University Press, 1992.

Index